"[A] winding journey through the most glaring, damaging and humorous typos, misprints, misidentifications, fuzzy numbers and obiticides in the history of journalism, from the accidental to the malicious." —*Publishers Weekly*

"Craig Silverman . . . turns what could have been a sudsy little stocking stuffer into a serious study of why journalists fail so often." —*American Journalism Review*

"*Regret the Error* is not an indictment of the media, or an apologia, but a reminder that in this age of instantaneous news, citizen publishing and online scoops getting it right still counts for something."
—J. D. Lascia, author of *Darknet: Hollywood's War Against the Digital Generation* and Senior Fellow, Society for New Communications Research

"The book is in effect a paean to fact checking and sound journalism, and it deserves to join [Evelyn Waugh's] seminal work [Scoop] atop every journalism school syllabus—and on the desk of every reporter and editor." —*The Walrus*

"Silverman takes the media to task, . . . call[ing] for greater efforts to reduce errors and to correct them." —*The Oregonian*

"Mixing humorous corrections taken from large and small newspapers alike, Silverman gives historical context to the current problems (he laments the demise of newspaper proofreaders) and then proposes solutions for busy newsrooms (such as random post publication fact checking). . . . [The book] is academic but never dry, as Silverman smartly breaks up what could be monotonous journo-speak with more than 300 amusing media corrections." —*Variety*

Regret the Error

Regret the Error

How Media Mistakes Pollute the Press
and Imperil Free Speech

Craig Silverman

UNION SQUARE PRESS
An imprint of Sterling Publishing Co., Inc.

New York / London
www.sterlingpublishing.com

STERLING and the distinctive Sterling logo are
registered trademarks of Sterling Publishing Co., Inc.

Library of Congress Cataloging-in-Publication Data Available

10 9 8 7 6 5 4 3 2 1

Published by Sterling Publishing Co., Inc.
387 Park Avenue South, New York, NY 10016
© 2007 by Craig Silverman
Introduction to the Paperback Edition © 2009 by Craig Silverman
Foreword © 2007 by Jeff Jarvis
Distributed in the United Kingdom by GMC Distribution Services
Castle Place, 166 High Street, Lewes, East Sussex, England BN7 1XU
Distributed in Australia by Capricorn Link (Australia) Pty. Ltd.
P.O. Box 704, Windsor, NSW 2756, Australia

Book design and layout: Oxygen Design/Sherry Williams, Tilman Reitzle

Sterling ISBN 978-1-4027-5153-0 (hardcover)
Sterling ISBN 978-1-4027-6564-3 (paperback)

For information about custom editions, special sales, premium and
corporate purchases, please contact Sterling Special Sales
Department at 800-805-5489 or specialsales@sterlingpublishing.com.

Contents

Introduction to the Paperback Edition

I FIRST LEARNED of an error in this book even before its publication in November 2007.

Robert Basler, a senior editor at Reuters, e-mailed me in October to point out an error he had found in the advance copy I had sent him. "Don't shoot the messenger," he wrote, "but on Page 115, the last entry in the Common Errors chapter, you mention the *South China Morning News*. You may be right, but as somebody who lived in Hong Kong for eight years, I've only heard of the *South China Morning Post*."

Basler, who went on to use *Regret the Error* as a textbook in a journalism class he taught at George Washington University, had responded to my request for readers to contact me if they spotted an error in the book. He was, of course, correct: the paper's name is the *South China Morning Post*. So, shortly after receiving his e-mail, I posted a correction to the book's Web site. It was the first of what would, as of this writing, total twelve corrections.

Basler's correction was followed roughly twenty-four hours later by one from *Slate*'s media critic, Jack Shafer. He correctly noted that Apple Inc. was still called Apple Computer Inc. in 2006 when the company was embroiled in a lawsuit brought by Apple Corps, a company owned by the Beatles. (I had also incorrectly called the band's company Apple Music.)

Soon, Aldous Russell, a man who frequently spots typos on RegretTheError.com, reported a misspelling of "Fresno" in the book. He was joined by retired proofreaders, a university professor, and other kind folks who demonstrated their skills as volunteer copy editors. Bless them all.

Though I regret each of the errors that led to these corrections, I'm grateful that eagle-eyed readers took up the challenge and helped me fix mistakes contained in the first edition of this book. I hope that all of the errors have been discovered and corrected, and I encourage you to continue to spot errors in this edition. As was the case with the hardcover, you can report an error and read and subscribe to all of the book's corrections at http://book.regrettheerror.com. I look forward to hearing from you.

The e-mails and letters detailing my mistakes were just one portion of the feedback I got for this book. I was also granted the Arthur Rowse Award for Press Criticism for *Regret the Error,* which I was honored to receive from the National Press Club. When I traveled to Washington, D.C. to accept the award in July 2008, I made one important stop before the ceremony: the Newseum, D.C.'s museum devoted to the news business.

Though the recently re-opened museum boasted a brand-new $450 million facility, I must confess that the first thing I did was head to a bathroom, camera in hand. Once inside, I was greeted by this text:

To Err Is Human, To Correct Divine

Just as some dive bars fill their men's rooms with strange newspaper stories or photos of scantily-clad women to occupy the eyes of patrons, the Newseum has covered the walls of its restrooms with notable corrections and errors to offer up some amusing accuracy-related content. (If it weren't for the fact that the Newseum contains other interesting displays about accuracy and bias, I might have taken offense to the placement of the topic.)

"Even the best newspapers make mistakes," reads a small plaque placed inside the restroom. "The flubs on these walls . . . include headlines that don't mean what they say and corrections that admit truly embarrassing errors."

Among the unfortunate headlines displayed in the restroom was "Crowds Rushing To See Pope Trample 6 To Death." A murderous pontiff would no doubt attract a crowd, but obviously that wasn't the real story. One of the best errors showcased was a weather map of the United States, replete with different markings and shading to depict meteorological trends. Below it was this caption: "Shaded parts of map locate areas occupied by Israel since 1967." This must have been shocking news to residents of Wisconsin, Iowa, and Illinois, all of whom resided in the aforementioned shaded regions.

Apart from the restrooms, the Newseum display about media

accuracy included some of the famous errors detailed in this book, such as "Dewey Defeats Truman" and the erroneous reporting about the Sago Mine disaster of 2007. Like errors and corrections themselves, the display was amusing, informative, and important. But you can only spend so long chuckling at the mistakes of the past before your mind turns to the errors and corrections of the present. This brings me to some important research that came to light just before this book was published.

In late 2007, Scott Maier, a leading newspaper-accuracy researcher and an important source for *Regret the Error*, revealed some of the findings from his latest study, *Tip of the Iceberg: Published Corrections Represent Two Percent of Factual Errors in Newspapers*. In it, Maier checked to see if the 1,200 factual errors he had identified in U.S. newspapers in a previous study were corrected by the papers in which they originally appeared. No one had ever looked at this before, as for decades the focus has been on identifying the number of errors—not how many errors are actually corrected by newspapers. As the title of his paper indicates, Maier found that roughly only *two percent* of the verified factual errors were ever corrected.

"While it is not plausible or arguably even desirable for every newspaper error to be detected and corrected, this study shows the corrections box represents the 'tip of the iceberg' of mistakes made in a newspaper, therefore providing only a limited mechanism for setting the record straight," Maier wrote in *Tip of the Iceberg*. "The findings also challenge journalists' widely held perception that errors, when detected, are commonly corrected."

ONE OF THE QUESTIONS I am most frequently asked is whether things are getting better or worse. Are journalists making more errors than they did years or decades ago? Are we correcting more of them? (These questions are often followed by a request for me to name the worst newspaper; unfortunately, the body of accuracy research doesn't offer a definitive answer.)

The final chapter of this book outlines some of the innovations taking place in relation to accuracy and corrections, but I fear that not enough news organizations are embracing them. Overall, we're holding to practices decades—or even centuries—old that are, as evidenced by Maier's research, woefully inadequate. And given the current economic challenges facing newspapers in particular, I fear that things could indeed get worse.

Some papers are attempting to practice addition by subtraction by cutting or buying out newsroom staff in the hope that the reduced costs can combine with a more entrepreneurial workplace culture to help bring about change and a return to those wonderful newspaper profit margins of yesteryear.

That's all well and good in theory, but the dangerous reality is that today's journalists are required to do more with less. Reporters don't just file for a print edition; they now also file daily or hourly copy for a Web site. They may also be asked to contribute to a blog or a podcast, or to do video and photographic work. Though I do believe every journalist should be trained to tell stories in a variety of ways, the fact is that over-working people while also reducing the ranks of copy editors who provide quality control is a recipe for disaster. This potential worst-case scenario already played out in a small way at the *Orlando Sentinel*.

In October of last year, the *Sentinel*'s public editor wrote a column that warned of a "frightening" spike in the paper's number of corrections. "In the past three months, the newspaper has corrected more than a third more errors of its own making on average than it did during the relatively placid prior five months," wrote Manning Pynn in a column, "Errors expose need for editing," published on October 28, 2007. He reported that the previous three months "have accounted, thus far, for significantly more corrections of internally generated errors than the newspaper averaged in that three-month period during the prior five years."

Something had caused a rise in the number of errors and corrections at the paper. Pynn shared what he believed to be the cause.

"When the *Sentinel* tightened its financial belt back in June, it lost a wealth of seasoned veterans, many of them editors," Pynn wrote. "Those journalists not only wrote headlines and captions. They also scrutinized the work of reporters—correcting spelling, straightening out syntax, double-checking facts—before publication. With fewer people to do that now, less of that important work gets done, and the result is more published errors."

The Internet has increased the potential for fact-checking, collaboration with readers, and more effective corrections, but, with many newsrooms struggling to maintain the problematic status quo, innovation is not the norm. As a result, things seem to be getting worse and many of the papers that have reduced the number of copy editors and reporters could find themselves in the *Sentinel's* situation.

"Every business' success depends on the reliability of its products or services," wrote Pynn. "If their reliability declines, people are less likely to buy them. Newspapers are particularly susceptible to that phenomenon."

Think about Maier's findings and the *Sentinel* example and apply them to another industry. Would you buy a car with such a high failure rate? Would you buy food from a company that only caught two percent of contaminations? Likely not. So why do we accept such a low standard in journalism? And why aren't we doing more to improve the quality of our product?

Thanks in large part to the Internet, journalism is undergoing significant changes. The profession and its product are evolving, but the same can't be said for error prevention and corrections. This period of transformation is the ideal time to reexamine and recommit to attaining accuracy in reporting.

In the midst of all this change, however, one thing that has remained constant since this book was published is the onslaught of worrisome and hilarious errors and corrections. (Some fall into the category of being hilariously worrisome.) Whatever the future holds for accuracy and journalism as a whole, it seems certain that the river of errors and corrections will continue to flow for decades to come.

The Best Corrections of 2007–08

In an article in Monday's newspaper, there may have been a misperception about why a Woodstock man is going to Afghanistan on a voluntary mission. Kevin DeClark is going to Afghanistan to gain life experience to become a police officer when he returns, not to shoot guns and blow things up. The *Sentinel-Review* apologizes for any embarrassment this may have caused.   —*Sentinel-Review* (Ontario)

✦

In the May 25 "Explainer," Michelle Tsai asserted that an eight ball is about 10 lines of cocaine. While the size of a line depends on personal preference, most users would divide an eight ball into more than 25 lines.   —*Slate*

✦

A headline on a report in The Caucus roundup yesterday, about *The New York Post*'s error in reporting that Senator John Kerry had chosen Richard A. Gephardt as his running mate in 2004, misstated the famous headline in *The Chicago Daily Tribune* in 1948 when the paper declared the wrong winner in the presidential race. The headline was "Dewey Defeats Truman," not "Dewey Beats Truman."   —*New York Times*

✦

An error occurred in the story "Weather Blamed in Death," which appeared in Wednesday's edition. In the story, it's stated that the "Oasis shelter is the one in the city that accepts people." The sentence should have read "The Oasis shelter is the only one in the city that accepts intoxicated people." We apologize for the error.   —*The Daily Herald Tribune* (Alberta)

✦

An answer in yesterday's edition of Isaac Asimov's Super Quiz was wrong. As every proud Canadian knows, the second-largest country in the world is Canada, not Ukraine. Ukraine's nice but Canada's a lot bigger. —*Toronto Sun*

✦

'Gossip Girl': In Sunday's Calendar section, the Monitor column about "Gossip Girl" misquoted two lines of dialogue between characters discussing one's relationship. It read: "Jenny: 'Is that why we went dessert?' Elise: 'You went dessert?!?!?!'" The correct lines on the show were: "Jenny: 'Is that why we went to third?' Friend: 'You went to third?'"

—*Los Angeles Times*

✦

In a report on page 3 of *The Australian* on April 10, "Girl from the Gong to take on the world", it was stated that a contestant at the Miss World Australia beauty pageant had said she "believed in injustice and inequality". This was incorrect. The contestant said: "I believe in justice, equality and integrity." *The Australian* apologises for the error. —*The Australian*

✦

An obituary on July 21 of Shirley Slesinger Lasswell, who marketed memorabilia and toys based on A. A. Milne's children's books about Winnie the Pooh, misspelled the name of the department store that agreed to let her set up Pooh Corners for children. It is Neiman Marcus, not Nieman Marcus. (The *Times* has misspelled the company's name in at least 195 articles since 1930.) —*New York Times*

✦

A HEADLINE in Monday's *Daily News*, "He regrets his role in 'postal' vid," implied that Richard Marino, the subject of a

YouTube video, was sorry for an incident in December at a Brooklyn post office. Marino, in fact, is not sorry. The *News* regrets the error.   —*New York Daily News*

✦

An article in Wednesday's Calendar section about an English-language newspaper in Mexico City referred to the many U.S. ex-patriots who live there. It should have said expatriates.

— *Los Angeles Times*

✦

A caption on Saturday with a picture showing a Pakistani man on his bicycle carrying a painting of his son, who he says was abducted by Pakistani intelligence agents in 2001, misspelled the name of the Pakistani capital. It is Islamabad, not Islambad.   —*New York Times*

✦

OUR STORY on the price of tomatoes last week misquoted Alistair Petrie, general manager of Turners and Growers. Discussing the price of tomatoes Petrie was talking about retail rate not retail rape. We apologise for the misunderstanding.

—*Sunday Star-Times* (New Zealand)

✦

Australian cricketer Don Bradman was carried, not curried, off the field during the Ashes series in August 1938 (Heroic Hutton leads England to 903, page 12, the archive, November 6).

—*Guardian* (UK)

✦

In "They live by night," page 4, G2 August 27, we wrote about a man who beat bats to death with a dingy paddle; we meant dinghy paddle.   — *Guardian* (UK)

✦

If readers of the *Book Review* have been considering picking up a little conversational Hindi, they would probably do well to not begin with the sample list of words in the Jan. 7 review of "Sacred Games," a novel by Vikram Chandra that sprinkles untranslated Hindi throughout its English text. Indian readers pointed out that while most of the Hindi terms in the review were innocuous, several were in fact obscene suitable for Chandra's tough-guy characters, no doubt, but not for the *Book Review*, where editors failed to check the meaning of the words in the novel's glossary.   —*New York Times Book Review*

✦

A front-page article yesterday about the role that Barack Obama's wife, Michelle, is playing in his presidential campaign rendered incorrectly a word in a quotation from Valerie Jarrett, a friend of the Obamas who commented on their decision that he would run. She said in a telephone interview, "Barack and Michelle thought long and hard about this decision before they made it" not that they "fought" long and hard.
                                        —*New York Times*

✦

Clarification: A story in yesterday's Nation pages about Mitt Romney mixing up Barack Obama and Osama bin Laden said that Fox News Channel president Roger Ailes had previously used the similarity between the names Osama and Obama to mock the senator. Fox News says Ailes was making a joke aimed at President Bush, not Obama, when Ailes said in a speech to broadcast executives in March: "And it is true that Barack Obama is on the move. I don't know if it's true that President Bush called Musharraf and said, 'Why can't we catch this guy?'"   —*Boston Globe*

✦

Army Spec. Hugo Gonzalez was misidentified in two photo captions with the Oct. 1 installment of the Left of Boom series, and his rank was incorrect on Page One. Also, in some editions of the Oct. 2 installment of the series, the full name of an EFP, a type of weapon used by insurgents, was incorrectly given as "explosively formed perpetrator." It should have been "explosively formed penetrator."   —*Washington Post*

✦

A story on Page B4 on Wednesday about foraging for edible mushrooms contained a photo of amanita muscaria, which is a poisonous and hallucinogenic mushroom. It was a copy editor's error.   —*Portland Press Herald* (Maine)

✦

A report "From Bombay to Rajasthan" ("Newscape" page, January 8, 2007) stated that actor Elizabeth Hurley will wear "a 4,000-pound sari by designer Tarun Tahiliani" during her wedding in March. While one reader wondered how she would be able to lift the 1,800 kg sari, another reader said there are possible fears about the bride being reduced to pulp by its weight. It was an error. The word "pound" was used instead of the currency symbol for pound sterling (£).   —*The Hindu*

✦

We misspelled the word misspelled twice, as mispelled, in the Corrections and clarifications column on September 26, page 30.   —*The Guardian* (UK)

NOTABLE APOLOGIES

An article about Lord Lambton ("Lord Louche, sex king of Chiantishire", News Review, January 7) falsely stated that his son Ned (now Lord Durham) and daughter Catherine held a

party at Lord Lambton's villa, Cetinale, in 1997, which degen-
erated into such an orgy that Lord Lambton banned them from
Cetinale for years. In fact, Lord Durham does not have a sister
called Catherine (that is the name of his former wife), there has
not been any orgiastic party of any kind and Lord Lambton did
not ban him (or Catherine) from Cetinale at all. We apologise
sincerely to Lord Durham for the hurt and embarrassment
caused.   —*Sunday Times* (UK)

Michael Platt's editorial on July 21, 2008 may have inadvertently left the impression that General Motors in some way
supported neo-Nazis. That was not the intention of the line in
question and the *Sun* greatly regrets not being more clear in
the story. The *Sun* apologizes to GM, its dealers and customers.
General Motors has employees in six continents, 192 coun-
tries, 23 time zones, and works in more than 50 languages. GM
strives to create a culture and a business environment based
upon inclusion, mutual respect, responsibility, and understanding of all people.   —*Calgary Sun*

On December 22, 2006, *The Australian* published an article on
page 28 titled, "Coffa backs measures to restore order". In it,
The Australian incorrectly stated that Ms Van Tienen had been
found guilty by the Australian Sport Anti-Doping Authority of
trafficking drugs and banned from participating in weightlift-
ing for two years. Ms Van Tienen has never been charged or
convicted of drug offences, has never been banned from the
sport, nor has she ever been involved in an organised drug
ring. *The Australian* apologises unreservedly for any hurt or
embarrassment caused to Ms Van Tienen by the publication.
                                          —*The Australian*

In a report about the Scottish elections, an editing error led to us wrongly suggesting that John Swinburne of the Scottish Senior Citizens' Unity Party had been accused of allegedly causing a breach of the peace by running amok in a polling station with a golf club (Recrimination follows chaos over new Scots voting procedures, page 5, May 5). We apologise to Mr Swinburne for any embarrassment or distress caused.

—*Guardian* (UK)

In Friday's article on Liz Hurley's wedding it was wrongly stated that the actress is holding a pheasant shoot on the Sunday after the ceremony. Game shooting is of course illegal on Sundays and the pheasant season ended on Feb 1. We apologise for the error and accept that if any shooting is to be done it will be by the paparazzi, who have no season and do not observe the Sabbath.   —*Daily Telegraph* (UK)

On May 6 under the headline "Grease chiefs hit by pounds 8k Gest list" we said that David Gest had made a string of backstage demands before agreeing to appear on the show including a DVD of himself being played in his dressing room together with various refreshments served at specific temperatures and chauffeur-driven cars for his friends. In fact, David did not make any of these demands which, we have now discovered, were circulated as a hoax by an unknown person and we apologise to David Gest for publishing them.

—*Mirror* (UK)

We were wrong to say in our headlines (yesterday, front page and page 4) that the report of Judge Rupert Bursell QC into a complaint of drunkenness against Dr Tom Butler, the Bishop of Southwark, had concluded that Dr Butler was drunk. Judge

Bursell did not hear any evidence or reach any conclusions as to the truth of the complaint. We apologise to Dr Butler for the distress and embarrassment this must have caused him.

—*Times* (UK)

✦

Our item about Slough in the last issue said the leader of the Tory group on the council was Cllr Diana Coad. In fact that honour currently falls to one Derek Cryer. "Lady" Diana, who is also the party's parliamentary candidate for the town, merely behaves as if she is leader. Apologies to the invisible man.

—*Private Eye* (UK)

Foreword

NOBODY'S PERFECT—not even journalists . . . especially not journalists. Reporters and editors make mistakes. Indeed, we are probably more likely than most to do so. For just as bartenders break more glass because they handle more beer, so journalists who traffic in facts are bound to drop some along the way.

Yet too often, we won't admit that. What is plainly obvious—even a matter of liturgical confession for people of many faiths—is heretical to the reporting cult: People are fallible. But we journalists too often believe we are not. We were trained to seek and attain nothing less lofty than truth. Accuracy. Objectivity. We were the trusted ones. Impartial experts. Fair and balanced.

Alan Rusbridger, editor of London's *Guardian,* said at a 2007 meeting of the Organization of News Ombudsmen at Harvard, "Since a free press first evolved, we have derived our authority from a feeling—a sense, a pretense—that journalism is, if not infallible, something close to it. We speak of ourselves as being interested in the truth, the real truth. We're truth seekers, we're truth tellers, and we tell truth to power." But then he quoted Walter Lippman from 1922: "If we assume that news and truth are two words for the same thing we shall, I believe, arrive nowhere."

It is time for journalists to trade in our hubris and recapture our humanity and humility. And the best way to do that is simply to admit: We make mistakes.

Craig Silverman's examination of the art of the correction in his blog and now this book could not come at a better time for journalism. For the public's trust in news organizations is falling about as fast as their revenues are (and, yes, those facts may be related). One way to earn back that trust is to face honestly and directly the trade's faults. The more—and more quickly—that news organizations admit and correct their mistakes, prominently and forthrightly, the less their detractors will have grounds to grumble about them.

But for journalists, to admit mistakes is to expose failure; corrections, in this logic, diminish stature and authority rather than enhance them. In my experience, some reporters and editors have tended to think that if they just ignored a mistake for long enough, it—or at least its memory and stench—would fade away.

But now that journalists' readers and sources can be heard via their personal printing presses on the Web, it is no longer possible to ignore errors or, worse, to hide them. As Ken Layne, an early blogger, warned mainstream media in 2001: "We can fact-check your ass." And fact-check we bloggers do.

At first, most journalists I knew resented this new layer of editing by the masses. In September 2004, bloggers took the allegedly three-decades-old documents that Dan Rather used as the basis of his putative exposé of George Bush's military service and only hours later exposed them as clumsy computerized forgeries. But Rather waited twelve days to respond, and when he did, he dismissed the bloggers as partisan operatives (a story Craig will tell in greater depth in the pages that follow). If Rather had sincerely sought the truth, his response to the bloggers should have been: "Thanks. I don't know as much as you do about typewriters and word processors. So let's get to the facts together." Instead, he barricaded himself in his castle until he fell off his throne—or rather, his anchor chair.

But journalists' attitude toward their new army of fact-checkers soon changed. Contrast Rather's performance with Reuters' two years later. In August 2006, bloggers—among them the same one who helped debunk the Bush documents, Charles Johnson of LittleGreenFootballs.com—showed how a photographer working for the news service had embellished the image of smoke from explosions caused by Israeli bombs in Beirut. Reuters immediately pulled those photographs off its wire, investigated, soon fired the photographer, reorganized its photography staffing and procedures, and investigated technology to help prevent tampering. But most important, Reuters publicly thanked Johnson and the bloggers. In so doing, it was saying to him and to its readers and sources: We all respect the truth. We're all in this together.

But this discussion should be about more than just errors and corrections. This is about new and better ways to gather, share, and verify news. And it is about a radically different and improved relationship between journalists and the public they serve. These changes in the culture and practice of journalism will not just bolster journalism's reputation but also expand its reach and impact in society.

Still, our discussion does start with the error. For it is through the error and the correction that the public has been let into the news to improve it. That—and the rare letter to the editor that makes print—had been the only chinks in the castle walls around journalism. But now, thanks to the Internet, the public and journalists can do so much more together. The correction is only the beginning of a long list of new means of collaboration.

Consider the notion that news should be not a product but a process. We have thought of news as a thing—finished, complete, and polished—simply because that was what old media required: The story could be printed or broadcast just once, and then it was history—so, by God, you'd better get it right the first time, for there was no second time.

But now look at how news can be covered: A reporter may blog an idea for a story and ask the public what they know and want to know, what and whom to ask. The reporter also may get that idea directly from a reader writing on his or her blog. In the last year or so, this has become commonplace in newsrooms that once shunned blogs. Reporting has unquestionably improved as a result. Next, the reporter may share notes, interviews, and questions with the public, who now can help by providing information and corrections before the story is completed. I have seen this, too. Today, stories are more and more often being published on the Web before they go to print—this has become policy at a number of the world's leading newspapers, including the *Guardian* and *Telegraph* in London. This means that a story can be read and corrected, again, before it is published. Once it is printed, though, it need no longer be discarded as fish wrapping, and it need no longer enshrine errors in archival eternity. The story can and should live on, with conversation around it, on a newspaper's site or on the blogs that link to it, and with not only corrections but also more facts and reporting and new perspectives.

As is their wont, bloggers have taken this process one step further: We often put out stories that are unfinished—half-baked, as we call them.

This is not because, as some traditionalists would wish to argue, we are irresponsible or lazy. It is so we can get the full story faster by saying, in essence: Here's what I know, and here's what I don't know. What do you know? We reach a fuller set of facts and understandings together.

Also consider the bloggers' generally accepted ethic of the correction: When we make errors beyond a simple typo, it is important for us not only to correct them, and quickly, but also to acknowledge our mistakes. We often strike through the original error, in case an early reader linking to us relied on that mistake as fact. I await technology that will also allow us to send out alerts of our corrections to those who read or wrote about what we said: the ability to subscribe to content and be told when it is updated.

Further, the Internet also enables us to change the very structure of articles and even of interviews. Why shouldn't a quote in an article link to its spot within an entire interview? Not that most readers would want to dig through such raw news gathering, but in case they do want to investigate, they may. The real significance of this is that quotes need no longer be taken out of context, because we can link to them in their context. Thus we would eliminate an entire class of errors.

The nature of the interview itself changes, too, as subjects more frequently demand to conduct interviews via e-mail. This allows them to craft their responses and not be subject to the spoken missteps and gotcha moments inherent in live interviews. This also supplies sources with a complete record of the conversation, to be used to check against a reporter's work and to be made public.

So now, on the Internet, the public has its own means of both verification and response. Now we can argue with the guy who buys ink by the barrel. We have bits by the barrel. This process can be so effective that Susan Crawford, a professor at New York's Cardozo Law School, has theorized that libel laws and litigation have become less necessary. "Libel law," she blogged, "seems much less relevant. Rather than sue, you can just write back."

So far, we have been focusing mostly on how new technology can help prevent and correct errors. But this same technology can also help foster a relationship among professionals and amateurs that is so much richer and more productive than in the past—a relationship that, I believe, may ultimately both save and extend journalism. For just as members of the public may now correct an error or fill in a fact, they also may join in the process of reporting. I call this networked journalism. Gannett has reorganized its newsrooms in part around this concept. Jay Rosen, a journalism professor at New York University, established NewAssignment.net to experiment with open, group-reporting projects. I see citizens recording town meetings that newspapers cannot afford to cover and using the Internet to let their neighbors hear. Techniques such as these expand journalism even as journalistic institutions are shrinking.

Taken together, these changes radically advance the relationship between professional journalists and the public, shifting the field of encounter from errors and confrontation to collaboration and respect. Rosen has written that journalistic professionalism has served too often to separate journalists from the public they serve. Some regret that the line between professional and amateur is blurring. I do not. I prefer the level playing field. I also prefer seeing journalists in the communities they cover, not just as chroniclers, but also as help-mates. As more amateurs commit more acts of journalism, it is in their interests and those of journalists and society for them to do it better. And so the role of the journalist may shift to enabling and edu-cating—to helping these amateurs get the facts they want and get them reliably. Thus the journalist corrects the public as the public corrects the journalist.

As it is possible for any of us to become reporters, it is also true that we must all become editors. For as Craig makes clear when he cites examples of the viral spread of misinformation, the speed of news today and our ability to see current, unedited, unverified reports necessitates that we in the audience become better at distinguishing raw from refined news. This will become only more pronounced as more news is disseminated live. The next time there is, God forbid, a disaster covered by citizens with camera phones, they will likely send both photos and video to the Internet live, as the news occurs. So we all may share the vantage point of witnesses to news, but we will not have the perspective and time that reporting gives us to vet that news. We will get more news more quickly—which is good—but also more misimpressions. This necessitates better training in media and news literacy, so we can spot or at least suspect the errors as they are spread.

As much as some would wish that journalism would be practiced in the future as it has been in their own lifetimes, there is no denying or resisting the changes taking place in technology, culture, and media. The *Guardian*'s Rusbridger discussed a few of those changes in his speech before the ombudsmen.

First, more American news outlets are beginning to follow, if timidly, the European model of newspapering. The *Guardian* has no problem saying it is liberal—indeed, its mission is to be the world's leading liberal voice. In the United States we coyly dance around such admissions. Some journalists were shocked when the first *New York Times* ombudsman, Dan Okrent, called that paper liberal; others were hardly surprised. Fox News still insists on calling itself only fair and balanced; the joke is that this phrase has become synonymous with conservatism. I say those are lies of omission. Journalists do have perspectives and, yes, opinions. Their decisions about what to cover and how to cover it cannot help but reflect that. I won't start a debate about the merits and prospects of an objective press—this foreword would go on forever—but I do think that dropping the institutional voice for a human voice is just more honest. Said Rusbridger,

> BUT IT'S PERHAPS INEVITABLE that, the more you move from reporting to advocacy, campaigning, and persuasion, the more people will question you. Any force in society which attempts to exert active strong influence can't be surprised to find people wanting to question everything from your motives to your methods.
>
> In other words, handing down tablets of stone and telling people "this is how it is" is a less persuasive proposition than it once was. It's laborious to recite the numerous surveys of trust, which show that journalists are not invariably regarded as dealers of the unclouded truth. As an industry, we tend to react to such surveys with disdain or hurt or contempt.

In the words of the Millwall football chant, "No one likes us, we don't care."

But journalists can no longer stand apart. As Rusbridger pointed out, in the old days—a few years ago—the public had "few independent ways of verifying a newspaper or broadcast account, certainly on the day it was published or broadcast. Now a huge amount of information is simultaneously released." He continued,

> WHAT DOES THAT MEAN? It means that inquiring, suspicious, or specialist readers (by which I mean people with a particular interest in a particular subject) will swiftly be able to test your journalism for accuracy or bias against any published information. Of course, we still have sources of information not available to just anyone. But today there are millions of fact checkers out there. Millions of them have their own blogs or websites. So we can refuse systematically to correct or clarify our journalism, but we would be foolish to imagine that it will therefore go uncorrected or unclarified. It will: all that will happen is that it will take place elsewhere.

The net of this, Rusbridger said, is that journalism is not about "delivering the truth, the whole truth, and nothing but the truth. No one believes that anymore if they ever did." And journalism is not "an infallible way of ascertaining what is going wrong around us." Instead, "It is something more fluid—a much more iterative thing than the tablet of stone. It is about us saying, 'this is how it seems to us; it's not the definitive word on the subject by any means; some of you will know more about this; we can collaborate to try to get closer to the truth on this story; this is how you can contribute.'"

News is a process. It is a process of trying to get ever closer to truth, to find more facts now with more hands, to see the story through new perspectives, to fill in the voids and find the shape of news together.

One last point: I certainly do not want to seem to be cavalier about errors, even if I do argue that we are entering an age when we will more often publish first and edit later, even if I advocate publishing half-baked work online so we can cook it together, even if live news brings more misimpressions, even if I propose breaking down the walls between professional and amateur journalism. None of this is an excuse for making mistakes. Quite the contrary: Accuracy must become more attainable through the help of technology and with the aid of more people in the process. That, I believe, is Craig Silverman's quest: to reveal the art of the correction, the virtue of fixing your mistakes, the value of driving closer to the truth.

In the end, this is about instilling an ethic of transparency—even about our fallibility and foibles—in journalism, professional and amateur. It is about being unafraid to speak in our imperfect human voice instead of hiding behind the cold castle walls of the institution. It is about forging a new relationship of collaboration with the public we serve. It is about our shared goal of a better and more accurately informed society.

We all make mistakes. That's not the question. The question is what we do next.

Jeff Jarvis
New York City
2007

Introduction

THIS BOOK, AND THE WEB SITE that spawned it, was born of a single, remarkable "clarification" that appeared on the front page of Kentucky's *Lexington Herald-Leader* on July 4, 2004:

> IT HAS COME to the editor's attention that the *Herald-Leader* neglected to cover the civil rights movement. We regret the omission.

It was published as part of the paper's special package about the fortieth anniversary of the passing of the Civil Rights Act in the United States. In preparing the retrospective, the paper discovered a disturbing lack of material in its own archives. Neither the *Herald* nor the *Leader*, the two local papers that merged in 1983, had devoted any regular coverage to the movement that led to the passing of the act.

"They catered to the white citizenry, and the white community just prayed that rumors and reports would be swept under the rug and just go away," Rev. Thomas Peoples, a former leader with the NAACP, told the *Herald-Leader*. Decades after committing its sins of omission and prejudice, the paper opted for a brief, brave, and remarkable front-page admission of omission.

Prejudice and a desire to pander to their core readership had led the two papers to ignore the facts of the day. And so, forty years later, the *Herald-Leader*'s current staff felt the need to acknowledge their predecessors' failures. In just twenty-one words, it attempts to correct errors of omission and unprofessionalism from decades before. Can such a short, straightforward correction actually have any effect? Is it a waste of time? Are corrections in general a waste of time and space? For me, it inspired many key questions about press errors and corrections.

Corrections, usually tucked at the bottom of page A2 in a newspaper or at the end of a magazine's letters page, are the standard way for a publication to admit its errors. Broadcast news outlets, infrequently, read corrections on the air, or post them to their Web sites. Corrections are often boring and incoherent. Few readers notice them, and those who requested them are often dissatisfied with the result; they would prefer that the error was never made in the first place. Yet, in spite of their failings, corrections, born of ignorance or error, can be remarkably insightful.

The *Herald-Leader*'s correction was published on the front page—the rarest of locations. I couldn't help but wonder how many less newsworthy but equally necessary corrections went unread due to their placement within sections or on the back side of the front page.

A few months before the *Herald-Leader*'s admission, I had written an outline for a Web site that would track and report on media errors and corrections. I viewed it as a way to use the power and convenience of blogs to deliver content and analysis that was lacking in the media world. I had written my two-page proposal and then forgotten about it for a few months; this correction made me look at it again.

On October 13, 2004, I made the *Herald-Leader*'s belated correction the first post on the site. I also included other recent noteworthy corrections such as this one from the September 30, 2004, edition of my local paper, Montreal's *Gazette*:

> A CAPTION BELOW a photograph of a demonstrator in a monkey suit on Friday, Sept. 24, may have contained erroneous information. The caption claimed the photograph showed "angry anglophones" voicing displeasure over Bill 22 in 1974. In fact, it is impossible to determine the linguistic background of the demonstrator in the monkey suit.

Only in Quebec could the linguistic background of a person in a monkey suit be an issue worth noting in a correction. In just three sentences, this correction offers elements of the factual, the absurd, and the society that gave rise to it. Clearly, corrections are more than just simple statements of error and regret. I became fascinated with them, their history, and the issue of media accuracy in general.

This book is ostensibly about accuracy, errors, and corrections in newspapers, magazines, online news outlets, and radio and television news broadcasts—all said to be about news and information. But, in a larger sense, we're all focused on the same thing: trust. In journalism, nothing is possible without trust. Journalists must be able to trust their colleagues and managers, trust their sources and reporting abilities, and trust that the public wants to hear the hard, necessary truths along with the comfortable ones that so easily dominate the news.

If the press does not have the trust of the people it strives to inform, enlighten, and, occasionally, inspire or enrage, it ceases to fulfill the lofty role it claims in a democratic society. Errors and inaccuracies, and the obfuscation of them, erode the fundamental trust journalists require to carry out that role. This book is about trust: how it can be destroyed by errors, how the press can regain it by rededicating itself to accuracy, and why it is perhaps more important now than it has ever been before.

The 2007 *State of the News Media* report, a massive annual survey published by the Project for Excellence in Journalism, stated clearly that for the American public there has been "more than 20 years of growing skepticism about journalists, their companies and the news media as an institution. As we have noted in other reports, since the early 1980s, the public has come to view the news media as less professional, less accurate, less caring, less moral and more inclined to cover up rather than correct mistakes."

These disturbing trends are directly linked to the issue of accuracy. "Despite the relative popularity of newspapers . . . people don't really believe a whole lot of what their daily newspaper tells them," said the report. "For that matter, they don't believe much of what any news medium has to say."

In 1985, 84 percent of Americans said they believed most of what they read in their daily newspaper. By 2004 that number had fallen to 54 percent. The public has doubts about the ability of the press to accurately report the news, and to admit its mistakes when it fails to do so. A Pew survey in 2002 found that only 23 percent of Americans believed that the press is willing to admit its mistakes. It had inched up to 28 percent by 2006, not exactly a ringing endorsement.

In Canada, a 2007 poll asking people to rank the trustworthiness of professions found that only 26 percent of people trusted journalists, with a related category, "other members of the press," earning the trust of 22 percent of respondents. According to the poll, journalists are trusted more than lawyers and auto mechanics by only 1 percent. (Though we're still more trusted than CEOs, car salesmen, and politicians—a hollow victory, to be sure.)

The studies and polls conducted during the past several years on the public perceptions of press accuracy are numerous and largely consistent. Robert J. Haiman summarized recent findings in *Best Practices for Newspaper Journalists*, a handbook prepared for the Freedom Forum in 2000:

> IN THE 1999 ASNE Credibility Study, a national random sample of readers had an identical result: Factual errors in news stories corrode the credibility of newspapers publishing the mistakes.
>
> In a 1994 survey of Chicago-area readers by Northwestern University researchers David Nelson and Paul Wang, accuracy was found to be first among characteristics that most bothered readers about newspapers. In a Louis Harris & Associates survey commissioned in 1996 for the Center for Media and Public Affairs, only a bare majority of those surveyed agreed that the media "usually get the facts straight." And, in a 1998 Media Studies Center national poll, 86 percent of respondents said they believed that stories "often" or "sometimes" contained factual errors.

These findings may lead some to think there was at one time a golden period in journalism when journalists enjoyed total or near-total trust from the public, when accusations of bias, incompetence, or malice weren't regularly leveled at the profession, and when people consumed news with total faith. While we have seen a decline in trust and believability over recent decades, the truth is that what's in the press has never been viewed as akin to the word of God. From the early newspapers of the seventeenth century to our advanced, global news operations of today, the public has always had its suspicions about the accuracy of news reporting, and has always had ample reason to have them. The basic criticisms of the press in the twenty-first century are no different from those that were lev-

eled centuries ago. Even with all the advancements in the training of journalists and how they gather and report news, the fundamental issue of
accuracy and the lack thereof persists. Today, however, external pressures
and the media environment heighten the importance of accuracy and
exact a higher toll for errors. Factual errors have never been more publicized; mistakes have never been more costly.

In his book *The Kingdom and the Power*, Gay Talese noted that, in the
1960s, the internal politics and decision making at the *New York Times*
rarely found their way "beyond the thick walls of the *Times* building."

Talese speculated that "if there were reporters and columnists from
other publications each day watching and questioning the editors of *The
Times*, following them around and analyzing their acts and recording
their errors, if *The Times*, were covered as *The Times* covers the world,
then [the editors and their paper] would lose much of the dignity and
decorum that [they] now [seem] to possess."

Those words today seem prophetic, not just in respect to the *New
York Times*, but in the case of the entire oft-maligned mainstream press.
(An important note: this book is filled with examples of errors and corrections from the *Times*. Rather than viewing this as an indictment of
the paper, it is important to note that the *Times* is perhaps the most scrutinized and reported-on news organization in the world, a situation
born of its influence. Its errors therefore make up a significant portion
of those on record.)

The press today relentlessly reports on the press, obsessing over triumphs and failures, decisions, mistakes, and the personalities behind
them. So too do the external media watchdog organizations that salivate
over evidence that speaks to bias, inaccuracy, or hubris in the press.
Blogs and other online news and commentary operations add another
layer of scrutiny (and, frequently, ridicule). In this new climate of
scrutiny, few things attract more attention than errors or ethical lapses.

"Alerts of journalistic failures are coming more frequently from politicians, bloggers, mainstream press critics and, with more ways to add their
own voice, even citizens themselves," noted the 2007 *State of the News
Media* report. "Perhaps most important, with more choices, the public can
easily see the limits of what any one news organization is offering."

Today, the era of thick walls blocking the flow of information from the newsroom, or repelling the inquiries and accusations of outside parties, seems almost quaint and nostalgic. The reporting of the *Times*, and of other major news organizations, is itself reported on with some approximation of that paper's dedication to covering the world.

The press operates under a heavy watch. The level of scrutiny its critics apply to everything it does—from its fixation on the legs and ratings of Katie Couric to its serious journalistic failures—is akin to that which the press applies to public officials or corporate executives (perhaps its exhaustive coverage of celebrities excepted). When the fashion police of *Us Weekly* begin lambasting frumpy reporters at press conferences, we'll know the profession has truly gone meta mad.

Today's culture of scrutiny and criticism in which the once-sacred Gray Lady often finds herself under interrogation is revealing longstanding inadequacies of reporting methods and the difficulties the press faces in attempting to provide accurate information. For criticizing the press, the instrument of choice is facts. Spotting factual errors in press coverage has become a mission for groups and individuals who treat it like a blood sport. This has both exposed the existing, troubling level of reporting errors and increased their impact. The small mistakes—typos and such, errors that used to go unnoticed except for the rare correction—are now cataloged and publicized. Individual reporters are tracked, their mistakes logged and noted, their work unremittingly examined and critiqued. In England, there is a blog devoted solely to the perceived inaccuracies of Victoria Newton, a columnist for the *Sun*. In the United States, the work of Alessandra Stanley, the television critic for the *New York Times*, is scoured for errors, thanks to her having falsely accused Geraldo Rivera of "nudging" a rescue worker out of the way in New Orleans so he could get on camera. (Her error was compounded by the paper's initial refusal to correct it.)

Thanks also to the massive amount of information online and in databases, the ability to fact-check and spot a mistake is greater than ever before. Because of blogs, e-mail, and other technologies that put mass media in the hands of anyone with an Internet connection, the ability to publicize errors is also more powerful and far-reaching. Communications technologies have grown, advanced, and, more important, simplified to such a great extent that the power to publish, disseminate, and attract attention is no longer dependent on buying ink by the barrel or launching satellites.

We are living in an age of fact checking by the public; at the same time, within the press the practice of checking is on the decline. This spells disaster for the error-prone news media.

Writing in *Forbes* magazine, Rupert Murdoch agreed that "people's expectations of media have undergone a revolution. They are no longer content to be a passive audience; they insist on being participants, on creating their own material and finding others who will want to read, listen and watch."

The people formerly known as the audience, to borrow the formulation made famous by New York University journalism professor Jay Rosen, are no longer passive consumers of information. They question, criticize, and, using other forms of media, make their own contributions. The news monopoly once held by major media organizations is being eroded as people acquire the means and motivation to, as the journalist Dan Gillmor put it, "commit acts of journalism."

As trust in "official" journalism wanes, many other newslike operations are evolving to fill the void. When people stop trusting the media, believing the media, they go elsewhere. Raising the level of accuracy in the press is, I believe, one critical way to ensure the survival of quality journalism within both the mainstream media and the new sources of news that are emerging on what seems a daily basis.

At the core of this changing landscape is the concept of quality. "Quality is more important than ever, because the marketplace is more ruthlessly competitive," wrote Murdoch.

Journalistic quality is usually expressed as a mixture of accuracy, solid reporting, and strong writing in a professional, ethical environment. This concept of "quality" journalism is often at the heart of the argument against blogs and other new news media put forward by established media organizations as a differentiator. Professional journalists and the heads of large news organizations contend that their work is more professional, more accurate, and therefore of higher quality and more trustworthy than the work of less-established news organizations or external critics. Yet the public believes them less and less, and more than seventy years of media accuracy research confirms the validity of their skepticism.

While some see the new world of blogs and decentralized media as a race away from quality and toward rumor and baseless opinion, we are in fact in the midst of a quality competition for news consumers. Those who innovate and demonstrably show their quality have much to win. Those who cannot or will not get their facts straight, and be transparent about their errors and their process to prevent and acknowledge them, will lose.

Media errors exert an untold—and, of course, unchecked—amount of power on our world. The living are bumped off and the dead are exhumed and inserted in today's headlines. Thousands become millions, men become women, and the innocent are instantly judged guilty. Errors are also the source of much humor, and have been for centuries. I have attempted to offer in this book some of the most egregious, hilarious, and fascinating of history's media errors. But more important, I have sought to provide what I believe is the first comprehensive examination of the level of accuracy in the press and the impact of errors. There is much to shake one's head at; many examples of errors and corrections are simply shocking, or sidesplitting, and I cannot hide my pleasure at presenting some from recent times. But there is a larger, more urgent issue to consider.

People rely on the press for information that informs their daily lives. When that information is incorrect and fails to be corrected, or is unduly influenced by outside forces—sources, corporations, or governments—that attempt to manipulate, this fundamental source of important information becomes corrupted. This has a damaging effect on society as a whole, which in turn contributes to the erosion of the free press. The flow of accurate news and information is essential in a democracy, and the press, which is meant to be a bastion of free speech and the exchange of ideas, has a moral and professional duty to act, not just as a disseminator, but as an arbiter of information. When the press makes mistakes, especially egregious ones, it gives ammunition to those who would curtail its power through increased regulation or legislation that could potentially restrict press freedom and have a corollary effect on freedom of speech. The press is one of the most powerful venues in which freedom of speech is exercised; the act of publication or broadcast is speech itself. When the seemingly powerful media cannot exercise its freedom, average citizens naturally suffer the impact.

If the press is hamstrung by oppressive governments, unduly constrained by courts, or "chilled" by overly restrictive libel laws, it cannot carry out its role as a check and balance on the institutions of government and society. In the case of *New York Times Co. v. United States*, U.S. Supreme Court Justice Hugo Black wrote, "Only a free and unrestrained press can effectively expose deception in government." That case involved the famous Pentagon Papers, an internal Pentagon report about the Vietnam War. It was leaked to the *New York Times* and the *Washington Post* in 1971 by military analyst Daniel Ellsberg after he'd initially tried to make the report available to Congress. The documents revealed important information about the U.S. government's decision making and views on the war—information that was contrary to the public statements and declarations of top government officials. The government filed injunctions to stop the newspapers from publishing the contents, and the case went all the way to the Supreme Court. In a 6-3 decision, the Court deemed that the government had no right to restrain publication of the Pentagon Papers.

This case is an example of how the press can act as a check on a government that is keeping the truth from its citizens. The "free and unrestrained press" Justice Black wrote of must not be taken for granted. If the press defaults on its commitment to present the facts, it loses the trust and support of the public and becomes vulnerable to restraint.

Errors are a major contributor to an erosion in the level of trust in the press. Once this trust begins to be lost, the rights of the press and indeed of speech itself are threatened. It is then a matter of time until laws are enacted that impinge on the press's right to publish accurate reports and alternate views that inform and encourage public discourse.

Accuracy helps build the trust that ensures public support of a free press. Errors—especially uncorrected ones—have consequences not

only for the people they affect but also for the society as a whole. It's
time to view them with the seriousness they demand.

"Although many journalists may think that spelling and grammar
errors, wrong names, wrong titles, wrong addresses, wrong dates and
other similar mistakes have relatively little to do with the press's credibility, the public sees it otherwise," wrote Robert J. Haiman in *Best
Practices for Newspaper Journalists*. "In all of our roundtables, the frequency of errors was cited as a major reason why the public is
increasingly skeptical of what it reads."

By words and policies, journalists are committed to the pursuit of
accuracy, but the deeds do not match up. Today's media environment is
exposing this deficiency, further eroding the credibility of the press.

Decades of research have shown a direct link between the number
of errors the public spots in a particular media outlet and that outlet's
loss of credibility. Along with the data compiled by the massive State of
the News survey, earlier work also pinpointed a link between accuracy
and credibility. A 1988 paper in *Journalism Quarterly* combined the
results of four earlier surveys and stated plainly that "the public thinks
that the media could report more accurately and impartially."

This clear yet unalarmist statement becomes more urgent when
one realizes that in the nearly twenty years since it was made, the public
perception of press accuracy and believability has dropped.

At a time when the newspaper industry in particular is looking for
ways to stem the loss of daily circulation and create growth online, not
only is allowing these corrosive errors to continue ethically unacceptable; it's simply bad business. As Howard Tyner, then the editor of the
Chicago Tribune, put it in 2000, "The slightest excuse is sufficient [for
readers] to bail out. People get very angry when they see mistakes,
especially mistakes that go uncorrected. It's a credibility issue. If
people are thinking about getting rid of you anyway, why serve up a
big softball?"

All the ethical and professional arguments in the world can be mar-
shaled in the name of accuracy, but perhaps, in this time of falling
revenues, the most persuasive is the business argument. Take, for
example, how the value of a typical newspaper is calculated. When

Philip Meyer, one of the leading journalism scholars working today, asked two prominent newspaper brokers to estimate how much of a publication's valuation was "goodwill," they "both gave the same answer: 80 percent. That leaves only 20 percent for the physical assets," he wrote in *The Vanishing Newspaper*.

Meyer describes goodwill as "the organization's standing in its community. More specifically, it is the habit that members of the community have of giving it money. In accounting terms, it is the value of the company over and above its tangible assets such as printing presses, cameras, buildings, trucks, and inventories of paper and ink." When asked if part of goodwill was also the perceived credibility and believability of a newspaper, Meyer replied, "Absolutely."

Meyer's research revealed two links between credibility and the financial health of a newspaper. In one study, he found that papers with a higher ranking of credibility are able to better maintain their circulation. Another Meyer study revealed a link between higher credibility and an increase in the rate a newspaper was able to charge for its advertising.

"If you are trusted you retain your readers longer and you get more for your advertising," Meyer told me. At a time of stagnant or falling circulation and audiences, accuracy is today as much an economic imperative as an ethical and professional one.

There will never be a time of 100 percent accuracy in the media. This is admitted by every journalist, and it is the reality. There are too many outside forces and factors, and too many inadequate and flawed internal processes that afflict journalism. There is also the human factor. Journalists are not robots; they have failings just like other human beings.

The press has perpetually struggled with accuracy issues, but rarely is this reality communicated to the public. By ratcheting up the public's expectations through sloganeering and self-righteous declarations—"the most trusted name in news," "fair and balanced"—the press contributes to the problem. Yet what processes and innovations have been made to back up such claims? Given the pitfalls inherent in the news-gathering process and the current lack of fact checking in most newsrooms, the press should replace slogans with a more transparent, realistic portrait of how the news is gathered and verified, or not, and communicate with the public about how journalism works, and how it often doesn't. It would help people understand the intrinsic challenges to accuracy that journalists face every day. They could then perhaps accept the reality that the news will never be perfect—but only if they are assured that the people bringing it to them do adhere to standards, do make an effort to verify their information, and are willing to be honest about it when they get something wrong. This kind of orientation and new level of honesty would go a long way toward gaining the public's trust if combined with a concerted effort to prevent errors and offer more effective ways of correcting those that do occur.

The press today is struggling to keep its self-defined role in society as the voice of the public because the public now can have a voice of its own. Despite the negative view the citizen media inspires within many newsrooms, this is an exciting, revolutionary time for journalism. The profession is being pressured to reinvent itself and deliver on its promises of accuracy and quality.

The good news is that the technologies helping to bring so much trouble to the journalism establishment are also the means by which a new standard of quality, accuracy, and accountability can be defined and met. It's time to embrace accuracy and drive toward a new standard of verification and correction in the press.

Though spotting choice corrections and publicizing and analyzing errors have become a part of my daily life, I look forward to the time when the well runs dry. That will mean the accuracy challenge has been met, and real commitment, innovative processes, and new technologies have made a reality of the "quality" that professional news now claims to have. Sadly, it will also mean I will never again be struck by a correction for a decades-old transgression, or by one about the linguistic background of a person in a monkey suit.

It's a trade-off I can live with.

Statement of Accuracy

O NE OF THE CENTRAL ARGUMENTS of this book is that errors occur too frequently in journalism. It is essential that the press work harder to prevent them and, once they are discovered, that it take all necessary steps to correct them. Upton Sinclair had no reservations about making claims to total accuracy in his 1919 book *The Brass Check: A Study of American Journalism* when he wrote,

> YOU MUST GRANT MY CLAIM concerning this book—that it is a book of facts. There are no mistakes in it, no guesses, no surmises; there are no lapses of memory, no inaccuracies. There are only facts.

Given my subject matter and conclusions, I think such hubris ignores reality and invites disaster.

In writing this book I have done my best to rely on quality sources of information, and to make these sources known to you through endnotes. In addition, this book was reviewed by my editors for content, accuracy, and style. All of us are acutely aware of the need for this book to meet the highest standards of accuracy, but the final responsibility and blame rest with me. Any factual error, typo, inelegant sentence, or other mistake is mine alone.

I also provided selected chapters to experts who could offer their take on the overall veracity of my research. Other sources quoted in this book were also given the opportunity to review specific sections. All offered excellent feedback and edits, but the ultimate responsibility for the accuracy of the entire book rests with me.

Even with these efforts, I must be clear in stating that I expect to have made errors. That is the rule, not the exception. In the spirit of accuracy, I now encourage you to set this book down and visit http://book.regrettheerror.com. The page labeled "Corrections" will list any and all of the known errors in this book and offer the corrected text. It also offers you the opportunity to sign up and have the latest corrections automatically e-mailed to you as they are issued, and on the same page you can also subscribe to an RSS corrections feed. I have also detailed the errors I have made in my previously published journalism in the Afterword of this book.

If you believe you have found a factual error in this book, please fill out the Error Report Form located in the Corrections section of the Web site. Please be specific in describing the location and content of the mistake, and also, if possible, offer me the correct information, with a citation of your source.

If you do not have Internet access, I have included an "Error Report Form" at the end of this book. You can complete this form and mail it to me. You can also check a box on the form to have me mail you corrections to the book as they emerge. I do, however, ask that those with Internet access use the Web site to report errors, send comments, and check for corrections. The printed form is a courtesy for those without Internet access.

I also want to hear from you if you disagree or agree with an opinion, conclusion, or argument offered in the book, or have additional information to offer. The Web site will publish a selection of letters from readers who disagree (or agree) with the content of the book, and I will include these communications as a means to further the discussion. (I will contact you if I intend to publish your letter.) I would love to have your contribution. You can use the error form mentioned above to send me your thoughts.

An issue of debate among journalists is whether it is possible to draw too much attention to errors and corrections. The fear is that this could unjustifiably diminish public confidence in a particular news outlet. The argument is that most errors are not of a "serious" nature and therefore do not warrant more attention than a simple correction notice. I hope my transparency and the resources I have dedicated to collecting and publicizing errors will in fact enhance your experience.

If you can suggest ways to improve upon this existing structure, I would love to hear from you.

CHAPTER 1

A BRIEF HISTORY OF MEDIA ACCURACY AND ERRORS

THE OLDEST SURVIVING ENGLISH-LANGUAGE newspaper was published in Amsterdam by Pieter van de Keere in 1620. He was a map and print engraver by trade, but certainly not a proofreader. At the bottom of the second and last page of the surviving edition is the date: "the 2. of Decemember." The history of the English-language press begins, at least on paper, with a typo. And if you skip ahead almost 325 years, this is the kind of journalistic error you will see in print on any given day:

> AN OCT. 19 [2004] ARTICLE on songwriter John Bucchino incorrectly stated that he doesn't read. The sentence should have said he doesn't read music.   —*Dallas Morning News*

Step back a century and a half and you'll find this egregious error in the *New York Daily Times* (precursor to today's *Times*) of June 12, 1852:

> WE ARE ASSURED BY THE FRIENDS of Mr. William O'Conner, that the account of his insanity, given by our reporter yesterday, was entirely unfounded. He is of sound mind, and has not been missing, as was reported. We cheerfully make the correction.

A cheerful correction for the *Daily Times;* less amusing for Mr. O'Conner.

Errors, inaccuracies, and outright fabrications have appeared in all forms of written media ever since stylus was put to papyrus, though news itself predates literate societies. The desire to communicate is inherent, and it breeds a desire to share new information and gather important intelligence, which begets the concept of news and what would become journalism and the news business. News is a natural human need. "Human beings exchanged news long before they could write," wrote Mitchell Stephens in *A History of News*. "They spread news by word of mouth on crossroads, at campfires or at markets. Messengers raced back from battlefields with reports on victories or defeats. Criers walked through villages announcing births, deaths, marriages and divorces. Stories of unlikely occurrences spread, in the words of one anthropological report, 'like wildfire' through preliterate societies."

While all people enjoy good news and gossip, it is accurate news that matters most to society. The desire for factual information is an inseparable component of news and has emerged as the foundation of modern journalism. It is also the foundation upon which people and societies make important decisions and formulate their worldviews. The quality of information is paramount in everything from business and war to personal relationships and the press. The Chinese philosopher Confucius believed that a government required three things to function: weapons, food, and trust. Of the three, however, he said that "without trust we cannot stand." Consistently factual information builds trust, one of the cornerstones of society.

Accuracy is at the core of how the media builds trust. Ensuring the quality of reported information has always been a constant struggle, a pursuit dependent on the technology and resources available at the time and, of course, on the honor and skills of sources, reporters, and publishers.

New technologies, like faster ships, took news farther faster, and the printing press introduced the ability to make exact copies of a document, thus reducing copying errors; the telegraph enabled news to travel instantly over long distances with total fidelity; radio and television sent sound and images to the world; the Internet has further increased the reach of news and enabled it to be delivered in a multimedia environment. The change over time is remarkable: In the late fifteenth century it took two years for news of the death of a Turkish sultan to reach England. In 1963, 68 percent of Americans knew that President Kennedy had been shot within a half hour of the event.

Today, people learn of major news events within minutes, sometimes even seconds. Though the news medium can accelerate the message, acceleration doesn't necessarily guarantee accuracy; rather, the technological advancements that enable incorrect reports to travel farther and faster can also increase the dissemination of errors. News travels fast, but it doesn't always travel well. Accuracy has never been— and never will be—an easy goal to attain.

The history of journalism as a profession begins primarily with the early newspapers of the seventeenth century. But the history of accuracy as a codified professional ethic within the press begins to emerge only in the twentieth. "About 80 years ago, newspapers invented the doctrine of objectivity to assure the public that its news was factual and fair," wrote Stephen J.A. Ward, a former reporter with *Canadian Press* and a professor of journalism at the University of British Columbia, in his 2004 book, *The Invention of Journalism Ethics.* This is important to remember in any look at media accuracy: It has a relatively short history as a true ethical and professional pursuit. Old habits die hard, and ingrained perceptions inside and outside the press are difficult to change. As Ward concluded, "Five centuries after the first periodic papers, journalism still struggles to avoid debasement, let alone live up to its democratic duty."

The role of the press as a check on the powerful and a critical element of democracy requires that it live up to high standards in regard to accuracy, fairness, and professionalism. When it fails, the public feels it has been let down, fooled, or even betrayed. The stakes are high; in the early twenty-first century, people's expectations of the press may seem low, but they have risen over the course of hundreds of years. Certainly journalists don't mind talking about their invaluable role in society.

The history of accuracy and media errors reveals much about the struggles of today's press, not to mention what it provides in the way of some undeniably colorful and shocking examples of media errors that truly stand the test of time.

Oral News

NEWS TODAY IS VERY MUCH a product: *news*paper, *news*cast, *news*letter. Sometimes we pay for a news product and hold it in our hands; other times it is given to us much the way it was provided tens of thousand of years ago or earlier, when the development of language gave birth to oral news. This form of news would spread from person to person, village to village. Preliterate societies recognized the importance of news and eventually developed systems for gathering and distributing it. But oral news has obvious limitations.

As it passes from one person to another, the information inevitably changes. Early societies tried to reduce error by establishing the job of messenger—a person whose sole role was to ensure the speedy, faithful distribution of news. Kings, chiefs, or merchants, for example, would dispatch human messengers, and these people were the owners of the message. They controlled the news. But they also recognized the need to verify their message, to provide whatever proof or facts could be offered to convince their intended audience of its veracity. "A Bedouin scout's report on the fertility of a pasture could hardly be doubted if he was carrying an armful of grass," according to *A History of News*. But this was not always possible.

Though our news systems have evolved into sophisticated organizations using advanced technology, the news we seek out today is not altogether different from what commanded the attention of our preliterate ancestors. News passed on by mouth could travel with impressive speed at the time, but so could rumors: Inevitably, spoken news would change every time it was passed on from person to person.

Written News

THE INVENTION OF WRITTEN LANGUAGE created the ability to faithfully produce a record of events, a huge advance over the mutable nature of oral news. Still, the act of writing something down didn't make it inherently accurate. It was then as it is today: The owners of the means of news production—writing skills, messengers, printing presses, Web sites, television stations—are in control of what is disseminated.

Written systems date back to as early as 3100 BCE, and the advent of this form of communication and documentation enabled records of recent or historical events to be set in permanent form. Ancient Greek writers such as Herodotus and Thucydides wrote accounts of history and of their own times, respectively, in the fifth century BCE. Even then, they recognized the need for accurate news and were aware of the difficulties in gathering it. Thucydides explained his reporting method in the introduction to his account of the Peloponnesian War. It's a paragraph that could just as easily have been written by a journalist of today:

> WITH REGARD TO MY factual reporting of events . . . I have made it a principle not to write down the first story that came my way, and not even to be guided by my own general impressions; either I was present myself at the events which I have described or else heard of them from eye witnesses whose reports I have checked with as much thoroughness as possible. Not that even so the truth was easy to discover: different eye witnesses gave different accounts of the same events, speaking out of partiality for one side or the other, or else from imperfect memories.

In 59 BCE, ancient Rome produced a daily accounting of government news, the *acta diurna,* written on papyrus and posted in a public place. As official government publications, the *acta* were not dispassionate, complete records of the day. They were what the government deemed important to disseminate to the Roman masses and to those at the far-flung reaches of its empire. They were a major source of written news in the world for at least 280 years.

The Chinese Han dynasty, which dates from 206 BCE to 220 CE, also distributed written newsletters to officials in its provinces, and paper is reported to have been invented in China in 105 CE (though a 2006 discovery suggests it was in use even a century before). These *tipao* (*pao* meaning "report") continued for centuries as official government reports and were later made available to other members of society. As is often the case, privately created newsletters later supplemented these official government reports.

By the fifteenth century, handwritten newsletters were making the rounds in Europe, and kings used them to celebrate their major triumphs and spread the news to their subjects. But nothing was more important to the development of news and journalism than Johan Gutenberg's invention of the printing press in the mid-fifteenth century. Though other printing systems predate his invention, Gutenberg's press was a quantum leap forward for news production and dissemination. It also had a major effect on the ability to reduce errors. The letterpress prevented errors of reproduction, but accuracy was and is still determined by those who produce the accounts.

The printing press enabled news to reach a larger audience at a vastly reduced cost, though it was not the death knell for oral news exchanged in coffeehouses, at home, and in city streets. In the sixteenth century, news was still being called out by criers in the streets and recited in the form of poems, or "news ballads." These more primitive forms of news remained necessary because illiteracy was still prevalent in society and so the old methods of oral news held fast. Also, government controls often prevented enterprising reporting, while news-gathering methods remained disorganized and ultimately untrustworthy. Propaganda flowed freely from the printing press, and there were no established news organizations outside of the government.

The sixteenth century did, however, see the emergence of "newsbooks," one-off chronicles of current events, usually recounting battles, matters of state, or tales of a magical or supernatural nature. Though largely unreliable as sources of news, newsbooks signaled the advent of journalism and of the news business—because they relied on a paying audience. To attract an audience they typically featured fantastic tales, salacious gossip, or polemical tirades alongside timely articles that had the appearance of accuracy. Newsbook publishers recognized the need to claim truthfulness and honesty. One English newsbook author in 1548 pledged, "I shall never admit for any affection towards countree or Kyn, to be so partial, as wil wittingly either bolster the falsehood or bery the truthe." This declaration was followed by a string of insults aimed at the pope. In offering sensational stories to ensure sales, we see in newsbooks the origin of the conflicted nature of journalism that is evident today.

Birth of the Newspaper .

THE SEVENTEENTH-CENTURY PRESS

THE MODERN NEWSPAPER is widely accepted to have begun in Europe during the seventeenth century. This was when newsbooks evolved into newspapers that adhered to a set frequency of publication and a mix of news and comment. Newspaper publishers didn't have established reporters working specific beats and cultivating sources, so they often reprinted the stories of any other publication they could get their hands on, or simply published the news brought to them by the captain of the latest ship to make port. These limitations made accuracy a luxury; fiction was widely available, but truth was in short supply.

Publishers knew that if no one believed and trusted their product enough to buy it again and again, their business would fail, so to cultivate a sense of trust they constantly trumpeted their dedication to truth and accuracy. The language of accuracy and facts is prevalent in these early pages, but their content belies such claims. These precursors of our mass media, in response to the public's ongoing desire for accurate information, helped enshrine the concept of accuracy as a fundamental value of the news business. From these early roots, the concept of factual reporting born of objectivity slowly began to take hold in the European and North American press.

In 1614, the author of a one-off newsbook sought to assure his readers that, despite the lies other "pamphlet-pressers" may have foisted on the public, the tales contained in his publication were true. And so, "passing by what's past, let not our present truth blush for any former falshood-sake," he suggested. Then he launched into a tale of a gigantic serpent that had been discovered living thirty miles from London. But the author of the serpent tale went beyond assuring readers of his honor to convince them of the tale's truth; he also listed the names of three local witnesses who could "certifie the truth of all that has been here related." Claims of an ethical nature began to merge with the use of verifiable sources to create the impression of accurate reporting.

In 1681, one English publication expressed its role as delivering news, "without any reflection upon either persons or things, giving only that are matter of fact." This pure view of facts had been present in the work of scientists such as Copernicus and Galileo, who used the facts of carefully constructed and argued experiments to bring new truth to light. Scientists were joined with historians such as Francis Bacon, who declared that a historian must report with impartiality and obey "the rule of writing nothing but Matter of Fact." The Royal Society of London, founded in 1660, later pushed this philosophy of fact, making its motto "Take Nobody's Word for It."

The newsbooks and early newspapers of the seventeenth century extolled accuracy and facts with rhetorical flair, but what they published in reality had no semblance of truth and accuracy. Newspapers peppered their pages with scandalous, often totally false accounts worthy of today's most sensational tabloids, and political and religious partisanship was rampant. Facts and accuracy were largely the stuff of slogans and marketing copy.

There was no defined method for professional reporting, no code of ethics, and news was often delivered by horse-drawn carriage, relayed by ships' captains, or lifted from news sheets delivered from such places as Amsterdam, where English-language news sheets were common. Assessing the quality of incoming reports was nearly impossible, and an inaccuracy reported in one publication would eventually snake its way around Europe, thanks to the reliance on republishing to fill the news hole.

Publishers of the time were also wary of angering the ruling class and the church for fear of seeing their press carted off or smashed to pieces. As their ongoing operations depended on their being in the good graces of the Crown and the church, any publisher with a licensed press who claimed to be a dispenser of truth could be trusted to deliver only the approved version. People continued to want the facts, and, powerless to deliver them, publishers just continued to restate their claims to accuracy and factuality.

One paper, the *Faithful Scout*, promised "to encounter falsehood with the sword of truth." The *True Informer* declared that "truth is the daughter of time" and promised to sift through incoming reports because they are not "to be taken or credited at the first hand." The newspaper *Mercurius Civicus* bore the subtitle "Truth impartially related from thence to the whole Kingdome, to prevent mis-information."

Readers were often left to judge the trustworthiness of a particular publication by the ferocity and eloquence of its editor's declarations of honesty and ethics, or on other more important characteristics of the time, such as whether they were Catholic or Protestant. One could assume that readers lent their loyalty and patronage to publications that reflected their points of view. In the areas of politics and religion, people wanted the truth as they saw it, and the publications of the day were happy to oblige. In fact, the papers excelled at delivering polemical tirades.

The English press of the mid- to late seventeenth century is important for its recognition of the public's desire for accurate reporting born of facts. Lip service to this ethic was seen as a competitive differentiator, a form of branding that could mean the difference between brisk sales and a debtor's life. Indeed, "from the beginning, newspapers were operated to make money," according to English press historian Joseph Frank.

Readers then, as now, demanded much from their news sources; few enjoy having their beliefs questioned, and even fewer will pay for the privilege. The bias of readers could be a frustration for editors, among them Thomas Gainsford, famous at the time, who appears to have taken his claims of honesty to heart. "In one [1624] issue, Gainsford thanks a reader for correcting a previous erroneous story that located the Antichrist's birth in Babylon," wrote Ward, perhaps offering evidence of one of the earliest reader-induced corrections on record. Two years later, a full correction notice appeared in another English publication: "In our laste newes where it is spoken of the ship of Schoonhouen, which is cast away upon the Coast of Portugall reade that it was bound for the East, and not the West Indies." The idea of correcting an error was seen even then as good practice, a way to demonstrate to readers that the publication adhered to a standard of accuracy.

Claims of truth and accuracy were not limited to the English press of the time. In France, Cardinal Richelieu sought to control distribution of news in the late seventeenth century, offering an exclusive right to publish to the *Gazette de France*, operated by Théophraste Renaudot, now considered the father of French journalism. "In one thing I yield not to anyone—in the search for truth," he declared.

Near the end of the century, the first newspaper appeared in what would become the United States, under the leadership of Benjamin Harris in Boston. Harris was no stranger to publishing, or controversy. He had previously edited a Whig newspaper in London and was jailed for printing a seditious pamphlet. With no future in England, he left for the colonies soon after his release. His first issue of *Publick Occurrences Both Foreign and Domestick* appeared on September 25, 1690. In the prospectus for his publication he expressed a desire to track down factual reports and expose liars. He also provided what is perhaps the first formal corrections policy on paper. Harris wrote that "nothing shall be entered, but what we have reason to believe is true, repairing to the best fountains for our Information. And when there appears any material mistake in anything that is collected, it shall be corrected in the next." He then expressed the belief that it was not enough to simply correct a mistake. No, an editor must "trace any such False report, so far as to find out and Convict the First Raiser of it, he will in this Paper (unless Just advice be given to the contrary) expose the Name of such Person as A malicious Raiser of false Report."

Harris's effort was short-lived. Though he intended to publish monthly, he was shut down four days after distributing his first issue. The governor and council declared that he had published "Without the least Privity or countenance of Authority." His accuracy was also called into question with the condemnation of his "sundry doubtful and uncertain Reports." Even then, accusing publishers of inaccuracies was seen as a powerful way to dismiss their work, not to mention being grounds for closure. Harris's knack for upsetting the authorities once again felled his publishing venture.

Before the publication of *Publick Occurences*, the governor of Massachusetts had allowed a news broadside titled *The Present State of the New-English Affairs* to be published in 1689. Though not a true newspaper— it had no set frequency and was sanctioned by the government—it is noteworthy for its front-page subhead: "This Is Published to Prevent False

Reports." American journalism historian Frank Luther Mott calls it "an acknowledgement that one of the great functions of the printing of news is to correct the inevitable abuses of rumor." With these humble and ineffectual beginnings, the press was on its march toward accuracy and factual reporting.

The Eighteenth Century and the Fourth Estate

THE DAWN OF THE EIGHTEENTH CENTURY brought a flowering of publishing and journalism. In 1709, London was home to more than thirty papers, though only one, the *Daily Courant*, was published daily. By 1792 there would be fourteen daily papers in London. France, between 1600 and 1789, produced more than 1,267 different publications, many of which focused on areas of science and art. Germany's first regularly published daily paper was published in 1718, and France's in 1777. The United States saw its first daily paper, the Pennsylvania *Evening Post*, arrive on May 30, 1783. Newspapers now abounded, but accuracy was still elusive. One journalist of that century complained that reports "daily and monthly arouse mankind with stories of great victories when we are beaten, miracles when we conquer, and a multitude of unaccountable and inconsistent stories which have at least this effect, that people are possessed with wrong notions of things, and wheedled to believe nonsense and contradictions."

The rise of the weekly and daily periodical brought with it the now common notion that the faster the pace of news, the greater the propensity for error. "The chance of making a reporting error (and having one's error detected) increased as did the quantity of hurried, poor-quality newspaper writing," wrote Ward.

The rush to meet deadlines was becoming a reality—and affecting quality. The periodic press of the eighteenth century realized it needed to please and serve readers if it wanted them to purchase the next issue. Their financial survival depended on maintaining the trust of readers, and accuracy was accepted as fundamental to this mission. Benjamin

Harris's earlier expression of a correction policy began to take hold in a more informal way. "[Publishers] started producing weekly or biweekly newssheets on sale from a public office where people could come back and say 'That report doesn't jibe with reality,'" Stephen Ward told me in an interview. "They had to try and retain the reader's confidence."

Publishers responded to the demands of daily publishing by hiring news gatherers—reporters—to cover events and other news. They sat in on trials and gathered information from shippers and farmers for reports about port activity and crops. Much of the news was still dependent on the arrival of ships with fresh information; when they were delayed, something had to fill the pages, or, as we say today, feed the beast. The English papers of that century, along with the boring stock and shipping tables, also traded in rumor and innuendo. Some news came via a chain of people and sources, most of which were impossible to independently verify. These reports ran as is.

In England, news gatherers were given a fresh source of information when, in 1771, the House of Commons allowed reporters inside; the House of Lords followed in 1775. Reporters sent to Parliament were restricted in that, initially, they were not allowed to take notes. They had to write their stories from memory, which had obvious limitations. When asked if the newspaper accounts were faithful to his comments in the House of Commons, one member of Parliament replied, "Why, to be sure, there are in that report a few things which I did say, but many things which I am glad I did not say, and some things which I wish I could have said."

Partisanship was ever present in many reports about politics, but newspapers of the day also saw themselves as sources of amusement, information, and important matters of commerce. "They covered a wide range of topics and their opinion of their role in society grew," wrote Ward. "By mid-century, newspapers grew increasingly fond of claiming that their factual news and impartial judgment were more important to the public than the polemics of the partisan journals."

Factual, impartial reporting continued to be the mantra of many contemporary newspapers, even those that were staunchly in favor of one political party. Some newspapers evolved the idea of what would become known as objectivity, not as a guiding principle of their profession, but because it was seen as what readers wanted. John Walters I founded what would later become the famous London *Times* in 1785, and struck out on a mission to be a "faithful recorder of every species of intelligence," but challenges remained.

"The lack of a proper system of news-gathering made for far too much reliance upon rumor," according to Frank Luther Mott. "Sometimes rumors were printed, with warnings against them; and the heading 'Important—If True' was not uncommon."

Also increasingly common were correction-like statements revealing the failings of previous reports, meant to display the publication's devotion to accuracy, or at the very least the appearance thereof. The *American Herald*, a newspaper published in Boston, on August 30, 1790, printed a notice that acknowledged the failings of a previous report. "We are informed, that a vessel arrived in Cape-Ann last Friday, the Captain of which says he spoke with a British packet, bound to Halifax in a short passage from England, the Commander of which gave him to understand that War was declared by England against Spain." This convoluted statement was basically a correction: The war was indeed on, and it was England who declared it against Spain. We regret the error.

In France and America, the eighteenth-century press was involved in delivering much more than the latest shipping news or word from abroad: It was instrumental in helping foster revolution. Though not every paper of the day preached against the British in the colonies or castigated the royals in France, the century saw the emergence of the idea of a free press dedicated to the public good and the ideals of democracy.

At the lofty end of the spectrum, the press was there, as the voice of the people, to serve as a check on the powerful. Yet this was also a time when a partisan press was the rule, and the century saw the introduction of government control in the form of a 1712 Stamp Act in England, and a similar one in 1765 in the American colonies. Though not direct censorship, it required printers to purchase a stamp for each sheet of paper, putting enormous financial pressure on the printers of the day.

They could survive only by gathering large paying audiences. As a result, newspapers were often inseparable from the causes or political parties they endorsed. This guaranteed them a reader base, though it often laid waste to truth and accuracy.

Edmund Burke, as later reported by Thomas Carlyle in *On Heroes, Hero Worship, and the Heroic in History*, is widely credited with expressing a more philosophical view of the press in a speech he made in the English Parliament. Carlyle wrote that Burke looked to the reporter's gallery and declared them the "Fourth Estate" of Parliament, intimating that publishing and reportage were inextricably linked to democracy. This concept was furthered when the importance of a free press was enshrined in the constitutions of France and the United States. "The embryonic journalism ethics of the early seventeenth century had culminated in a public ethic," wrote Ward. "The public ethic had begun with the rather simple notion that a periodic press wrote for readers and therefore owed the public reliable and factual news. The public ethic, by about 1800, had become a more complex theory based on the idea of a free press, as enshrined in the American and French constitutions."

By the end of the eighteenth century, the ideal of faithful, accurate reporting had merged with the new responsibility of the press to the people in a democratic society.

The Nineteenth Century
FROM EXCESS AND ERROR TO RESPONSIBILITY

L INKING THE FUNCTION OF THE PRESS to the fundamental principles of democracy elevated the role of journalist from scandalmonger and mere recorder of speeches, fires, Parliament, and so on to a major force and influence in society. This newly established role of the newspaper, and the press as a whole, elevated it in people's minds, but there were many individuals for whom newspapers were too expensive to play a part in their daily lives. This would change, particularly in nineteenth-century New York, where the newspaper would flourish and evolve into a form of mass media that everyone could afford, thus contributing to its ever-increasing power and importance in society.

This was the century when newspapers sprouted up all over the United States. Accuracy and factual reporting continued to be their mantra, yet in their pages, inaccuracies and bias were rampant. "These journalists were interested in information, even anxious for information, but they were not yet worshipful of information," wrote news historian Mitchell Stephens. "Occasionally, they would ignore news that challenged their preconceptions: Federalist newspapers in America underplayed the more optimistic reports on Napoleon's fate; Republican newspapers were far more likely to swallow the false reports that French forces had regained the offensive."

The press of this important century would abuse its power and trade accuracy for circulation; it would also launch vitriolic partisan attacks. "When, in the early nineteenth century, political parties and fast cylinder printing presses developed, American journalism became mainly a branch of the party system, with very little pretense to neutral authority or ownership of the facts," wrote Nicholas Lemann in the *New Yorker*.

Along with faster presses, another invention of this century proved essential to news dissemination. On May 11, 1844, Samuel Morse sent the first intercity telegraph message using Morse code. Though he was not the inventor of the telegraph, his improvements to that communication system soon made it an essential tool for newsrooms. The nature of telegraphy also lent itself to the simple communication of facts, which played a role in the emergence of the "inverted pyramid" style of news writing, which began an article with its most important facts. As the London *Times* informed one of its correspondents, "Telegrams are for facts; appreciation and political comment can come by post."

This century would eventually see facts elevated to new heights, but only after decades of hoaxes, journalistic fabrications, and exaggerations had turned people and institutions against the press.

CHAPTER 2

MASS MEDIA: BORN OF A BIG LIE

I N THE LAST WEEK OF AUGUST 1835, the New York *Sun*, one of three daily "penny papers" in the city, offered a portentous front-page story under this headline:

GREAT ASTRONOMICAL DISCOVERIES
Lately Made
BY SIR JOHN HERSCHEL, L.L.D, F.R.S, &c.
At the Cape of Good Hope.

Credited as a reprint from the official-sounding *Edinburgh Journal of Science*, it began by whetting the appetite of readers with a flourish of hyperbole:

> IN THIS UNUSUAL ADDITION TO OUR JOURNAL, we have the happiness of making known to the British publick, and thence to the whole civilized world, recent discoveries in Astronomy which will build an imperishable monument to the age in which we live, and confer upon the present generation of the human race a proud distinction through all future time.

Reprinting articles from other journals and newspapers was common practice. Clearly, however, this was no ordinary article. And in New York, it was the *Sun*'s alone.

The man behind the discoveries was Sir John Herschel, a well-known astronomer of the time who was also the son of an even more renowned astronomer. The article said that Herschel was using a "telescope of vast dimensions and an entirely new principle" to make "the most extraordinary discoveries in every planet of our solar system."

Using his new device, it said, Herschel observed objects on the moon up close and had once and for all answered the question of whether life exists beyond earth. As an afterthought, the article also noted that Herschel had "solved or corrected nearly every leading problem of mathematical astronomy." This was only the beginning. Another article, already "preparing for the press," would be "found of incomparable importance to some of the grandest operations of civilized life."

The affordable "penny papers" had only begun publishing in New York two years prior to the *Sun*'s astronomical story, and three had already sprung up. It was boom time. With this sensational story, the *Sun* had a scoop that was certain to grab the attention of readers in New York's increasingly crowded newspaper market.

The article said that Herschel's mission to build a more powerful telescope led him to collaborate with Sir David Brewster, the Scottish physicist who had invented the kaleidoscope in 1816. It even credits Brewster with "ingenious" suggestions regarding optics in an article in the *Edinburgh Encyclopedia*. (A citation to page 664 was provided for anyone who wanted to look it up.) As the two men exchanged ideas on how to pump up the power of current telescopes, Herschel made sudden, fantastic progress, causing Brewster to spring from his chair "in the ecstasy of conviction" and exclaim, "Thou art the man!" Inspiration had struck.

Lengthy detailed descriptions followed, of the power and dimensions of the magnificent scope, along with digressions into the principles of astronomy for less learned readers. All served to assure the public that the world's most fantastic telescope was indeed installed at the Cape of Good Hope in South Africa with the eye of one of the world's preeminent astronomers firmly set upon it.

The *Sun*'s story was initially accepted as the scoop it claimed to be. William Griggs, who published an analysis of the moon hoax in 1852, said he was standing outside the *Sun*'s offices on the day the first installment appeared. He wrote of seeing crowds clamoring for a copy of the newspaper and said the public greeted the tale with "voracious credulity." He wrote, "The almost universal impression and expression of the multitude was that of confident wonder and insatiable credence." This early acceptance would diminish as the *Sun*'s series advanced and Herschel's findings became increasingly fantastic.

Benjamin Day was the twenty-four-year-old editor and publisher of the paper; tall tales and scandalous reports were a staple of Day's *Sun*. His vision for the *Sun* had been to create a lively paper for the workingman that was more entertaining than the stoic six-cent journals. To achieve this, the *Sun* eschewed politics and listings of recent shipping activity, preferring to run humorous stories or tales about duels and local drunks. In early editions, Day lifted his stories from other papers. He also reprinted their ads to create the impression that the *Sun* was already a success. Clearly, ethics and accuracy were not on his mind. He had a young family to support and needed his new venture to succeed.

"*The Sun* editors sometimes abused the great power at their disposal, and their inexperience caused them more than a few troubles with the law, especially libel suits," wrote Susan Thompson, a journalism professor at the University of Alabama, in her paper, "Rising and Shining: Benjamin Day and His New York *Sun* Before 1836." "Also, the emphasis on fiction passed off for fact severely undermined the progress toward a professional standard that would eventually embrace the ideal of objectivity in news reporting."

The next morning's edition, which hit the streets on August 26, 1835, continued with a second installment of the moon report. It tracked Herschel on his way to South Africa while in the company of Dr. Andrew Grant, a pupil of his father's who discovered the planet Uranus and now worked with Herschel; Lieutenant Drummond of the Royal Engineers; and a "large party of the best English mechanics."

At their destination they erected the massive scope on pillars that rose 150 feet into the air. On the evening of January 10, after testing the device on lesser elements of the sky, they aimed squarely for the "eastern limb" of the moon. The time was 9:30 p.m. Their first sighting was a formation of basaltic rock that was "greenish brown" in color.

Covering the shelf was a dark red flower that Dr. Grant said was "precisely similar to the Papaver Rhoeas, or rose-poppy.

"This," he declared, "was the first organic production of nature, in a foreign world, ever revealed to the eyes of men."

The tale, now being told in the voice of Herschel himself, led readers through a series of discoveries, each more amazing than the last. From the rock and flowers came a "lunar forest." Dr. Grant seemed to wipe a tear from his eye as he deemed the trees the same firs "as I have ever seen cherished in the bosom of my native mountains." The trees led to a mountainous descent that held a lake (or inland sea; the men weren't sure), and then a beach of white sand ("fairer shores never angels coasted on a tour of pleasure," said Dr. Grant). It continued with the emergence of a deep ocean flowing with high tides. The moon was quickly revealing itself to be a pristine paradise, but the men were not yet satisfied. As Herschel noted, "Our chase of animal life was not yet to be rewarded."

A few hundred words later, the chase ended. Herschel spotted a mass of "brown quadrupeds" in another region of forest. He said they resembled bison. Some readers might have found bison a bit tame for the moon, and it was as if Herschel and his scope could sense the disappointment: "The next animal perceived would be classed on earth as a monster. It was of a bluish lead color, about the size of a goat, with a head and beard like him, and a single horn, slightly inclined forward from the perpendicular. The female was destitute of horn and beard, but had a much longer tail. . . . This beautiful creature afforded us the most exquisite amusement."

In the early days of the series some journals reprinted the text outright, while most New York papers condemned it as an outrageous lie. (A month after the series ended, the *New York Herald* reported that the "ingenious hoax is going the rounds still. Every paper that we receive from the West brings it back again. The Bowery Theatre has dramatized it, and now Hannington [a museum] has actually put it on canvas, and placed it for exhibition in his diorama.") The credibility of the articles was quickly being eroded as the discoveries piled on.

At the time, Herschel was known to be at the Cape of Good Hope using new equipment to examine the sky. But the *Sun*'s series was published when there were no telegraph wires to aid in communication, and the mail took weeks to reach England. Not that it mattered. Any letters sent to the *Edinburgh Journal of Science* for confirmation would have gone unanswered, since that particular journal had ceased publication before the articles ran.

The *Sun*'s tale was, of course, a complete fabrication. But the paper wasn't finished yet. The third installment continued with tales of islands, lunar palm trees, volcanoes, and a new assortment of familiar yet exotic animals. They included gold and blue pheasants, miniature zebras and reindeer, elk, moose, horned bears, and the "biped beaver." The fourth installment introduced a species of creatures that came into view after descending from the lunar sky and landing softly on the ground. After the creatures folded away their large wings, the men watched as they walked erect and dignified. The winged walkers were four feet tall and covered almost entirely in copper-colored hair. Their faces had a fleshy color and showed a level of intelligence that was "a slight improvement upon that of the large orang outang, being more open and intelligent in its expression, and having a much greater expansion of forehead."

The group named them *Vespertilio-homo*: man-bats.

And near the man-bats was a giant edifice, ruby in color, that they named the "Ruby Coloseum."

The next day's *Sun* brought word of massive mountains, more oceans, and a huge temple built of polished sapphire. In the sixth and final installment, the man-bats were seen eating fruit and socializing;

An image of the "Ruby Coloseum" reported in the Sun*'s moon hoax of 1835. To make extra money, the paper produced prints such as this one for sale to the public. (Provided by MuseumofHoaxes.com.)*

discoveries were made of the composition of the rings of Saturn; and then a fire destroyed significant parts of the powerful telescope.

Indeed, the damage was done. The series ended with a note from the editor of the *Sun*:

> THIS CONCLUDES THE Supplement, with the exception of forty pages of illustrative and mathematical notes, which would greatly enhance the size and cost of this work, without commeasurably adding to its general interest. —*Ed Sun.*

With that, the *Sun* concluded one of the longest and most audacious fabrications in the history of the media. Though it was published to help draw more readers to the paper, Day, its sensationalist editor, could not have imagined that the series would endure for so long, and be spun and respun with equally specious facts for nearly two centuries.

The hoax also came at a critical point in the history of newspapers. There were two types of newspapers in New York: the six-cent journals of commerce read by the upper class, and the recently launched penny papers, like the *Sun*, that cost a single penny and were aimed at the masses. The penny papers represented a significant shift toward mass media. Their circulation model was contingent upon amassing the largest number of subscribers possible, rather than cultivating a targeted, elite audience. Before the penny papers took hold, the largest paper had been the six-cent *Courier and Enquirer.* It sold 4,500 copies a day.

To draw readers, not only did papers begin to compete for the news of the day, but they also came up with the most outlandish—and often false—news that could be found, or imagined.

The *Sun*'s two rivals, the *New York Transcript* and the *New York Herald,* caught off guard by the moon discoveries, proceeded to demean and mock their competitor's exclusive. The *Transcript* went so far as to invent a character, Captain Thomas Tarbox, that it claimed was with Herschel during the discoveries. In one of the Tarbox articles, the captain reported seeing two of the man-bats fighting a duel with swords: "I consider the discovery I made, a most important one, inasmuch as it proves that some of the inhabitants of the moon are as great fools as those of the earth—to prefer settling a quarrel with edged tools when every sailor knows that the only genteel method of doing the thing is with the bare fist," he wrote.

The *Herald*'s attacks were delayed because a fire had destroyed its offices and printing press three weeks earlier. But once the presses began to roll again, the *Herald* lit into "the impudent *Sun*—the unprincipled *Sun*—the mercenary *Sun*—the low-bred *Sun*—*The Sun* that hoaxes the public—that tells untruths for money."

The *Herald*'s editor, James Gordon Bennett, in the very first issue of his newspaper, in 1835, had attempted to stake out the high journalistic ground. "We shall endeavor to record facts on every public and proper subject, stripped of verbiage and coloring," he declared. Some no doubt found it ironic; the *Herald* was often criticized for its emphasis on gruesome, sensationalized stories of murder and salacious tales of sex scandals—a formula that persists today. In 1840, it would even become the enemy in a "moral war" waged against it by other newspapers.

The same fire that temporarily put the *Herald* out of business would also provide essential, and until now, buried, information that links the inaccuracies of the media during the *Sun*'s days to today. The moon hoax represents more than just a scurrilous new low in the history of the news media's inaccuracy, though that is no slouch of an achievement—the press has been unable to get the facts of this story right at any point during the last 170 years.

In August 2002, almost exactly 167 years to the day since the *Sun* ran its first moon installment, *US News & World Report* published a special issue about "the art of the hoax." One of its stories was a retelling of the moon hoax.

"The New York *Sun*'s army of loudmouthed paperboys marched down the steamy streets of the city in the summer of 1835," it began. "They shouted out headlines no one could resist: Beavers, bison, and bat-boys had been discovered on the moon. Daily sales of *The Sun* skyrocketed from 4,000 to 19,000—making it the world's most popular paper and launching a new kind of journalism."

The meteoric rise of the *Sun*'s circulation during the moon series has become one of the foundations of the hoax story. It is mentioned in nearly every account of the hoax that can be found in newspapers, magazines, and books, and on the Internet. The success of the hoax is cited as the source of the *Sun*'s growth, and also a major factor in the rise of the penny papers during the *Sun*'s time.

The penny papers did usher in a new form of publishing and with it a new type of mass media journalism. The *Sun*'s hoax was also a key event in establishing the popularity of the paper. But reports of the *Sun*'s circulation gains are questionable at best, adding a modern level of deception to the hoax of 1835.

On the fourth day of the hoax, the *Sun* printed a notice that pegged its circulation at 19,360. "We do not hesitate to say that our circulation is the greatest of any daily paper in the world, (the daily edition of the London Times being only 17,000)," it boasted. "Our only present difficulty is to strike off a sufficient number for the demand."

The *Sun* could have achieved that circulation during the hoax. By its own admission, however, this actually represented a *decline* in its circulation from what it had been twelve days earlier, when it ran this notice:

ENORMOUS CIRCULATION—At the time of penning this paragraph—5 P.M. Wednesday afternoon—the enormous number of twenty-six thousand copies of yesterday's edition of The Sun had been issued to carriers and sold at our counter, and our publishing office is still thronged with persons waiting to be supplied:—our press, though a double cylinder, not being able to print them as fast as they have been demanded. We may safely assert that no other one paper in the Union, nor in the world, ever sold as many papers in one day, as we did yesterday.

That day—August 13, 1835—was just after the massive fire burned the *Herald* temporarily out of business. While this was a onetime event, it represented a greater circulation spike than the hoax had delivered. Since the early days of the hoax, however, that has not been the story. Searches in newspaper archives turn up thousands of hits on the hoax, with a great number repeating the tale of increased circulation. There is no doubt that the hoax series provided a lift in the *Sun's* circulation. But it was not an unprecedented increase, and not the largest the paper had experienced.

From the 1800s through the 1900s and into the 2000s, the hoax has been kept alive by a media that preferred to take the facts at face value. It added exaggeration to the initial fabrication, rather than set the record straight.

Fortunately, it is Alex Boese's job to challenge accepted wisdom, especially when it comes to hoaxes. Boese is the founder of MuseumofHoaxes.com and the author of three books on the subject. While pursuing a master's degree at the University of California at San Diego, he selected the moon hoax as his thesis topic and, over the course of two years, read the *Sun* as well as many other papers from the time. Though he never finished his thesis, his work represents perhaps the only accurate retelling of the hoax and its impact.

Boese provided me with the *Sun's* earlier circulation claim, and clippings from many of the paper's competitors. In addition to revealing the circulation fallacy, he also debunked the equally retold tale that the public and other papers fell for the hoax en masse. In reality, the *Sun's* competitors were not fooled for a second. Nor were the majority of high-class journals in New York. (Boese found that two of them—the *Mercantile Advertiser* and the *Daily Advertiser*—did, in fact, profess their belief in the *Sun's* series. As Boese wrote in his unfinished dissertation: "For this, they were roundly mocked by the other papers.")

"There was a huge amount of skepticism at the time of the moon hoax," Boese told me. "I tried to look at every newspaper I could get my hands on, and only a few papers I found kind of suggested they believed it. That's completely different from the accounts."

Over the last nearly two centuries, the *Sun's* hoax has been kept alive and given the polish of misreported history, making it all the more audacious. No doubt, Benjamin Day would be proud.

Hearst, Pulitzer, and Sulzberger
A BATTLE FOR THE SOUL OF JOURNALISM

HOW DO YOU LIKE the Journal's War?" asked the front page of William Randolph Hearst's *New York Journal* for two days in 1898. This evocative question likely elicited a common response from his readers of the day: just fine.

In April of that year, war broke out in Cuba between Spain, who controlled Cuba, and the United States. This war, which lasted 113 days and resulted in an American victory, would eventually become famous for what is said to have helped cause it, and for a single piece of communication that supposedly sums up this period in journalism. That communication was a telegram exchange between Hearst and illustrator Frederic Remington, who had been sent to Cuba in January 1897 with correspondent Richard Harding Davis. They were there to report on the Spanish rule of Cuba and provide the *Journal* with images and reports from the volatile colony. After their arrival, Remington is said to have cabled Hearst that "everything is quiet. There will be no war. I wish to return." Hearst famously replied, "Please remain. You furnish the pictures and I'll furnish the war."

This exchange is legendary in the annals of journalism and has become known as the perfect encapsulation of the period of "yellow journalism" that took hold in New York at the end of the nineteenth century. With the passage of time and the work of journalism scholars, however, it has now been widely debunked. "It is often cited as exhibit 'A' in the dubious argument that Hearst fomented the Spanish-American war of 1898," according to W. Joseph Campbell, a historian of yellow journalism who amassed evidence to suggest that the exchange never occurred. Remington did in fact leave Cuba, but it was at the behest of Davis, an experienced correspondent, who had asked him to go. Davis remained and filed reports about executions at the hands of the Spanish, and other matters, reports that did help provide the *Journal* with the kind of on-the-spot examples of Spanish crimes it desired. Hearst was gung ho for conflict, and over time he came to be blamed for starting the war. To say that Hearst's paper caused the war is an exaggeration, but he and his paper were certainly invested in seeing it happen and did their best to create public support for it. In fact, Hearst viewed that kind of activist agitation as the core of a new form of journalism.

Though the existence of the famous telegram has proved doubtful, Hearst's view of journalism made many feel that he could have sent such a message. Hearst, along with publishers such as Joseph Pulitzer, was at the forefront of a new kind of journalism that captivated readers in New York and elsewhere. He called it the "journalism of action." Campbell wrote that Hearst "argued newspapers were obliged to inject themselves, conspicuously and vigorously, in righting the wrongs of public life, and in filling the void of government inaction and incompetence." The *Journal* itself outlined its mission in the words "The new journalism does things; the old journalism stands around and objects."

In pursuing this vision, prior to 1898, the *Journal* was one of the leading voices calling for war with Spain over Cuba, and one reporter for the paper even went so far as to organize a jailbreak for an imprisoned woman being held by the Spanish in Cuba. More than the imagined telegram, that incident is a shining example of the "journalism of action." One can also look to the *Journal*'s headlines of the time to see its role in helping beat the drums of war. On February 18, 1898, it declared, "THE WHOLE COUNTRY THRILLS WITH THE WAR FEVER."

Hearst's paper is today best known for its part in "yellow journalism," a practice at the end of the nineteenth century that saw him pursue sensationalist reporting in competition with Joseph Pulitzer's higher-circulation *New York World*. That time is commonly viewed as a low point in journalism, a period when the two press magnates sought to outdo each other with the most lascivious, outrageous, and attention-grabbing reporting possible. In the course of trying to destroy each other, they came close to destroying the reputation of the press itself. Yet it was the failures of such papers as the *World* and the *Journal* that proved most important to journalism and accuracy. Their excesses and the ensuing public outcry set the stage for journalism to look inward and pursue a less activist, more restrained, and dispassionately factual model. This helped give birth to the professionalized, accuracy-seeking press we find today in democratic societies.

Key to this evolution was another paper of the time, a small-circulation daily that was purchased out of bankruptcy court in 1896 by a young Adolph S. Ochs. It was the *New York Times*, and Ochs had his work cut out for him. In New York, papers such as the *Journal, Sun, World,* and *New York Commercial Advertiser* were already beating the pants off the *Times* in circulation and influence. Ochs looked at his competition and saw an opportunity to set his broadsheet apart. In October 1896, he purchased a huge advertising sign in Madison Square and spelled out his new slogan in red lights, "All the News That's Fit to Print."

Behind the slogan was Ochs's plan for a paper that "offered a detached, impartial, fact-based paradigm that embraced innovative technologies emergent in the late nineteenth century but eschewed extravagance, prurience, and flamboyance in presenting the news," wrote Campbell in his book, *The Year That Defined American Journalism,* a single-year study of the occurrences of 1897. Ochs himself set out his vision for the paper in a memo to staff on August 19, 1896. He spoke of a "sincere desire to conduct a high-standard newspaper, clean, dignified and trustworthy" and how this required "honesty, watchfulness, earnestness, industry and practical knowledge applied with common sense." Ochs's goal was to "give the news impartially, without fear or favor, regardless of any party, sect or interest involved."

His was to be a paper of decency, and this meant toning down political partisanship and scandalous content, and offering trustworthy reporting. In his own reserved way, he was going to war with the *Journal* and the *World,* among others. It was a battle for readers, but its legacy would cast it as a battle for the soul of journalism itself.

Ochs sought to set himself apart from the "new journalism" of the yellow press, while also pursuing a more straightforward approach than the *New York Commercial Advertiser,* then the city's oldest paper. J. Lincoln Steffens, the *Advertiser*'s city editor, was shunning professional reporters and instead recruiting young men who could tell a story with literary flair. Ochs found a place for his paper in the middle of the road, with a focus on dispassionate, professional reporting, an emphasis on business news, and, critically, a reduced price. (In fact, he reduced the price to one cent from three cents in October 1898 in large part due to a disgruntled associate who threatened to expose the *Times*'s inflated circulation numbers to advertisers. So not all was ethical in the *Times*'s house.) This was the beginning of what would eventually make the *Times* the "paper of record."

Michael Schudson wrote in his 1978 book, *Discovering the News*, that the *Times* represented one of the "two journalisms" of the late nineteenth century. It was the "journalism as information" model, whereas the Pulitzer and Hearst papers were "journalism as entertainment." Campbell's study of the journalism of 1897 notes that these papers all provided a mix of entertainment and information, but the dichotomy between the journalism of action, or "public journalism," and the *Times*' more reserved model was clear.

Much like the penny press from the early part of the century, the activist papers sought sensational, colorful, captivating stories. Because journalists had not yet dedicated themselves to the ideal of total accuracy and there were no widespread ethics in the profession, inaccurate and outright false reporting was still common. Edwin L. Shuman wrote a handbook for journalists in 1894 and advised that it was acceptable for a journalist to make up aspects of a story he had not seen firsthand as long as these details didn't pollute the overall truth of the story. The practice was "perhaps excusable as long as the imaginative writing is confined to non-essentials and is done by one who has in him at least the desire to represent the truth," he wrote. Shuman called it one of the "most valuable secrets of the profession at its present stage of development. Truth in essentials, imagination in non-essentials, is considered a legitimate rule of action in every office. The paramount objective is to make an interesting story."

Another common maneuver in the industry was for newspapers to mock, demean, and ridicule one another in order to sway the paying public. Ochs's paper accused the *Journal* of practicing "freak journalism," and Pulitzer's paper took to calling its competitors "derelicts of journalism." Near the end of the century, Charles Dana, editor of the New York *Sun*, declared, "I have never published a falsehood." Pulitzer retorted, "That is another lie."

It was a competitive environment, where sniping at the crosstown rival was commonplace, and these criticisms often took the form of accusations of unprofessionalism, inaccuracy, or recklessness. In one example, Pulitzer's *World* was thrilled in early 1897 to trumpet its proof that a major story in the *Journal* turned out to be in error.

On February 12, the *Journal* had given huge billing to Richard Harding Davis's report that Spanish police had boarded an American ship headed for Florida and strip-searched three Cuban women suspected of carrying messages to anti-Spanish-rule forces in America. The *Journal's* front-page headline read, "Does Our Flag Protect Women? Indignities Practiced by Spanish Officials on Board American Vessels. Richard Harding Davis Describes Some Startling Phases of Cuban Situation. Refined Young Women Stripped and Searched by Brutal Spaniards While Under Our Flag on the Olivette."

But the story was not totally accurate, and Davis would later write an account explaining the mistake and laying the blame at the feet of Remington, the illustrator, who drew a picture showing the women being searched in the presence of men. Men had not, in fact, taken part in any strip search. After the *World* learned of the mistake, it ran a front-page story under the headline "'Tale of a Fair Exile.' Senorita Arango's Own Story of the Olivette 'Search Outrage.' A Statement to the World. She Loved Cuba for Whose Freedom All Her Brothers Are Now Fighting. Visited them in Camp; Banished, She Denies Richard Harding Davis' Story that Men Saw Her Stripped and Searched."

Davis, so upset by Remington's incorrect image and the headline it wrought, never worked for Hearst again. The *World* was thrilled with its exclusive. Though its own reporting was of no higher standard, it never missed an opportunity to point out the errors of the competition.

Given this environment, it was no surprise that the *Times* and particularly the *Sun* were thrilled when, on February 4, 1897, the Newark Free Public Library's trustees voted to cancel subscriptions to the *Journal* and the *World* due to their content. By May, the boycott had reached ninety other institutions. This was a reaction to the yellow press and its supposed descent into the gutter due to its use of caricatures, gossip, and other scandalous fare. The boycott was spurred by a bill proposing to restrict the printing of caricatures and illustrations of people without their consent. The bill would have seriously restricted the ability of the papers to publish commentary in an illustrated format, and therefore have been a threat to freedom of the press and freedom of speech. The bill and boycott were initially popular with some politicians and members of the public who deemed what these papers published to be unsuitable and often wholly inaccurate. The publishers faced a fine of $1,000 and even prison time for doing what today is common practice. The boycott eventually waned and the bill was defeated—good news for the press as a whole—but it proved to be a powerful rebuke to the journalism of Hearst and Pulitzer—and yet another example of how incorrect reporting can threaten freedom of the press and freedom of speech.

THE SPANISH-AMERICAN WAR of 1898 and the *Journal*'s boisterous support for it would be another key death blow to the "journalism of action." (Though support for the war was widespread among newspapers of the day, there were marked differences in how they behaved. Hearst's paper managed to distinguish itself by being louder and more outrageous than the rest.)

The benefit of hindsight has served to reduce the amount of blame laid at the feet of the yellow papers for starting the war. They played a role but not a decisive one. What is true, however, is that the lead-up to the war, and the war itself, was the low point of a low period in journalism, a time when its excesses and errors led to the rise of a more dispassionate, fact-based model of reporting that would be adopted as the vision of a more professionalized press. In many ways, the Spanish-American War was the last loud gasp of yellow journalism. Without yellow journalism, we might not have the journalism of today. Times were changing, and the *Times* was on the ascendant.

"As the century progressed, violations of the truth, while they were certainly not eliminated from journalism, began to be looked upon more seriously," wrote Mitchell Stephens in *A History of News*. "Accuracy had become a sacred duty because facts increasingly were held sacred."

By the end of the nineteenth century, the period of yellow journalism had drawn to a close and participants such as Pulitzer began working to move journalism in a more respectable, professionalized direction. With this shift, the *New York Times* began its ascent to its place as the most influential newspaper in America, if not the world. Near the end of the century, Pulitzer placed a prominent notice of the new ethic on a newsroom wall at the *New York World:*

"THE FACTS—THE COLOR—THE FACTS!" read one sign. "ACCURACY! ACCURACY! ACCURACY!" commanded another. Pulitzer saw the writing on the wall, but in another sense: The journalism of action and the era of yellow journalism were over. In 1913, due to his recognition of the difficulties in distinguishing "that which is true and that which is false," Ralph Pulitzer, Joseph's son, created a Bureau of Accuracy and Fair Play at the *World,* and with it came the first newspaper ombudsman.

The Twentieth Century
ACCURACY AS CODE

As JOURNALISM ENTERED the twentieth century, it was flourishing, and it was obsessed with itself. By 1915 there were well over 2,000 daily English-language papers in the United States, with another 160 in other languages. This massive growth would eventually lead to some contraction in the industry, and news chains and wire services had already sprung up to serve the growing empires of men such as E.W. Scripps and Randolph Hearst.

After the wars of yellow journalism, Joseph Pulitzer was in the process of resuscitating his reputation; in 1902 he approached Columbia University to discuss funding a journalism school along with a series of prizes for the best in journalism and other literary pursuits. He set forth his vision for the Pulitzer Prizes in the 1904 edition of his will, which specified that, among other awards, four of them should be given for journalism. He left the future awards and subjects open to determination by an advisory board. The first Pulitzer Prizes would be handed out in 1917.

Also in 1904, Pulitzer expressed his vision for his journalism school in an article in the *North American Review*. "Our Republic and its press will rise or fall together," he wrote. "An able, disinterested, public-spirited press, with trained intelligence to know the right and courage to do it, can preserve that public virtue without which popular government is a sham and a mockery. A cynical, mercenary, demagogic press will produce in time a people as base as itself. The power to mould the future of the Republic will be in the hands of the journalists of future generations."

Columbia's Graduate School of Journalism opened on September 30, 1912, a decade after Pulitzer had first raised the idea. By that time, the University of Missouri's program was four years old, and today claims the title of the world's first journalism school. Many more would follow, and by 1996, 54 percent of newspaper newsroom employees held an under-graduate degree in journalism or communications, according to a survey by the American Society of Newspaper Editors. With journalism schools cropping up at universities all over North America and beyond, news organizations took up the march toward professionalization, a process inextricably linked to the importance of accuracy.

The early twentieth century was critical for the growth and accept-ance of accuracy in the North American press, and its evolution would influence other journalists around the world. But this period also saw some notable failures of fact. On November 7, 1918, the United Press wire service, today known as UPI, reported that World War I had ended—four days before the official armistice. The report was corrected that day, but it did appear in newspapers and had a significant effect on the wire service's reputation, according to one expert.

"It was a major gaffe," Billy G. Ferguson, who worked for UPI for forty years and is the coauthor of *Unipress: United Press International Covering the 20th Century*, told me. "It drastically affected UPI's growth thereafter. For a long time American editors wouldn't take up a UPI report without having an AP [story as confirmation]. They said it was because UPI was reckless. It was a stain on UPI's reputation, but also a hallmark of UPI's enthusiasm and push to get the news in a competi-tive manner."

Another now-famous example of error came a year later when the *New York Times* printed story after incorrect story about how the Bolsheviks in Russia were being soundly defeated. When the revolution was successful, the paper had a lot of backpedaling to do. Though errors and outright fabrications were on their way to becoming enemies of journalism, in the early stages of the newly sanitized press they still occurred, as they do today. It is inevitable that mistakes will be made, but what matters for accuracy is the clear determination to eliminate errors, acknowledge those that occur, and institute a high ethical standard within the press.

In the early twentieth century, errors were acknowledged to be bad for business and bad for journalism. So the industry responded. For the first time, codes of ethics were adopted in newsrooms to guide the daily work of reporters and editors. Accuracy was always at the core of these statements. Professional ideals were finally being put down on paper as ethical statements rather than advertisements. The press was, in effect, making a promise to the public about what it would do and why it could be trusted.

"I have no thought of saying The Associated Press is perfect," wrote Melville Stone, the general manager of AP, in 1914, adding that "the thing it is striving for is a truthful, unbiased report of the world's happenings . . . ethical in the highest degree."

The AP's current "Statement of News Values" says, "We abhor inaccuracies, carelessness, bias or distortions. It means we will not knowingly introduce false information into material intended for publication or broadcast; nor will we alter photo or image content. Quotations must be accurate, and precise."

The American Society of Newspaper Editors first adopted its "Canons of Journalism" in 1922. Its current version, called the "Statement of Principles," includes the dictum "Every effort must be made to assure [sic] that the news content is accurate, free from bias and in context, and that all sides are presented fairly. Editorials, analytical articles and commentary should be held to the same standards of accuracy with respect to facts as news reports. Significant errors of fact, as well as errors of omission, should be corrected promptly and prominently."

By the 1930s, the ethics of journalism and the reverence for accuracy were finally being clearly articulated and standardized within newsrooms, and journalists—once derided, ridiculed, and looked down upon—were being trained at some of the world's leading universities. "By the 1930s . . . a revolution in ethics had occurred," wrote Ward.

Though newspapers had proclaimed their values and preached truth and accuracy for at least four hundred years, one of the most significant changes was that, in the twentieth century, people—journalists included—began to truly believe these claims and expect them to be visible in the journalism of the day. The result was that, among the public and in the halls of power, expectations were raised as to how the press would behave and conduct its daily work. The loud proclamations of the new profession of journalism—ethical, accurate, and an essential part of a free society—now came with the academic and policy credentials to back them up. There was no turning back. Accuracy had arrived as both an ethic and an expectation.

CHAPTER 3

REGRETS, MORE THAN A FEW

THE 1948 U.S. PRESIDENTIAL ELECTION was held in a time
before daily tracking polls, sophisticated voter research, and other
tools of the trade today. Nevertheless, it looked like it was going to be
easy to call.

New York governor Thomas E. Dewey appeared to be on his way to
a clear victory over incumbent Harry S. Truman. Public opinion polls
showed that Dewey was well ahead, even cruising. Truman, who was
elevated to the presidency after Franklin D. Roosevelt died, had less
money for his campaign and, it appeared, little hope. The press had
largely written him off.

It seemed the headlines declaring a Dewey victory were already
being cast into hot lead, ready for the press.

"Dewey Defeats Truman"

IN THE SPIRIT OF HIS STATE MOTTO, "Show me," Truman, a
former haberdasher from Independence, Missouri, decided to ignore
the polls and the press and take his campaign on a whistle-stop tour of
the country. When his train stopped at stations large and small,
Truman, standing on the platform of the last car, gave impassioned
speeches that rang true with voters. The crowds waiting to greet him got
bigger at every stop, and soon the call "Give 'em hell, Harry!" caught on
with his supporters. In the end, he traveled "21,000 miles, stopping in
more than 250 cities, and delivering more than 300 speeches." But
when he and his wife, Bess, went to cast their votes in Independence,
on November 2, 1948, his chances still looked grim.

That same day, workers at the *Chicago Daily Tribune* were preparing for their final bit of election coverage. They were struggling. The skilled workers who operated the Linotype machines—huge, clacking creations that turned type into small bricks of lead used to make the printing plates for a daily newspaper—were on strike. Members of the powerful International Typographical Union had been off the job at all of Chicago's six daily newspapers since November 1947. (In the end, the strike would last for twenty-two months.)

"The printers promised 24-hour-a-day picket lines around the six Chicago dailies," reported *Time* magazine when the strike began. "The publishers promised they would print anyway, by photoengraving. The papers began a frantic scramble to hire typists. The *Sun* hired 80 and set up day and night shifts. All the papers buckled down to give Chicago its daily news, in spite of the strike."

And so, a little less than a year later, on Election Day 1948, the *Chicago Daily Tribune*, like the five other papers in the city, was preparing to put out its election editions without its speedy Linotype machines and the workers who operated them. Substitute workers were in the composing room; the hulking Linotypes were silent.

As returns slowly came in from polling stations across the country, the deadline for the first edition approached, and the *Tribune* was forced to make a call on whether to declare the election in Dewey's favor. His returns looked solid, but there were many states still to file their returns, even in the eastern part of the country.

The inexperienced staff needed to get moving, and the paper didn't want to lose out to its many local competitors. The newspaper couldn't wait for the news.

"A call was made to the paper's Washington correspondent, Arthur Sears Henning, who had been wrong just once in the previous 20 years," the *Tribune* would later report. "He stuck by his prediction that it would be Dewey."

The first edition of the paper, made available by 7:30 p.m. on election night, carried the front page headline "GOVERNOR DEWEY CLAIMS VICTORY." The 9 p.m. edition, the second of eleven editions put out by the paper throughout that evening and into the next morning, declared, "DEWEY DEFEATS TRUMAN."

Only newspaper collectors remember the first edition, and almost nobody remembers editions three through eleven. But the second edition of the *Chicago Daily Tribune*, dated November 3, 1948, is today one of the most recognized press errors in history.

It was by no means the first or last incorrect presidential election headline by a newspaper. In the 1876 race between Rutherford B. Hayes and Samuel J. Tilden, many papers mistakenly gave the victory to Tilden. In 1916, the *San Francisco Examiner* put Charles Hughes in the White House instead of Woodrow Wilson.

In 2000, many different newspapers, Web sites, and broadcasters made errors in calling the race between George W. Bush and Al Gore. Four years later, prior to Election Day 2004, the *New York Post* made a

Harry S. Truman celebrates his 1948 presidential victory by displaying the erroneous front page of the Chicago Daily Tribune. *(From the Collections of the St. Louis Mercantile Library.)*

major gaffe when it declared on July 6 that Democratic candidate John Kerry would name Representative Dick Gephardt as his running mate. Kerry's choice turned out to be John Edwards.

"So call it 'Dewey Defeats Truman,' call it a 'Gaffe-hardt,' call it a chicken farm's worth of egg on our face—just remember that we're striving every day to bring you the most informative, the most enlightening and, yes, the most amusing newspaper in town," apologized the *New York Post* on July 7, 2004.

On the night of November 2, 1948, as more returns poured in, the *Tribune* began to see its error. It sent its trucks out to collect the mistaken second edition. Many copies had already been sold, but a good portion was reclaimed from sellers. One copy, however, began a trip that would secure the headline's place in history.

After his victory, Truman set out for Washington aboard his train, Victory Special. Early in the trip, on November 4, his caravan pulled into Union Station in St. Louis. "Thousands of St. Louisians swept aside police lines and swarmed over the tracks in Union Station when the President's train pulled into St. Louis this afternoon," reported the *New York Times.* "Crowds behind a glassed-in fence yelled, 'Open the gates or we'll break them down.'"

Along with the more than ten thousand supporters there to greet the train was Pierce W. "Pete" Hangge, a photographer with the St. Louis *Globe-Democrat.* He and other press photographers snapped photos of Truman and the adoring crowd.

Standing on the rear platform of his train car at a podium embossed with the presidential seal, Truman held up a copy of the *Tribune* to show the crowd the headline: "DEWEY DEFEATS TRUMAN." Thousands erupted in cheers. Truman kept playing to them. "Several times the president raised the newspaper and turned about so that all sections of the crowd could have a look," wrote the *Times.*

Many photographers got a shot of a smiling Truman brandishing the paper, but Hangge took the shot that has today become one of the iconic images of electoral triumph and press inaccuracy. It shows a beaming Truman seeming to lean over and thrust the paper out into the crowd. At the center is the paper, its headline large and loud.

Thanks to that photograph, people all over the country got a laugh at the *Tribune's* expense. The next day, the *Chicago Sun-Times* ran a front-page photo of Truman mocking its competitor. Later, the president had the headline turned into a paperweight that he kept on his desk in the Oval Office.

Even though the pollsters, the prognosticators, and many political reporters had been wrong about what election night would reveal, the *Tribune* became the emblem of error. But it was not the only publication to have erred on its front page. Few recall what Truman did after he finished having fun with the *Tribune.* Setting down that paper, he repeated the routine with the November 6 issue of the *Billboard* (today known as

Billboard magazine). Its cover, according to the *Times,* "showed a singer holding a big placard portrait of Mr. Dewey." The headline read, "OUR NEXT PRESIDENT."

But Hangge's shot was of Truman with the *Tribune,* and so no one remembers *Billboard'*s folly. Few are also aware of the other mistakes contained in the famous edition of the *Tribune.* That edition of the paper was in fact a comedy of errors. The printers' strike made it impossible to properly and quickly set and correct type. That meant the *Tribune* relied on typewriters instead of Linotype machines, and on less-skilled workers. Through a combination of human error and insufficient technology, "The front page was done with a typewriter because nobody knew how to run the Linotype machines," I was told by Rick Brown, who was for thirteen years the publisher and editor of *Collectible Newspapers,* the newspaper of the Newspaper Collectors Society of America. "They typed out the columns one at a time and then glued them down. If they made an error in the vote totals, they'd go back and just 'X' out a digit. If it said 762 votes for Dewey but the correct number was 782, they'd go back to where '6' was and keep hitting '8' until it was a lot darker [than the 6]."

Someone responsible for gluing down the typewritten columns also managed to place five lines of text upside down in a below-the-fold story. The incorrect headline was, of course, the worst mistake of all. As is often the case with errors large and small, many factors came into play to deliver this famous front-page disaster.

The election results were also late coming, so the paper had incomplete information on which to make its news judgment; it had to take an educated guess, and it guessed wrong. This was partly the fault of the editors and the reporter who made the call, and partly the result of the incorrect Gallup Polls and internal *Tribune* data that had made Dewey look like a sure thing. Their reporting failed them, and their sources did as well.

The errors in the "Dewey Defeats Truman" edition of the paper were the result of a series of unique but related failings that converged on one evening in 1948: the strike, the polls, the staff, the technology on hand, the deadline, and in the end, a mistaken assumption by one of the paper's respected reporters. But in the debacle's aftermath, the paper was not in the mood for introspection or self-analysis.

The *Tribune* addressed its error in a story titled "Never Again, We Hope." It placed the blame largely on the pollsters and their "alleged science."

"We were dim on Dewey from the start," it also declared.

"Having been bitten as badly as the next one, we hope that we have the courage to swear off these sessions with the crystal ball in the future," it said. "Divination and inspection of the entrails ought to be left to the vanished priests of ancient Rome. The science is too fallible."

And that was all. The paper moved on, but the photograph and story live on. The *Tribune*'s desire to get past its error and not look at root causes beyond the failure of pollsters and their "crystal ball" is still commonplace in today's press. But even the most basic of errors have a provenance. They happen for a reason, or, frequently, for a variety of them.

As a result, errors tell many truths about journalism.

A Theory of Error

THE STUDY OF HUMAN ERROR began, unlikely enough, with a tin of cat food and a teapot. The aptly named James Reason, then a professor of psychology at the University of Manchester in England in the late 1970s, was at home making tea for himself and preparing to feed the hungry cat nipping at his heels. After removing the lid on the cat food, he swiftly dumped its contents into an open receptacle nearby, not realizing that it was his teapot. As he would later determine, both the pot and the cat's bowl were used for holding things, but his brain failed to distinguish between the two. The result was a teapot full of brewed cat food.

That single moment of absentmindedness became Reason's Newtonian apple, a perfect, accidental moment of inspiration. Reason, who is now a retired professor emeritus of psychology at the university, realized that "a new research topic was literally under his nose. In tracing the causes of absent-minded incidents, [he] began an exploration of human error." Reason started cataloging examples of error and working to track their origins. As with his food-in-the-teapot experience, he discovered that "you begin to see the kinds of conditions that create [error], where you have for example two objects, like a teapot and a cat's bowl, which are for putting in, you just get the wrong ones in."

With his books *Human Error* and *Managing the Risks of Organizational Accidents*, Reason established himself as the leading researcher in human error and became a sought-after consultant for workplace and organizational safety and error management. His work has been applied to the airline industry to help reduce pilot error and crashes, to the shipping industry to help prevent oil tanker spills and other errors, and to the nuclear industry to prevent another Chernobyl. More recently, he was a leading voice and consultant in major international initiatives to provide better patient safety in the medical profession. These are all what he calls "high reliability" industries—in which errors can have catastrophic results, and failure is not an option. As does journalism, these professions rely on a mix of highly trained people to work in a high-stress, time-sensitive environment with a variety of processes and technologies.

While even the worst journalistic error is hardly akin to an airline crash or reactor meltdown, the press plays an essential role in the flow of critical information that affects every part of our lives. When this information is incorrect or misrepresented, the consequences can be serious to both individuals and society as a whole. As for the press, errors exact a high toll on its credibility, which, in turn, causes people to look elsewhere for information. The result of fewer readers or viewers then affects the bottom line. Typically, people don't die when the press errs (though it has happened in extreme cases), but media mistakes are a threat to society, free speech, and the media itself. As such, it would benefit the press to think of itself as a "high reliability" industry in the context of Reason's work. The fact that journalism doesn't put as much emphasis on error prevention and management as does the airline industry is one of the reasons why—even though accuracy is acknowledged as a fundamental of journalism—media errors are so commonplace.

Along with Reason's research into the cognitive malfunctions that can cause us to drop cat food in a teapot or type one word when we mean another, he pinpointed "error traps" that exist outside of our minds. He found that many industries create environments, technologies, and processes that repeatedly produce, or force, the same error. In other words, he found that human error is rarely the result of humans alone. This is particularly important to remember because technology plays an increasingly relevant role in reporting and journalism.

One of the most famous examples of an error trap occurred during World War II. As new planes with new technology were being developed and deployed by the United States, there was an alarming increase in the number of crashes and other accidents in combat and training; to explain it, the term "pilot error" came into much more frequent use. It seemed suspect to blame it all solely on the pilots, so Lieutenant Colonel Paul Fitts and his air force colleague Captain Richard Jones began interviewing pilots to try to determine the cause of the incidents. They soon noticed a pattern: Pilots frequently reported that the controls inside the cockpit were confusing or inconveniently placed. The cockpit was trapping pilots into making errors.

"The strong link between inadequate design and 'pilot error' was buttressed by one of Fitts and Jones's most compelling findings: almost all the pilots interviewed reported that they sometimes made errors in the cockpit, *regardless of their level of skill and experience* [emphasis in the original]," wrote Kim Vicente in his 2003 book, *The Human Factor: Revolutionizing the Way People Live with Technology*. The air force responded by redesigning or modifying the cockpit controls, and, once the error traps had been removed, "pilot error" was reduced or eliminated altogether. This literally saved lives, not to mention a lot of very expensive aircraft.

This attention to the system in which a person operates is one way of managing error. But there are still spectacular failures in industries where safety is of paramount importance and detailed controls are built in. Often they are due to "active failure"—that is, when a human subverts the system. "At Chernobyl, for example, the operators wrongly violated plant procedures and switched off successive safety systems, thus creating the immediate trigger for the catastrophic explosion in the core," Reason wrote in the *British Medical Journal* in 2000.

At their core, errors are a result of both the human factor and the system in which we operate. To prevent and manage errors—Reason observes that a 100 percent error-free industry or practice is unattainable—one must address the human element alongside the system people interact with and the tools they use.

In journalism, a reporter who produces a story that contains an error is expected to take the blame. Whether reporters misspell someone's name or misquote a source, the error is largely seen as theirs and theirs alone. If a computerized spell-checker fails them, it's not considered an excuse; the industry ethic is that the journalist must own up to it. The same holds true for an error introduced in the editing process. A copy editor who ineptly recasts a sentence and thereby causes a mistake is required to accept blame, which, when a correction is made, then attaches to the media outlet as a whole.

Even though corrections do not name the reporter or editor responsible for the error, the individual's accountability for it is part of the essential contract of journalism: Publishers and broadcasters are expected to do their best to report accurately and fairly and are required to acknowledge and correct any errors they make. The public, as with other industries, is willing to accept a certain level of error—if it is acknowledged and corrected. But what about error prevention? How many errors are too many for the public to accept?

In the early nineties, the Centre for Asia Pacific Aviation surveyed air travelers about their attitudes toward airline safety and error. "We concluded that the public generally accepts that accidents are relatively rare and commercial airline flying very safe relative to the alternatives," Peter Harbison, the center's chairman, wrote in a 2007 article. "But we also concluded that once a threshold of accidents was reached, this confidence would be seriously eroded and would significantly deter travelers from flying."

The same holds true for journalistic errors: There is a threshold at which public trust begins to erode. As research from Philip Meyer and others has shown, errors have a deleterious impact on the credibility of a newspaper. In fact, accuracy is one of the most effective predictors of newspaper credibility. Simply put, more errors equal less credibility. As people begin to see what they consider to be too many errors, they disengage and may eventually tune out altogether. The practice of

accepting blame and providing accountability in journalism acknowledges the human side of press errors, and a concerted effort to track
and correct mistakes builds trust.

The accountability of the press is partly due to professional ethics,
but also—and perhaps even more importantly—to help ensure the all-
important accuracy of the public record and free flow of accurate
information in a democracy. Without accurate reporting, a democratic
society will suffer. The consequences of media errors beg for the kind of
study applied by the air force in World War II, but research into the
cause of press errors is dwarfed by a focus on counting those that do
occur, as I explore in Chapter 4.

Thanks to research that began in 1936, we have a reasonable concept of how accurate daily newspapers and television news are, what
their most common errors are, and how often they are corrected.
Causation, however, is largely left to assumptions or simplified varia-
tions on "I goofed" or "I forgot" or "I was misled." This lack of insight
contributes to the ongoing occurrence of journalistic errors.

Media errors are born of any number of factors, both human and
systemic, some of which are under the press's control. The most
common causes of error, however, are sloppy, hurried reporting; bad
typing; careless editing; unwarranted assumptions; faulty memory; inef-
ficient processes; inelegant technologies that create error traps; or,
occasionally, outright incompetence or malice. Poor note taking can
leave journalists staring blankly at their notebooks wondering exactly
what they were thinking, or what that source on the street said to them.
The rush of a deadline will often cause a newspaper reporter to rely on
memory rather than research; a hurried copy editor may insert errors
where there were none. The editing process, which moves copy from
one person to another, provides numerous opportunities for the introduction of new errors. Spell-checkers fail; incorrect graphics, photos, or
sound clips are broadcast; sources lie . . . the list goes on. But there is
no definitive list.

"There are as many reasons for [sic] errors as there are occasions:
sloppiness, mishearing, misstatement, mischief," said Jack Fuller, the
former president of the Tribune Company. "But the reader of the news

does not care about reasons anymore than the driver of a new automobile cares why his door handle came loose. Error is the journalist's responsibility, regardless of the cause."

This quote, while noble, illustrates the bias in journalism toward what Reason calls the "person approach" to human error. The assumption is often that a mistake is solely the result of one person's failings. We blame the pilot and rarely inspect the cockpit. As a result, journalism largely ignores the "systems approach" and neglects the environment and technologies that also contributed to the error. This one-sided view helps ensure that media errors continue.

"By focusing on the individual origins of error it isolates unsafe acts from their system context," Reason wrote. "As a result, two important features of human error tend to be overlooked. Firstly, it is often the best people who make the worst mistakes—error is not the monopoly of an unfortunate few. Secondly, far from being random, mishaps tend to fall into recurrent patterns. The same set of circumstances can provoke similar errors, regardless of the people involved."

Working under deadlines causes errors, as do the technologies used by reporters every day; and the newspaper system whereby a story goes from a reporter to an editor and onward until it reaches the page-layout and printing stage is rife with weaknesses and opportunities for error. Yet any blame is laid solely at the feet of the person seen as being directly responsible—to the complete exclusion of the process that contributed to the error. Every stage in the production of a newspaper, broadcast, or other news product is designed with some controls to prevent error, and yet each of these stages also has the ability to introduce or even force errors. This reality is what caused Reason to develop his "Swiss cheese" theory.

This theory holds that errors will occur when each element in a series of prevention and detection systems—reporters, spell-checkers, copy editors, and so on—fails in succession. Because every system has its vulnerabilities, each is like a slice of Swiss cheese—some solid areas, but also a lot of holes. "The presence of holes in any one 'slice' does not normally cause a bad outcome," according to Reason. "Usually, this can happen only when the holes in many layers momentarily line up to permit a trajectory of accident opportunity—bringing hazards into damaging contact with victims."

When all of the players and systems in journalism fail in succession on the same fact or element of a story, thus exposing a hole in their "slice," an error will pass through, and end up in the paper or on the air. (This is the journalistic version of what Reason calls a "hazard.") The holes occur either because of existing deficiencies—the inability of a spell-checker to recognize all proper names, for example—or because of new "active failures" introduced somewhere in the process. Perhaps a source unwittingly or purposely provides erroneous information, or, in the worst-case scenario, a reporter makes something up. *The Daily Tribune* of Cartersville, Georgia, was forced to offer a sheepish apology to readers after its process, or lack thereof, led to an embarrassing typo on its front page of March 26, 2007. The lead headline of that day's edition read, "MEN THREATENED WITH GUN WHILE WORKING ON ONE OF *THEM'S* CARS" (emphasis added).

Er, that should have been "One of Their Cars." It was an obvious mistake that scores of readers noticed. Yet how did the paper miss this glaring error? "The headline on the lead article in Tuesday's issue of *The Daily Tribune* news is a poor example of journalism, and the fault is entirely mine," wrote Joe Hiett, the paper's managing editor the next day. "I could try to offer excuses but won't because I cannot."

Hiett wrote the headline, and so he did the proper thing for a journalist and fell on his sword. Yet he also indicated several factors that contributed to the error: The paper did not have a policy that ensured that every headline was read and checked by others. He also noted that "we do have Associated Press style manuals, we do have spell check on our computers (albeit not very advanced programs), but we do not have a grammar check in our programs." These may seem like excuses to some, but they are in fact valid factors that led to the error. In this case, he was in many ways the sole slice of cheese and, as a result, the error easily found a hole to pass through and ended up in the paper.

Reason said errors usually occur because of a combination of latent conditions and active failures. His background in cognitive psychology led him to examine and classify the types of errors that humans are prone to make. But his work has also contributed greatly to a wide variety of professions and practices that have devised their own definitions and categories of error. One of the most applicable comes from Donald A. Norman in *The Design of Everyday Things*. He placed errors into two main categories: slips and mistakes.

Slips occur when we are fully aware of the correct action and intend to carry it out but accidentally make an error. Here is a journalistic slip, as published in the September 22, 2006, edition of the *Orange County Register*: "The pot growers had tapped into an irrigation line for landscaping around the gated community of Stoneridge, and had rigged up a network of white, 3/4-inch PVC piping to grow the *cannibals*" (emphasis added).

The last word was supposed to be "cannabis." Whoever wrote and edited the story knew it should have been cannabis, but a slip caused the error. As the slip passed through each layer of editing, no one caught it. The original slip, possibly made by the reporter, was therefore not identified by the spell-checker because "cannibals" is a correctly spelled word. The subsequent layers of editing and production also failed to catch the error. No one actually thought the network of piping was meant to grow cannibals, which is why it's classified as a slip, not a mistake. A mistake results from conscious action and thought. The *Chicago Daily Tribune* initially calling the 1948 election for Dewey instead of Truman was a mistake. The paper made a conscious decision.

Donald Norman wrote that "most everyday errors are slips. Intend to do one action, find yourself doing another. . . . The study of slips is the study of the psychology of everyday errors—what Freud called 'the psychopathology of everyday life.' Some slips may indeed have hidden, darker meanings, but most are accounted for by rather simple events in our mental mechanisms."

Slips occur because of what a *Chicago Tribune* editor referred to unscientifically as "brainlock." A person is aware of the correct word, date, or spelling, but something causes him or her to replace it with an error. Reason's work helped quantify brainlock and trace its origin, and media accuracy research over roughly the past seventy years has shown slips to be the most common form of factual error in newspapers and television news. The good news is that slips are preventable. The correct information is on hand, or it can easily be found online, by phone, or by another easy method; it may even reside within one's own mind. In the end, something prevents it from finding its way into the final product, and the systems designed to catch the error fail in succession.

After the *Tribune* instituted a rigorous error-tracking program, its editor concluded in 2000 that the data showed "at least one-half to two-thirds of all errors in the newspaper were preventable; most occurred through reporting or writing mistakes or were introduced during the editing process." Unlike true mistakes in the Donald Norman definition, slips don't have to happen. This is good news in that it presents a clear place for accuracy programs to begin. The bad news is that, because slips are so obviously preventable, readers have a low tolerance for a preponderance of them. By not addressing slips, the press demonstrates its unwillingness to treat accuracy in a manner commensurate with its stated commitment to the accuracy principle of journalism. This makes journalism a low-reliability profession as opposed to the high-reliability fields it should strive to emulate.

Mistakes encompass errors that are the direct result of conscious, incorrect decisions. "Mistakes result from the choice of inappropriate goals," according to Norman. "A person makes a poor decision, misclassifies a situation, or fails to take all the relevant factors into account." Just as slips can be the result of a psychological or subconscious blip, mistakes often trace back to our brains, but they can equally be caused by the system we operate within.

"We make decisions based upon what is in our memory; memory is biased toward overgeneralization and overregularization of the commonplace and overemphasis on the discrepant," according to Norman. There are times in journalism when a reporter so badly wants to *believe* something that he or she makes all the facts, or lack thereof, fit that idea. (Reason would call this "active failure.") For individual journalists, avoiding error in everyday reporting requires a unique mixture of critical thought and analysis, and, at the same time, the ability to quiet other parts of the brain to prevent the classic slips of relying on faulty memory or assumptions.

Mistakes occur when journalists make poor decisions or draw wrong conclusions; slips often occur in the act of producing journalism: writing or editing an article or script, or reading it on air. Mispronouncing the name of an accused criminal during a broadcast is a slip; having the wrong name altogether due to poor reporting is a mistake. To prevent and manage both types of error, it is essential to evaluate the people as well as the processes, policies, and technologies that guide their everyday work.

Aside from simply confirming the maxim that to err is human, the research into the origin of human error provides an explanation for why media accuracy is such a challenge. A multitude of factors are involved. Errors are rarely the result of one person's failings, and, as Reason's work has proved, they are not exclusively the province of poorly trained or lazy individuals. Journalists have their own internal thought processes, biases, and inherent failings to contend with. In addition, they are pushed by editors, pulled by sources, harangued by critics, pressed by deadlines, and stifled by a lack of resources. The tools they use every day in their work are often filled with error traps and other latent conditions that can subvert even the most conscientious worker. That errors are so common in journalism is not a shock; they are indeed part of human existence.

But just because errors will inevitably occur doesn't mean the press should resign itself to their existence. The lesson of high-reliability industries demonstrates that an industry or profession *can* eliminate many errors and manage the rest to attain a level of acceptable, measurable, explainable error. This achievement requires

- an understanding of the nature of human error;
- a strong commitment to addressing the issue; and
- an investment in accuracy.

As an industry, journalism and broadcasting have invested huge amounts of time, money, and resources in higher-quality printing presses, better cameras and microphones, faster means of news dissemination, better design, and any number of areas that improve the quality of how a newspaper, magazine, or broadcast looks, feels, sounds, or is accessed. A story can be sent around the world in a matter of sec-

onds by wire service or satellite uplink, and the quality of these trans-
missions improves constantly. Faster, brighter, in color, more
convenient, on demand . . . the media focuses on these things every day.
But accuracy—described as fundamental to news by everyone in the
profession and the public alike—just doesn't rate as an area for major
investment. The quality of the actual product receives nothing comparable to the news media's investment and innovation in the means by
which it is distributed. Why work so hard to get a product on the shelves
and in a pretty box if it doesn't work as it's supposed to? In the end,
quality is what makes for success.

A strong commitment and a modicum of time and capital investment in improving accuracy could reap tremendous rewards in
credibility, and credibility would inevitably produce economic benefits
for print, broadcast, and other news media. Fortunately, even with their
lack of focus on the cause of error, journalists already have much of the
essential data required to begin a serious campaign for accuracy.

Over the past seventy years or so, a series of alarming reports have
provided a clear picture of errors: how frequently they occur, what the
most common forms of error are, what effect errors have on journalism,
and whether journalism is acknowledging and correcting the majority
of its errors. Taken together, this research provides ample evidence that
the level of error in daily journalism is not only constant but potentially
increasing, and it is also diminishing the level of public trust and support for the press. Unfortunately, perhaps because most journalists
don't make a habit of reading academic journals, this research has not
prompted an industry-wide call to quality of the kind we've seen in other
industries and professions. It's time to change that.

CHAPTER 4

THE TRUTH ABOUT
MEDIA ERRORS

IN 1934, A RESPECTED NEWSPAPERMAN, magazine editor, and Iowa State College professor by the name of Mitchell V. Charnley was hired by the University of Minnesota's journalism school, which had officially opened in 1922. Charnley would go on to write books about reporting and radio news and become a distinguished member of the faculty, but one of his most important achievements and contributions to journalism goes largely unmentioned outside of academia. "As common as the layman's superficial generalization that 'the newspaper is always wrong' is the newspaper man's defense that the wonder is that so few errors get into print," he wrote in an academic article published in 1936. "But, as far as I have been able to discover, neither has had reliable information on which to base his belief." Charnley was speaking to the lack of data regarding press accuracy. Newspapers had been around for centuries, but at the time, no one had a true grasp of just how accurate daily journalism was. As Charnley put it, most journalists insisted the work they did was remarkable for its accuracy in the face of news-gathering challenges and deadline pressure. The reading public, however, had its suspicions. No one knew the truth about media accuracy. Charnley decided to try to provide an answer.

Print Media Errors

THE RESULT WAS "Preliminary Notes on a Study of Newspaper Accuracy," which was published in *Journalism Quarterly* in December 1936. It is widely acknowledged as the first study of newspaper accuracy. In the more than seventy years that have passed since his groundbreaking work, there have been no less than seven similar independent studies using the methodology Charnley developed. Along with work that has examined errors in broadcast media and other areas, these studies provide data that offer the most comprehensive answer to the essential question: How accurate is the press?

Charnley's method was to collect local news stories from three daily papers in Minnesota, and mail them, along with a questionnaire, to sources cited in the articles. He chose stories that were meant to be "wholly objective," meaning he excluded opinion columns, sports stories, and other articles "in which there was visible subjectivity." Each source was asked to fill out a questionnaire, which Charnley then used to identify errors present in the article and classify them in groups such as incorrect dates, misspellings, and incorrect names. His method has been used and updated over time, in particular to separate objective errors (errors of fact) from subjective errors (errors of opinion or perspective).

This methodology opens the door for sources to vent their own opinions or bias, but it also attempts to provide a framework to separate the pure errors of fact from those that involve personal perception, which are also valuable in their own right. Nearly six hundred of the one thousand questionnaires sent out by Charnley and his team came back completed. In the end, the study found that just under half of all the local news stories were said to have contained an error. The most common error type was errors of "meaning," perhaps the most subjective category, followed by the incorrect reporting of names and titles. Charnley also noted that 14.5 percent of the errors reported by sources had appeared in previous stories in the same paper. Lessons were not being learned; corrections were not being issued.

The study concluded with his expressing the hope that other researchers might take up the cause and perform similar surveys that go beyond geographical boundaries and use a larger sample size. His wish would be granted, and subsequent studies would largely confirm Charnley's findings, though many of the most comprehensive of them returned higher error rates. According to this research, newspapers have not improved their level of accuracy over the last seventy years. In fact, they appear to have gotten worse.

"Among academic studies, the proportion of stories that sources found with errors has ranged from a low of 41 percent to as high as 60 percent," wrote Scott R. Maier, a journalism professor at the University of Oregon who has conducted two such studies; one was a survey, published in 2005, of 4,800 news sources cited in fourteen newspapers spread out across the United States. "Newspapers conducting their own accuracy studies tend to receive a more positive review, with some reporting sources finding errors in fewer than 10 percent of stories."

Maier previously spent twenty years as a working journalist and has emerged, along with Philip Meyer at the University of North Carolina, as one of the premier media accuracy researchers. That is something he admits to finding amusing. "In my early years as a reporter, my evaluations would always describe me as a strong reporter and good digger who needs to work on accuracy," he told me in an interview. "In my final years [of reporting] I finally got the message." He started double-checking the facts in every story he wrote, and cut his own errors in half.

Maier's comprehensive 2005 study, conducted with Meyer and a team at UNC and the Oregon Survey Research Laboratory, revealed that "sources found errors in 61 percent of local news and feature stories, an inaccuracy rate among the highest reported in nearly seventy years of accuracy research." This is the most exhaustive, most recent study of its kind, and its findings are the most distressing ever. In an article outlining the research, Maier calls the data "sobering" and says it provides "empirical evidence corroborating the public's impression that mistakes pervade the press. In about every other article, sources identified 'hard' objective errors about which there should be little dispute, such as names or addresses."

Maier says the results surprised him, especially since journalists are on average more educated than ever before, and because professional organizations such as the American Society of Newspaper Editors have occasionally worked to raise awareness of the importance of accuracy. "With all the attention given to accuracy I figured maybe [newspapers] would do a bit better," he told me. "Instead we found the opposite. . . . I'm not sure it shows newspapers are getting worse, but it certainly shows accuracy is a persistent problem and far more prevalent when you can find an error in every other story."

Echoing Charnley's 1936 declaration about the dichotomy between how journalists and the public view accuracy, Maier says errors are "far more persistent than journalists would think and very close to what the public insists, which I had doubted."

Aside from the high number of factual errors, the research also found that "subjective errors" should not be dismissed out of hand as bias or "merely differences of opinion. . . . Subjective errors have a stronger negative association with credibility than factual errors." Errors in general have been proved to have an effect on the perceived credibility of a newspaper, but subjective errors in particular exact a higher toll. Categories of subjective errors in Maier and Philip Meyer's study included "My quotes distorted or out of context," which sources claimed in 21 percent of stories; "Interviews with others distorted or out of context" (14 percent); "I was not identified the way I wanted to be identified" (11 percent); "Gratuitous references to my race or appearance" (2 percent); "Story was exaggerated" (12 percent); and "Story was sensationalized" (18 percent). In *The Vanishing Newspaper,* Meyer sums up the error data by saying one could "pick any local story from a daily newspaper, and the chances are better than ever that a source mentioned in that story will find something wrong with it."

Dan Gillmor, a respected journalist who worked at the *San Jose Mercury News* before leaving to dedicate his time to citizen journalism projects, agrees. "Here is a fact, and I say it with regret after almost 25 years of professional journalism experience," he wrote on his Center for Citizen Media blog. "Almost every article gets something wrong, from the source's perspective. . . . Every journalist should have the experience of being covered by journalists. Nothing would improve the craft more."

The issue of a source's claims of error versus what journalists acknowledge as errors is important to note. They don't always agree about what constitutes a mistake. A 1982 study by William Tillinghast found that reporters at the *San Jose Mercury News* agreed with sources' claims of error less than 25 percent of the time. Internal newspaper surveys conducted with sources also trend lower than independent studies. Gilbert Cranberg compared his independent accuracy survey results for the *Des*

Moines Register with those of the paper itself. "The difference in result was striking," noted George Kennedy in a 1994 article for *Newspaper Research Journal.* "The *Register* received complaints of inaccuracy from only 14 percent of sources. Cranberg got such complaints from 63 percent."

Maier summarized the contradictory findings in a 1999 paper while studying for his doctorate at the University of North Carolina. "In a review of 24 dailies that conducted accuracy checks, 15 percent reported that 90 percent or more of their stories were error free," he wrote. "Investigators speculate that fear of offending the newspaper and differences in research rigor may account for the disparity in accuracy rates. Researchers also have found that there is often disagreement between sources and reporters over what is error."

Meyer attempted to resolve the source-versus-reporter issue in a 1988 study that compared source claims of error with those acknowledged by reporters. "The flaw with the [source survey] is that it doesn't differentiate between things where the source is just pissed off and a real error," Meyer told me. To fix this, in cases where the reporter and source disagreed about the accuracy of a specific fact or claim, a third party (a high-level editor) was brought in to make a final determination. The result was a finding that roughly 25 percent of stories contained verifiable errors.

The source survey method, often referred to as the "accuracy check," undoubtedly has its weaknesses, but it has been refined and updated over the past seventy years to remain the most accepted and trusted of all accuracy studies. Though by no means perfect, this methodology offers the best data available, and the findings show a distinctive and disturbing trend.

Charnley's 1936 study found that 46 percent of local news stories contained an error. A 1965 study, which received feedback on only 143 stories, found an error rate of 41 percent, the lowest rate ever recorded in an independent study. Subsequent studies have found error rates of 54 percent (1967), 60 percent (1967–68), 52 percent (1974), 47 percent (1980), 55 percent (1999), and 61 percent (2005). These studies provide an overall picture of accuracy and, with some overlap, they looked at different-sized newspapers in different regions all over the United States. From larger papers such as the *Miami Herald* and *Philadelphia Inquirer* to small publications such as the *Grand Forks Herald*, in terms of circulation size and geography, the combined studies crisscrossed the entire United States.

The range of findings—roughly between 40 percent and 60 percent—suggests a middle ground for newspaper error rates. (A 1985 study by Larry L. Burriss is the only accuracy check to look at news magazines. He found that more than 90 percent of the stories examined were considered accurate by the sources, further feeding the notion that magazines are more accurate than newspapers. This is not surprising when one considers the extra time magazines have to prepare stories, and the fact that, in 1985, most of the leading newsweeklies still had full-time fact checkers on staff. This is no longer the case at *Time* or *Newsweek*.)

One can and should assume that not all papers are equal when it comes to accuracy. For example, the 2005 survey found an "objective" error rate—meaning errors of fact and not interpretation—of 57 percent in the *Boulder Daily Camera*, while the *Charlotte Observer* had a rate of 45.1 percent. The subjective error rates for the same papers were 54.6 percent and 40.6 percent, respectively. Standards and resources vary from paper to paper, and yet the overall findings have an undeniable ring of consistency.

The cumulative effect of this research, brought into stark reality with the 2005 survey, is a troubling picture of newspaper accuracy. Based on this data, one can assume that close to half of the local news stories in most American newspapers contain at least one error. Aside from being unacceptable, it's downright shocking to most journalists, many of whom are unaware of these studies.

Broadcast Errors

GUY KEWNEY WAS SITTING in a waiting room at a BBC TV studio in London, in May 2006, when he looked at the TV monitor and saw a man being interviewed whose caption identified him as Guy Kewney. It was a live BBC broadcast. "There were several surprising things about my interview," he would later note, including the fact that, despite the identification of the guest as the editor of newswireless.net, a technology news site, his television persona seemed to know very little about technology. Also unlike the man on TV, "I'm not black. . . . I'm fair-haired, blue-eyed, prominent-nosed, and with the sort of pale skin that makes my dermatologist wince each time I complain about an itchy mole," he wrote. "I'm a walking candidate for chronic sunburn damage."

Kewney was expecting to be interviewed on the air about the lawsuit between Apple Corps, the Beatles' company, and Apple Computer Inc., the technology company. A studio manager had mistakenly called the reception area instead of the room where Kewney was waiting and asked whether "Guy" was there. As misfortune would have it, a man named Guy Goma had recently arrived for a job interview with the BBC. He soon found himself being fitted with a microphone and plopped into a chair in front of an interviewer.

"Guy Kewney is the editor of the Web site newswireless, good morning to you," said the interviewer. At this point, Goma realized the mistake, and a mixture of fear and shock passed over his face, causing his mouth to briefly open in surprise. He finally settled on a polite reply of "Good morning," delivered with a faint hint of a French accent.

"Were you surprised to see this verdict today?" he was asked.

"I was very surprised to see this verdict to come on me, because I was not expecting that. When I came they told me something else and I'm coming . . . a big surprise," he said.

"A big surprise," repeated the journalist, perhaps wondering why this man claimed to be an expert. But she soldiered on, asking him more questions until the segment ended.

"Apparently," wrote Kewney, "the unflappable Mr. Goma assumed the whole thing was some kind of initiation prank. His own speciality is data cleansing, and (my source inside the Beeb tells me) [he] was a little upset that nobody asked him about his data cleansing expertise."

The mistake provided days of fodder for the British papers, and the BBC issued an apology. Like newspapers, broadcast news often makes errors of misidentification, but a live broadcast can take an error to a whole new level. This is not to suggest that the carefully scripted evening network newscasts don't also make mistakes. In March 2005, NBC

News, acting on incorrect information from two State Department offi-cials, declared that the judge presiding over Saddam Hussein's trial had been killed. A death had occurred, but that of a different Iraqi judge.

As in the BBC mix-up, live broadcasts can also produce instant errors of a unique nature, such as when a reporter for a local CBS sta-tion in New York was delivering a live bit about a MetroCard scam outside a subway station. Suddenly, two men appeared behind him and began chanting the names "Opie" and "Anthony," two shock jocks on XM Satellite Radio. "What the fuck is your problem, man?" demanded Arthur Chi'en, the reporter. He was later fired.

Broadcast news also played a huge part in the instant dissemination of the incorrect information about miners trapped in a mine in Sago, West Virginia, in early 2006. In this case, an unverified statement—call it a rumor—that twelve miners were alive traveled as breaking news to air, live. (This incident is explored in more detail in Chapter 9.)

Along with these major mistakes, television news suffers from smaller instances of error, often coming in the form of typos on graphics. During the Mark Foley congressional page scandal in the fall of 2006, Fox News mistakenly labeled Foley as a Democratic repre-sentative instead of a Republican, causing many to charge the organization with bias. In early 2007, a CNN report about the where-abouts of Osama bin Laden carried the headline "Where's Obama?", making an incorrect reference to Illinois senator and presidential can-didate Barack Obama. "We want to apologize for that bad typo," anchor Wolf Blitzer later said in a rare on-air apology. "We also want to apolo-gize personally to Senator Barack Obama. I'm going to be making a call to him later this morning to offer my personal apology." (CNN is not alone in making this mistake. Senator Ted Kennedy confused the two during a 2005 speech.)

News broadcasts suffer from inaccuracies just like every other form of journalism, but when it comes to accuracy, newspapers are by far the most studied and scrutinized media. This is in part due to their impor-tant role in society and within the media itself. Many broadcast newsrooms begin the day by looking through the morning papers and scanning the newswires, in addition to monitoring the twenty-four-hour news channels. They scan for major news that requires coverage. Newspapers are also a tangible product, which means they more easily lend themselves to the kind of study devised by Charnley, and they later become part of the public record in the form of archives and databases. "Television is much more fleeting," Paul Giacobbe, ombudsman for WJAR-TV in Providence, Rhode Island, told the *American Journalism Review* in 2003. "Someone may hear or see a mistake, but then the story is over and they're on to something else. A newspaper is read and reread. There is more of a sense of permanence."

The ethic of running corrections on a regular basis is therefore more widespread in print. "While newspapers often run corrections, TV stations are not always forthcoming about admitting mistakes," wrote Andrea Miller, then a doctoral student at the University of Missouri's journalism department, in a 2002 research paper. Her paper looked at the ethical dilemmas wrought by breaking news—and how many television news departments fail to weigh the issues before going on air with new information.

"Despite one study's finding that as many as one-third of the stories on local TV news have inaccuracies, only a sixth of the stations run corrections as often as one a month," she wrote. "Many news directors believe admitting mistakes might cause viewers to lose confidence in their news. Is the rationale that by not admitting mistakes we are serving the greater good? Or is the greater economic good of the station being served instead?" Airtime is expensive, and devoting even a few seconds to a correction is seen as a significant use of time.

The suspicion that economic factors or concerns about public perception cloud the media's willingness to correct errors is widely held among readers and viewers. It's often reflected in the public's general unwillingness to request corrections or point out errors (examined in more detail in Chapter 10). In the case of broadcast news, surveys in the Charnley model showed that errors do occur on a regular basis; a later survey of station managers also confirmed the frequency of error. The lack of a formalized corrections structure in broadcast news makes the existence of errors all the more disconcerting.

By comparison, on any given day in most markets, the local newspaper will run significantly more content than the average local evening newscast. There are more words, more facts, more contributors, more sources, and a wider variety of information in the newspaper. This means that more errors will occur purely on the basis of volume.

The 1999 study cited by Miller found a 30 percent error rate in TV news broadcasts. A 2002 study updated the methodology and sent sources the actual video of a story, rather than just a transcript. The study's researchers found that

> SOURCES WERE generally pleased with the so-called factual accuracy of the stories in which they appeared. However, more than one-third of the respondents in that study thought that important information had been left out of the stories. Nearly 20 percent indicated that their interviews had been taken out of context. The respondents rated the seriousness of the subjective errors to be higher than the seriousness of factual errors.

A 2004 study, also using the accuracy check method by sending tapes to sources, revealed an error rate of 35 percent in television news stories. "In measure after measure in this pilot project, there is significant loss of credibility at three key levels—the story, the journalists and the news organization itself," wrote authors Gary Hanson and Stanley Wearden of Kent State University. "This may help explain the steady decline in the public's perception of the news media's credibility." (Radio news has, to my knowledge, never been studied.)

Sources are not the only people who are studied for broadcast accuracy. A telephone survey conducted with seventy-five broadcast news decision makers in large and small markets in the United States found that respondents were largely in agreement about the most common broadcast news error. "The answer in one word: spelling," wrote Gary Hanson in the 2003 paper about the survey, meaning that on-screen graphics often misspelled names or other information. "The mispronunciation of names by newscasters and reporters was another common error listed. Other errors mentioned less frequently were the lack of checking on the background of stories, a lack of general knowledge of the local area, minor factual errors in stories, material left out of a story because of time requirements and unintentional bias due to misunderstanding the subject matter."

As with newspapers, sources claim a high number of "subjective" errors in news broadcasts and view these with the most severity. One frequent complaint is that the images don't match the story, or that a quote was too brief or was used out of context. There are some medium-specific differences to take into account. The combination of images with spoken words creates a different environment for error. Print publications also tend to have more space for source quotations, and therefore many TV sources end up feeling unsatisfied with their amount of airtime. They had a lot more to say, but most newscasts don't have the time to let them say it. The sound bites selected often leave sources unhappy.

The news managers were also asked about the frequency of errors in their reporting. Twenty-seven percent said errors occur every day, 50 percent said they happen once or twice per week, and only 1 percent said they never happen.

To ensure accuracy, the television news business adheres to what is supposed to be an industry-wide accuracy practice: script review. This is a process whereby different members of the news team vet scripts for a broadcast. For a daily local newscast or major network evening newscast, a top producer or story editor will often see every script meant for air. The practice is less prevalent at twenty-four-hour news stations that deal with breaking news or favor a chat- or talk-show format. According to Linda Mason, CBS News senior vice president for standards and special projects, the *CBS Evening News* fact-checks every script for broadcast, though she also acknowledged that this is not a foolproof practice.

The 2003 survey of newsroom managers found that script review does occur, but it lacks standardization. Rarely is there one designated fact-checker in a TV newsroom. "In most cases, the scripts are read by supervisors and anchors," wrote author Gary Hanson. "Scripts in smaller stations tend to be reviewed by the news director. In larger stations, other levels of management conduct the review." Some stations will perform a full "review" that includes fact checking, but in many cases scripts are read only for clarity, continuity, and narrative, much like what a copy editor at a newspaper reads for. A major network broadcast such as the *CBS Evening News* will typically invest more time in fact checking, but errors occur in small and large broadcasts, and a major difference between TV news and newspapers is that corrections are not a standard part of a broadcast.

TV news and newspapers have many differences in the way they gather and present the news, but they have a common bond: errors. Though print media in general are more faithful practitioners of corrections, they are equally responsible for the constant dissemination of errors that are never acknowledged or fixed.

Uncorrected Errors

WHILE IT IS EASY TO HARP ON THE LACK of corrections in broadcast media, there is a larger, more urgent issue of error that pervades all news media. Based on the data available, the number of errors that are actually corrected is only a small fraction of the total errors committed. This means that not only is the error rate a problem in newsrooms, but the number of corrected errors compared to the overall error rate appears to be minuscule.

Journalists have a responsibility to prevent and correct error—not only for the sake of professional ethics and public expectations, but also for the public record and the press's role as a midwife of free speech. They are failing in their mission when they don't hold up their end of the accuracy bargain, and that failure is compounded when existing systems fail to correct most of the errors that occur.

For example, the *Boston Globe* published 57,893 stories in 2005 and ran 1,018 corrections the same year, giving it a rate of correction of less than 2 percent of all stories. A closer look at this low number reveals that some stories may have had no corrections, while others may have had several; the term "stories" in the *Globe* tally comprised not just hard news stories but also columns and editorials (which still use facts, though perhaps fewer than an average hard news story, and have not been the subject of accuracy studies), and other stories that fall outside the category of local news and features. (Perhaps local news or feature stories are more prone to error, but no one has studied this.) Stories chosen for accuracy checks are those that are presumed to be objective reports built on hard facts; they are perfect for such studies because accuracy and correction matter most in this form of journalism. Their sources also tend to remain readily available for later research purposes.

In the *Globe*'s case, the City and Region (local) section was responsible for the most corrections in 2005, with 237. It is one of the largest sections of the paper, so one could expect the bulk of the corrections to be associated with it. Because these stories are about local events and people, their sources are usually located within the community and have easy access to the paper; this makes them more likely candidates for correction.

I selected the *Globe* because it is one of few papers that track and catalog their corrections and also make the total number of stories available along with the data. I compared it with the *Philadelphia Inquirer* because the two papers are of relatively similar size and that paper was included in Maier's 2005 survey. The *Globe* was not. Based on circulation, the *Globe* is the thirteenth largest paper in the United States; the *Philadelphia Inquirer*, with roughly 100,000 more subscribers, is ranked eleventh by 2006 data from the Audit Bureau of Circulation, an independent body. In Maier's 2005 survey, he states that the *Inquirer* had an overall error rate of 60 percent. Sources reported purely factual "objective errors" in 45.2 percent of stories. Yet the *Globe*, a comparable paper, had an overall correction rate of roughly only 2 percent. Though the comparison is inexact, the gap is troubling, even if one were to choose the 25 percent error rate found by Philip Meyer in his 1998 paper that used the input of reporters and a third party to evaluate claims of error.

"There are mistakes that go unnoticed by staff or unreported by readers," admitted Richard Chacón, the *Globe*'s ombudsman, in an article that revealed the numbers.

Even allowing for the fact that this is not an exact comparison, it is impossible to ignore the huge gap between the number of errors per story and the number of corrections per story. Somewhere in the middle is the actual number of factual errors per article in an average daily news-paper, and therefore a commensurate number of corrections that should be published. Allowing for source bias and error, this true error rate is not as a high as Maier and Meyer's finding of 60 percent, but it certainly can't be as low as 2 percent, even if you believe that the *Globe* is a demon-strably more accurate paper than the *Inquirer*, or others in the study.

What this means is that newspapers are not preventing, catching, or correcting a huge number of errors in daily reporting. Since television news runs so few corrections and has been shown to have error rates as high as 35 percent, one can assume that broadcast news is also commit-ting manifold uncorrected errors. The corrections that are published and broadcast are the tip of the iceberg, and the ice runs very deep.

The reasons why sources don't ask for corrections, and why papers are often reluctant to provide them, is addressed in Chapter 10; the issue here is uncorrected errors, what I consider to be the silent killer of journalism and press credibility, and a genuine threat to its role as a conduit and upholder of free speech in a democratic society.

Uncorrected errors are the worst kind of mistakes because they remain in databases, archives, and online forever, feeding future inac-curacies and continuing to anger the public. When I spoke with Philip Meyer about uncorrected errors, he drove the point home with a per-sonal story. "Years ago, the *Wall Street Journal* misspelled my name," he said. Meyer requested his correction and then "checked back fifteen years later and it was still incorrect." Uncorrected errors that reside in databases influence future reporting and feed the cycle of inaccuracy. Reporters and others return to them again and again, and pass along the incorrect information. Online versions of articles that contain uncor-rected errors also have a dangerous level of permanence. John Carroll, the former editor of the *Los Angeles Times*, spoke about this issue in a 2004 speech at the University of Oregon.

"Like a factory on a river, daily journalism is an industry that pro-duces pollution," he said. "Our pollution comes in the form of errors. America's river of public discourse—if I may extend this figure of speech—is polluted by our mistakes. A good newspaper cleans up after itself." Carroll's form of waste management was of course the correction. Specifically, it was to ensure corrections made their way into databases and into the text of the original article, as well as into the print edition of the newspaper. "Thus," he said, "we keep the river clean."

Unfortunately, as many examples demonstrate, this form of cleanup is not being undertaken, even for well-publicized mistakes.

In March 2003, the United Kingdom's *Sunday Telegraph* was the first to report that "schools across Britain have been ordered by local authorities to abandon the ancient tradition of serving hot cross buns at Easter so as not to offend children of non-Christian faiths." Headlined "HOT CROSS BANNED: COUNCILS DECREE BUNS COULD BE 'OFFENSIVE' TO NON-CHRISTIANS," the story ignited a public outcry over political correctness gone wrong, and several other papers climbed aboard. It even made papers in the United States. "These people are silly asses," one Conservative member of Parliament told the paper.

The *Sunday Telegraph*'s story quoted several "spokespeople" explaining the decision. "We are moving away from a religious theme for Easter and will not be doing hot cross buns," said one who, like the others, was not named. "We can't risk a similar outcry over Easter like the kind we had on Pancake Day. We will probably be serving naan breads instead."

You may have guessed that the report was completely false. In fact, most schools never served hot cross buns in the first place. "It was a figment of the reporters' imaginations and the *Sunday Telegraph* eventually carried an apology," wrote Roy Greenslade on his *Guardian* blog in April 2007. (He also wrote about the incident for the *Guardian* in 2003.) "But this was never appended to its Web site story, and the result has led to the story being recycled some four years later."

Due to the *Telegraph*'s negligence in correcting its error online, the tale of the banned hot cross buns was prone to fresh appearances. In 2007, it was the *Cayman Net News*, an online newspaper, that published a story mentioning England's "blanket bun ban." This caused one of the London boroughs accused of crossing the buns off its menu to issue a denial to a local newspaper.

"So the failure of the *Sunday Telegraph* to put a note on its website archive—as it promised at the time to do—has led to the pernicious lie being resurrected," Greenslade wrote. "Isn't it about time that it sorted this out? Or will [the boroughs] be called on to deny these claims every Easter for the rest of the century?" As of this writing, the article remains uncorrected.

Occasionally, a long-uncorrected error can be rectified if a source steps forward to bring it to the attention of a media outlet. Or, if someone on staff happens to notice a recent mistake, a good corrections editor will search the archives to see just how long it has gone uncorrected. The latter circumstance led to the *New York Times* correcting a long-running mistake in the paper, on November 16, 2006:

> AN OBITUARY ON MONDAY and in some copies on Sunday about Isadore Barmash, a retired business reporter for *The New York Times*, rendered incorrectly the name of a department store that he wrote about frequently. It was Gimbels, not Gimbel's. Gimbels, which closed in 1986, has been referred to correctly in *The Times* more than 500 times since 1980 and incorrectly more than 120 times; this is the first time the error has been corrected.

A former *Times* editor spotted the misspelling and pointed it out to Greg Brock, the paper's corrections editor. "When we were alerted to the misspelling, my boss said: 'Hmm. I wonder how many times we have corrected this?'" Brock told me. "So we looked. Zilch." Gimbels has now been added to the paper's internal list of names to watch out for.

Unfortunately, many errors go uncorrected for decades or even centuries, and pass from one medium to another. "The historical error can be very much like the virus that spreads from book to book," Ron Chernow, the National Book Award–winning author of *Alexander Hamilton* and other works, told the *New York Times Book Review*.

"Falsehoods . . . seep into the record, infecting newspapers and magazines, which often rely on books as main sources," the article read.

Uncorrected errors are the waste of the journalism industry. They spill into the public realm, the information stream, and ultimately, the historical record. Studies show that readers sense that not all errors are corrected, and some readers even go so far as to feel that the press makes an effort to hide some of its mistakes. A 1999 survey by the American Society of Newspaper Editors (ASNE) found that 40 percent of the public said they "sometimes" see corrections for errors in the newspaper, while only 19 percent believed they "always" appear. Journalists see it differently, with 58 percent saying they always see corrections for errors in the newspaper.

By not making an effort to discover and correct errors, the press squanders the existing goodwill and trust of the public. The 1999 ASNE survey found that 78 percent of people who saw a correction for an error "felt better" about their newspaper. Said one respondent, "Stress accuracy. If there's a mistake, admit it. People are more likely to believe you. Don't hide it in small print. Let them know you want them to know your mistakes." This echoes what the aviation industry's research confirmed: that the public has a threshold for error.

People accept the reality that errors will occur, especially in daily newspapers or in breaking news on television. But they will not accept egregious errors, a steady stream of easily preventable mistakes, or the unwillingness of the press to own up to its failings. The correction of errors is an integral part of journalism. Until better error-prevention strategies are implemented, the media must make a stronger commitment to cleaning up mistakes.

An acceptable level of error would be one that does not erode trust and credibility in the news outlet without hamstringing journalists who want to engage in challenging reporting that may result in errors. To achieve this acceptable level, error prevention must be introduced, and all resulting errors must be corrected. "Nothing is more crucial to a news organization than its reputation for accuracy, and nothing is more crucial to establishing this reputation than the honest, timely, and public admission of errors," said press scholar Charles D. Whitney.

The standard ethics statements for journalism organizations and individual outlets all state in one form or another that when mistakes occur, the press is responsible for correcting them. "Accuracy is a fundamental of journalism, but mistakes sometimes occur," reads the note at the end of every correction in the *Albany Times Union*. "The *Times*

Union's policy is to acknowledge errors promptly." A similar statement reads, "The *Akron Beacon Journal* is committed to fairness, accuracy and objectivity. We recognize that errors occur and are eager to make corrections, which are published here."

The act of correction is supposed to provide a measure of accountability and disseminate the correct information to its audience. In doing so it also serves a higher purpose: to ensure that, as society's source of accurate, important information, the media remains a bastion of free speech.

With a combination of effective error detection, correction, and prevention, journalists can move to producing journalism that has a proven, acceptable rate of accuracy. Standards can be raised so that the only errors the press makes are forgivable ones, which are corrected as soon as possible, and in an equitable manner. The public has an inherent sense of forgiveness for acceptable errors. The current, low standard of accuracy is squandering this goodwill. Accuracy should be seen not as a burden, but as the core of journalism's purpose. Accuracy is, in fact, an enabler of great journalism.

The Necessity of Error (No, really)

AT NOON ON OCTOBER 25, 1973, Bob Woodward and Carl Bernstein, then two young *Washington Post* reporters in the midst of their dogged reporting on the Watergate scandal, were having lunch with their literary agent and an editor from Simon and Schuster at the Hay-Adams hotel in Washington.

They were hoping to sell what would later become *All the President's Men*, but their minds were elsewhere. A story of theirs that had been on the front page of that morning's *Post*, headlined "TESTIMONY TIES TOP NIXON AIDE TO SECRET FUND" was gnawing away at them. In fact, it briefly made them consider resigning from the paper. The story contained an error the duo feared could harm it, their work in general, and their careers. It said that President Nixon's chief of staff, Bob Haldeman, controlled a $350,000 slush fund for CREEP, the Committee to Re-elect the President, from his post in the White House. What they wrote was true, but they had made an error of attribution. The story said that the proof of Haldeman's involvement had come from grand jury testimony by Hugh Sloan, the treasurer of CREEP, who had resigned after the infamous break-in at the Democratic National Party offices in the Watergate apartment and office complex. Their error was that Sloan, though he had confirmed the fact privately, had not told the grand jury that Haldeman controlled the fund. The *Post*'s story was true, but this single error, which didn't change the fact of Haldeman's involvement, threatened to unravel all the good work they and their editors had done.

That morning, after the *Post* story appeared, Sloan, pursued by reporters, issued an on-camera denial that he had told the grand jury that Haldeman controlled the special fund.

"It was the worst day emotionally during the twenty-six months that Woodward and Bernstein covered Watergate," wrote Alicia C. Shepard in her book, *Woodward and Bernstein: Life in the Shadow of Watergate.* Bernstein would later admit, "We were careless in hearing what we wanted to hear. We didn't ask the right questions. We made an assumption of logic that what Sloan told us, he told the grand jury, and we were wrong."

It was, in fact, the second error the duo had made in their Watergate reporting. A story on October 6 had wrongly accused three men of receiving the information from illegal wiretaps put into Democratic Party headquarters before the Watergate burglary. (I decline to rename them here, since the stigma of false accusation stuck with them for a long time and was not fully erased by the subsequent disclosure of the mistake.) As Woodward and Bernstein would later write in *All the President's Men,* the "three men had been wronged. They had been unfairly accused on the front page of *The Washington Post,* the hometown newspaper of their families, neighbors and friends."

The difference was that the White House and CREEP had chosen not to pile on against the paper for that previous mistake. The error in the Haldeman story, however, brought forth a denunciation from Press Secretary Ron Ziegler, who gave his regular press briefing at the same time Woodward and Bernstein were suffering through their lunch meeting. "I don't respect the type of shabby journalism that is being practiced by *The Washington Post,*" he told reporters.

This mistake threatened to derail the *Post*'s reporting and impugn its credibility. "We took a giant step backwards in our credibility at that time," *Post* executive editor Ben Bradlee later said. "It was a very tough thing on us. It kind of underlined the whole thing and the fragility of where we were. It was hard to win and so easy to lose."

After lunch, Woodward and Bernstein walked back to the newsroom, using copies of the *Post* to shelter them from the rain. They were "tired, frightened and confused," according to their own account in *All the President's Men*. Eventually, they realized the root of their error, after they'd talked with Sloan's lawyer, tracked down an FBI source and his superior, and finally talked with Sloan himself. In the meantime, Bradlee had bought the time Woodward and Bernstein needed to get to the truth by issuing a statement to the media: "We stand by our story."

The media eventually backed off the inaccuracy, and the article's central claim was proved true. It was a sloppy error but not a damaging one. Woodward and Bernstein's work would continue.

It is nearly impossible today to imagine a newspaper being able to overcome the errors made in the course of the *Post*'s Watergate reporting and still be able to push the story to its ultimate conclusion. The *Post*'s initial mistake of wrongly naming three men, and the subsequent hairsplitting but very public denial by Sloan, then followed by Ziegler's denunciation, would, in today's environment, have been picked up and pursued relentlessly by the media, from the mainstream press to partisan blogs. The reporters would have been hard-pressed to buy the extra time they needed to learn the truth from Sloan. Bradlee, who went through roughly thirty different versions before he decided on that brief but unequivocal statement of support, may have found it difficult to stand by the story. (Bradlee is quoted in a footnote in *All the President's Men* saying, "'By this time I was up the river with these two reporters. I can remember sitting down at the typewriter and writing about thirty statements and then sort of saying, "Fuck it, let's go stand by our boys."'")

One of the commonly held maxims of journalism —and indeed the motto of the Web site Regret the Error—is that "mistakes happen." Many argue that not only are errors inevitable in the press, they are in fact the by-product of journalism itself. Or, in the words of former *Los Angeles Times* editor John Carroll, mistakes are the "pollution" of our industry.

Though I'm reluctant to make the case for errors, it needs to be said that they are indeed a reality and always will be. What we in the press need to do is destigmatize them, and reduce the number of easily avoidable ones; then errors that originate from outside sources or hard-hitting reporting can be placed in context, understood, and corrected.

Complex, investigative reporting is hard work. It should be given a higher standard of checking to ensure that it's not undermined by mistakes, but some stories are under such wraps, their investigation deliberately thwarted by those affected by them, that reporters rarely find a straight line to the facts. This kind of situation breeds some of the toughest calls in journalism. But if the pursuit of an important truth is suspended by a seemingly inconsequential mistake, or by the efforts of those who seek to conceal the truth from reporters, it is a loss to society.

Admittedly, Woodward and Bernstein didn't just spell someone's name wrong; in one case they went so far as to name the wrong perpetrators of a scandalous act. But what if that error had shut down their reporting? What if it had caused the administration and other groups to exert so much pressure on the *Post* that it had aborted the Watergate story entirely? The criminal acts perpetrated by those associated with the Watergate scandal could have gone unpunished, and the society might never have known about the illegal operations that were orchestrated by the White House, the seat of their government.

Time and again I've preached that there's no such thing as "small errors," and in Chapter 8 I offer examples of errors with profound consequences. But my belief that there are no small errors doesn't mean I subscribe to the unrealistic notion that 100 percent accuracy, 100 percent of the time, is possible. Before I am accused of being an error-lover, let me be clear: We can and must significantly reduce the number of errors in the press. And we can and must do a better job of acknowledging and correcting them.

By making these newfound commitments, we can find a level of acceptable error, one the public will tolerate, that will also create an environment for great journalism. To achieve this acceptable level it is imperative that journalism do a better job of preventing and correcting all errors; that means attacking uncorrected errors and instituting new measures to eliminate preventable ones. As the saying goes, you learn by making mistakes. Enterprising and important journalism should not be stifled by a wholly unrealistic expectation of accuracy.

This is a challenging section for me to write because I know some will see it as an endorsement of errors and others will think it is a watering down of my stance on accuracy. It is neither. I'll let Philip Meyer explain: "A newspaper with a zero level of factual errors is a newspaper that is missing deadline, taking too few risks, or both," he wrote in *The Vanishing Newspaper.* "The public, despite the alarms raised [in studies by the industry], does not expect newspapers to be perfect. Neither do most of the sources quoted in the paper. The problem is finding the right balance between speed and accuracy, between being comprehensive and being merely interesting."

The public has a capacity for forgiveness for an error that, for example, was printed as a result of erroneous information supplied by the police department. What they don't accept are sloppy errors that easily could have been prevented, or errors that result from lazy or malicious journalism.

The research into media accuracy and credibility reveals several truths. First, the number of errors in the average daily newspaper, broadcast, or online news story is much higher than the rate of corrected errors. There is a serious gap between errors and corrections, and this means that journalism is not cleaning up its own mess. We are polluting the information stream and, as a result, free speech and democracy itself. Another important conclusion is that the public and journalists themselves agree that the press is making too many errors. But the third truth is in where the necessity of errors resides: The public is willing to accept a certain amount of mistakes as long as they are not particularly egregious, harmful, or malicious; it does not have an unrealistic expectation of accuracy. The public wants to know what we got wrong; this information helps it judge a news source's credibility. People are more suspicious of media outlets that never publish corrections, never admit their mistakes. To make good use of this forgiveness and expectation of error, we have to do a better job of preventing, acknowledging, and correcting our errors. This enables journalism to function and flourish.

The Corrections
MULTIPLE OFFENSES

A CAPTION ON THE TOP PHOTO on Page E1 Tuesday should have identified the person on the left as Shelli Pittman, a Brower family friend. Also, the article incorrectly stated the cause of death for a child the Browers were in the process of adopting. He died of encephalitis. Also, while the Browers say they would like to adopt the biological sister of Anthony and Michael, whom they are adopting, she is in the custody of her biological father.

—*Star Tribune* (Minnesota)

An article last Sunday about street fighting referred incorrectly to the Ultimate Fighting Championship and the Pride Fighting Championships, two televised fighting leagues, and misstated the title of a Spike TV series. Both organizations do indeed ban a number of tactics; neither is "no holds barred." The series is called "The Ultimate Fighter," not "The Ultimate Fighters."

An accompanying picture caption referred incorrectly to the hold demonstrated by Jim Arvanitis. It was a rear-naked choke, not a guillotine choke.   —*New York Times*

In a Comment piece headed, We must not forget how war was won, page 22, May 7, we wrote of "the genocidal destruction of the Jewish and gypsy (sic) populations". Gypsy takes a capital G. The stylebook says so: Gypsies u[pper]c[ase], recognised as an ethnic group under the Race Relations Act, as are Irish Travellers. The point has been made in corrections on the following occasions: December 7 1999; March 3 2000; May 4 2000; March 3 2001; July 25 2001; August 1 2001; September 1 2001; December 14 2001; February 19 2003; September 29 2004; March 3 2005.   —*Guardian* (UK)

AN ARTICLE ON THE FRONT OF THE DEC. 9 Lake section about the Tavares City Council described incorrectly a story that Tavares Mayor Nancy Clutts e-mailed to a city official about the dangers of electromagnetic bombs. The story, e-mailed in June when Clutts was vice mayor, does not mention how aluminum may protect people from such bombs, as the *Sentinel* was told. The incorrect information was repeated on the continuation of Lauren Ritchie's column on Page K9 Dec. 18; in an article on the front of the Lake section Dec. 19 and on the continuation on Page G4; on the continuation of an article on Page H3 Dec. 22; in Ramsey Campbell's column on the front of the Lake section Dec. 26; on the continuation of an article on Page H3 Dec. 31; and in a letter to the editor by K.O. Williamson on Page K8 Jan. 1.   —*Orlando Sentinel*

A brief report incorrectly referred to Nottingham as the gun crime capital of England and the least-secure university town with a third of students being victims of muggings (University crime, August 17). In fact, the first description is untrue, the second was based on statistics for the whole of Nottinghamshire, not just the city, and the third was a national statistic.

—*Times* (UK)

A July 4 story about Scottsdale, Ariz., misspelled the name of resident Bob Amento. The story also cited a proposed "SOB" ordinance but incorrectly stated what that term stood for. It means "sexually oriented business." The story also said several celebrities lived in Scottsdale when they actually live in the adjacent community of Paradise Valley. In addition, the article cited a real estate index that listed $1.1 million as the median home price in Scottsdale. That index by a real estate broker referred to single-family homes in a residential section of the city, not all types of homes in all parts of the city.   —*Chicago Tribune*

The Report Card on the Schools, published by *The Inquirer* on March 6, contained some incorrect information.

The percentage of students in the class of 2004 taking the SATs at Ridley High School in Delaware County was 79 percent. The daily teacher absentee percentage for the Willingboro School District in Burlington County for last year was less than 1 percent.

The Lindenwold, Pine Hill and Winslow School Districts in Camden County offer grades pre-K to 12. Students in the Berlin Township and Clementon districts attend Pine Hill secondary schools. Chesilhurst students attend Winslow secondary schools. Waterford students feed into the Hammonton secondary schools.

The percentage of teachers at Holy Cross High School in Burlington County who are certified by the state is 83 percent.

—*Philadelphia Inquirer*

✦

A front-page article on June 21 about evangelical Christians in New York City referred imprecisely to Tony Carnes, a sociologist and a writer for the magazine *Christianity Today*. (The error also appeared in articles on Dec. 13, 2004, and Nov. 5 and 14, 2004.) He is the director of a social sciences seminar at Columbia University; he is not on the faculty.

—*New York Times*

✦

Several articles early this year about a Navy submarine that crashed into an undersea mountain in the Pacific Ocean on Jan. 8 misstated the precise location. It was just north of the Equator, not in the South Pacific. The error appeared on Jan. 11, 12, 15 and 23, Feb. 12 and March 13. The location, first classified, was later specified by the Navy as 7 degrees 44.7 minutes north latitude and 147 degrees 11.6 minutes east longitude.

—*New York Times*

THE LAKESIDE TOWN OF COBOURG, ONTARIO was mentioned last Saturday in separate accounts about old friends meeting— once in a cutline in the Life section and twice in a Travel section story about trains. The parallels continued with spelling— it was wrong in all three places. (A guest writer did have it right in a Father's Day submission to Life that day.) The *Star* regrets the errors.   —*Toronto Star*

❧

In the story on film critic David Thomson ("Citizen Thomson," May 1), it was reported that Thomson's father had sparred with boxing heavyweight champion Max Baer. He was a sparring partner for British boxer Tom Heeney. The story also said that the third edition of Thomson's "The Biographical Dictionary of Film" was published in 1996. It was published in 1994. It was also reported that Thomson showed personal courage in his friendship with gay documentary filmmaker Kieran Hickey because of anti-gay sentiments in London in the 1960s. In fact, Hickey was not openly gay at the time.

—*Los Angeles Times*

❧

An article on Jan. 25 about a guilty plea by Leonard F. Pickell Jr., former president of the James Beard Foundation, to a charge of grand larceny misstated the year he became president. (The error also appeared in articles on Dec. 14 and Dec. 16, 2004, and Sept. 20, 2004.) Mr. Pickell took office in 1995, not 1994. The error came to light during the editing of a recent article on the case.   —*New York Times*

❧

CHAPTER 5

COMMON ERRORS

ROUGHLY EVERY JANUARY, ombudsmen and public editors at newspapers in the United States begin preparing their annual corrections column. Driving this ritual of fallibility is the fact that many newspapers have begun collecting their corrections in internal databases to track the frequency of errors, their location in the paper, and the most common mistakes. I have come to look forward to this annual rite of disclosure, and sometimes find myself saddened when a paper declines to share its data.

Internal corrections databases are by no means the rule within newspaper operations. There are still only a handful of papers that keep records, and the resulting columns usually spend more time placing the numbers and errors in context—other papers make errors, too!—than guiding readers through the past year in errors. Many of the ombudsmen also resist the urge to purge their paper of some of the more egregious and amusing mistakes and corrections, though some allow themselves to have a little fun. John Temple, the editor of the *Rocky Mountain News*, takes it upon himself to share the corrections data, and his column about the paper's 2005 totals included an admission that "spellcheck changed the name of Leucadia National Corp. to La-De-Da National Corp. And we published it."

Temple's column also provided a fairly straightforward description of the basic journalistic corrections philosophy. "At the *Rocky*, our policy is to correct errors we notice ourselves or that are brought to our attention by readers," he wrote. "Not only is it the right thing to do, but if we didn't, our electronic archive would contain inaccurate information that very probably would be picked up and repeated in future stories."

When combined with the accuracy-check research, these columns offer insight into the most common errors at different newspapers, and the industry in general. Based on this data, it is indeed those classic slips, or cases of so-called brainlock, that dominate the lists. The reader's representative for the Minnesota *Star Tribune* wrote that the paper's errors "usually [sic] aren't complicated, they're brain burps by someone working fast, often someone who knew the correct information or easily could have checked." She then ticked off her paper's list of common errors: "name spellings, e-mail addresses, historic events or records, math, whether a picture matched the name in the caption, whether the country was marked correctly on a map."

That list would resonate at most newspapers or other media outlets. Indeed, more than seventy years of accuracy research, and the corrections data from newspapers, reveals a consistent grouping of common mistakes. Anything involving numbers or math continues to be a challenge for journalists, as are names and titles, photo identifications, geography, and quoting people correctly. While this list may seem to reside at the more acceptable end of the spectrum of error—plagiarism and fabrication are relatively rare—these are exactly the kinds of preventable errors that drive readers and journalists crazy, and that have a corrosive effect on the press. Each type of the most common regular slips and mistakes deserves its own examination, and all are the subject of corrections collections in this book. It is also necessary to call out two of the more egregious causes of journalistic error: unreliable sources and malicious reporters. While these species are fortunately less prevalent than are helpful, knowledgeable sources and professional, ethical journalists, their transgressions attract a higher level of attention and exact a greater toll on the press. They also demonstrate that the lack of accuracy controls within newsrooms inevitably engenders highly damaging mistakes. A system, or lack thereof, that allows the smaller common errors to persist will inevitably give rise to more egregious mistakes and transgressions.

Names and Titles

PAINTER JACKSON POLLOCK, actor Dan Aykroyd, the company formerly known as Philip Morris, former secretary of state Madeleine Albright, writer Edgar Allan Poe, and Focus on the Family leader James Dobson have few things in common in real life. But they all belong to a not-so-exclusive club of notable people whose names are regularly botched in reporting. They are joined by an unending parade of average citizens, politicians, sports figures, celebrities, and other famous and not-so-famous folks who find themselves misnamed or incorrectly titled in the press.

Mitchell Charnley's 1936 newspaper accuracy study revealed that the misspelling of names and titles was the most common factual error. Nearly seventy years later, Scott Maier and Philip Meyer's 2005 study suggested that newspapers have improved in this area, yet it still ranks as one of the most common errors.

Obviously, someone's name is an incredibly personal thing. When even one letter is wrong, sources feel as though the story wasn't actually about them, or as if they never really said what they were quoted as saying. It also tells them that perhaps the reporter who prepared the story is less than conscientious in his or her work.

Jackson Pollock was Jackson Pollack at least 66 times in the *New York Times*. Dan Aykroyd was misspelled at least 45 times in the same paper; Philip Morris was bungled at least 128 times, and Madeleine Albright was wrong at least 40 times, according to the paper's own calculations. But the misspelled name champion in the *Times* appears to be Theodore C. Sorensen, an adviser to President John F. Kennedy. A correction on March 12, 2007, said the paper "has misspelled Mr. Sorensen's surname more than 135 times in headlines and articles during the 50-plus years he has been a Democratic adviser and well-known author."

Some names trouble a specific publication, while others appear to induce errors across the board. After I saw a string of corrections regarding the spelling of Edgar Allan Poe's middle name, a database search turned up close to a dozen other recent examples in papers ranging from the *Commercial Appeal* in Memphis to the *Chicago Tribune*, the *Wall Street Journal*, and the Associated Press. The same sense of déjà vu struck me after reading yet another correction stating that James Dobson was not a reverend, pastor, minister, or evangelical, all of which he is often described as being. Though he heads a religion-oriented organization, Dobson is in fact a PhD. Looking through the Nexis news database, I discovered he has been given a religious moniker at a minimum of more than twenty times by the press since 1985. The list of repeat offenders includes the *Washington Post*, *Newsweek*, and the *Chicago Tribune*, among others. Dobson was also the subject of a religion-related correction from Denver's *Rocky Mountain News* on November 24, 2006:

> AN ARTICLE AND HEADLINE on Page 17A Thursday incorrectly stated that James Dobson, founder and chairman of Focus on the Family, believes people who don't practice what they preach should undergo an exorcism. His quote, in a TV interview about reaction to the firing of evangelical leader Ted Haggard for "sexual immorality," was: "Everybody gets exercised (worked up about it) when something like this happens, and for good reason."

When it comes to names, one can perhaps understand the difficulty of "Aykroyd" or the unconventional spelling of "Madeleine." But it's not only those with strange or difficult names who suffer. In fact, the more difficult the name, the more scrutiny it seems to attract, given its obvious perils. My searches in Nexis turned up not a single correction involving the misspelling of the names of singer Engelbert Humperdinck or Zbigniew Brzezinski, who served as national security adviser to Jimmy Carter. The *Hartford Courant*, *New York Times*, and *Houston Chronicle* did, however, get the latter's title wrong, and the *Times* also incorrectly reported the title of his book, *Power and Principle*, in 1983. But "Brzezinski"? No sweat.

Some of the most well-known and simple names are also misspelled. "President George Washington's first name was misspelled in an editorial in Monday's @Issue section," noted the *Atlanta Journal-Constitution* on February 21, 2006. Donald Rumsfeld was referred to as "Donald Armsful" in a headline on a front-page article in the *Denver Post* on December 3, 2006.

Two weeks later, the same paper misspelled the name of Qwest, a major employer in the

MEMO JUST BEFORE RESIGNING

Donald Armsful's classified note to the White House acknowledged the strategy was not working and suggested several options to avoid the appearance of losing.

By Ann Scott Tyson
The Washington Post

   Washington — Two days before he resigned from the Pentagon, Defense Secretary Donald Rumsfeld sent to the White House a classified

The Denver Post *misspells "Donald Rumsfeld" on its front page. (From Sanchmo's Lessons Learned, http://sanchmo.blogspot.com.)*

Denver area that the paper frequently covers. Rumsfeld has also been referred to as the secretary of state by the *New York Times* (corrected on March 26, 2006, and again on September 30), and the Raleigh *News & Observer* (September 12, 2006).

Florida governor Charlie Crist bears a conventional name, yet it triggers a common slip born of its similarity to a much more famous leader's name. Several Florida newspapers have published corrections after spelling his last name "Christ." It's perhaps forgivable considering that in January 2007 his own office made the same mistake.

"A page on the governor's Web site listed his agency appointees under a headline 'The Christ Team,'" reported the Associated Press. "A spokeswoman says it's just a typo. But it's a common one."

Though his last name appears to be the most error-inducing element of his moniker, Crist has suffered other naming errors as well. "The first name of Florida Gov. Charlie Crist was incorrect in the 'Noted' column in Sunday's @Issue," admitted the *Atlanta Journal-Constitution* on April 16, 2007.

Then there are entire articles that seem hopelessly lost when naming *any* names. From the *New York Times* of March 20, 2005:

AN ARTICLE LAST SUNDAY about the re-emergence of Paris as the world capital of fashion misspelled the given name of a designer of luxury fashion products. He is Marc Newson, not Mark. It also misspelled the surname of a fashion designer who acknowledges Paris's debt to immigrant cultures. He is Bernhard Willhelm, not Wilhelm. The article also misspelled the name of an American underwear and clothing company whose T-shirts were compared with couture. It is Hanes, not Haines.

Name errors are not exclusively misspellings. Those unfortunate enough to share a name with an accused individual are often mistaken for criminals. This phenomenon exists largely in smaller communities where there are perhaps only a handful of people sharing the same name. Inexact reporting can tar them all. Still, one can never be sure his or her name is safe, regardless of geography. The *Lexington Herald-Leader* felt the need to further clarify one of its reports, publishing this correction on March 4, 2007:

> COURTNEY RAE BISHOP, 32, a psychologist for the Fayette County Public Schools at Millcreek and Athens-Chilesburg elementaries, is not the same as Courtney Diane Brundige Bishop, 24, who is charged with murder in the death of her infant son, Caleb Eli Bishop.

The titles attached to names also fall victim to error, but some of the more notable errors deal with song, book, television show, or film titles. "On the cover of some copies of *TV Week*, which was printed in advance, the title of Ken Burns' upcoming documentary is incorrect. The title is Unforgivable Blackness, not Intolerable Blackness," read a correction from the *Dallas Morning News* on January 17, 2005. The *Virginian-Pilot* put a positive spin on the Chris Rock show *Everybody Hates Chris* by calling it *Everybody Loves Chris*.

Just as the *New York Times* has struggled with certain names time and again, the *Los Angeles Times* has recently proved to be an unreliable source of song titles. Between January and February 2006 it ran a series of corrections for off-note reporting:

IN MONDAY'S HEALTH SECTION, an article about disco-themed fitness classes misnamed three songs. The correct titles are "Dim All the Lights," not "Dim the Lights"; "Le Freak," not "Freak Out"; and "Brick House," not "Brickhouse." [Corrected January 24, 2006]

AN ARTICLE ABOUT the duo OutKast in Sunday Calendar misidentified three song titles: They are "Hey Ya!," not "Hey Ya"; "The Way You Move," not "I Like the Way You Move"; and "Ms. Jackson," not "Miss Jackson." [February 1]

A QUICK TAKES ITEM in Wednesday's Calendar section said that at a Las Vegas benefit, Celine Dion and Elton John sang duets of "Sorry" and "Saturday Night." The correct song titles are "Sorry Seems to Be the Hardest Word" and "Saturday Night's Alright (for Fighting)." [February 23]

The *Washington Post* joined in with its own errant song title in a correction to a concert review that, "misstated the title of a song by the group Camera Obscura. The title is 'Lloyd, I'm Ready to Be Heartbroken,' not 'Lloyd, Are You Ready to Be Heartbroken?'"

I could offer up hundreds of examples of Republicans being described as Democratic politicians, and vice versa, but suffice it to say that when there are only two main choices and the information is readily available, the press still manages to flub the facts.

This is the common thread that runs through naming and title errors: the correct information is almost always easily found in a matter of seconds or minutes. These preventable slips are maddening to sources and inexcusable for journalists.

The Corrections
NAMES AND TITLES

A CRIME WATCH REPORT IN THE NOV. 7 Community Extra section erroneously identified Kent resident Bertram Haft as being arrested for leaving a Citgo station without paying for beer valued at $2.58. Haft was actually the person who reported the theft to police. The error was made by a correspondent.

—*Akron Beacon Journal*

In a photo caption that accompanied a Feb. 7 article on clothing designer Cynthia Steffe, Ms. Steffe was pictured second from the left. In some editions, she was misidentified. In addition, the name of the NBC television series "Law & Order SVU" was incorrectly referred to as "Law & Order SUV" in some editions.   —*Wall Street Journal*

Wednesday's editorial about the lobbyist Jack Abramoff gave the wrong name for the president of Gabon in one reference. It should have been President Bongo, not President Gabon.

—*New York Times*

A March 9 Food article misidentified the founder of the Food Blog Awards. She is Kate Hopkins, not Kate Hudson.

—*Washington Post*

In a March 20 story about a world water forum, The Associated Press erroneously described Gana Unnayan Sangstha as an aid worker. It is the name of a nongovernmental organization in Bangladesh that one of the participants in the forum was associated with.

—Associated Press

✦

In an article headed "Battle for the flag in a party poles apart", which was published on January 4, 2006, it was reported that Waverley councillor John Wakefield was "a former member of the Communist Party". Mr Wakefield is not and never has been a member of the Communist Party. The error is regretted.

—*Daily Telegraph* (Australia)

✦

In a March 17 story about protests planned against the Iraq war, The Associated Press erroneously identified Jeremy Straughn as a political socialist at Purdue University. He is a political sociologist.   —Associated Press

✦

An arrest warrant was issued by Wadsworth police for Tasha Appel of Akron on a domestic violence charge. Police said the Oct. 10 incident involved Appel shoving and threatening her mother, Peggy Mitchel, 42, of Wadsworth at the Mitchels' Main Street residence. An item in the "Crime Watch" on Sunday incorrectly named the victim as the suspect.

—*Akron Beacon Journal*

✦

The Tracy M. Brand who works for the Fairbanks North Star Borough risk management department is not the Tracy M. Brand whose arrest on driving while intoxicated charges was reported in Sunday's News-Miner.

—*Fairbanks Daily News* (Alaska)

✦

IN A CAPTION ACCOMPANYING a page 13 article titled "Gala Art
Gallery hosts Albin Brunovski exhibit," in the Saturday, March 4,
edition of the *Turkish Daily News*, the title of "Albanian
Ambassador Jonuz Begaj" was mistakenly written as "Lebanese
ambassador." We apologize for any inconvenience.

—*Turkish Daily News*

❖

A report in *The Daily Telegraph* on February 24, 2006 entitled
"A bad trip for Nimbin" included a photograph of a Nimbin
street. Some readers may have identified Mr Mark Richardson
from the photograph and inferred that Mr Richardson was
involved in drugs. Readers should note this inference is
not correct.   —*Daily Telegraph* (Australia)

❖

A story in Wednesday's paper said incorrectly Richer Lapointe,
the owner of the hardware store where Karla Homolka was
employed, had been convicted of hashish possession during
the 1980s. In fact, the person convicted was another man with
the same name.   —*Gazette* (Canada)

❖

In a story ("Renowned Professor Nailed in Kiddie Porn Case")
Professor William Cockerham of the University of Alabama
was mistakenly identified as the suspect in a federal child
pornography case. The suspect, named Professor William
Cockerham, never taught at the University of Alabama, but
teaches at Fresno Pacific University.

Both professors have the same names, however Professor
William Cockerham of Alabama is an internationally
renowned educator, while the professor with the same name in
Fresno is only known in his own community.

I am sincerely sorry for this error. Professor William
Cockerham of the University of Alabama should never have

been identified with the William Cockerham of Fresno Pacific
University.   —AxcessNews.com

＊

Richard Scott, a psychologist testifying in the kidnapping and
rape trial of defendant William Thimiogianis, was mistakenly
referred to in place of the defendant in a report in Thursday's
Metro section.   —*St. Louis Post-Dispatch*

＊

In some editions Wednesday, a quote with a Page A1 story
about Israeli troops in the Gaza Strip incorrectly described
Israeli military spokeswoman Capt. Noa Meir as a senior
Hamas leader.   —*Sacramento Bee*

＊

Alan Dean Campbell was the arresting officer in a warrant
arrest for burglary. He was mistakenly listed as the arrested
person in the For The Record section on Page 5 of Wednesday's
edition. The person arrested was Andrew Lee Weddle, 19, 4150
Bockhofer Road.   —*Palladium-Item* (Indiana)

＊

The obituary of a former Irish prime minister, Charles
Haughey, on June 14 quoted one of his former cabinet members, Maire Geoghegan-Quinn, in the same paragraph as a
mention of his longstanding mistress. The mistress, whose
name was not given in the article, was Terry Keane. We apologize for any implication that it might have been
Geoghegan-Quinn.   —*International Herald Tribune*

＊

James Uriah Courtney wrongly appeared in a Porirua drink-driving list on September 9. Mr Courtney was not convicted of the charge, which was withdrawn by police.

—*Dominion Post* (New Zealand)

❖

BECAUSE OF A REPORTER'S ERROR, a story on Page One Tuesday transposed the name of Advance Ambulance dispatcher Ed Gates with that of Charles Slagle, a man charged with stealing a credit card from a dead man. Gates and Advance Ambulance are helping police with the case.

—*Plain Dealer* (Ohio)

Typos

WHEN IT COMES TO ERRORS, the typo is by far the most common and hilarious. This blanket term can apply to any misspelling or incorrect word usage. While the majority of typos are simply incorrectly typed words that become unintelligible, or entirely different words, they also take the form of incorrect grammar or usage. As is frequently the case, a spell-checker run rampant can also deliver a typo.

A typo is a classic "slip" in that the cause of error is accidental, rather than a result of incorrect thinking or assumptions. One of the more celebrated and (sometimes incorrectly) retold recent typo tales came in the closed captions of an edition of ABC News's *World News Tonight* broadcast on April 22, 2003. It has been cited again and again in articles about media errors, and, as is often the case, some of its factual details have been altered over time. The most common mistake is that it aired on CNN.

Peter Jennings, the program's late anchor, delivered a report about Federal Reserve chairman Alan Greenspan's health, noting that he was "in the hospital for an enlarged prostate." But viewers reading the captions were told he was suffering from an "enlarged prostitute."

The mistake was later acknowledged by an ABC spokeswoman who said, "We strive for perfection, but when you're typing that fast, there are occasional mistakes. We regret the error."

Because it was first reported in a *Washington Post* gossip column, Andrea Mitchell, an NBC News correspondent and Greenspan's wife, was given the last word. She chose well.

"He should be so lucky," she said, elevating it from an

> **Storyline:** The Senators, down 3-1, try to stay alive. Ray Emery will be in goal, not Dominik Hasek.
> **Positives:** Zdeno Chara led everyone in ice time with 30 minutes, 50 seconds in the fourth game . . . Teppo Numminen led the Sabres with 24 minutes, 59 seconds. . . Christoph Schubert and Daniel Alfredsson led the Senators with four shots each. . . Ales Kotalik led the Sabres with five shots. . . Mike Grier led the Sabres in hits with five. . . Chara, Schubert, and Fisher had four each for the Senators. . . Jason Spezza won 11 of 15 faceoffs (73 per cent). . . The Sabres outshit the Senators 32-28. . . The Sabres also blocked 18 shots to Ottawa's 11. . . Wade Redden's shooting percentage was 100 per cent: He scored on his only shot.

An unfortunate May 2006 typo from the Ottawa Citizen.

amusing typo to an anecdote journalists can't resist telling and retelling.

It's difficult to know exactly when CNN was first given credit for the error, but an April 2005 article about corrections in the *Quill*, which is published by the Society of Professional Journalists, is one culprit. How fitting.

Though every journalist hates to make a typo, and many a typo has haunted the dreams of copy editors, it's one category of error we can't help but feel a certain amount of affection for. Typo of the Year is also invariably among the most popular corrections in RegretTheError.com's annual roundup of the year in media errors and corrections. Some recent honored candidates include the *Dallas Morning News* referring to a woman as a "socialist" instead of a "socialite," which is undoubtedly one way to ruin a Texan's social standing; a Liverpool newspaper changing the Welsh National Opera's acronym (WNO) to "winos" throughout a story; the *Ottawa Citizen* reporting that a hockey team had been "outshit" rather than "outshot" by a competitor; and the same paper quoting a man talking about his "little seedy store" as opposed to his "little CD store." The correction of the year for 2005, published in the *Denver Daily* News on July 27, was also due to a typo:

THE *DENVER DAILY NEWS* would like to offer a sincere apology for a typo in Wednesday's Town Talk regarding New Jersey's proposal to ban smoking in automobiles. It was not the author's intention to call New Jersey "Jew Jersey."

The Jews turned up again when a photo caption in Minnesota's *Star Tribune* of May 14, 2006, reported that, "Kentucky Derby winner Barbaro grazed in the paddock Wednesday. He will try to win the second jew of the Triple Crown on Saturday."

A correction from the March 29, 2004, edition of *The Australian* has also become legendary:

A STORY HEADLINED "Syria seeks our help to woo U.S." in Saturday's Weekend Australian misquoted National Party senator Sandy Macdonald. The quote stated, "Syria is a country that has been a bastard state for nearly forty years," but should have read, "Syria is a country that has been a Baathist state for nearly forty years." *The Australian* regrets any embarrassment caused by the error.

Narrowing the field down to just these few initial howlers caused me considerable strain, as there is no shortage of hilarious, scandalous, and altogether shocking typos. They are as remarkable as they are profuse. Readers tack them up on fridges, post them on their blogs, and recount them at dinner parties. Journalists always have their own worst typo story ready for the telling, or have filed away one from a colleague or competitor.

A front-page typo from the July 11, 2006, edition of the San Francisco Chronicle.

Though typos are one of the more reliable sources of humor in the press, they can also be distracting and damaging, and readers do notice. Typos matter.

A 1999 survey revealed that 35 percent of the U.S. public finds spelling or grammar mistakes in their daily newspaper more than once a week, while 21 percent claimed to spot them daily. Seventy percent of journalists see them more than once a week. Readers notice the smallest of typos, even if they elude journalists and editors.

"Each misspelled word, bad apostrophe, garbled grammatical construction, weird cutline [photo description], and mislabeled map erodes public confidence in a newspaper's ability to get anything right," noted the report from the American Society of Newspaper Editors. "One focus group even laughed out loud when asked whether mistakes ever appeared in their paper."

In explaining its "winos" error to readers, the Liverpool *Daily Post* offered up a frequent excuse for its error: the spell-checker.

"The problem arose when the computer spell checker did not recognise the term 'WNO' (Welsh National Opera). A slip of the finger caused it to be replaced with the word 'winos,'" noted the paper's acting editor in a column. "All stories in the *Daily Post* go through a series of checks for error, but unfortunately this one slipped through the net. It just goes to show that it's hard to beat the good, old-fashioned dictionary."

Spell-checkers are of course that inelegant feature contained in most computer word-processing programs. They have been the cause of many typos largely because the spell-checker regularly turns nonstandard words into something else entirely, as I will further explain in Chapter 11 when looking at their role as an ineffective replacement for proofreaders. The consequences can be amusing (think "Baathist" and "bastard," for example), but the perils of the spell-checker sometimes seem to outweigh its perceived benefits.

When Pope John Paul II passed away in 2005, an article in the *Daily Press* of Newport News, Virginia, quoted Cardinal Joseph Ratzinger, today known as Pope Benedict XVI, as saying, "Today we bury his remains in the earth as a seed of immorality." Er, that would be "immortality." A spell-checker may have changed a misspelling to the wrong word, or it simply missed the incorrect usage entered by the writer. Spell-checkers can determine if a common word is misspelled, but they rarely save a writer from a usage error. That requires the human touch.

Rather than an incorrect or misspelled word, some typos are in fact the result of something that's not there. Lose a "not" or "less" or other modifier, word, or even single letter, and suddenly a sentence can take on a remarkably different tenor, as this *Guardian* correction from November 21, 2005, illustrates:

> IN EDITING CAMPBELL ROBB'S Public eye piece, page 10, Society, November 16, we lost the word "less", altering his assessment of the way in which larger charities were said to dominate the field at the expense of smaller ones. Here is his comment with the word restored: "While the bare statistics regarding the charity sector may give this impression, the reality is more complex and less depressing."

Or this from the *Los Angeles Times* of August 24, 2005:

> AN ARTICLE IN THURSDAY'S California section quoted Jay Young, a Colorado man brought in to capture an alligator in Harbor City's Lake Machado, as saying he was "far better" than Crocodile Dundee. Young says that his quote was that he was "far better looking" than Crocodile Dundee.

And this from the *Boston Globe* of the day before:

> BECAUSE OF A REPORTING ERROR, a quotation in a story about Rolling Stones fans in yesterday's Living/Arts section misidentified "Happy" as a son of Keith Richards. It is a song.

Typos are a result of the writing and editing process, and the tools journalists use to aid them in it. Readers understand that they will occur but can't help wondering why a profession that puts a premium on words can't spot the clunkers that leap from the page over a morning coffee. As such, typos, no matter how amusing, speak directly to a lack of quality control and oversight in the press.

The Corrections
TYPOS

A FILM REVIEW IN WEEKEND on Friday about "Le Pont des Arts" misspelled a word in the title of a Monteverdi madrigal that a character sings on a recording. It is "Lamento della ninfa," not "ninja."   —*New York Times*

◆

In the original version of this report, *Newsweek* misquoted Falwell as referring to "assault ministry." In fact, Falwell was referring to "a salt ministry"—a reference to Matthew 5:13, where Jesus says "Ye are the salt of the earth." We regret the error.

—*Newsweek*

◆

Mr Smith said in court, 'I am terribly sorry. I have a dull life and I suddenly wanted to break away.' He did not say, as we reported erroneously, 'I have a dull wife and I suddenly wanted to break away.' We apologise to Mr Smith, and to Mrs Smith.

—*Daily Mail* (UK)

◆

In our review of The Who at Leeds University, page 36, June 19, we attributed to Pete Townshend the exclamation, "You are wank!" [sic]. We are assured that what he actually told the audience was, "We are all back." Apologies.

—*Guardian* (UK)

◆

THE SEPT. 20 WASHINGTON SKETCH, about a news conference held by former secretary of state James A. Baker III and former congressman Lee H. Hamilton, said that Baker was bothered by the questioning and whispered "malicious" to Hamilton, unaware that he could be heard on the audio feed. Baker says the word he spoke was "militias."   —*Washington Post*

❖

Fulsome and fulsomely were again used in error in a complimentary sense. It means excessive or insincere in an offensive or distasteful way—Collins (Prayer Book Rebellion, page 14, G2, August 7, and Domenech's quiet revolution is winning friends, page 2, Sport, July 8).   —*Guardian* (UK)

❖

A listing in Sunday Calendar said hot dogs would not be allowed at the Scandinavian Autumn Fest and Marknad on Sept. 17 at Vasa Park in Agoura. No canines will be allowed at the event.   —*Los Angeles Times*

❖

The Nazi laws prohibiting Jews marrying aliens, mentioned in the Writ large column, page 13, June 12, banned marriages with Aryans, not aliens.   —*Guardian* (UK)

❖

An article in the main news section Wednesday about Sigmund Freud's granddaughter Sophie incorrectly referred to Asperger syndrome as a severe form of autism. According to the National Institute of Mental Health, Asperger syndrome is at the mild end of the autism spectrum, a range of five pervasive developmental disorders that includes autistic disorder. Also, the story quoted Sophie Freud as saying, "Young people

need to be thought to think." The correct quote was: "Young
people need to be taught to think."   —*Chicago Tribune*

＊

An article on Sunday about young American Jews whose plans
to visit Israel have been complicated by violence in the region
incorrectly rendered a word in a quotation by Jerome A.
Chanes, a faculty scholar at Brandeis University who special-
izes in American Jewish culture. He said, "Most of the yeshivas
are in and around Jerusalem, and there are always security
problems there"—not "sectarian" problems there.

—*New York Times*

＊

The man extolling the virtues of breast milk, mentioned in
When is breast best?, page 9, G2, January 18, believed that it
had given him remission from prostate cancer rather than
prostrate cancer.   —*Guardian* (UK)

＊

A story in Thursday's *Bee* incorrectly quoted Sen. Tom
McClintock, R-Thousand Oaks, on comments he made in a
subcommittee hearing about a proposed $5 million appropria-
tion for the California Partnership for the San Joaquin Valley.
Sen. McClintock should have been quoted as saying that if the
appropriation were approved, the state would be "buying $5
million worth of prattle." The reporter misheard the senator
and wrote, "buying $5 million worth of crap." The error was
confirmed by listening to an official audio recording of the subcommittee hearing.   —*Fresno Bee*

＊

IN A STORY PUBLISHED Aug. 19 on the United Church of Canada's national conference, delegate Robert Pike was incorrectly quoted as saying he wanted to punch a church leader for a comment he made on aboriginal stereotypes. In fact, Pike said he felt like he was punched in the stomach after hearing the comment by Rev. Keith Howard.

—*National Post* (Canada)

+

A "seering" new documentary referred to in the heading for Up front, page 2, Film & Music, August 11, was in fact "searing".

—*Guardian* (UK)

+

The Mini Page, a children's syndicated feature that runs inside the second section of the Sunday comics, recently made two errors. In the April 10 edition about Wind Waves, Tsunamis and Tides, it incorrectly stated that the sun orbits Earth. The sentence should have read: "The orbit of the moon around Earth and Earth around the sun creates forces affecting tides." In the March 27 edition about the Netherlands, the name of Philips Electronics, a Dutch company, was misspelled.

—*Washington Post*

+

In a story appearing on Sun-Sentinel.com on July 24 titled "Die pods: The mortality rates of iPods have some users fuming," an Apple spokeswoman's comment was written in a way that was misleading. The article should have stated that iPods are designed to last "for years," not that iPods are designed to last four years.   —*Sun Sentinel* (Florida)

+

Calorie-counting slimmers would nibble on a sliver of cheese rather than a slither. —*Daily Mirror* (UK)

✦

We inadvertently misquoted veteran peace campaigner Pat Arrowsmith when we said she was going to stand up and martyr herself by admitting overlooked convictions in Newbury magistrates court (People, page 8, July 21). She said she was not going to become a martyr. —*Guardian* (UK)

✦

A story on Page B-1 of Tuesday's Alaska section about Keith Landers' murder trial incorrectly quoted a family friend saying from the witness stand that the defendant told her his wife had been "unfair" to him. She actually said his wife had been "fair" to him. —*Anchorage Daily News*

✦

In last week's story "Marine Corps Making Progress with Distributed Ops Experimentation," a reference to the initial "sweat package" of the experimentation should have read "SUET package," explaining this stands for small-unit enhancement training. —*Inside the Navy*

✦

Editor's note: A review of Pearl Jam that appeared in Monday's *Inquirer* incorrectly characterized the audience's response to the keyboardist at Saturday's show. The audience was not booing Kenneth "Boom" Gasper, but cheering him on by chanting his nickname. —*Philadelphia Inquirer*

✦

A STORY ABOUT THE GOOGLE Trends service on page A1 of
Monday's *Tribune* cited a wrong word as one of the top search
terms of Salt Lake City users. The actual word was "boogers."
Due to an editing error, it said the word was "bookers."

—*Salt Lake Tribune*

If NYSE Group Inc. completes an acquisition of Euronext NV,
short sellers might abandon their positions in NYSE. An
Ahead of the Tape column yesterday mistakenly said short sellers would abandon their positions if NYSE "pulls out of" the
deal, when it should have said "pulls off" the deal.

—*Wall Street Journal*

In an article about the British Film Institute's new digital
media initiative (The public spirit award goes to . . .), page 16,
Film & Music, September 8, we said the BFI, despite government subsidies, is "woefully overfunded". The writer meant, of
course, woefully underfunded.   —*Guardian* (UK)

We described the actor Julie Graham as omniscient in an article about the shallow casting pool for television dramas
(Haven't we met before? page 37, September 8). We meant to
say she was omnipresent, or seemingly present everywhere,
rather than all-knowing.   —*Guardian* (UK)

A story on Tuesday's front page about contract negotiations
between a teacher's union and the Sutter County Board of
Education should have used the word "parity" instead of
"parody."   —*Appeal-Democrat* (California)

A story in Saturday's Section A on David Brewer's selection as the next superintendent of the Los Angeles Unified School District quoted Brewer as saying: "A good friend came up to me and said, 'Dave, why wait? Why wait to help disadvantage children?'" The quote should have read: "A good friend came up to me and said, 'Dave, why wait? Why wait to help disadvantaged children?'"   —*Los Angeles Times*

✦

Bill Clinton's speech at the Labour conference was a paean of praise for Tony Blair. A peon is a menial worker or peasant. (Page 6, September 28).   —*Daily Mirror* (UK)

✦

In our report Russia's big spenders flaunt their fortunes, page 23, October 28, we referred to the shopping sprees of "the hoards of rich". As a reader writes, the Russian rich may have hoards of money, but collectively they move and shop in hordes.   —*Guardian* (UK)

✦

A review of Wikinomics on Tuesday should have said, "This is not another book about profitless Internet start-ups." The word "not" was inadvertently omitted.   —*USA Today*

✦

Because of an editor's error, a sentence on page 8D on Tuesday in a story about Rockies prospect Hector Gomez buying a bus was changed from "On the back he put 'Los Peloteros' which in Spanish means 'The Ballplayers'" to "he put 'Los Plotters' which in Spanish means 'The Pallbearers.'"

—*Denver Post*

✦

An article in the Feb. 6 Arts section implied incorrectly that Eva Zeisel was involved in a plot to assassinate Joseph Stalin. That was the unsubstantiated charge made to arrest and imprison her.   —*Washington Post*

A film review on Wednesday about "Little Miss Sunshine" referred incorrectly to contestants in the fictional children's beauty pageant of the title. The critic intended to compare the contestants to underage prostitutes, not to "underage fleshpots."
                                                 —*New York Times*

A headline on Page One on Saturday should have made clear that Oregon Health & Science University will be studying the effects of meth, not cooking it.   —*Oregonian*

An item in the Observer column on March 14 reported that Ludwik Dorn, Poland's minister of the interior, had said some former police officers used the services of prostitutes. A more correct translation was that they had a "wide social life".
                                                 —*Financial Times*

In a report about the CIA leak scandal, page 4, October 29, we said "[Karl] Rove found Mr. Bush as a gland-handing good ol' boy trading on his family name and his charm." That should be glad-handing not gland-handing.   —*Guardian* (UK)

A Jan. 5 "Recycled" incorrectly stated that a federal rather than a state appeals court reversed Andrea Yates' convictions. Also the term "matricide," which refers to killing of mothers, not killing by mothers, was misused.   —*Slate*

In our note on the Channel 4 programme *The Sperminator,* page 20, G2, yesterday, we referred to the "sperm doner." Someone who donates is a donor. A doner is a type of kebab.

—*Guardian* (UK)

Language department, from page 7, January 24, where, referring to a mass burial site, we said, "In it were at least 150 bodies, interned in more than five layers . . ." That should be "interred."

—*Guardian* (UK)

An editorial in Friday's paper incorrectly stated that Florida Cresswell, a candidate for state representative in the 28th District, was convicted in 1999 of battery and stealing Tupperware. In fact he was convicted of stealing a battery from a van as well as Tupperware that was inside the van.

—*Chicago Tribune*

In the article "Prostitute found strangled in burning flat" on C1 on June 23, the head of Kowloon West regional crime unit, Senior Superintendent Leung Ka-ming, was quoted as saying: "It was a small fire and solvent was used in the incident." The quote should have read: "It was a small fire and no inflammable solvent was used in the incident." The error was introduced in the subediting process.   —*South China Morning Post*

A FRONT PAGE ARTS & LEISURE article today about Russian chanson music, a popular but banned genre, incorrectly translates the last word of a proverb. It is "Don't rule out prison or poverty," not insanity.   —*New York Times*

＊

The *Advocate*, in Saturday's editions, misquoted East Baton Rouge Parish School Board member Bill Black.

Black was quoted as saying, "Every year we lose hundreds of thousands of textbooks."

Black actually said, "Every year we lose hundreds of thousands of dollars worth of textbooks."

The *Advocate* regrets the error.

—*Advocate* (Louisiana)

＊

We said that Manfred Alexander had had "a spell in prison in Switzerland and a period of interment" when we meant internment (An act of true friendship, G2 page 2, March 29). Interment is burial, internment is detention.

—*Guardian* (UK)

＊

When we said that the shadow attorney general had prevaricated in the Commons to make time for discussions elsewhere, we meant procrastinated (Champagne, pizza, and snatched sleep, page 5, March 12). To procrastinate is to delay; to prevaricate is to speak with intent to deceive.

—*Guardian* (UK)

＊

'Sheep might be dumb . . . but they're not stupid' (News, last week) said that studies in Oxford showed that a Caledonian heifer called Betty had managed to bend a piece of wire to construct a hook and retrieve food from a jar. Betty is, in fact, a

New Caledonian crow, a creature perhaps better adapted to
bending wire than a cow.   —*Observer*

*

In a Comment piece, Don't rush to judgment, page 30,
November 27, we said: "Russia has killed people abroad, it is
true, and recently. In 2004 two military-intelligence agents
blew up the Chechen separatist leader Zelimkhan Yandarbiyev
in Qatar (the Americans helped)." The Americans helped cap-
ture the agents, not to assassinate Yandarbiyev.

—*Guardian* (UK)

Numbers

O N J A N U A R Y 2 2 , 2 0 0 6 , *60 Minutes* aired a report by correspondent Bob Simon about the oil sands of Alberta, Canada. The story
focused on the enormous amount of oil contained in the province, and
how current mines were likely just scratching the surface. In one clip,
Simon dug his hands into the oil sand at one mine and commented
that it felt like topsoil except instead of trees, "it grows money." A new
gold rush was on, and the surrounding towns couldn't keep up. It was
a compelling piece of journalism. Simon used some big numbers to
drive it home.

"There are 175 billion barrels of proven oil reserves here," he said.
"That's second to Saudi Arabia's 260 billion but it's only what companies can get with today's technology."

One mine was using the world's biggest truck. "It's three stories
high and costs $5 million," he said. "It carries a load of 400 tons of oil
sands, which means, at today's oil prices, each load is worth $10,000
dollars."

Legendary oilman T. Boone Pickens was given airtime to talk about
how much money his hedge fund has invested in the oil sands. "We're
managing $5 billion here," he said. "And, about 10 percent of it is in the
oil sands. So, it's the largest single investment we have."

Simon thought about the numbers for a moment and then said, "Ten percent of 5 billion? I flunked math."

Pickens indulged him and said that equaled $500 million.

In a story built upon staggering numbers—billions, millions, tons, stories—it seemed surprising that an accomplished correspondent couldn't move a decimal point on $5 billion. Was Simon just playing to the camera to get Pickens to say the number himself? Or was he afraid to attempt the calculation in his head and risk making a mistake, therefore ruining the take and losing the natural exchange by having to repeat it?

If Simon is like many journalists, he probably felt a pang of fear at the realization that he needed to perform a piece of arithmetic on the fly, and on camera, even during a taped interview that could later be edited. He is also like many journalists in that he felt it okay to portray himself as someone who "flunked math." After all, journalists work with words and pictures. Math is for scientists, bankers, mathematicians, and engineers. They do the math, and reporters quote them. That's how it works.

The truth, however, is that math and numbers are used in all types of reporting. Yet we often have a fear of them that causes us to hesitate when making calculations, or we accept numbers or statistics without giving them a second look. Whether it be census figures, polls, sales figures, television viewing habits, or other data, numbers can speak volumes, and they litter all manner of stories: dates, statistics, dollar amounts, telephone numbers, addresses. A story without numbers is often considered weaker than one with them. If you are trying to write a so-called trend piece about a particular product or activity becoming popular, it's essential to find some numbers to back it up.

"There is something so magical about numbers," said Don Gibb, a journalism instructor at Ryerson University in Toronto. "You come back with numbers and just toss them into a story, or even better than that you toss them into a quote, and somehow that gives it authenticity."

The reality that journalists need and use numbers so frequently, combined with a level of discomfort with them, leads to the current situation in which numerical errors rank among the most common type found in the press.

"Deploying numbers skillfully is as important to communication as deploying verbs, but you won't find many media practicing that philosophy," wrote Max Frankel, a former top editor at the *New York Times*. "Most schools of journalism give statistics short shrift and some let students graduate without any numbers training at all. . . . The media's sloppy use of numbers about the incidence of accidents or disease frightens people and leaves them vulnerable to journalistic hype, political demagoguery and commercial fraud."

THERE ARE THREE MAJOR CATEGORIES of numerical errors: incorrect calculations or interpretations made by a reporter; a typo that, for example, adds a zero or mangles a phone number; and incorrect numbers that are provided by a third party and then, without proper scrutiny, are passed on by the media.

The greatest danger with numerical errors goes far beyond a dropped zero or poor calculation. Journalists use math and numbers to formulate arguments and create stories that illuminate the true nature of our world. When calculations are botched or the reporting misses the larger points, it can contribute to false assumptions about entire nations or groups of people. Once reported, these mistakes become part of the public record and are often impossible to correct. They will be reported and cited again and again, further burying the truth, as I will illustrate.

"It is instructive that many of the causes attributed to numerical errors—i.e., carelessness, oversimplification, poor editing—are violations of basic journalistic standards," wrote Scott Maier, a University of Oregon journalism professor and accuracy researcher, in a study about math errors. "What appears to be lacking is a willingness to question numbers that don't make sense."

While math and numbers can appear to be solid and exact things, they often contain a multitude of nuances. Numbers hold within them amazing amounts of insight, but they frequently contain a bevy of traps and subtleties that get lost in the news cycle.

"Mathematics is not primarily a matter of plugging numbers into formulas and performing rote computations," wrote John Allen Paulos in *A Mathematician Reads the Newspaper*. "It is a way of thinking and questioning that may be unfamiliar to many of us, but is valuable to almost all of us." The latter is a concept any journalist would embrace, but we lack the appreciation and skill with numbers to realize it. Research also suggests that the fear of numbers that exists in many journalists is also a factor in error. Journalists often scare themselves into mistakes.

The issue of journalists and math was the subject of a 2003 article by Scott Maier. He conducted a mail survey of 1,000 sources cited in math-related articles in the Raleigh *News & Observer* and found that "news sources identified an average of two stories with numerical errors in each newspaper edition." He also administered a basic math test to reporters and discovered that, despite the "profound feelings of mathematical inadequacy" professed by writers and editors, their basic math skills weren't terrible. "Nearly one in five journalists missed more than half of the questions posed," Maier noted. "But, surprisingly, strong performers in math outnumbered the weak performers."

When I spoke with Maier, he said some journalists admitted to being "terrified" of math. He theorized that the perception of journalists being awful with numbers is so ingrained that even those with the necessary skills feel reluctant to use them. They think they don't know what they're doing even when they do. They fall victim to a self-fulfilling prophecy.

Research has shown that anxiety can specifically affect one's ability to do math. A 2007 study by Mark Ashcraft, a psychologist at the University of Nevada Las Vegas, found that students taking a big math test were affected by their level of anxiety. "It turns out that math anxiety occupies a person's working memory," said Ashcraft. (I of course have to note that an early version of a Reuters article about the study misspelled his last name as "Ashcroft" and also flubbed the spelling of "Las Vegas." Fortunately, no numerical errors were made in the piece.)

Maier concluded that the cause of error could often be traced back to sloppiness. "For example, incorrectly reporting the size of a jury or reporting a percentage twice in the same paragraph reflects carelessness, not numerical ignorance," he wrote. "There was little evidence that errors occurred because reporters miscalculated numbers."

I have come to the same conclusion after tracking number-related corrections since 2004. The vast majority are not the result of poor math; they occur because of the same slips that cause typos and so many other types of common errors. They are careless errors made when the correct information is known and on hand. The results can vary from the obvious (millions instead of billions) to the hilarious, as this admission from the *Florida Times-Union* demonstrates:

> A TOLL-FREE NUMBER to a non-partisan organization tracking the election turned out to be painfully wrong. Instead, the wrong number referred callers to a sex talk service. Of course, this never should have happened, since the newsroom's policy is that all phone numbers should be called before publication.

The paper's policy of calling all phone numbers is sound practice, but someone forgot to follow through. Incorrect phone numbers and addresses are common numbers errors and, aside from simply directing people to the wrong location or contact, can have surprising consequences. Sharon Burnside, the former public editor of the *Toronto Star*, invited readers to examine two cases of number-related error to see the consequences:

> ASK ACCOUNTANT MARVIN VISSMAN, who spent Tuesday referring phone calls for The Fixer [a column in the paper], instead of concentrating on year-end tax returns, because the contact number printed with the popular local column was wrong.
> Ask the Menak Thakkar Dance Company. Information published last weekend from the 2004 South Asian Heritage Festival calendar, instead of the 2005 calendar, had them performing the wrong work, on the wrong day, at the wrong time. This year, the troupe is not even associated with the festival.

Even the smallest numerical slip can have repercussions for members of the public. One of the most common sets of numbers in any paper is the lottery picks from the night before. City papers still run these on a regular basis, and often err and print older numbers or otherwise mangle them. After watching the constant printing of lottery-related corrections, I found myself waiting for the day when one person opened a morning paper to see his or her numbers listed in error. As it turned out, I didn't have to wait long or look far.

Ulysee Maillot spread open his Sunday edition of Montreal's *Gazette* on August 13, 2006, and checked the lottery numbers from the night before. He compared them with his ticket and slowly ticked off each number against those in the paper. The draw was for $43.2 million, the second largest in Canadian history. And Maillot's numbers matched.

He started thinking about how he was going to spend the money. Within a few hours, however, he felt sick.

"I never said a word," he later recalled. "I was weak, I was sweaty, I was so upset."

The lottery numbers were wrong; the paper had mistakenly printed Wednesday's numbers, not Saturday's.

Maillot was the truly unlucky soul I had been expecting. He decided to fight back against the paper by telling his story to other media outlets. He also hired a lawyer who threatened to sue the *Gazette*. The coverage, and threat of a lawsuit, caused the paper's publisher to write an apology.

"We have no reason to doubt the sincerity of Mr. Maillet's claim that he had thought for a short while that he had won a lottery," wrote publisher Alan Allnutt, misspelling the man's name in the process. "But *The Gazette* publishes about 100,000 words and numbers every day and we simply cannot guarantee all the information's accuracy. In the last 20 years we have published nine corrections of Loto [Loto Quebec] numbers. I wish I could say it was fewer, but then we have published lottery numbers on about 7,200 mornings in that time period."

It seems that when numbers go awry in the press, the reaction is to fight innumeracy with . . . numbers. Journalists, it seems, just can't get enough of them (right).

THE PRESS'S HUNGER FOR NUMBERS in all manner of stories also leads to a fixation on them in governments, companies, and organizations of many kinds that seek to earn coverage; they make a huge effort to gather the kind of data that journalists love to receive. Having some juicy numbers in a press release can mean the difference between an ignored communication and one that inspires a story. Unfortunately, many of these numbers are born of dubious practices or massaged past the point of reality. Once they're contained in a press release or report, many journalists treat them as gospel, happily passing them along without a second look. In doing so, the press is both a creator of and a conduit for numerical errors.

"Let's face it, we often report poorly because we fail to understand statistics, or take them into account, or demand them, or get bamboozled by phony or unreliable numbers," wrote Victor Cohn in an adaptation of his book *News & Numbers: A Guide to Reporting Statistical Claims and Controversies in Health and Other Fields*. Cohn, a widely respected science writer for the *Washington Post*, who passed away in 2000, wrote one of the great texts on numbers and the press. He attempted to offer some basic principles for evaluating the numbers that flow into newsrooms on a daily basis, and give reporters and editors the skills necessary to present them accurately.

"We can be better reporters if we understand a few basic principles—the laws of probability and chance, statistical power, troublesome variability and inevitable statistical biases—to learn the probable truth of the things we are told, to weigh and question claims, to judge the contentions of scientists, doctors, environmentalists, politicians, economists, whomever," he wrote.

The danger is that dubious numbers take on a level of certainty when they make their way into the press and, ultimately, the public record. This sometimes causes an echo-chamber effect whereby incorrect numbers appear in one publication and are then repeated again and again in the press and by outside sources. A number arrived at in a newsroom and made public is picked up by organizations or people who see it as a validation of their views. They use it in their communications, and this causes other press outlets to use it again.

Writing in *Harper's* in 1964, Otto Friedrich recounted the tale, told to him by a researcher at *Newsweek*, of one fact-checker tasked with determining how many soldiers were in the Sudanese army. The checker scoured newspaper clippings and called the Sudanese embassy in Washington. No answer could be found. Eventually, the checker was told to make an educated guess. The number 17,000 was arrived at and inserted into the article. Friedrich describes how the article made its way to Khartoum, "where the press complaisantly reprinted it and commented on it."

These local press accounts were dispatched back to the Sudanese embassy, "and one day a Sudanese Embassy official happily telephoned the *Newsweek* researcher to report that he finally was about to tell her the exact number of men in the Sudanese army: seventeen thousand."

The problem persists. In May 2006, U.S. attorney general Alberto Gonzales announced the implementation of his department's Project Safe Childhood to fight against online sexual predators. "We are in the midst of an epidemic of sexual abuse and exploitation of our children," he said in a press release. "Project Safe Childhood will help law enforcement and community leaders prevent, investigate, and prosecute sexual predators and pornographers who target our children and grandchildren."

Gonzales also used a frightening statistic to drive home the importance of his message. According to *Legal Times*, he said, "It has been estimated that, at any given time, 50,000 predators are on the Internet prowling for children."

The *Legal Times* investigated the shocking figure, wondering where it came from. It received an answer from the attorney general's press secretary, who said, "That number is actually pulled from [NBC newsmagazine] 'Dateline' and other media outlets."

Dateline has built a mini-franchise in the form of its recurring series *To Catch a Predator*. Host Chris Hansen and his team work with— and pay—a watchdog group called Perverted Justice to go online pretending to be underage kids and see if predators approach them. If one makes contact, they set up a meeting at a location that *Dateline* fills with hidden cameras. Local police officers wait in the wings. The perps walk into the house expecting to meet their underage target but are instead confronted by Hansen. After he questions and condemns them, the police take over.

It's a solid ratings hit for NBC, and Hansen also wrote a book about the topic. (The fact that NBC has paid Perverted Justice as much as $100,000 to participate in the operation caused many in the media, including myself, to question the ethics of the project. Journalists aren't supposed to pay for stories. *Dateline* feels strongly that the arrangement is ethical, especially given the results of the work.)

So where did *Dateline* get that huge number of 50,000 predators? The *Legal Times* reported that Hansen cited "law enforcement officials" as the source in one broadcast. After being contacted for comment, Hansen said "this is a number that was widely used in law enforcement circles," though the publication noted he "couldn't specify by whom or where."

Hansen referred reporters to Ken Lanning, a former FBI agent who works with the show. But he couldn't confirm it, either.

"Was it just a WAG—a wild-assed-guess?" Lanning said. "It could have been."

In fact, Lanning said 50,000 was the magic number used in the 1980s to estimate the number of children abducted by strangers every year. In that same decade, he said, it was the number used by the press to estimate the number of people killed by satanic cults. As far as numbers go, 50,000 is big enough and round enough to attract attention and instill a sense of fear.

"For some reason the number 50,000 keeps popping up," Lanning said. "Maybe because it's not small and not large. It's a Goldilocks number."

In a subsequent interview with *On the Media*, a public radio program, Hansen said *Dateline* used the number in the first two editions of the series but had not used it since then. Someone, however, forgot to tell the attorney general. After being out there for so long, the dubious claim of 50,000 online predators is likely to continue to appear in the press and elsewhere.

In that same radio program, Carl Bialik, who crunches numbers in a column for the *Wall Street Journal*, commented on the way dubious figures make their way into the news and other reports.

"An interesting phenomenon of these numbers is that they'll often be cited to an agency or some government body, and then a study will pick it up, and then the press will repeat it from that study," he said. "And then once it appears in the press, public officials will repeat it again, and now it's become an official number."

As long as the number works for a story, or a tale someone outside the press is spinning, it's considered usable. Numbers will usually be challenged only when they don't fit with the angle chosen by a reporter or editor.

The need for a higher level of numeracy and scrutiny within newsrooms has been proved in a series of studies. They looked at how numbers used by the press have contributed to false or misleading perceptions of specific groups of people or particular social issues. Maier reported, "Journalistic innumeracy has been found to contribute to inaccurate and misleading stories regarding African-Americans, banking, child abuse, drug abuse, education, the homeless, political polls, the poor, science, Social Security and Medicare, technological and natural disasters, and other topical issues." Few would care to stand up and speak on the behalf of online predators to say they are nowhere near as prevalent as the "Goldilocks" number of 50,000 suggests. But other communities or professions are frequently and incorrectly maligned by fuzzy numbers.

One example from Maier's list (each subject area has been the focus of at least one study or article), in fact, reveals the origin of that fanciful "Goldilocks" number, and how it helped pave the way for much incorrect reporting about child abuse.

John Walsh, today widely known as the host of *America's Most Wanted* and a crusader for victims of crime, suffered the tragic, brutal loss of his son after the boy was kidnapped and murdered in 1981. A few months later he testified before a U.S. Senate committee about the abduction of his child by strangers. As he would later do with his television series, Walsh was trying to use his personal loss to raise awareness about the reality of child abduction. In preparing for his testimony, he sought numbers to back up his cause. It seems the U.S. Senate is as addicted to numbers as the press is.

"We were told not to come here without some statistics," he testified. And then he offered a staggering one. Walsh said that 50,000 American children were abducted by strangers every year. It was the birth of Goldilocks: a big, fat, round number that fit just right for senators and the press.

As with the magical *Dateline* figure that was spawned from his testimony, Walsh later admitted, "I can't defend those figures." But the number stuck and was reported again and again. "The panic he had helped start, aided and abetted by the media, had swept the nation," wrote Richard Wexler in "Understanding Child Abuse Numbers," a sidebar to an article in the spring 1993 issue of *Nieman Reports*, a publication of the Nieman Foundation at Harvard University. "And what did the media learn from all this? Apparently, not much."

Wexler reported that a 1990 study for the U.S. Department of Justice found that the real number of abductions is "no more than 300, and probably less."

But the 50,000 figure remained. In 1982, the Associated Press reported that "of the 50,000 stranger abductions, 5,000 children are returned unharmed, while 5,000 are found dead." Two years later, the AP was still using the number, stating flatly that "strangers abduct 50,000 children a year." The number has diminished over time, and Walsh's recanting of it likely helped. In 1984, the *Los Angeles Times* published an article questioning the numbers.

"There's no way there's 50,000 stranger abductions a year!" it quoted James Wootten, the deputy administrator of the office of juvenile justice and delinquency in the U.S. Department of Justice, as saying.

Wexler's article went on to catalog the other numerous, dubious child abuse statistics manipulated by interested parties in order to stoke public anger. For the most part, the press accepted them at face value and without objection.

Wexler wasn't attempting to diminish the seriousness of child abuse. Rather, he was calling for an accurate representation of the problem. "The first step towards finding real solutions is getting a real understanding of the numbers," he wrote.

The challenge for the press is to wade through and question the prepackaged figures pimped by organizations and special interests, while also working to combat the fear of numbers many journalists have. The media embraces the power of numbers and uses it to deliver strong reporting. But the rampant innumeracy and lack of questioning means that, all too frequently, the numbers reported every day in every medium simply don't add up.

The Corrections
FUZZY NUMBERS

IN AN ITEM IN YESTERDAY'S paper on how Kirstie Alley lost
75 pounds, it was incorrectly stated that she "ate . . . twenty-six,
seven, eight thousand calories a day."

The correct figures are six, seven, eight thousand calories a day.
—*New York Daily News*

In a G2 feature, How to . . . improve your swimming, page 27,
August 31, our advice struck a chilling note when it recommended finding a pool "heated" to 28F. That is below freezing
point. We meant 28 Celsius (82F).   —*Guardian* (UK)

Sunday's Section A described the Illinois Senate race as close.
A poll taken in mid-September showed Democratic candidate
Barack Obama with a 51-percentage-point lead over Republican
Alan Keyes.   —*Los Angeles Times*

Any number divided by zero is undefined, not zero as reported
last Sunday in a Starship article about the number zero. Zero
divided by zero is also undefined. The *Star* regrets the error.
—*Toronto Star*

In an article about the adverse health effects of certain kinds of
clothing, pages 8 and 9, G2, August 5, we omitted a decimal
point when quoting a doctor on the optimum temperature of
testicles. They should be 2.2 degrees Celsius below core body
temperature, not 22 degrees lower.   —*Guardian* (UK)

An article in the Sept. 17 Calendar section about "Gloomy Sunday" said the movie cost less than $200,000 to make. Its budget was $5.2 million.   —*Los Angeles Times*

+

A story in the Dec. 13 Business section about MetroPCS referred to 4.5 potential customers in the D-FW area. The correct number is 4.5 million.   —*Dallas Morning News*

+

A story in last Sunday's @issue section on food safety said that four companies control 80 percent of the nation's meat market and thus have a "virtual monopoly" on the market. A counterpoint piece should have said four companies owning 80 percent does not constitute a monopoly.

—*Atlanta Journal-Constitution*

+

An editorial Thursday, "A wise pause on nurse ratios," mistakenly said some hospitals had been "trying to get by with 15 or more nurses per patient." The reference was to the number of patients per nurse.   —*San Francisco Chronicle*

+

GLOBAL TEMPERATURES could rise by 7.7C by the end of the century, that is by 2100, not by 3000 (Global warming predictions are underestimated say scientists, page 3, May 23).

—*Guardian* (UK)

+

An article in Saturday's Your Home section committed overkill by advising readers to smother grass with a much-too-thick layer of wet newspaper. The article should have suggested using a layer that's about 12 sheets thick, not 12 inches. The reporter erred.   —*Akron Beacon Journal*

✦

The June 1 story "The Corporate Takeover of U.S. Intelligence" mistakenly stated that 70 percent of the approximately $48 billion U.S. intelligence budget given to contractors amounted to "roughly $42 billion." Seventy percent represents approximately $34 billion. The error has been corrected.

—Salon.com

✦

An article in Business Day yesterday about bidders for *The Philadelphia Inquirer* and *The Daily News* misstated the price that the newspapers are expected to bring in some copies. It is $600 million, not $600,000.   —*New York Times*

✦

In paragraph 4, please read . . . $112 million-budgeted film . . . instead of . . . $112-budgeted film.

—Reuters

✦

In an Aug. 19 story, The Associated Press erroneously reported the acreage that the president of Ecuador's Chamber of Agriculture said was covered by ash from the Tungurahua Volcano. The figure was nearly 50,000 acres, not nearly 500,000.   —Associated Press

✦

A caption in the World Cup special section Friday misstated the year that Germany hosted the Olympics before World War II. It was 1936, not 1946.

—*International Herald Tribune*

✦

A Jan. 21 Magazine article incorrectly said that 350 rail cars could carry 4 million tons of coal. It would take about 40,000 typical cars, or 350 to 400 typical coal trains, to carry that amount.

—*Washington Post*

A Week Ahead item in Monday's Calendar section said that in Albert Brooks' new film, "Looking for Comedy in the Muslim World," Brooks' character was asked to go to India and Pakistan and write a 500-word report on what made 300 Muslims laugh. The character was asked to write a 500-page report.

—*Los Angeles Times*

A recipe in the Entrée section Sunday for Three-Grain Breakfast Cereal misstated the calorie count for a one-third cup serving. The serving contains 185 calories, not 18.

—*Milwaukee Journal Sentinel*

We gave an unlikely figure of 14m tonnes of snackfood consumed during transmission of the Superbowl, which would be almost half a tonne for every American (What we've learned, page 28, February 11). We meant 14m kilograms.

—*Guardian* (UK)

There was a decimal slip in our Super Bowl snack food correction yesterday. The mistaken figure of 14m tonnes would be almost 0.05 tonnes of food for each American and not almost half a tonne.   —*Guardian* (UK)

A story on Page 4B of Thursday's Metro & State section about teenagers seeking abortions incorrectly stated there were about 50,000 teen abortions in Florida last year. The story should have said there were nearly 50,000 teen pregnancies.

—*Miami Herald*

◆

The project to turn the old Colman School in Seattle into an African American museum with apartments on the upper floors will cost about $20 million. A previous version of the story left out the word "million."   —*Seattle Times*

◆

An Op-Ed article on Saturday, about pay for airline pilots, misstated what the top salary for a pilot in 1924 would be in today's money. It would be about $93,000, not $1 million.

—*New York Times*

◆

On Tuesday's editorial page, the letter "Enjoying MySpace" contained a percentage error. The letter stated, "Six million people use MySpace, and if 600 become news items, that's only 1 percent." Six hundred is 0.01 percent of 6 million.

—*Daily Press* (Virginia)

◆

Halliburton 1st-quarter earnings surge . . . Please read in the second paragraph "$488 million" . . . instead of . . . "$488."

—Reuters

◆

An article in Business Day on Wednesday about an experiment to link slot machines in Las Vegas casinos to a central computer network misstated the number of machines being tested by the Treasure Island casino. It is 16—not 1,790, which is the total number of machines in the casino.

—*New York Times*

In last week's wine column, mention was made of a Chambertin Clos de Beze 1006. That, of course, was a 1996.

—*Business Times* (Singapore)

Sunday's Metro Page B8 weather report may have led readers to believe global warming had assaulted Roseville with a high of 705 degrees. While it certainly was hot Saturday, that temperature was obviously incorrect. The correct high temperature was 104 degrees.   —*Sacramento Bee*

IN AN ARTICLE IS IT OK . . . to drink cow's milk? (Ethical living, page 26, G2, June 6), two mistakes were introduced in the editing. Comments which were made by an unnamed former dairy worker, whose mother runs an animal sanctuary, were mistakenly attributed to Gordon Tweddle for which we apologise. We also caused the writer to say that cows are responsible for "19% of global warming". In fact cows are responsible for 20% of methane gas, and methane gas accounts for 19% of global warming.   —*Guardian* (UK)

Yesterday's table of nutrients for frozen beef burgers on page
G0 6 gave the sodium contents in grams. In fact, the sodium
is measured in milligrams. We regret the error.
                                   —*Hamilton Spectator* (Ontario)

An article last Sunday about earmarks, the legislative practice
of setting aside money in spending bills for special projects,
included erroneous amounts, based on information in the
Congressional Record, for the Missouri Forest Foundation and
the Mystic Aquarium in Connecticut. Congress approved
$750,000 for the forest foundation, not $750 million; and
$400,000 for the aquarium, not $400 million.
                                              —*New York Times*

July 21 Style review of the movie "Clerks II" misstated the
budget of the original "Clerks." It was $27,000, not $230,000.
                                             —*Washington Post*

A story headlined "Johnson Electric tips rise in sales, margins"
on July 21 should have said Johnson Electric acquired Saia-
Burgess for US$548 million, not US$4.5 billion.
                                      —*South China Morning Post*

An Op-Ed article on Tuesday, about philanthropy by billionaires,
misstated the amount of Warren Buffett's donation to the Bill
and Melinda Gates Foundation. It is $31 billion, not million.
                                              —*New York Times*

An article July 2 about plans for the Burlington Municipal Airport's plans to buy an airport hangar misstated the length of the airport's paved runway. Its length is 4,300 feet, not 45,300 feet.   —*Milwaukee Journal-Sentinel*

❖

An article in Business Day on Thursday about the proposed merger of the law firm Dewey Ballantine with Orrick, Herrington & Sutcliffe misstated the estimated profit per equity partner at Dewey Ballantine last year. It was $1.24 million, not $1.24. The article also referred incorrectly at one point to Morton A. Pierce, chairman of the management and executive committees, as Mr. Morton, instead of as Mr. Pierce.

—*New York Times*

❖

AN OCT. 15 SPORTS ARTICLE incorrectly identified Nick Bax as a runner for St. Albans School in England. He runs for the school of the same name in the District. Also, the article described Bax as having trailed another runner for the first 4,000 kilometers of a race. It was the first 4,000 meters.

—*Washington Post*

❖

A property transaction published in the Sept. 17 Real Estate section contained a typographical error. The house at 140 Mildred Ave., Syracuse, was sold for $85,000, not $849,000. The corrected transaction appears below.

—*Post-Standard* (New York)

❖

A chart in Business Day on Wednesday with an article about Google's share price surpassing $500 misstated the performance of New River Pharmaceuticals, which was listed among the best-performing initial offers. Shares of New River increased 1,154 percent through Tuesday since its offering in August 2004, not 527 percent. In addition, two companies listed in the chart, New River and Atlas America, did not reflect the split-adjusted share prices. The split-adjusted price for New River was $4, not $8; and for Atlas America, it was $10.33 instead of $15.50.   —*New York Times*

*

The Nov. 10 Broadsheet item "He or she?" indicated that two percent of every 1000 babies are born with ambiguous genitalia. This description was both confusing and incorrect. In fact, while it's difficult to determine precisely how common intersexuality is, estimates range from one in 2,000 births to one in 4,500 births. The item has been corrected.

—Salon.com

*

A report in the New York pages yesterday in the new feature headed "Ink," about the Rev. Al Sharpton"s weight-loss plan, misstated the frequency of his workouts in some copies. He exercises three times weekly, not three times a day.

—*New York Times*

*

CHAPTER 6

UNRELIABLE SOURCES AND MALICIOUS REPORTERS

I N APRIL 2004, THE LONDON BUREAU of Reuters moved a story on the wire that boasted a perfect confluence of news: average people using cool new technology to engage in dirty, anonymous sex in public places.

"British commuters take note," it warned, "the respectable person sitting next to you on the train fumbling with their cell phone might be a 'toother' looking for sex with a stranger."

The story explained that "toothing" was the latest in tech-enabled fornication. It was "where strangers on trains, buses, in bars, and even [in] supermarkets hook up for illicit meetings using messages sent via the latest in phone technology."

The new phone messaging technology was Bluetooth, thus the name "toothing."

CNN grabbed the story, and publications including London's *Telegraph*, the BBC, and a host of technology news sites all piled on with stories of their own. Toothing—which was spurred on by an online message board filled with posts from eager "toothers"—was the new flash mob, a perfect media-ready meme.

The only hitch in this international story was that toothing didn't exist. There were no lonely commuters sending out explicit offers for a quickie in the washroom. Two Englishmen, Ste Curran and Simon Byron, had made up all the posts on the message board. The pair dreamed up the idea of toothing as a buzzword ripe for media consumption. They decided to unleash it and see if the media was as gullible as they expected them to be.

They were right.

Unreliable Sources

N OW, YEARS LATER, FEW OF THE media outlets that wrote about toothing have run a correction to advise readers of the false information. To cap toothing's error-riddled media ride, an April 2005 episode of *CSI: Miami* entitled "Killer Date" featured a plotline in which an investigator loses his badge after toothing his way into a sexual encounter outside a club.

Toothing is but one example of the continuous stream of egregious errors and outright fabrications foisted on the media by unreliable sources, hoaxers, liars, and others seeking exposure or notoriety. The absence of effective checks and balances to prevent people from having their way with media organizations means readers and viewers are regularly treated to fake and otherwise incorrect stories. In these examples, the conscious fibbing and manipulation by a source combines with the willingness of journalists to take newsworthy stories at face value and rush them out into the world. Unreliable sources take advantage of the news media's need to find an untold story or locate a great source to illuminate the news of the day. This is what unreliable sources feed on. Those who understand how journalism works often find it shamefully easy to manipulate journalists into reporting something false or misleading.

From conscious hoaxers like the men of toothing, to companies or organizations that spin their numbers and facts past the point of reality, the existence of such unreliable sources outside the media means that overworked (and occasionally just plain gullible) journalists have to keep up their guard at all times. The lack of rigorous fact checking at most news organizations, combined with the push to always get something fast and first, results in errors great and small. From invented tales of toothing to incorrect reports about arrests or other occurrences, unreliable sources frequently fool the press, and we're all worse off because of it.

Recent years have brought sources bearing tales of naked skydivers in Sweden, and a man passing himself off as an executive for Dow

Chemical and announcing live on the BBC that the company was willing to admit responsibility for one of the world's worst environmental disasters. Other examples found Slate.com and the BBC reporting that cows have accents, *Sports Illustrated* reporting that a West Virginia football fan defecated in the stands during a game, the *Toronto Sun* reporting that a fake virgin was seeking 5 million hits on his Web site within thirty days to be able to have sex with a female friend, and a Massachusetts paper saying a student at UMass Dartmouth was visited by federal agents after requesting a copy of Mao Zedong's *Little Red Book*. Hoaxes, the lot of them.

As I write this, the *Fresno Bee* this morning apologized to readers after printing the tale of a "fat, blind goldfish rescued off a lawn and reunited with his owner." It began when a woman placed a classified ad in the paper stating, "Found: Large, obese goldfish. Approx 11 yrs old, blind as a bat." The ad later appeared on *The Late Show with David Letterman*, and a woman soon claimed the fish was hers.

"Bernadette Planting was reunited Tuesday with her pet goldfish, Charley, almost two months after he disappeared from her above-ground pool and weeks after Charley had become a minor media celebrity," read the initial *Bee* article.

The next day, the two women were outed in a story about the hoax. "Journalists are trained to be skeptical, but at some point we have to take people at their word," said Betsy Lumbye, executive editor and senior vice president of the *Bee*. "We're disappointed that these ladies weren't honest, and disappointed that we didn't catch the hoax."

One major weakness within the press is what I call the desire for the perfect source. Journalists are always looking for that one great source to help illuminate a story, someone whose personal tale illuminates one of greater suffering, or a greater good. A source that *is* the story, rather than someone who can just talk about it. This is hammered into every reporter on just about every beat. Get me someone to hang the story on, goes the editor's cry. Find the perfect source to draw readers into the story, and your editors will thank you.

The search for the perfect source is an everyday part of journalism. Rising gas prices? Don't just get a talking head from an oil company, analyst firm, or NGO—find Joe Sixpack who left his car at home all week. Even better if he owns a Hummer and knows how to give good quote. Or, as the folks in TV say, is a "good talker."

Every story is supposed to be humanized so it can speak to the average reader or viewer. And so journalists trudge out into the streets, send out mass e-mails, and needle friends, family, and contacts for that one perfect source.

The news media is addicted to the perfect source. Along with the occasional fake perfect source or untrue tale, this addiction usually results in paint-by-numbers work. How many times a day do we encounter stories that begin with a single person's tale? You can almost count the words until you hit the inevitable "Joe Sixpack is like [number] other people in [insert city/state/province] who [insert hobby/problem/etc]."

Ah, the human touch.

People like hearing about other people. All the better if it's someone they can relate to. It's a standard, albeit transparent, practice. It also leaves journalists open to manipulation. Some people seek to be the perfect source in order to gain some kind of benefit for themselves. Some just think they're being helpful by offering the reporter what he or she seems to want. Much like journalists, sources make mistakes. Police departments often err in supplying information to the news media, as do people who send press releases, community announcements, and other information. This prepackaged news is then passed on without further research. For example, the *International Herald Tribune* published a correction on March 14, 2007, after one of its sources backtracked on a claim:

AN ARTICLE MARCH 3 about the slaying of Ken Gorman, a supplier of medical marijuana in Denver, included an erroneous estimate from Allen St. Pierre, the executive director of the National Organization for the Reform of Marijuana Laws, of the number of legal marijuana providers who have been killed nationally. St. Pierre says he can only verify six killings since 2003, not the 20 since 1997 that he earlier estimated.

The *Los Angeles Times* had to publish a correction on January 24, 2007, after it discovered that one source, interviewed to provide an honest assessment of a health clinic, turned out to have a conflict of interest:

> AN ARTICLE IN MONDAY'S Health section about walk-in clinics described Carrie Clemens' visit to Lindora Health Clinic, reporting in a positive way her experience as a patient at the clinic. Clemens is also an employee of Lindora Inc. but did not acknowledge this fact when asked about her place of employment. *The Times* learned of it after publication of the article.

I bowed to an unreliable source when a column I wrote for the *Globe and Mail*, a national newspaper in Canada, stated that "the Retail Council of Canada estimates that stores across the country lose up to $8 million per day to employee theft." I used numbers provided to me by the council. The day after the story appeared, I received an e-mail from my source telling me she had made a mistake. Employee theft accounted for only 40 percent of the $8 million. In the case of source errors, the journalist shares some of the blame for not doing the proper due diligence.

Sometimes reporters do significant, patient research to verify a source's claims. This requires time and dedication. It's a luxury not afforded in many of today's skeletal newsrooms. Often almost no fact checking is done, except for larger investigative stories or those that appear in magazines with fact-checking departments. Usually, the source is taken at his or her word; the reporter trusts his or her gut. This is risky. It's also the rule, not the exception.

The level of checking depends on the story. Reporters who are out to gather a few man-on-the-street quotes about the topic of the day don't bother to check on the people they talk to. The worst that happens in these cases is someone decides to have a little fun and give a fake name, like Heywood Jablome. (Hey would ya blow me?)

The *New York Post* quoted "Heywood Jablome, 41, a Manhattan real estate agent" in a 2001 story about coffeehouses. Two years later, the *Post and Courier* of Charleston, South Carolina, reported that during a protest police "officers escorted Heywood Jablome away." In 2007, the New York *Daily News* referred to Jablome as "that ubiquitous source who unfailingly turns up in some unsuspecting scribe's story every decade or so." We should be so lucky.

Paul Van Valkenburgh was a more committed impersonator, and it was only after his death that he was revealed. Van Valkenburgh spent part of his life claiming to be the writer of the hit song "Itsy Bitsy Teenie Weenie Yellow Polka Dot Bikini." When he died, in September 2006, his loving wife contacted the Associated Press to report his passing and note his contribution to the world of music. AP wrote the story, and it was widely published. To explain one questionable aspect of the tale, the man's wife said Van Valkenburgh had assumed the name Paul Vance in crediting himself for the song. Just a day after the story's release, the real Paul Vance, a seventy-six-year-old man living in New York, stepped forward and told the AP, "Do you know what it's like to have grandchildren call [sic] you and say, 'Grandpa, you're still alive?'"

Van Valkenburgh's widow said, "It's such a long time ago. To have it come out now, I'm kind of devastated."

In this case, it took an incorrect report to inspire a personal correction that was perhaps decades in the making. A little more checking prior to publication would have saved the real Paul Vance from fielding phone calls about his demise—and saved his grandkids a lot of confusion and concern.

Aside from the average person who fibs at the expense of the media, or seeks to impersonate someone famous or relatively unknown, there are stories that seem to pin everything on the tale of one, usually hard-luck, person. The reporter will spend time with the person, trying to coax out colorful anecdotes and details, to learn as much as possible in order to tell the story with authority. The extra effort can, in the best cases, result in a powerful personal tale that illuminates a larger truth. In the worst cases, you get a story in which the person is not what he or she claims to be. The individual is, in short, a liar.

This form of the dangerous perfect source—the liar—was exemplified by a story in the *New York Times* in 2006, a front-page tale of the iconic "man in the hood" whose photo became a signature image of prisoner abuse at Abu Ghraib prison. The *Times* thought it had scored an in-depth interview with a person whose experience could best tell the story of how some Iraqis have been put in tragic situations due to the invasion. After the story ran, Salon.com raised questions as to whether the *Times* really had the man in the hood. When the *Times* took the time to fully check his story, it agreed. It wasn't the man. The paper published an Editor's Note, on March 18, 2006, that began:

> A FRONT-PAGE ARTICLE last Saturday profiled Ali Shalal Qaissi, identifying him as the hooded man forced to stand on a box, attached to wires, in a photograph from the Abu Ghraib prison abuse scandal of 2003 and 2004. He was shown holding such a photograph. As an article on Page A1 today makes clear, Mr. Qaissi was not that man.
>
> *The Times* did not adequately research Mr. Qaissi's insistence that he was the man in the photograph.

The note then stated that other media outlets such as PBS and *Vanity Fair* had also cited Qaissi as the man in the hood. So he seemed to be a bona fide source. The truth was that he had merely convinced others of his tale. Everyone was wrong. In a strange twist, however, an investigation by *Times* public editor Byron Calame revealed "clear evidence of the error had existed in an unnoticed 2004 *Times* story." The paper had failed to unearth evidence residing in its own previous reporting.

Using the *Times'* archives, Calame found that "in an article on May 22, 2004, the paper had correctly identified the man in the photograph as Abdou Hussain Saad Faleh." Calame also noted that the paper felt Qaissi's claims were validated because he had been cited by other news organizations. In judging the veracity of his claims, it looked to other news outlets as sources, and they also failed the *Times*. It was a cascade of error born of one unreliable source.

"The *Times's* decision to treat Mr. Qaissi's claims as credible was 'influenced' by the awareness of similar earlier reports in *Vanity Fair* and on PBS that had gone unchallenged," wrote Calame. "But those reports weren't mentioned in *The Times* until they were invoked in the March 14 story and the Editor's Note. Readers of the original story, I believe, deserved to know that secondary sources were influencing *The Times*'s acceptance of Mr. Qaissi's claims."

In this case, the truth was there to be found, but the news organization didn't push hard enough to find it. That people lie comes as no shock. More difficult for the news media is the barrage of press releases and pitches that constantly flow in from government, organizations, companies, and other entities. Contained within this multitude of faxes, e-mails, and tips whispered in an ear are often unreliable "facts" and figures. The press is charged with vetting these sources, evaluating their information, and examining their motives. Incorrect information is of concern, as are instances of omission. When sources take hold of a story and guide a willing reporter, other viewpoints and facts can be left unreported. A frequent saying in journalism is that you are only as good as your sources. When sources are wrong, so too are journalists. Evaluating the pedigree and honesty of a source is critical to accuracy because sources themselves are so critical to journalism.

Reporters cultivate people in the know about certain issues and areas. Occasionally, to protect someone who is providing important information that could jeopardize his or her safety or position, reporters will allow a source to remain anonymous. This became en vogue after Woodward and Bernstein revealed the existence of Deep Throat in a book about their Watergate reporting. Since then it has evolved to the point where people who don't warrant the protection of anonymity demand it in order to shield themselves from having to stand by their remarks. This back channel of anonymous attacks and whispers puts the onus on a reporter to evaluate whether a source is being honest, and if the person warrants such protection. When a source is unnamed, neither the audience nor other journalists are able to assess the quality of the individual's information.

As sexy and mysterious as it may seem to have an anonymous source in a story, their use has become too commonplace, and it's enabling individuals to manipulate coverage. Leonard Downie, the top editor of the *Washington Post*, described the current climate of sources and the rumors they push in a 2004 letter to readers. He wrote that "Internet-borne rumors, talk-show speculation and sophisticated spinning by newsmakers who want to influence how the news is reported while hiding their responsibility for doing so" represent a challenge to accurate reporting.

When people don't have to attach their names to a comment or piece of information, they feel liberated to say things they otherwise wouldn't. This works well in the case of whistle-blowers who seek to offer journalists information that will enable them to investigate something unjust. For spin doctors or political operatives, anonymity offers a means to conceal skullduggery.

Fortunately, more and more news organizations are rewriting their guidelines about anonymous sources to ensure that only those who warrant the cloak of anonymity receive it, and that their audience is given an explanation for why it was granted. Readers, listeners, and viewers have a right to know where the news and information they get is coming from. If that's not possible, they should be told why. Articles littered with anonymous sources, be they "a senior administration official" or "someone with knowledge of the deal," distance the audience from the story because they are unable to fully judge its veracity.

The danger of anonymous sources is that journalists are at the mercy of people who can say whatever they want without being held accountable for it.

The most serious recent example of manipulative anonymous sources came during reporting about weapons of mass destruction in Iraq. Leading up to the invasion of Iraq in 2003, there was a series of articles in the *New York Times* that relied on sources, including anonymous ones, who proffered documents to make the case that Iraq had weapons of mass destruction. *Times* reporter Judith Miller, a Pulitzer Prize winner, wrote a series of reports in 2001 and 2002 that cited information from sources she had cultivated over the many years she spent covering terrorism, bioweapons, and other important issues related to national security.

On December 20, 2001, she reported, "An Iraqi defector who described himself as a civil engineer said he personally worked on renovations of secret facilities for biological, chemical and nuclear weapons in underground wells, private villas and under the Saddam Hussein Hospital in Baghdad as recently as a year ago."

On April 21, 2003, reporting from within Iraq after the invasion, Miller wrote, "A scientist who claims to have worked in Iraq's chemical weapons program for more than a decade has told an American military team that Iraq destroyed chemical weapons and biological warfare equipment only days before the war began, members of the team said."

In Miller's case, she had a long-standing relationship with Ahmed Chalabi and his organization, the Iraqi National Congress. As an organization committed to toppling Saddam Hussein, it had a vested interest in making the case for WMDs and for the need for an invasion. These sources were self-interested to the highest degree. Whether you believe the invasion was justified in spite of the absence of WMDs or not, the reality is that news reports chronicling their existence played a major role in galvanizing public support for the war. In hindsight, it was discovered that there were no WMDs in Iraq. The information provided by Chalabi and others was incorrect. Not enough effort was made to investigate their claims and balance their self-serving point of view. The failure of the news media—the *Times* is not alone, though Miller became the reporter most linked to this issue—to dig deeper and question the information flowing from agenda-driven sources let the sources dictate the coverage of the day, a situation no journalist feels comfortable in.

Cultivating sources is, of course, a part of every journalist's job. The police reporter with the best contacts on the force will often get the story before anyone else. The political correspondent with access to top administration officials and high-level bureaucrats will be fed information that others don't get. This symbiotic, or parasitic, relationship is at the core of journalism. Sources need coverage just as much as the media needs sources. And the journalists who manage to collect the best sources guard them at all costs, occasionally even going to jail to protect them.

"She is possessive of her sources," *New York Times* executive editor Bill Keller told *New York* magazine in an article about Judith Miller published in June of 2004. (The story was aptly titled "The Source of the

Trouble.") One of the criticisms leveled against Miller was that she became beholden to her sources, addicted to access. That, and her unwillingness to share her sources and information with fellow *Times* journalists who might have questioned it, was viewed as one of the reasons for her inaccurate reporting.

Daniel Okrent, the paper's first public editor, wrote that "in *The Times*'s W.M.D. coverage, readers encountered some rather breathless stories built on unsubstantiated 'revelations' that, in many instances, were the anonymity-cloaked assertions of people with vested interests." Okrent's column appeared six days before the paper published an Editor's Note admitting its failings in regard to the reporting about WMDs in Iraq.

The note began by saying that, after a review of its work, the *Times* "found an enormous amount of journalism that we are proud of." But it also acknowledged what critics had been saying for months or even years: Many of its reports came from unreliable sources offering unsubstantiated information. "We have found a number of instances of coverage that was not as rigorous as it should have been," read the note. "In some cases, information that was controversial then, and seems questionable now, was insufficiently qualified or allowed to stand unchallenged. Looking back, we wish we had been more aggressive in re-examining the claims as new evidence emerged—or failed to emerge."

In summarizing a 1999 conference session about sources at the Nieman Foundation for Journalism at Harvard University, John F. Kelley called sources "the bearer of the kernel of information that starts the journalistic ball rolling or helps speed it along."

Sources are a critical component of journalism, but when they are not kept at an appropriate distance or subjected to the necessary amount of scrutiny, they can cause an incredible amount of damage to news organizations and to the public's perspective. The reality is that the media, which is grappling with huge cuts in newsroom staff and pressure to publish news-making stories in order to compete in a fragmented media landscape, will continue to be tripped up by its infatuation with the perfect source. Anonymous sources will always exist, even in cases where they shouldn't, and liars, hoaxers, and others out for self-gain will continue to call up newsrooms and pitch reporters. The onus is on reporters and editors to keep an appropriate distance from sources while also questioning their motives. Reporters should always ask themselves that classic question: *Qui bono?* Who benefits?

Malicious Reporters

F EW THINGS ELICIT MORE ANGER and cause more hurt within the profession of journalism than when one of its own commits a serious ethical lapse on purpose. Journalists such as Jayson Blair, the disgraced *New York Times* reporter who plagiarized, fabricated, and fooled colleagues time and again before being exposed in 2003, are viewed as the serial killers of the journalism community: strange, troubled psychos who operate outside the norms of the profession.

Mistakes are a part of daily journalism, but the idea that a journalist would commit them purposely is abhorrent and perplexing to reporters and editors. Why make something up when you can just make a few more phone calls and find the answer? Why steal someone else's words when you could interview the same sources, or attribute the information to them? Why make up a source when you can easily find one?

It's easier than ever before to detect literary theft and journalistic fiction, and there are also more people looking to spot it. But the parade of plagiarists and fabricators continues: student journalists, noted columnists, editorial writers, beat reporters, and Pulitzer Prize winners. According to the known instances, they make up a tiny proportion of working journalists. But they are among the most famous.

Journalists view the mind of the plagiarist or fabricator as a place of mystery and malice, the root of a troubled soul and a professionally bankrupt colleague. Their offenses are often referred to as the "sins" of journalism; they are rarely forgivable and always damaging. When they are caught and exposed, they sabotage their own career (though the most famous of their kind can usually count on a book deal), and they bring shame on their employer and the profession as a whole.

The name of a sinful journalist is never far from the lips of a critic of a particular publication or broadcaster. If you hate the *Times*, you love

Jayson Blair. If you're suspicious of the *New Republic*, the *Washington Post*, or *USA Today*, Stephen Glass, Janet Cooke, and Jack Kelley, three other famous fabulists, are your patron saints. Those who already believe in the incompetence or malice of these organizations view such incidents as confirmation of their lack of ethics and proper quality control. The plagiarist and fabricator are ammunition for critics, and the scourge of the profession.

Instances of plagiarism and fabrication are far less frequent than the barrage of factual errors. But the dastardly, damaging nature of the offenses means they punch far above their weight. They are also the subject of much discussion and psychoanalysis. Why, wonders the press, do these people lie, steal, and fictionalize? Why, wonders the public, are they often not caught until after they have done it again and again? These questions are rarely answered to anyone's satisfaction.

The offenders themselves offer a variety of responses. Some say personal issues outside of their job caused them to take shortcuts to fulfill their duties. Some aspire to greatness and see fabrication or plagiarism as a means to deliver the kind of reporting craved by editors, readers, and awards committees. Others blame those around them, saying the working environment, or culture, of a particular institution marginalized them, or forced them into a corner. They say they are the product of their surroundings, or of the profession. But who wants to hear the criticisms of an admitted plagiarist or fabricator? They have already been discredited.

Malicious journalists share a lack of ethics and professionalism that many of them developed early on. Jayson Blair and Janet Cooke, before they landed at the *Times* and the *Washington Post*, respectively, had both lied on their resumes and had been guilty of ethical misconduct. Some journalists who have committed such major offenses are found to have developed the habit while in journalism school, where they were supposed to be taught the standards of the profession. This suggests that journalism schools could play a stronger role in detecting and exposing the plagiarists and fabricators of tomorrow.

Writing in *Maisonneuve*, a magazine and accompanying Web site published out of Montreal, a pseudonymous former journalism student explained how she had developed her habitual fakery. "I started fabricating stories at the beginning of my second year," wrote "Kate Jackson" in a story entitled "Confessions of a Teenage Fabulist." Faced with the pressure to write a newsworthy story every week for one of her classes, she simply started making up interviews, sources, and quotes. And she got wonderful grades. As a result of continual praise from her professor and the ease with which she earned it, she continued to fake her stories:

IN TOTAL, I WROTE NEARLY A DOZEN fraudulent stories over two semesters, sticking to soft news and human-interest pieces. I often drew upon my social life for inspiration, "covering" local events I attended and imaginatively filling in the blanks instead of doing actual background research. My stories were pithy and concise, just like we'd been taught, earning me the straight-A average required to stay in the program. Each time a fake story was handed back to me with praise, I was both pleased and stunned that I had gotten away with it again. I guess it would have been impossible for one professor to fact-check almost one hundred student stories every week; we were, it seems, working on the honour system.

As are the vast majority of working journalists. Only a handful of newspapers use rigorous preventative procedures or technologies to catch plagiarism before—or after—it makes its way into print or goes on the air. Fact checking is used at many major magazines, but it is a discipline that is on the decline. Though it can be extremely effective when done expertly, it too has weaknesses. The working conditions within newsrooms remain largely favorable to the copycats and fabulists of today and tomorrow. The major danger to their continued presence appears more and more likely to be the regular readers, blogs, and media-monitoring organizations that increasingly scour the mainstream press for mistakes and other failures. The truth is that newspapers and magazines rarely discover instances of plagiarism or fabrication on their own. They are often alerted to it by outside sources or organizations—or, as is often the case, by the publication the work was stolen from. Journalists are reasonably proficient at exposing plagiarists and fakers, just as long as they don't sit at a nearby desk.

In her essay, "Kate" wrote that she eventually dropped out of her journalism program, and now, years later, she wonders, "How many Jayson Blairs—or Kate Jacksons, for that matter—have you trusted today? I guess you'll never know."

In 2007 she was working in film and television where "couch-bound research is much more appropriate and accepted, and there's always the safety net of situating my work as a critical interpretation rather than empirical truth." Small comfort for her oblivious employer, no doubt.

There are those, like "Kate," who are just too lazy to do the work of reporting properly. Because of the lack of controls in newsrooms or the weakness of fact-checking procedures, they get away with a cribbed sentence or paragraph here, an invented quote there. Then they become addicted, and seemingly forget how real reporting is supposed to be done. Others are highly praised achievers who show great promise, but falter under pressure. They are people whose drive for success outstrips their sense of professional propriety, exemplified by Janet Cooke and her legendary fabrication of the world's most perfect tragic youngster.

"Jimmy is 8 years old and a third-generation heroin addict, a precocious little boy with sandy hair, velvety brown eyes and needle marks freckling the baby-smooth skin of his thin brown arms," began her story, "Jimmy's World," which was published on the front page of the *Washington Post* on September 28, 1980.

A few paragraphs down comes the inevitable "Jimmy is not alone" perfect-source sentence: "Heroin has become a part of life in many of Washington's neighborhoods, affecting thousands of teen-agers and adults who feel cut off from the world around them, and filtering down to untold numbers of children like Jimmy who are bored with school and battered by life."

Cooke knew she needed the perfect source to tell her story and get it on the front page. So she invented him. He was so perfect he earned her a Pulitzer Prize, which she later had to return.

Bereft of professional ethics, Cooke made up what she knew her editors wanted—what every editor wants. This doesn't excuse her actions. Her overarching ambition set in motion a series of events that sullied the reputation of the *Washington Post* just a few years after its Watergate triumph.

Just as some unreliable sources are revealed to be liars, out for personal gain, the same is unfortunately true for some journalists. Jack Kelley, a former foreign correspondent for *USA Today*, according to the paper's 2004 investigation, was discovered to have "fabricated substantial portions of at least eight major stories, lifted nearly two dozen quotes or other material from competing publications, lied in speeches he gave for the newspaper and conspired to mislead those investigating his work."

One can find good and bad in any profession, but when a journalist goes bad—or was never good in the first place—it will impact people far beyond the newsroom walls. Just as the triumphs of the press are made public, so too are its failings. As they should be.

Since 2005, I have kept a record of occurrences of plagiarism and fabrication by journalists. Over the two years, I have noted close to forty incidents, and there were undoubtedly more that I missed. Some were deemed to be onetime, accidental offenses wherein a reporter forgot to attribute a sentence or quote to another source. Others—in fact the vast majority—were far worse.

In November 2005, for example, the *Californian* newspaper in Bakersfield revealed that it had found instances of plagiarism and fabrication in at least twenty-nine stories written by one reporter. Her previous employer then investigated her work and turned up two more. Just two months later, the *Press Enterprise*, a newspaper in Bloomsburg,

FROM THE EDITOR

News interviews suspect; reporter resigns

Press Enterprise editors have been unable to verify the authenticity of interviews in 24 stories written by former staff reporter Kate York between Aug. 23 and Jan. 2. The reporter has resigned.

The suspect material was included in otherwise accurate stories, mostly as man-in-the-street interviews that purported to convey comments by local residents on news events or trends. An audit of the stories in question uncovered 46 such names that cannot be found in the phone book or on the Internet, in voter registration or property records, or in the newspaper's own electronic archive of stories published since 1994.

York, an experienced reporter who had been with the paper a little more than four months, defended the interviews as accurate and truthful. When asked by editors to provide notes as proof, she resigned, effective immediately, saying she no longer wanted to work for a news organization that did not trust her reporting.

In 2001, the Press Enterprise dismissed a reporter after he admitted making up an interview with a shopper in the Columbia Mall. The newspaper has a zero tolerance policy for fabrication.

JIM SACHETTI
Editor

The Press Enterprise, *a newspaper in Bloomsburg, Pennsylvania, published a note from the editor in its January 17, 2006, edition concerning a reporter who fabricated interviews in twenty-four of her stories for the paper.*

Pennsylvania, announced that one of its reporters had fabricated interviews in twenty-four stories.

One of the stranger incidents was revealed to me when I came
across an article in the *Toronto Star*, in late December 2006:

> MOON GOD DRINKING PRODUCTS CO., a skin care company in
> China, has offered a bounty of 1,000 yuan ($144) for every
> typographical or literary error found in a day's editions of four
> Chinese publications in an attempt to embarrass journalists
> into better writing. Hao Mingjian, who came up with the idea
> for the bounty, said that "China's press has lost its polish in the
> past decade or two," which "reflects a chaotic cultural environ-
> ment and shows people lack a sense of responsibility." We
> applaud Hao's initiative, but we have learned over our years at
> the *Star* that it is impossible to embarrass journalists. Public
> humiliation is our stock in trade.

I was thrilled by the ingenuity of the Chinese entrepreneur and
planned to make note of his gambit on RegretTheError.com. But as I
searched for more reports about this error bounty I became puzzled,
and then horrified.

I initially found the same item reported on the Web sites of the
Wisconsin State Journal and the *Rocky Mountain News*. The latter credited it to Reuters, but my searches in a news database turned up
nothing recent like it from Reuters. The *Wisconsin State Journal* had
credited Randy Cassingham in its report, so I decided to contact
Randy, a former journalist who runs a Web site and weekly newsletter
called *This Is True*, which catalogs strange-but-true items about our
world. Via e-mail I asked him where he'd found the story, and he confirmed it was from a Reuters report. Except it was a Reuters report
from a decade ago. Cassingham had recently been ill, and to satisfy his
subscribers, he'd decided to reprint some of his favorite items from a
decade earlier.

It was clear that the newspapers in question had spotted his item
and failed to notice the disclaimer about its date, so they'd run it as a

new story. The *Star* didn't credit Cassingham or Reuters, which alone is unprofessional, but then I compared Cassingham's report with the *Star*'s. Except for the comments about its being impossible to embarrass journalists, the article was completely plagiarized from *This Is True*. Understandably, Cassingham was livid.

"It's patently obvious where they got this story," he told me. "That they didn't check their Reuters wires for corroboration is shocking—it's no wonder that there is scandal after scandal of embarrassing plagiarism, made-up stories, and other malfeasance by newspapers these days."

I contacted the *Star* to alert it of the theft and then posted a story on RegretTheError.com. (I also made one error: Because the article was unsigned, I referred to it as an editorial. In fact, it was printed in the paper's Arts section.)

I received confirmation from the *Star* that it would look into the incident, but none of my follow up e-mails were answered. Days later, on January 4, 2007, the paper published a correction:

> LAST SATURDAY'S EXACT CHANGE story, about a Chinese skin care company offering money to readers who find errors in four Chinese publications on a particular day, should have credited Randy Cassingham's This is True web site and should have indicated quotes from his story. Written in 1995, it was re-posted on the site last month. The *Star* regrets the errors.

No admission of plagiarism. No apology to Cassingham. The reporter responsible for the story was never named, nor was his or her previous work examined for other incidences of plagiarism. The irony of plagiarizing an article that dealt with the inaccuracies of the press was rich fodder in itself. But the more serious issue is that the paper declined to offer a full admission and explanation to readers, or engage in a proper investigation of how a ten-year-old story was stolen and copied from a Web site. The episode was, in effect, swept under the rug.

The existence of photo-editing software such as Photoshop has also given rise to a new category of malicious journalist: photo manipulators and even photographic plagiarists. The most famous recent incident involved Adnan Hajj, a contributing photographer for Reuters. During the conflict between Israel and Lebanon, or more specifically Hezbollah, in the summer of 2006, it was revealed that Hajj had manipulated some of his photos to make them more dramatic. In one instance, plumes of smoke were made larger and darker. Another saw him increase the number of flares dropped by an Israeli fighter plane. Reuters fired him and removed all of his previous photos from its archives.

As a rule, news photographers are not allowed to alter images in any way except to adjust their size and make other minor changes that do not impact the overall composition. Whenever a designer combines images for graphical effect to illustrate a story, or makes other changes to create an artistic presentation, the news organization is supposed to add a note to readers in the cutline—the description of the photo.

"There is no graver breach of Reuters standards for our photographers than the deliberate manipulation of an image," said Reuters global picture editor Tom Szlukovenyi.

ANOTHER NOTABLE TREND of recent years is the tendency to dismiss an incidence of theft as "accidental plagiarism." Certainly, some reporters do accidentally fail to attribute information, or, as is often the case, the reporter claims to have confused his or her own writing and notes with research gathered from other sources. Proper attribution can also sometimes be removed in the editing process. Occurrences such as this usually result in a reprimand for the reporter and a brief acknowledgment by the paper, but when it comes to how the press handles them, they also serve to highlight two serious problems in journalism.

First, only a handful of news organizations use plagiarism detection services or software to check work before or after publication; meanwhile, these services, which compare words and phrases against those published online and occasionally in other databases, are becoming more and more common in universities and other academic institutions. (Even the K–12 private school where my mother works in

Halifax, Nova Scotia, uses one.) But in news organizations, these "accidental" acts of plagiarism are not caught before they hit the paper or Web site. Detecting them could save a lot of embarrassment for those writers who have seen their sloppiness, or that of an editor, brand them with a scarlet letter. It could also help catch the work of true plagiarists before it makes its way into the news.

The second element of note is that not enough publications will undertake an examination of a writer's previous work to determine if an apparent incidence of plagiarism was in fact a onetime occurrence. Reporters who are respected staffers with unblemished records will be taken at their word or, at a minimum, will be given the benefit of the doubt. The problem with this honor system is that the truth can be sacrificed. A reporter whose work is not scrutinized after a single incident is never fully cleared *or* fully exposed. And even if the publication believes the reporter's story about the accidental nature of the offense, some readers won't.

Doing the research and fully clearing a reporter's name is in everyone's best interest. Unfortunately, this type of investigation rarely happens unless the misstep in question relates to fabrication or substantial amounts of plagiarism in a single article. The lack of an effective, standardized process within newsrooms for handling plagiarism ensures that those who have committed many previous offenses that are lurking in the archives are not exposed and ousted from the profession.

The saga that resulted from a November 10 editorial in the *Star Tribune* of Minnesota offers a prime example of the dangers that befall a publication that declines to fully investigate an incident of plagiarism the first time around. After that editorial was published, the conservative PowerLine.com blog noted that several of its passages were similar to work previously published in the *New Yorker*. The charge was reviewed and the paper ran a brief Editor's Note to explain the incident:

> IT HAS COME TO OUR ATTENTION that the Nov. 10 editorial "Americans Need Their Congress Back" contained phrases that should have been attributed to Hendrik Hertzberg of the *New Yorker*. We owe readers an explanation of how this happened.

The writer, who properly attributed other views included in the editorial, took notes on the Hertzberg piece, intending either to directly quote him or otherwise include some of his views, which coincided with the editorial staff's opinions on problems in Washington. Later, in consulting these notes, the writer inadvertently failed to distinguish which parts were direct quotes and which were paraphrased ideas, resulting in the writing of phrases that included an unattributed, improper mix of the two plus other points about Congress.

The paper took the writer's explanation at face value and explained it to readers as nothing more than an unfortunate accident. The paper's reader's representative, Kate Parry, followed with a column offering further explanation, but she noted a couple of troubling points. Because editorials are unsigned, she wasn't able to ascertain who was responsible for it so she could examine the issue on behalf of readers. Her efforts to identify the party were rebuffed by the paper. That, wrote Parry, "meant I couldn't get answers to what would be natural questions in the minds of readers: Was the employee disciplined? Were previous editorials by this writer checked for signs of plagiarism?"

Parry wrote that "there are really only two reasons plagiarism occurs, one far worse than the other, but neither is good. Intentional plagiarism is a theft. Unintentional plagiarism reveals sloppiness. Neither inspires reader confidence."

The people at Power Line, who were initially alerted by a Minnesota man who spotted the similarities, were also dissatisfied. The paper had done nothing to prove it was a onetime, accidental occurrence. So Power Line decided to dig deeper. They soon discovered a second editorial that also borrowed from the work of Hendrik Hertzberg in the *New Yorker*. Finally, the paper named the editorial writer, Steve Berg, and commenced a full review of his work. But if Power Line hadn't stayed on the case, it never would have happened. Susan Albright, the paper's editorial page editor, penned another Editor's Note for readers:

WE WANT YOU TO KNOW THAT we are taking this matter very seriously. We have an obligation to everyone involved to be fair and deliberate in evaluating this; it is too serious a matter to jump to any conclusions without a thorough review. Since both of the editorials in question were written by editorial writer Steve Berg, the *Star Tribune* will conduct a review of his writing over the past year. During this review he will not be writing.

In my editor's note about the Nov. 10 editorial, I did not name the writer. The subsequent questioning of the earlier piece caused us to rethink that stance, since both were written by the same person and other writers were becoming objects of conjecture.

We strive to be candid about our processes and practices, so when the review is completed, I will be writing about this again.

Just over a month later, on December 17, the paper announced that its review had cleared Berg of any other incidents of plagiarism. Berg went back to work and maintained what he had always said: that the incidents were failures of attribution on his part, not acts of plagiarism. "Reacting to a right-wing blog, the newspaper found unintentional insufficient attribution in a fraction of 1 percent of my work," Berg was quoted by AP as saying. "I'll put that up against anybody."

Berg's anger is understandable. His career of more than three decades as a journalist almost came to an end. But his anger at Power Line is somewhat misdirected. His paper's initial mishandling of the incident greatly contributed to the questioning and complaints about his editorials, and put him at the mercy of outside forces. If the *Star Tribune* had investigated his previous work and found what it considered to be two isolated instances of sloppy attribution, the issue could have been put to rest. Instead, it rebuffed its own readers' representative and caused Power Line to do the work the paper should have undertaken in the first place.

In many of these examples, plagiarists or fabricators were rooted out by fellow journalists, though readers and bloggers are playing an increasing role. Jayson Blair, the disgraced former *New York Times* reporter, following his resignation in May of 2003 after his work came under questioning, was found to have plagiarized or fabricated in thirty-six of seventy-three stories examined by the paper. In the end, he was undone when he stretched a bit too far and stole from an article in the San Antonio *Express-News* that was written by a former intern at the *Times*, who knew him. That paper raised the issue with the *Times*, and Blair was finished.

But Blair's penchant for flagitious behavior was revealed earlier in his career. One hallmark of his deceit was a proclivity for lying about his whereabouts. Often, he would work from a bar instead of flying off on assignment to some ghastly, potentially dry locale. Before long, he was caught in his shape-shifting ways, and as a result the *Times* published this correction on October 23, 2001:

> AN ARTICLE IN SOME COPIES on Sunday about a benefit at Madison Square Garden for victims of the Sept. 11 terror attack misstated the price of the most expensive tickets. They were $10,000, not $1,000.
>
> The article also quoted incorrectly from a remark by former President Bill Clinton to the audience, many of them police officers and firefighters. Mr. Clinton said he had been given the bracelet of Raymond Downey, the deputy fire chief who died in the attack—not Chief Downey's hat.
>
> Referring to the terrorists, he said, "I hope they saw this tonight, because they thought America was about money and power. They thought that if they took down the World Trade Center, we would collapse. But we're not about mountains of money or towers of steel. You're about mountains of courage and hearts of gold, and I hope they saw you here tonight." He did not say "hearts of steel."

The next day brought another:

> AN ARTICLE IN SOME late editions on Sunday about the benefit concert at Madison Square Garden for victims of the Sept. 11

attack referred incorrectly to scenes in a short film made for the event by Woody Allen, "Scenes from a Town I Love," which showed New Yorkers talking on cell phones. An actor in one scene complained that his anthrax drugs had been stolen by muggers; he did not say the police took them.

Another man talked about opening Starbucks coffee shops in Afghanistan after the war; he did not say one had already opened there.

The article also included two performers erroneously among the participants. Bono and the Edge, of the band U2, were scheduled to appear but canceled before the concert.

Blair had begged off the concert to get drunk in a bar. He wrote about what he saw of the concert on TV. His editor was not pleased and gave him "a formal reprimand," but contrition was not one of the substances Blair was eager to swallow. He "lashed out at his superiors, telling them that the people who hired him were more powerful and important than they," according to *Hard News*, Seth Mnookin's book about the Blair scandal.

Blair's ambition was clear from his earliest days at the paper. In the end, his desire to curry favor with the "powerful and important" top editors made him lie and steal again and again to garner more prominent assignments.

One of the most difficult types of malicious journalists to detect is one who works hard to fly under the radar by inventing sources for seemingly commonplace articles. Witness the bland, workmanlike inventions of Christopher Newton, a reporter in the Washington bureau of AP. At least forty of his stories over a period of close to three years contained sources that didn't exist. His secret was an ability to conjure up real-sounding names and titles and attach to them quotes of no great interest or appeal. They were, in essence, as boring as the real sources he chose not to contact. (He was exposed in 2002.)

"Anyone who has used a database knows it is not an exact science," he quoted "John Martin" of *Consumer Reports* saying in one article. Jack Shafer of Slate.com cataloged the banality of Newton's genius, as expressed by executives at AP:

AP's SPOKESWOMAN Kelly Smith Tunney told the *New York Times* . . . the quotations went unnoticed because they were "innocuous" and "tangential." The sound bites "didn't raise any flags," AP Senior Vice President Jonathan Wolman told the *Washington Post*, because none of them were "very snappy or snazzy." In other words, nobody thought to dispute the AP quotations because there was no "there there" to dispute.

Usually, at some point, fabricators or plagiarists will seek to use their skills for professional gain. They will deliver a perfect quote or source that no one can locate, or concoct an entire story that will bring them to the attention of their peers. The delivery of a critical source at a moment's notice, or the exact telling detail sought by an editor, is the surefire way to please, but it is also the kind of behavior that can arouse suspicion. When malicious journalists manage to exercise restraint the way Newton did, it can become very difficult to root them out. This is a challenge that the press must take up in order to secure the reputation and reliability of the profession.

The Lesson Not Learned

FOR ALL THEIR INHERENT NEGATIVITY, instances of plagiarism and the like do inspire a healthy ritual of introspection and self-examination for journalists and the press. If not for these lost souls of the profession, the press would bump along at the same pace, ignoring the importance of quality controls, training, and oversight. These incidents bring an all-too-rare bit of attention to issues of quality control. The unfortunate reality is that, after a fresh scandal, journalists and editors soon begin to relapse into their old habits, as if the danger were behind them.

By not engaging in a serious, ongoing effort to learn from and subsequently prevent future ethical breaches, the press only guarantees they will continue to happen. In 1998, the *American Journalism Review* reported on a sense of urgency born of several incidents of malicious reporting:

THE VERY PUBLIC REPRIMAND of Pulitzer Prize–winning CNN correspondent Peter Arnett and the dismissals of two CNN producers for airing allegations that weren't rigorously verified, exposure of fabrications by *The New Republic*'s Stephen Glass and the *Boston Globe*'s Patricia Smith had sent a collective shudder through the magazine and newspaper industry. . . . The *Cincinnati Enquirer* had run a front-page apology for three days for a series on Chiquita Brands International written by staffer Mike Gallagher. In a June 28 story, the paper said Gallagher had deceived top editors and Publisher Harry M. Whipple about his reporting methods.

The ritual was repeated in the names of Jayson Blair and Jack Kelley roughly five years later. "In the wake of the Blair affair, news organizations throughout the country properly looked to how they do things," wrote Richard C. Wald in *Columbia Journalism Review* in 2003. "Truth is important to each one. Some commentators took glee in the *Times*'s pain. Yet it might happen to them. And, in essence, journalism searched inward."

Again and again, the cycle repeats.

Malicious journalists—plagiarists, fabricators, dishonest reporters, and unethical editors—exist because the profession enables them to. The "honor system" cited by the student fabricator remains in existence at most newspapers, magazines, and television and radio newsrooms. The fact checking used at some large magazines and occasionally employed by major television newscasts is also on the decline. Every journalist will agree that people like Jayson Blair and Stephen Glass have an effect on the profession and the public's perception of it, and yet a large-scale call to action and new commitment to weeding out the sinners in the profession has not been made. Or when it is, it is largely ignored.

When Peter Bhatia gave his final speech as the president of the American Society of Newspaper Editors in April 2004, he said, "One way to define the past ASNE year is to say it began with Jayson Blair and ended with Jack Kelley. . . . Make no mistake, these and other ethical breaches did horrible damage to our industry."

His speech was an admirable call to action. Bhatia, a top editor at the *Oregonian*, questioned many of the sacred cows of newspaper reporting and editing—such as the perceived inability to introduce a measure of fact checking into the 24/7 news cycle—and urged his colleagues to ponder some critical questions in light of the Blair and Kelley scandals:

> ISN'T IT TIME to say enough is enough? Isn't it time to attack this problem in our newsrooms head-on and put an end to the madness? Isn't it time to really dig deep and examine our operations in a way that goes far beyond memos and meetings? Are we really able to say we are doing everything possible to make sure our newspaper and staffs are operating at the highest ethical level?

He answered his own last question: "We are not."

I spoke with Bhatia three years after he made his speech, and asked him about the reaction to his strong words back in 2004.

"The feedback was very positive," he said, "but the test is over time."

Overall, he told me that he didn't think "anything came of" his specific suggestions to examine how antiplagiarism software could be used in the newsroom and how newspapers could develop a fact-checking process that worked within their difficult deadline constraints. One reason is that today many newspaper newsrooms have fewer reporters. The drive to produce more content for online editions and grow Web site traffic has, he says, also meant that fewer reporters are often doing more work.

"It's a hard thing to get on the front burner right now because [newspapers] are just thinking about how to prosper for the long term in the Internet era," he told me.

As with errors, there will always be those malicious journalists who fall through the cracks. But in an age of plagiarism-detection software, the ability to check sources instantly via e-mail or the phone or instant messaging, and the opportunity to use technology to track the errors of individual reporters and spot patterns, the possibility to prevent and catch this despicable species of journalist is greater than ever before. The root of the problem of malicious journalists is not being addressed, and so they continue to appear as always, and their colleagues, in hindsight, see that the signs were evident but, unfortunately, ignored.

Also often inadequate is how the press handles ethical breaches with its readers and the public. The *Times* dedicated an unprecedented amount of words to chronicling and deconstructing the Blair affair, but the response of many publications to serious journalistic lapses reflected in their pages is often nothing more than a couple of hundred words in a letter from the editor. We're sorry this happened, they say. We hope it won't happen again.

Missing in the aftermath of malicious reporting is a frank admission of how the incident occurred, and a concrete plan of action to prevent it from happening again. And so the press continues to suffer the damaging revelations of plagiarism and fabrication, and repeats ad nauseam the cycle of self-flagellation, followed by a return to the old way of doing things. All the better for the malicious journalists of today and tomorrow. Their future is secure.

CHAPTER 7

OBITICIDE:
DEATH BY MEDIA

ONE OF THE MOST POWERFUL and surprisingly common forms of media error is the report that a living person is dead. It's so frequent that I coined my own term to describe it. I call it "obiticide." Death by media error.

Obiticide is a damaging and embarrassing error for both the victim and the perpetrator. It calls into question the very processes by which news is gathered and disseminated. Surely standard procedures would call for confirmation from the family or a funeral home before noting someone's passing. What about employing a quick search of the archives before pronouncing someone long gone? Unfortunately, the press has no such thing as an enforced, universal standard for fact checking. This, along with the desire to be the first media outlet to report a prominent passing, greatly contributes to obiticide. If one outlet reports someone's demise, it's as good as gold for the rest; if editors are certain in their own minds that a particular person has passed on, they have few reservations about inserting the word "late" before the name in a story.

Many newspapers require that anyone who submits a paid obituary supply the name of the funeral home or a family contact that can verify the death. This reveals a sober truth: When it comes to obituaries, the factual standards applied by the *business* side of a newspaper are sometimes higher than they are on the *editorial* side of the firewall. This contradicts what most journalists and readers or viewers believe. And while some victims of obiticide get a laugh out of it, they also shake their heads, wondering how such a glaring mistake could have snaked its way through the editing process without being caught. Others spend the rest of their lives on earth battling the perception that they are gone, irrelevant.

Until a case of obiticide is solved, the victim resides in a nether-world where he or she lives and breathes the same as before, but, in the public eye, has ceased to exist. Some cases are never fully resolved, leaving the victim to suffer through frequent encounters that begin with "I thought you were dead!" For the famous in particular, media death, however fleeting, is a fate far worse than true expiration.

Highly visible people—politicians, actors, musicians, criminals—are today the most frequent victims of obiticide. But even before the emergence of newspapers, death reports were a major news item: "The most news-worthy event in many lives is, alas, their end," wrote Mitchell Stephens in *A History of News*. "Before the advent of the formal newspaper obituary, epi-taphs in prose or verse were the most common form of printed personal news." As an early example of obiticide, he notes that "in October 1525 criers in Paris announced that King Francis I of France had died in captivity, though he too was alive and would live for another twenty-one years."

Today's media puts a premium on the timely distribution of a well-prepared obituary. To make this possible, news organizations archive ("can") obituary files for use when someone notable passes on; they may even keep them current. A January 2006 report by *Editor & Publisher* said that the Associated Press alone has more than 1,000 canned obits on hand, with other major wires and newspapers maintaining similarly stocked databases. The *New York Times*, which had only 150 on hand in 2001, claimed more than 1,200 by early 2006. *Editor & Publisher* noted that "major papers continue to stockpile advance obits more than ever, while also devoting more writers to the dedications. Growing interest by readers in biographical pieces, along with an increased effort to present them more as stories than public notices, also adds to the renewed effort to stay one step ahead of death."

The AP makes sure to regularly update the content of its literary morgue, adding each new accomplishment or scandal as the person's life progresses. In the meantime, the predeceased carry on with their lives, rarely giving a second thought to the idea that somewhere in a newsroom a lone reporter is dutifully planning for their demise. This early preparation has many times resulted in a case of obiticide, leaving the press scrambling to explain its error, and resurrect the deceased. Sometimes, however, an instance of obiticide can have surprising, even positive consequences. This is the exception. The usual result is that someone living has been shunted into an early, erroneous grave.

In 1888, a French newspaper ran an obituary for Alfred Nobel, the Swedish physicist who invented dynamite in 1866. The headline declared, "The Merchant of Death Is Dead!" The obit described how Nobel had become a rich man by inventing something that enabled people to kill one another in mass numbers. Shame on him and good riddance, was the tone.

That same year, Alfred's brother Ludvig had died while staying in Cannes, France. In an example of laissez-faire fact checking, the French newspaper (and the others that followed) confused him with Alfred, who was also in France at the time.

The news spread quickly, even crossing the Atlantic. The *New York Times* of April 16, 1888, noted his recent passing in a more charitable tone. A front-page article in the May 24, 1888, edition of the *Decatur Daily Republican* (which was a reprint of an article in the New York *Sun*) reported, "The world has lost one of its greatest experimental chemists by the death of Alfred Nobel." That obit also made special mention of the success of Alfred's brother Ludvig in the petroleum industry. The April 22 edition of the *Atlanta Constitution* made do with a short, pithy note on page 12 that read, "Alfred Nobel, the inventor of dynamite, died the other day. He was a very quiet man, but his invention has made considerable noise in the world."

When the news reached Alfred in Paris, he was not pleased. Not only did he have to read his own often negative premature obituaries, but he was also in mourning for his brother. Alfred Nobel the famous physicist was alive and well, albeit in a rage. Ludvig, a successful oil entrepreneur, was dead. Erik Bergengren wrote in *Alfred Nobel: The Man and His Work*, "The world press, which for some reason confused the oil magnate Ludvig with the dynamite king Alfred, blossomed out in obituaries."

Nobel was not a man to let the errant obituary pass without doing something about it. Rather than simply pursue a correction or letter to the editor, many biographers report that he decided to create a legacy that would overshadow his controversial invention. Kenne Fant wrote in *Alfred Nobel: A Biography* that Nobel dedicated his fortune "to a cause upon which no future obituary writer would be able to cast aspersions." Nobel created awards for the people who "shall have done the most or the best work for fraternity between nations, for the abolition or reduction of standing armies and for the holding of peace congresses."

This was, of course, the Nobel Prize. But as is often the case, this tale, though frequently retold in books, by the media, and in inspirational talks, is not completely true.

"We have found several obituaries [from 1888] where Alfred's brother Ludvig is mistaken for Alfred," explained Olov Amelin, a senior curator at the Nobel Museum in Sweden, in an e-mail to me. "It would be interesting to find the first mention of the obituary being one reason for Alfred Nobel's decision to form a Prize, but so far I have only found rather late statements that this should be the case. So far we have to conclude that this is only one among many rumors that tend to grow around famous historical persons."

Completing this inauspicious Nobel circle 117 years later was the flawed report of the death of Harold Pinter, on October 13, 2005—the very day he received the Nobel Prize for Literature. Pinter, who was already suffering from lung cancer, had hit his head, and one UK television station managed to turn that into his demise. Certainly, he was one Nobel winner with whom Alfred Nobel would have felt a special kinship.

Nobel is not the only prominent figure whose premature death report precipitated a reaction of historical proportions. In early June of 1897, Samuel Clemens, better known as Mark Twain, was hiding away in London, still mourning the death of his eldest daughter, Susy, and working to make a dent in his considerable debt. (Some ill-conceived business ventures had drained coffers that had once overflowed with proceeds from his successful writing and speaking.) Now he worked diligently, joylessly, to churn out new work for publication. Meanwhile, Clemens's wife, brokenhearted by the death of her daughter, was growing increasingly frail.

Just a couple of months earlier, Clemens had written this line in
his notebook:

OF THE DEMONSTRABLY WISE there are but two; those who commit suicide, and those who keep their reasoning faculties
atrophied with drink.

Then, amid this melancholy, came a knock at the door. Clemens
opened it to find Frank Marshall White, a young correspondent from the
New York Journal. In his hand were two telegrams from his stateside
editor. It seems word had spread that Clemens, then 61 years old, was
gravely ill. Perhaps even dead. The editor had instructed his man via cable-
gram: "If Mark Twain dying in poverty, in London, send 500 words."
Displaying the cold calculation of a true newspaperman, he followed with
a second: "If Mark Twain has died in poverty send 1,000 words."
   Although Twain was under considerable financial and emotional
stress, he was not sick. But his cousin James Ross Clemens *had* been.
A doctor who worked in London, James Ross had recently paid his
famous cousin a visit and fallen ill while he was at his home. London
newspapers, learning that a man by the name of Clemens had fallen ill
at the address belonging to Twain, reported that the famous writer was
ailing. (Like the Nobel error, this shoddy reporting could have been
prevented had someone chosen to dispatch a correspondent to the
home of the great man.) And that was enough for the next day's edition. Earlier in the year, rumors of Clemens's desperate financial
situation had reached American shores. Now came word that he was
dying. Or was already dead.
   Clemens looked at the cablegrams. The paper had made a mistake,
and now he was faced with commenting on his pending, if erroneous,
demise. First he explained the error to the reporter, noting that his
cousin was now fully recovered. Then he let loose with one of his more
famous, and more misquoted, lines: "The report of my illness grew out
of his illness; the report of my death was an exaggeration."
   Twain walked away, his reputation for verbal pyrotechnics intact.
And the reporter had his quote. The mistake was quickly eclipsed by

Clemens's retort. As Ron Powers, Clemens's biographer, noted, "Within a day or so people around the world were repeating the key line . . . to one another, and realizing how long it had been since they'd had a jolt of Mark Twain's humor (if 'humor' it was). The remark . . . restored him to international attention."

After sending the reporter off, Mark Twain likely closed his door and sat down to ponder whether his death was indeed only worth 1,000 words. In the end, the media's error gave the world one of Clemens's most quoted lines. Some errors, though inexcusable, end up paying dividends.

Many prominent people join Clemens and Nobel on the obiticide victims' list. Bob Hope was killed off twice before his actual demise in 2003. Baseball great Joe DiMaggio was felled before his time, as was Rudyard Kipling, who wrote to the magazine that printed his obit: "I've just read that I am dead. Don't forget to delete me from your list of subscribers." James Earl Jones was pronounced dead in 1998 during a Pittsburgh Pirates radio broadcast. He had been confused with James Earl Ray, the man who murdered Dr. Martin Luther King Jr.

Obiticide is a frequent enough crime that some people choose to use it in their favor. They leverage the media's gullibility to fake their

In its December 3, 2005, issue, the Spectator, *a British magazine, corrected a previous report that Dr. Conor Cruise O'Brien was dead. It had also said he had been embarrassed to be Irish. Neither was true.*

CONOR CRUISE O'BRIEN

In our Politics column of 24 September 2005, Andy McSmith wrote: 'The late Conor Cruise O'Brien is reputed to have spent his final years embarrassed that he should have come from an insignificant country like Ireland.'

Dr Conor Cruise O'Brien is alive and well and proud to be Irish. *The Spectator* apologises to Dr Conor Cruise O'Brien for the offence caused to him by the untrue suggestion that he was embarrassed to come from Ireland.

own death. Legendary hoaxer Alan Abel executed one of history's most famous fake deaths in 1980. Abel had previously fooled the media into believing there was a Society for Indecency to Naked Animals. SINA's stated goal was to clothe naked animals around the world. He also fooled the press into covering another one of his inventions, Omar's School for Beggars, purportedly a school to train panhandlers.

In June 1980, with the help of his wife, a complicit funeral director, and ten associates, Abel fooled the *New York Times* into running his obituary. It began, "Alan Abel, a writer, musician and film producer who specialized in satire and lampoons, died of a heart attack yesterday at Sundance, a ski resort near Orem, Utah, while investigating a location for a new film. He was 50 years old and lived in Manhattan and Westport, Conn." Shortly afterward, Abel held a press conference to announce his resurrection. Soon after, the *Times* published this note:

OBITUARY DISCLOSED AS HOAX

An obituary in *The New York Times* on Wednesday reported incorrectly that Alan Abel was dead. Mr. Abel held a news conference yesterday to announce that the obituary was a result of a hoax he had arranged to gain publicity. He described himself as a professional hoaxer and said that about 12 accomplices had been involved in the deception.

Britney Spears was also temporarily killed off in a 2001 hoax perpetrated by two Dallas radio DJs, Kramer and Twitch. They announced on the air that Spears and boyfriend Justin Timberlake had been hit by a pretzel van in an automobile accident in New York. Spears was dead and Timberlake was in a coma, they said. Soon after, a Web page designed to look like it was from the BBC Web site was put online announcing the news.

"A Los Angeles police spokeswoman said her department spent the night answering calls from reporters and distraught fans of the pop couple," reported the actual BBC, which had lawyers intervene to pull down the hoax news page. The DJs were subsequently fired.

The Britney Spears hoax is a case of conscious media irresponsibility. The two DJs were attempting to solidify their reputation as premiere shock jocks and therefore should not be confused with a true news outlet. Yet their idiotic experiment reveals how easy it is for people in the media to spread an erroneous death report. In fact, they banked on it, assuming word would spread and they would receive credit for that day's big story. More press for them, and damn the consequences to Spears and the general public.

Abel, who managed to fool the *New York Times* into running his fake obituary, had needed an elaborate plan to get past the processes in place at the *Times*. This is because, unlike the DJs, he wasn't a member of the media. His word could not instantly be taken as fact or passed on as a reported rumor attributed to another news organization. His reputation as a media prankster also likely gave the *Times* pause, although clearly not enough. Essential to the success of his hoax was the complicity of a funeral home and his wife—two important sources that the *Times* did turn to in order to verify his demise. The paper had looked into the story, but nothing short of sending a reporter to inspect the body could have prevented the success of Abel's hoax. Call it the mark of a true professional hoaxer.

No media outlet should have to go to that length for verification, but this example does reveal the inherent flaws in even the best obituary confirmation processes. Those with enough will and resources can convince the media of anything, for a short while at least.

The parade of obiticide victims is endless. One of the more recent is Senator Jesse Helms. In March 2005, this correction appeared in the *Los Angeles Times:*

> A WEDNESDAY COMMENTARY on the nomination of John R. Bolton to be U.S. ambassador to the United Nations erroneously used the term 'the late Sen. Jesse Helms.' It should have said former Sen. Jesse Helms.

Retirement, it seems, is indeed death. So too is longevity, as evidenced by this November 30, 2005, correction from the *Pittsburgh Post-Gazette:*

> THE MORNING FILE had Arthur Schlesinger Jr. dead in an item published Nov. 29, 2005. This probably came as quite a shock to Mr. Schlesinger when he read The Morning File. The famous historian and one-time aide to President Kennedy is not deceased but 88. We are embarrassed but happy for Mr. Schlesinger.

Although not the most prominent victim of obiticide, actor Abe Vigoda, the primate-featured actor from *Barney Miller* and the first two *Godfather* films, deserves to be its most celebrated. In 1982, *People* magazine published a story referencing the "late" Abe Vigoda. But Vigoda was, and remains as of this writing, alive. (People still stop him on the street to tell him he's a dead ringer for the guy who played Fish on *Barney Miller.*)

Jeff Jarvis worked at *People* magazine from 1981 until he started *Entertainment Weekly* in 1990. On the occasion of the magazine's thirtieth anniversary he wrote about his fondest *People* memories on his media blog, BuzzMachine. Vigoda's death made the cut.

"After the reporter reported and the writer wrote, the editors edited and messed up the stories," he wrote. "Famously, one top editor changed a story to add the words 'the late' before Abe Vigoda's name. A researcher dutifully took those words out. The editor stubbornly put them back and that's what we published. Abe wasn't dead. But *People* said he was. So he took out a full-page ad in *Variety* with a picture of himself in a coffin, sitting up, reading the latest *People.*" (Most reports of the incident say the picture of Vigoda in the coffin ran in *People.* Evidence yet again of how one mistake breeds many.)

Vigoda battled the media grim reaper in stunning style. But some still think he's dead. The story of his mistaken demise has grown into an Internet legend and joke, but even that's not enough to convince everyone that he remains alive and well. In his case, the error has never been fully erased.

If you're one of those who think Vigoda has passed on, the best way to verify his status is to visit AbeVigoda.com. If all is right with Abe, his picture and the words "Abe Vigoda is alive" greet you. You can also refresh the page for an up-to-the-second status report, and there's a link to the song "Abe Vigoda's Dead (Premortem Mix)." Another Web site, Dead People Server, lists the life status of a wide range of celebrities. Its entry for Vigoda reads, "Abe Vigoda (actor)—Not dead yet. Born February 24, 1921. Fish on *Barney Miller*." When Abe's time does come, it won't be a surprise if the media exercises more caution than usual in noting his death. No need to rush; it's old news anyway.

Planned Obiticide

T HANKS TO THE THOUSANDS of canned obituaries lurking within media organizations, obiticide is usually a premeditated crime. The concept of canned obituaries often strikes nonmedia folks as a morbid, and perhaps self-fulfilling one. For large media organizations such as newswires, major dailies, or broadcasters, it is a necessity. There is an art to a well-written obituary, and offering a writer the time to do it right is something that benefits readers in the end. "The rule of thumb is the impact they've had, age, health situation, and if you hear rumors about somebody's health," said Jon Thurber, the *Los Angeles Times* editor in charge of that paper's obituaries. "You would not want to write Hugh Hefner's obituary on deadline."

These stockpiles of obits sit dormant in their databases, awaiting entry to the world at a moment's command. It's a perverse twist on the cycle of life. Babies are born and announced in the newspaper. Their life continues, sometimes also noted by the press, and gradually they begin the slide toward death. Somewhere, if they're lucky, an editor or producer assigns someone to write their obituary, and there it sits, eagerly awaiting the chance to announce its subject's demise. The media obituary is the final bow, a chronicle of achievement (or infamy) given to those deemed worthy enough to merit one. As evidenced by Alfred Nobel, the subject of an obituary will often take a keen interest in how his or her life will be remembered.

Charles Strum, the obituaries editor of the *New York Times* from 2001 until January 2006, told *Editor & Publisher* that, years ago, a writer was sent to interview screen legend Bette Davis for her obituary. As is often the case, she was not told of the purpose of the interview. "Not long after Davis brought out tea and snacks and began the interview," noted the magazine, "the Hollywood legend asked suddenly, 'Are you interviewing me for my obituary?'" The *Times* reporter admitted he was, "and she replied, 'Why the hell didn't you tell me?' Davis then went into the kitchen, made a pitcher of martinis, and they talked all night."

For Davis, the thought of a canned obituary was an honor. But the canned obituary is also a loaded missile, prone to the trigger itch of an editor who can send it speeding into the world. Unlike many of today's missiles, however, an obituary doesn't come with a recall button. The damage is instant, spreads rapidly, and is rarely undone by a correction.

CNN is one of many media outlets to see its preplanned obit work result in a fiasco. In spring 2003, a designer at CNN.com was tasked with preparing special obituary pages for several prominent people. Most were close to the end of their lives. One, Dick Cheney, was still relatively young, although his history of heart problems and current prominent political position made him a good candidate for a canned obituary.

A special Web page was created featuring a nostalgic picture of the predemised. At the top was a poignant quote from the person, and under that was the beginning of the text for the special obit. At the bottom of each page—they all used the same template—were links to more stories under the headings "Biography," "Features," and "Resources." The pages were housed in a part of the CNN.com site that was supposed to be password protected and therefore inaccessible to surfers and the Web-crawling tentacles of search engines such as Google. One day, however, the pages were left unprotected. Someone stumbled upon them and e-mailed the links to Fark.com, a popular news aggregation Web site, which publicized the pages to the world.

Soon thousands of Web surfers were looking at the strangely morbid, nearly identical mock-ups of Fidel Castro, Dick Cheney, Gerald Ford, Bob Hope, Pope John Paul II, Nelson Mandela, and Ronald

Reagan. The links spread around the Web, and surfers arrived in droves to gawk. CNN moved quickly to close off the pages, but their premortality preparations had been exposed, resulting in the world's worst case of mass obiticide.

On CNN's site, Bob Hope was called "the definition of entertainment for millions of fans throughout the 20th century." Cheney was dubbed the "loyal point man for two Bush presidencies." The pope, whose move to heaven was also prematurely declared in the days before his true demise in 2005, was a "great and controversial man." Castro's page featured his statement that "history will absolve me."

This was actually Hope's second experience with obiticide. The first time came on June 5, 1998, when a similar mistake caused the Associated Press to announce his death on its Web site. Staffers in the office of congressional majority leader Dick Armey informed their boss of Hope's passing, and he then asked Arizona representative Bob Stump to announce it on the floor of the House of Representatives. Stump did, saying, "It is with great sadness I announce that Bob Hope has died."

Stump's speech led news organizations to begin cranking out their own Hope tributes. Meanwhile, Hope was at home in Pasadena, California, eating his breakfast and wondering why the phone was ringing off the hook. Helicopters soon began circling overhead. His daughter Linda answered the phones and called the media to set things straight. But the missile had been launched and fallout was immediate. It was an embarrassment for the media—and the House of Representatives—and a massive headache for the Hope family.

News organizations prepare canned obituaries to do justice to their reports on the deceased; having a good database is also an advantage in today's competitive, scoop-oriented mainstream media. No media outlet wants to be the last one to get a decent obit up when someone prominent passes on, and if they can have it up first, well, that's something to crow about. It follows that the drive to break the news of a media magnet's death increases the likelihood of a premature report.

When things go wrong, however, media outlets are uncharacteristically happy to share the credit; take our scoop, please. Being the first to report a prominent death comes with bragging rights; making an erroneous call confers shame on an entire organization. Things become heated when an outlet's neck is on the line in an obiticide investigation. It's every journalist for himself, and the facts soon fall by the wayside.

One September night in 2005 I was having drinks with a group of fellow journalists in a Montreal bar. One person, a section editor at the Montreal *Gazette*, explained how, earlier that day, she had assigned one of her best political writers to chase down what turned out to be a dog of a story. That afternoon, CTV NewsNet, a twenty-four-hour cable news station in Canada, had broken into its regular coverage to report that Lucien Bouchard, the founder of the separatist Bloc Quebecois political party and former premier of the province of Quebec, had died at the age of sixty-six. This was all the more tragic because Bouchard, who had lost part of one of his legs to a flesh-eating disease, had made a full recovery and almost led the separatist forces to victory in the 1995 Quebec referendum.

CTV political expert Mike Duffy was put on screen and declared that Bouchard had had a "profound impact on Canadian history." Then anchor Kate Wheeler cut in with what the Canadian Press wire service reported was a "sheepish" grin, to say they were "happy to report Lucien Bouchard is alive and well." Killed off and resurrected in a matter of seconds. Behold the immediacy of the twenty-four-hour news cycle.

"I don't know why Radio-Canada has been reporting that but, indeed, now we're glad to report he's still alive," Wheeler continued. CTV credited (blamed) Radio-Canada, a publicly funded French broadcaster, with uncovering the story. Amid the confusion, the *Gazette* editor had her man call the Montreal law firm where Bouchard worked. He received nearly instant confirmation that Bouchard was still breathing.

Now the story moved from the death of a major political figure to an investigation of who was responsible for the specious scoop. CTV said it was Radio-Canada. In a press release, Radio-Canada struck back at CTV: "CTV NewsNet directly quoted Radio-Canada as having announced the death of former Quebec premier Lucien Bouchard this afternoon. In reality, however, this news was not reported at any time by either Radio-Canada or RDI, its 24-hour information network. Given the significance of this false report, Radio-Canada has asked CTV for a public retraction."

Catherine Cano, the news director of RDI, vented her anger to the Canadian Press news agency. "I'm so angry, I could sue," she said. "It's our credibility at play here."

There was, of course, a healthy dose of irony added to this mess. Journalists feel terrible when they make a mistake, but the truth is that most have no idea what it feels like to have one made about them. This was a rare role reversal for RDI, and they were livid.

Although CTV never confirmed what had happened, this is what caused the mistake: Prior to the erroneous announcement by CTV, RDI had aired a special tenth-anniversary package about the 1995 Quebec referendum. At one point, the broadcast addressed the illness that nearly took Bouchard's leg and almost cost him his life in the months before the vote. Apparently, someone at CTV saw the nostalgic footage of Bouchard, misunderstood the narration, and hit the proverbial Somebody Important Died button in the newsroom. And for a few seconds at least, Bouchard was indeed dead. CTV quickly corrected its mistake, but it fell far short of accepting responsibility for it or explaining to viewers how it happened. Its lack of interest in disseminating the truth about the incident added another level of incompetence to its initial error.

Obiticide and the Average Citizen

PROMINENT PEOPLE, be they politicians, actors, or musicians, are given the privilege (or burden) of a canned obituary treatment. But they are by no means the only people to perish by obiticide. Regular folks are murdered by the media on a regular basis. Worse, most don't have the means to purchase a corrective ad in *Variety*, like Abe Vigoda. In the aftermath of the error, they also know no one will build a Web site devoted to their longevity. These are silent deaths, fixed only by a small correction and/or an apology that few people read.

On November 21, 2005, former University of Akron president Dominic Guzzetta joined the long list of people shunted into an early grave by a newspaper. The *Akron Beacon Journal* reported he had been "posthumously" honored at a recent fund-raiser. In its resulting apology, printed the next day, the paper reported that he had received twenty-five phone calls by noon of the day it appeared. "I guess they wanted to be among the first to extend their condolences," Guzzetta told a *Journal* reporter. "I look forward to reading about my resurrection."

Anyone who is a "former" anything is much more susceptible to obiticide. Guzzetta left his post at the university and was "posthumously" honored. The same is apparently true for judges. An October 12, 2005, correction from the Cleveland *Plain Dealer* read:

> BECAUSE OF A REPORTING ERROR, Judge Thomas J. Parrino was mistakenly identified as "late" in Tom Feran's column on the front page of the Arts & Life section Tuesday. The judge is retired and living in Westlake.

Confusion abounds, and not just among journalists. When Ted Carlson, an announcer known as the "Voice of the Beavers" for his work calling Oregon State University basketball and football games, passed away in October 2005, he was the subject of many obituaries. (Just to be completely clear, Carlson was indeed dead.) But one reader of the *Corvallis Gazette-Times* mistook that Ted Carlson for her retired OSU journalism professor, also named Ted Carlson. She then sent a letter to the editor lamenting her former professor's passing. The paper, missing the error, ran it. The living Ted Carlson then spent the day fielding phone calls from shocked friends and relatives. He sent an e-mail to the newspaper to explain the mistake. Fittingly, he led with a familiar quote:

> WASN'T IT MARK TWAIN WHO WROTE that the news of his death was greatly exaggerated? Well, the *Gazette-Times* printed a letter to the editor (Nov. 2) from Susan Laird Endsley that noted the passing of her former journalism professor (me) and the Voice of the Beavers. Unfortunately, the Voice of the Beavers Ted Carlson died recently. Fortunately, I'm still hanging around. . . . I can't count the times when I was introduced to someone who would say: "Oh, Ted Carlson, Voice of the

Beavers." The last time it happened was in October at the WSU football game. Beaver rooters wanted a photo of themselves with the Voice of the Beavers. They got me instead.

Confusing people with the same name is common. But only the media can turn it into a case of obiticide.

The media acts as the public record, and obiticide is an example of how it can also undermine it. Someone who happens upon an erroneous claim of death may never locate the corrected information. Obiticide is an all-too-common media error, an all-too-powerful demonstration of the power of errors and their often profound effect on people's lives. We are more aware of this type of error because it so often involves celebrities or other prominent people whose coverage gets attention no matter what the story is. Perhaps a group of concerned actors, politicians, religious leaders, writers, and others who have seen their colleagues felled by obiticide could come together for an obiticide benefit concert, Still-Alive Aid. Many news outlets would feel it their duty to offer airtime to this worthy cause as a form of penance. But, of course, I could be dead wrong.

The Corrections

CONTRARY TO A STORY in today's What's On, Singer Lena Horne is not dead. The *Star* regrets the error.   —*Toronto Star*

+

In our report on Tuesday October 17 under the headline: Killer Coke, concerning the deaths of two men at the Westhaven estate, Dublin, following a drug overdose on Sunday, October 15, we mistakenly stated that the name of one of the deceased was one Philip Kenny. In fact the dead man was Roy Kelly, aged 30, from Huntstown Rise, Dublin. We are happy to correct the matter.   —*Mirror* (UK)

JAN. 18—A STORY WEDNESDAY on the late Dorothy Dandelske of

West Haven misidentified her husband, Donald, as being deceased. He is her widower.

—*New Haven Register* (Connecticut)

✦

A marriage license that ran in Tuesday's *Intelligencer Journal* mistakenly listed Kimberly Stoughton, mother of Jeremy J. Cunningham, as deceased.

—*Intelligencer Journal* (Pennsylvania)

✦

The *Times Herald* deeply apologizes to Richard Paul Smith, his family and friends.

A news story in Monday's edition incorrectly identified Richard Paul Smith, formerly of Conshohocken, as a victim of a fatal accident when in fact it was Richard A. Smith, currently of Conshohocken, who was struck and killed in State College, Pa., this past weekend. We also would like to extend our condolences to the family of Richard A. Smith.

—*Times Herald* (Pennsylvania)

✦

The *Gazette* would like to apologise to Martine Hopkins for incorrectly reporting last week that her father had died of cancer.

This was due to a misunderstanding for which the *Gazette* is to blame. In fact, her father is still alive.

The *Gazette* would like to apologise for any distress caused to Miss Hopkins, her father and their family.

—*Brentwood Gazette* (UK)

✦

Because of incorrect information provided to *The Sun*, an article about Charles Village in Sunday's Maryland section reported that Precious the Skateboarding Dog had recently gone "to the great skateboard in the sky." Precious is still alive.

—*Baltimore Sun*

✦

In our December cover story on the "Top Advisors Under 40" (page 34), we erroneously reported that a former partner of UBS advisor Brian K. Albach, had died. In fact, Albach's partner is still alive and retired from UBS in 2002.

—*On Wall Street*

✦

The television actor John Aniston is still alive. Incorrect information appeared in Shelley Fralic's column on this page Saturday.

—*Ottawa Citizen* (Canada)

✦

A letter to The Final Word in the Q section Sunday referred incorrectly to "the late Art Buchwald." Buchwald, a humorist, is alive.   —*News & Observer* (North Carolina)

✦

A Feb. 12 Metro article incorrectly reported that the parents of a teenager killed Saturday while fleeing D.C. police are deceased. Both parents of Kevin Thomas, 17, are alive.

—*Washington Post*

✦

A brief on Page 4B of the City & State section Sunday incorrectly stated that a shooting victim, Travis Lamont Bolden, in Durham died of his injuries. He is not dead.

—*News & Observer* (North Carolina)

Because of a reporting error, a story on Page A-1 of Sunday's *Times* incorrectly reported attorney Jack Furman was dead. He is alive.   —*Cape Cod Times*

✦

A headline in a letter to the editor on Friday's Readers' Page mistakenly indicated the subject of the letter, a World War II veteran, had died. He is alive. The *Post-Standard* regrets the error.   —*Post-Standard* (New York)

✦

An article in Sunday Calendar about a DVD anthology titled "Animated Soviet Propaganda" stated that famed Russian animator Boris Yefimov, who was interviewed by the anthology's producers, had died. Yefimov, who turned 106 in September, is alive.   —*Los Angeles Times*

✦

Heather Crowe, the former Ottawa waitress who became an activist against second-hand smoke after being diagnosed with lung cancer, is alive. Incorrect information appeared in yesterday's *National Post*.   —*National Post* (Canada)

✦

Elie Wiesel is alive and well and coming to Norfolk for a free lecture at 4 p.m. March 28 at Old Dominion University's Ted Constant Convocation Center. A review of the book "The God Factor" in Sunday's Daily Break section said incorrectly that Wiesel is deceased.   —*Virginian-Pilot*

✦

Wednesday's story about Canada's Walk of Fame inductees incorrectly referred to "the late Morley Safer." Safer is alive and continues to file stories as a *60 Minutes* correspondent. The *Star* regrets the error.   —*Toronto Star*

CHAPTER 8

MISTAKES
AND THE MISTAKEN

T HERE ARE SEVERAL WAYS a person can contract HIV, but one of the least known is via a newspaper. The *Arizona Daily Star* managed to infect one unlucky man, resulting in this correction on May 17, 2005:

> ERNIE PEREZ, WHO WAS A SPEAKER at the 22nd Annual International AIDS Candlelight Memorial Sunday, is not infected with HIV, the virus that causes AIDS. An article on B1 Monday mischaracterized remarks made by Perez during the ceremony, giving the opposite impression.

Every day the media performs other astounding feats through errors of misidentification. It regularly turns men into women, and vice versa. The accused become instantly convicted, businessmen morph into mobsters, families become terrorists, and parents are labeled recovering drug addicts.

Misidentification—be it by gender, criminal status, or relation— is one of the most common media errors. It is also one of the most damaging to the public and its perception of the press. When someone's gender is confused, or when someone accused of a crime is labeled guilty, the media treat it as a routine matter to be fixed with a correction and promptly forgotten. Not so for the people affected. For them it's a personal insult that lingers, an example of why the media can't be trusted.

Few average people will ever get their names in a newspaper or appear on television. When they do and their name is spelled incorrectly, or their son is described as their daughter, it has a lasting negative effect on their opinion of the media. They may never be interviewed again, but they will never forget the mistake. They will be asked about it by everyone they know who read the erroneous report or saw the program, and by many others who just heard about it. Having learned the hard way how error-prone the media is, and how ineffectual it is at correcting mistakes, they may never again trust what's in the paper or on broadcast news.

Errors of misidentification are all the more devastating for their victims because they are among the easiest to prevent. The accurate information is often literally in front of the reporter, or just a phone call or Internet search away. Deadlines loom, but the opportunity to prevent this type of error makes its prevalence all the more corrosive to public confidence in the media. The personal nature of a misidentification—it almost always involves a person—makes it all the more inexcusable.

Some errors, though ephemeral, can radically change a person's social stature, as was the case with Mary-Ann Thompson-Frenk, who was misidentified by the *Dallas Morning News* in June 2005. Columnist Norma Adams-Wade wrote a glowing profile of Thompson-Frenk's work to underwrite and help organize a conference called Religious Tolerance in a World of Spiritual Diversity. Adams-Wade referred to Thompson-Frenk as "a 28-year-old Dallas philanthropist, artist, socialist and spiritual devotee." Unfortunately, she is a "socialite," not a "socialist." The misidentification, though good for a laugh, would certainly have caused some confusion about her event.

By many newspapers' own admission, "misidentification" is one of the most common errors in the business. Christine Chinlund, the *Boston Globe*'s ombudsman until 2005, tallied her paper's corrections each year to calculate the number of errors the paper made in each category. Misidentification would often top the list. Her totals for 2004 found 1,031 errors in at least 58,922 stories written that year. "The analysis of types of errors shows 'misidentifications' led with 293, followed by 'misstatements' at 166 and 'misrepresentations' at 111," she noted in her January 2005 column. Chinlund wrote that some of the paper's more "serious" errors included "a main character misidentified; a criminal charge presumed but not filed."

The *New York Times*' collection of its funniest and most shocking corrections, *Kill Duck Before Serving*, dedicated an entire chapter to "Gender Benders," in which men became women and vice versa. Two other chapters, "Who's Who" and "Hello, My Name Is . . . ," focused on misidentifications of other kinds. If the "Paper of Record" can't get such straightforward facts right, some might logically question how well it does with other, more elusive facts. Mistakes such as these, though simple at first glance, steadily eat away at readers' confidence.

The best insurance against giving readers the wrong impression is, of course, not making the mistake in the first place. As Paul Moore, the public editor of the *Baltimore Sun*, noted in a December 2005 column, "While some of the errors . . . might elicit a chuckle, it is obvious that too many mistakes can seriously undermine a newspaper's credibility. On some days I worry that sloppy editing may be bringing *The Sun* to that point. With that danger in mind, journalists need to strive for perfection."

Misidentifications are indeed among the most horrifying, injurious errors of recent memory.

The Mobster and the Clown

IN APRIL 2005, the *Chicago Tribune* managed to commit perhaps the worst back-to-back misidentifications in media history when it labeled two average citizens prominent members of the mafia.

On April 27 the paper ran a graphic that showed the power structure of the Chicago Outfit mob. Listed was Frank Calabrese Sr., then sixty-eight, a "made" leader in the mob's Twenty-sixth Street crew. He was already in federal custody and had just been indicted for new crimes. The photo above his name depicted a man named Frank Calabrese, but it wasn't Frank Calabrese Sr., the mobster. It was Frank Calabrese, the founder of a successful Chicago printing company, and a horse owner. The paper mistakenly used a 1988 photo of him accepting an "Excellence in Manufacturing" award from Price Waterhouse.

To fix the mistake, the paper ran a front-page corrective article the next day. "At first, Frank Calabrese thought Tuesday's front-page *Tribune* story was simply another article about the mobster who shares his name," it began. It later noted, "Frank Calabrese the businessman did nothing wrong, but on Tuesday, was paying the price because he has the same name and the newspaper made a mistake." Calabrese told the paper, "It's aggravating. People assume things."

The paper interviewed Calabrese's lawyer, and Ken Menconi, the current president of the printing company that Calabrese founded. Menconi explained how, because of the story, he had to spend an inordinate amount of time on the phone fielding calls from customers. Some were amazed by the mistake; others feared they were in business with a less-than-ethical company, which raised Menconi's ire. "It's just that Frank built a great company and worked really hard on his reputation as an honest businessman," Menconi said. "We're just trying to build on his legacy here, and we don't want it ruined by this."

The *Tribune*'s misidentification had immediate consequences for Calabrese and his business. It impugned the credibility of a successful, ethical businessman and caused the company president to waste his workday doing damage control. The paper recognized the significance of its mistake by opting to run a corrective article rather than simply publish a correction that few readers would read. But the *Tribune* also made things worse by adopting a humorous tone in its subsequent article. It carried the playful headline "No Way, It's Not That Frank Calabrese."

The story was also remarkable for what it didn't include: an apology. There were no quotes from *Tribune* editors expressing regret. Calabrese, his lawyer, and a company representative were given the opportunity to talk about the error's fallout, but the paper failed to express any regret for it. It was a decision the *Tribune* would soon regret.

In addition to the corrective article, a short correction also ran in that day's paper, April 27, 2005:

A GRAPHIC EXPLAINING THE ALLEGED infrastructure of the Chicago Outfit mob on Page 18 of Tuesday's main news section incorrectly used a picture of businessman Frank Calabrese instead of mobster Frank Calabrese Sr. A story explaining the mistake appears on Page 1 of today's Metro section.

Again, no apology. The error itself was understandable: two men of roughly the same age from the same city sharing the same name were mistaken for each other. But it was, of course, preventable, and as is the case with many errors, it was the context of it, and subsequent actions (or lack thereof), that turned it into something truly alarming and legally actionable.

For the *Tribune*'s story the stakes were high. Identifying citizens as mobsters and placing them within a mafia hierarchy is a definitive act of condemnation. That makes it all the more imperative for the paper to check and recheck its information and images before it goes to press. The *Tribune* failed to do its due diligence. But it was the paper's playful, unapologetic tone in correcting the error that was the last straw for Frank Calabrese.

He subsequently sued the newspaper for one count of defamation and one count of invasion of privacy, seeking a minimum of $1 million for each count. The *Tribune* reported the filing and quoted its lawyer, Paulette Dodson saying, "It's unfortunate that he chose to take this step, even though we tried to make it right. We think we've corrected it in the paper, and we hope that that's sufficient."

It wasn't. The magnitude of the mistake and its consequences called for a public declaration of regret rather than a playful article devoid of an apology. Yet the only official comment from the *Tribune* came in the form of an empty statement from the company lawyer.

The same day the lawsuit story ran, April 28, the *Tribune* published another corrective article. The paper had misidentified *another* man as a Chicago mobster. The same mistake two days in a row led to corrective articles two days in a row. Yet the paper treated these similar errors differently.

The Calabrese photo had run on page 18 of the paper, but this second instance carried an even higher price for the man misidentified as a mobster. His picture ran on page 1, and the mobster with whom he was confused has a rather unfortunate nickname, thus adding insult to injury. The front-page photo was reportedly of Joseph "The Clown" Lombardo, a fugitive mobster who was the subject of an international manhunt. The photo ran under the headline "Have You Seen This Clown"?

Pictured was Stanley Swieton, an elderly Chicago man with no mob ties. He had simply had his picture taken when he was riding his bicycle one summer's day, managing to look quite dapper. Then, through an unfortunate chain of events nearly a year later, he was branded a mobster "clown" on the front page of a major American newspaper.

Roughly twelve months earlier, Val Carpenter, a college student, was working on a class project that had her snapping photos of people on bicycles. One day she spotted an elderly man with a unique sense of fashion riding a bicycle, cigar in hand. She stopped him, asked to take his photo, and pedaled off afterward. Over the ensuing year she occasionally ran into the man along the same path, and they would exchange polite greetings. She never asked him his name.

Then, the following April, she read a report in the *Tribune* about Joseph "The Clown" Lombardo being indicted. The story reported that, after his release from prison in 1992, Lombardo was regularly seen riding his bike while also smoking a small cigar.

Carpenter immediately grabbed her image from the year before. She noted the similarities: elderly man, bicycle, dapper dress, cigar. The neighborhood even made sense. She showed the photo to the paper, which then showed it to Lombardo's lawyer, Rick Halprin, for confirmation. (Frank Calabrese Sr.'s lawyer had not been offered the same courtesy.)

The paper would later report that Halprin had confirmed it was his client. Halprin disputed the report that he had provided a definitive identification, though he admitted saying that it could have been Lombardo: "At first glance, there are certainly striking similarities," Halprin told the *Tribune* in the corrective article about the misidentification. "I mean, how many guys of that age ride bicycles with cigars in their hands up and down Grand Avenue?"

The paper had treated the lawyer's initial statement about the similarity of the man on the bike to his client as confirmation. The *Tribune* thought it had a big scoop: the picture of an elusive mobster, freshly indicted for racketeering conspiracy, riding his bike without a care in the world just a few months earlier. It didn't seek further confirmation. The editors put it on the front page and the paper went to press.

On the day the paper ran Valerie Carpenter's picture, Stanley Swieton headed out to a medical clinic to get his blood pressure medication. He stopped to buy a *Tribune* and discovered that he was now a mobster and a "clown," which made the medication all the more necessary. Swieton, a retired janitor, was stunned. "I couldn't believe it," he said. "I don't want anything to do with the mob."

A feeling of panic and helplessness overcomes a person in Swieton's situation. The initial shock of seeing yourself identified as an international fugitive mobster is quickly followed by the realization that there are hundreds of thousands of copies of the newspaper all over the city. The story and photo are online, in databases. Any number of people are already gazing at him over their morning coffee, at their desk, or on their way to work. The information is out there as fact—it's in the paper, after all. What possible action could a simple citizen take to change people's minds? How much would the newspaper care about fixing its error? Most people are unfamiliar with the correction process at newspapers and magazines. They perceive the media as a large bureaucracy like the government, where it could perhaps take hours of explaining and navigating through a phone system to finally find someone who can help them. In the meantime, if you're Swieton, you're still being seen as a mobster.

The *Tribune*'s editors had failed to grasp the personal and professional trauma that its error the day before had caused Frank Calabrese. There was a distinct lack of empathy, which led to an almost insulting corrective article and a large lawsuit. The *Tribune* did not see the significance of the first error, but the second time around, the *Tribune*'s colleagues in the news media did not miss it. That evening, after a local TV reporter had tracked Swieton down, a throng of reporters arrived at his home, clamoring for interviews. TV cameramen and photographers asked him to pull out his green one-speed Schwinn bike and pedal up and down his driveway to re-create the image of the crime. It was a surreal scene—the man deemed to be a mobster clown on the front page of one of the largest newspapers in the United States performing a grotesque circus act to placate the very media that had made him a laughingstock only hours before. "I just want to clear my name and go back to my life," he told the *Tribune*.

The *Tribune*'s competitor, the *Sun-Times*, gleefully ran its own account of the mistake the next day. Writer Mark Brown contacted Halprin, the accused mobster's lawyer, who noted that Swieton "bears an uncanny similarity to Joey Lombardo, and if I were him, I'd find something else to do for a while," suggesting that Swieton might need to fear for his safety. The news just kept getting worse for the man.

In the end, he declined to sue the paper (though one wire service article about the errors carried a headline saying that both men had filed suit). Swieton's corrective article, unlike the one for Frank Calabrese, included a quote and an apology from *Tribune* editor Ann Marie Lipinski. "We sincerely regret our mistake," she said. "We strive for accuracy, but when we make an error we try to correct it. We are very sorry for this mistake and apologize to Mr. Swieton."

Although the back-to-back mob mis-hits were the same mistake, only one elicited an apology from the paper. The difference may have seemed negligible to the *Tribune*, but the man who didn't get an apology decided to sue. A successful businessman, he also had the means to pursue full legal action, whereas Swieton might have found the cost of legal proceedings prohibitive. Did Swieton get an apology because his picture ran on the front page? On what page does an error of this nature need to be published in order to elicit an apology?

The *Tribune* offered no explanation for its inconsistent actions. There was no internal procedure it could indicate to justify them, let alone explain to readers how it goes about selecting and confirming its pictures for each day's edition. The result was back-to-back errors that caused personal harm and embarrassment to two decent citizens, and revealed a major newspaper's internal incompetence and lack of empathy. Months after the suit was filed, I was told by a *Tribune* lawyer that the issue had been resolved, though she declined to elaborate. (My calls to Calabrese's company were not returned.)

The *Tribune* example is at the far end of the misidentification spectrum, but it is not alone in having had drastic consequences. Just a few months later, a Fox News pundit's misidentification caused a California family to be threatened and harassed by their community. The police even had to station a patrol car outside the family's home to take control of the situation.

The Terrorist

O N AUGUST 7, 2005, RANDY VORICK, his wife, Ronnell, and their three children were driving home from a visit to SeaWorld in San Diego. Three years earlier, the Voricks had purchased a home in La Habra, California, to be near Ronnell's parents. They weren't far from home when Randy's cell phone rang; it was one of their neighbors calling to tell him that someone on Fox News had just said a terrorist lived at their address. The commentator had read the address on the air, hoping to attract the attention of law enforcement.

The Fox personality was John Loftus, a former U.S. prosecutor and army intelligence officer on contract with the channel as a pundit. He reported that the house was occupied by Iyad K. Hilal, a man he accused of having links to the terrorists who had bombed London a few weeks earlier. Hilal, a grocery store owner, has never been charged with any crime. He was the previous owner of the Voricks' house.

Loftus was a regular contributor to Fox News who did a weekly segment, "Inside Scoop with John Loftus," every Sunday. That day he offered up Hilal's name and the Voricks' address, saying, "I thought it might help police in that area now that we have positively identified a terrorist."

For a brief period, a satellite image of the Vorick home, along with directions to it, was placed online by Fox News. For the Voricks, the repercussions were immediate. First came the call from a concerned neighbor. Simultaneously, the La Habra police began receiving calls from citizens alerting them to the presence of a terrorist in their midst. The next day the Vorick parents left for a previously scheduled cruise to Santa Catalina Island and Ensenada. The kids were put in the charge of Randy Vorick's brother and a babysitter. That same day the police stopped by to check on the family.

The *Los Angeles Times*, which broke the story of the mistake and ensuing consequences, reported, "When they returned [from their cruise] on Aug. 12, Randy Vorick said he had received several e-mails and messages on his cell phone from friends who told him that Loftus

had been interviewed on KFI-AM (640) radio and repeated his allegation about a terrorist living in La Habra. The radio station did not
broadcast his address."

In the ensuing weeks, drivers began stopping at the house to take
pictures; some slowed down long enough to yell profanities at the
family. Two Sundays after Loftus made the initial claim on Fox, the
Voricks were barbecuing on their patio when someone drove by and
shouted obscenities at them. A few nights later, someone lacking a dictionary spray painted the word "Terrist" on their house.

"I'm scared to go to work and leave my kids home," Vorick told the
Times on August 25. "I call them every 30 minutes to make sure they're
OK. . . . I keep telling myself this can't be happening to me. This can't
be happening to my family. But it is. I want our lives to be normal
again." The police began making routine patrols and eventually sta-
tioned a patrol car near the Vorick house to protect the family.

The mistake made by Loftus was, of course, heinous. The consequences are almost too much for most of us to comprehend. Imagine
arriving home from a day of family fun to discover that someone on
the number one cable news channel has labeled you and your family
terrorists. Then your home is vandalized and you find yourself in
need of police protection. All because someone in the media has
misidentified you.

As in the *Tribune* incident, the unwillingness on the part of Fox
News and Loftus to offer up a swift and meaningful apology and retraction left the Vorick family all the more incensed. In fact, it was only after
the *Los Angeles Times* contacted the channel and Loftus that they
admitted their error. This was despite the fact that Randy Vorick had e-
mailed Loftus to ask for an apology. "John Loftus has been reprimanded
for his careless error, and we sincerely apologize to the family," Fox
spokeswoman Irena Brigante told the *Times*, showing all the compas-
sion of a houseplant. (Loftus was later fired by Fox.) Loftus told the
Times that "mistakes happen." He also said, "I'm terribly sorry about
that. I had no idea. That was the best information we had at the time."

The *Times* reported that for Vorick "the apologies that came were
too little, too late." Contacted by e-mail for an interview, Loftus would

only say, "The matter has been satisfactorily resolved." He has posted an apology on his personal Web site. It reads, in part:

> I DID NOT REALIZE when I gave his address that Hilal had moved, and an innocent family was living there. I am heartsick that the family suffered harassment and anxiety as a result of my mistake. I take full and complete responsibility for my error in judgment. I will try very hard to ensure that I make as few mistakes as possible, and again apologize profusely to all of you, especially the Vorick family.

Aside from the pain and harassment suffered by the Vorick family, and the embarrassment to Loftus and Fox, the lasting effect of this incident is that it erased the confidence the Voricks and those close to them had in the media.

Incidents like this exact a high toll on the media. The marketing industry talks about "one-to-one" marketing in which there is strong, personal communication or a relationship between a product or brand and an individual consumer. Every misidentification, because it involves a person, is a form of negative one-to-one marketing for the media. Each person wronged by an error doesn't hesitate to tell his or her friends and colleagues about it. People will listen to Randy Vorick tell his story, and they will tell their friends, and it will be passed along for years to come. The result will be a new group of people who trust the media a little (or a lot) less than before.

The Voricks' story, however, did not end there. The *Los Angeles Times*, which wrote an admirable article about the mess, ran a correction in the paper the next day, August 26, 2005. It seems it had neglected to mention definitively that Hilal was not a terrorist.

> AN ARTICLE IN THURSDAY'S California section reported on statements made by John Loftus, a commentator for Fox News, describing grocery store owner Iyad K. Hilal as a terrorist. Although the article accurately quoted Loftus' expression of his opinion, *The Times* wants to make clear that Hilal has not been charged with any illegal activity and *The Times* is not

aware of any law enforcement agency or official that has identified Hilal as a terrorist. In addition, a previous story on Hilal, which ran in some editions of the California section on Wednesday, said that Omar Bakri Mohammed, a Muslim cleric formerly based in London, had identified Hilal last year in an interview in a newsletter as "leader of the U.S. branch" of an organization known as Hizb ut-Tahrir. Mohammed's interview actually identified a man named Iyad Hilal as the leader of a splinter group of Hizb ut-Tahrir that includes only "a few individuals." *The Times* regrets any confusion that may have resulted from these articles.

One more mistake to add to the pile. Hardly a surprise to anyone involved.

Doctors, Lawyers, and the Accused

THE *TRIBUNE* AND FOX NEWS errors show the profound consequences of misidentification. They are also powerful examples of how the media's response to a mistake can dictate its true impact. The everyday variety of these errors is of course less damaging, but not without harm. One frequent error of misidentification is that lawyers are mistaken for their clients, as illustrated by this July 2005 correction from the Montreal *Gazette:*

> A HEADLINE YESTERDAY over a story about police protocol in administering breathalyzer tests said incorrectly that Eric Sutton has been charged with impaired driving. In fact, as the story explained, Sutton is the lawyer acting for Mark Hughes, the person facing the impaired driving charges. The *Gazette* apologizes to Sutton for the error.

It did it again on March 23, 2007 when it published a photo of a lawyer instead of his client, a Montreal police officer, who pleaded guilty to thirteen counts of "sexually attacking" women and girls. The *Gazette* also ran a front-page correction and apology on December 14, 2004, after it confused a doctor investigating a charge of sexual misconduct with the physician accused of the crime:

FOR THE RECORD

Police officer Benoît Guay.   Lawyer Philip Schneider.

GAZETTE FILE PHOTOS

Defence lawyer's photo appeared

A photo in yesterday's paper incorrectly identified Montreal police officer Benoît Guay, who has pleaded guilty to 13 counts of sexually attacking girls and women. In fact, the photo showed Guay's lawyer, Philip Schneider. The Gazette apologizes to Mr. Schneider for the error.

The Gazette of Montreal apologizes for mixing up a lawyer with his client.

IN A STORY THAT APPEARED on Page A1 on Saturday, *The Gazette* reported incorrectly that Dr. Adrien Dandavino faces an allegation of sexual misconduct. In fact, Dr. Dandavino is acting as a syndic or investigator on behalf of the Quebec College of Physicians and is making the allegation of misconduct against another doctor, Rejean Vanier. *The Gazette* regrets the error and apologizes to Dr. Dandavino.

Misidentifications are very personal errors because they make someone into something they are not. Occasionally, this can be something that the subject of the error might not leap to correct, as in this *Los Angeles Times* correction from January 13, 2005:

A QUOTE IN AN ARTICLE IN Wednesday's Calendar section about the film "Kinsey's" eight-year journey to the screen suggested that the star of the film was an Oscar-winning actor. Liam Neeson was nominated for "Schindler's List" but did not win.

Perhaps Neeson held his tongue on that one. But most errors are less charitable, such as these three, all published during the last week of

February 2005. The first is from the *Fresno Bee*, which switched the identities of a driver and the pedestrian he hit and killed:

> A PEDESTRIAN KILLED in Hanford was misidentified on Page B2 of Tuesday's *Bee* as Daniel Richard Childers, 29, of Lemoore. The victim was Antonio Ornelas Sanzon, 48, of Hanford. Childers was the driver.

And these two from the *Boston Globe:*

> BECAUSE OF AN EDITING ERROR, the sex of one of the children of ceramist Jill Rosenwald was misidentified in Sunday's *Boston Globe Magazine*. Her 2-year-old, Loch, is a boy.

> BECAUSE OF A REPORTING ERROR, the late husband-and-wife design team Charles and Ray Eames were misidentified as brothers in yesterday's Galleries column in the Weekend section.

Not to give undue scrutiny to the *Chicago Tribune*, but it dealt another Chicagoan of good civic standing a bum hand, as this October 22, 2005, correction noted:

> A STORY IN THURSDAY'S Metro section about Leslie Ivy, a recovering drug addict who coaches a youth football team, mistakenly characterized two other coaches in the league. Charles Hemphill and Michael Phipps are coaches and neighborhood dads with no past drug addictions.

Imagine you're Charles Hemphill or Michael Phipps. You give your time to coach your kid's football team and one day a reporter shows up to practice. Maybe you'll be quoted in the paper, or get a nice picture of yourself and your child. So you speak to the reporter. Then the article appears and all of a sudden you're a recovering drug addict. How would that affect your opinion of the press? Would you feel comfortable talking to a reporter in the future? Likely not.

A correction admits the error; it does not erase it. It doesn't require something of the magnitude of the Calabrese, Swieton, or Vorick mistakes to erode trust in the media. This erosion then leads people to be less inclined to speak with the press, and less inclined to purchase newspapers or watch the news on television. Perhaps most important, it could make them reluctant to seek out the press to publicize a wrong or call attention to an important issue. As people disengage from the media, it hurts not only the industry and the profession but society as a whole. The result is that the picture presented by the media becomes distorted.

Tainted Images

PERHAPS IT WAS A VICTIM OF mistaken identity who coined the cliché of a picture being worth a thousand words (though the media would rarely offer that much space to correct an error). Sometimes the misidentified are never identified, as in the case of a truly embarrassing error from *Us Weekly* magazine.

In one of its typically photo-splashed stories about the celebrity breakup of actor Charlie Sheen and his wife, Denise Richards, the magazine ran a large photo of Sheen with his arm around a young, smiling blonde. She was identified as Ginger Lynn Allen, a porn star whom Sheen dated "on and off between 1990 and 1995." Just to be sure no reader could mistake her for anything else, her torso was branded with a large pink circle in which the words "PORN STAR" were stamped. Two weeks later, tucked away on page 11 of the magazine, was this correction:

> IN OUR FEATURE "Why She Left Him" [March 21, 2005], the woman identified in the photograph as former adult-film star Ginger Lynn Allen is neither Ms. Allen nor an adult-film actress. *Us* regrets the error.

What *Us* does not explicitly state is that it has no idea who the woman is—yet it asserts that she is not a porn star. She probably isn't, but *Us* is not exactly a reliable source at this point. The issue here is equity. The picture of the woman was large and prominently displayed. To top it off, *Us* literally branded her a porn star. Yet the resulting correction was tiny, tucked away, and lacking the necessary information: Who exactly is this woman? And how did the mistake happen? Two weeks later, the magazine still did not know who the woman was. And it was not about to make a large declaration of this in the correction.

Wrapped up in this mistake is the suggestion that any reasonably attractive blonde woman in a photo with Charlie Sheen from the early nineties could have been a porn star. His reputation made it

CORRECTION: *In our feature "Why She Left Him" [March 21, 2005], the woman identified in a photograph as former adult-film star Ginger Lynn Allen is neither Ms. Allen nor an adult-film actress. Us regrets the error.*

PORN STAR

Ginger Lynn Allen

Sheen dated the former adult-film star, now in her early 40s, on and off from 1990 to 1995. She later called him "the only man I ever really loved" but said, "When he's drinking and using, he's out of control."

Us Weekly's *erroneous photo identification and the resulting correction.*

seem plausible that he was sleeping with any woman photographed with him, and that she might very well have been a porn star or prostitute. This is not to lay blame on Sheen for the mistake. It's to highlight that the media will sometimes put aside evidence, or a lack thereof, and go with a supposition. Charlie Sheen and a hot blonde in the nineties? He must be sleeping with her. And he dated a blonde porn star then, so how far off could we be?

This "it could be true" mentality came into play on a late fall day along a Moscow road in 2005. Liam Lawlor, a former member of the Irish Parliament, was being driven to the airport. He had served three short stints in jail for failing to cooperate with a tribunal investigating corruption in Dublin's planning process. With him in the car were his driver and Julia Kushnir, a young woman who worked for a Prague law firm. She was serving as Lawlor's interpreter. Their car crashed, killing both Lawlor and the driver. Kushnir was injured but survived.

Shortly after the crash, the Moscow correspondent for the *Observer*, the Sunday edition of the *Guardian* newspaper, received a call from an editor at the *Sunday Independent* newspaper in Ireland. He had heard that Lawlor might have been in an accident. Nick Paton Walsh, the *Observer*'s correspondent, phoned the local police to look into it. The next day the *Observer*, the *Sunday Independent*, the *Sunday Tribune*, the *Sunday World*, the *Star on Sunday*, the *Sunday People*, and the *News of the World* all ran stories about the crash. All of them either stated outright or insinuated that the woman in Lawlor's company was a prostitute. And perhaps even an underage one at that.

The *Observer*'s story ran with the headline "Lawlor Died in Crash with Call Girl" and began, "Disgraced politician Liam Lawlor, who died in a car crash in Russia yesterday morning, may have been traveling with a young prostitute it emerged last night." This was, of course, false and defamatory to both Lawlor and Kushnir, the young woman, who was not a prostitute.

Denying that the *Sunday Independent* "got the story" from him, Paton Walsh told the *Irish Times*, "I rang an official police spokesperson and relayed only the contents of three conversations with this same person to their newsdesk, stressing at one point it was only a possibility the girl was a prostitute."

The "possibility" became a "probability" in light of some people's view of the "disgraced" Lawlor. Then it became fact when many newspapers printed it. Like the *Tribune*, Fox News, and *Us Weekly* errors, this mistake was born of a reckless disregard for fact checking and the lack of foresight to imagine how costly an error it could be to their outlet and to the mischaracterized party. The Lawlor and Sheen debacles also speak to preconceived notions about a person's identity, which in turn feed shameful misidentifications that wound people in the most personal of ways.

Preconceived ideas strike at the core of misidentifications. For that moment in time when the incorrect information is out in the world, it is perceived as fact. And those who do not scan the corrections will always take it as fact. That man has HIV, that parent used to be a drug addict, that doctor was a molester, that girl was a prostitute or a porn star. It taints the misidentified and colors our perception of them. As the media knows all too well, perception is reality, no matter how it is misreported.

The Corrections
MISIDENTIFICATIONS AND PERSONAL ERRORS

IN THE ARTICLE, "The return of citizen Kane" (Culture, October 23) we stated that the playwright Sarah Kane took her own life in a psychiatric hospital in 1999. In fact she was on a general ward in King's College hospital, London. We apologise to her family for any distress this error may have caused.

—*Sunday Times* (UK)

We said in error that the late playwright, Sarah Kane, had been sectioned under the Mental Health Act ('Suicide art? She's better than that', page 18, G2, October 12). She was voluntarily admitted to the Maudsley hospital, London, on two occasions and then discharged. We also gave the impression that she was under observation in a psychiatric wing when she took her life. This is inaccurate. She was in a general ward in King's College hospital, London. We wish to extend our apologies to her family and friends for any distress caused.

—*Guardian* (UK)

A picture on the cover of the Real Estate Section Friday was incorrect. The picture was not gangster Al Capone, but the actor Rod Steiger playing Capone.

—*Newsday* (New York)

A Nov. 10 article about the event Whose Role Is It Anyway? (tonight at the Hippodrome Theatre) included two errors. Windy Marshall, an actress who uses a wheelchair in the play Steel Magnolias, was incorrectly characterized as disabled. Also, Arena Players will present a scene from The Glass

Menagerie performed by African-American actors in traditionally white roles rather than a scene from The Meeting.

                                                —*Baltimore Sun*

❖

A Report on Business item on Wednesday misstated two facts
relating to Scott Paterson, the former head of Yorkton
Securities. Mr. Paterson remains married to his second wife.
Additionally, he was described by Peter C. Newman in his most
recent book as precocious, not precious.

                                                —*Globe and Mail*

❖

In a Nov. 7 story about the arraignment of Valerie Friend on
federal charges alleging she helped murder a drug informant,
The Associated Press reported erroneously that co-defendant
George Lecco had pleaded guilty in the case. Lecco pleaded not
guilty at his arraignment on Nov. 3.

                                                —Associated Press

❖

Because of an editing error, a story and headline on Page
A-1 of Thursday's *Times* included incorrect details about the
events leading to the arrest of Harold K. Isham Jr., 45, of
Middleboro. Isham's computer was in the possession of a
repair man in Bridgewater, who allegedly discovered porno-
graphic images on the computer and reported them to police.
No pornographic imates [sic] were found at Isham's parents'
Yarmouthport [sic] or in their computer.

                                                —*Cape Cod Times*

❖

An article in Sunday's Local section on the estate sale of former
Gov. Elbert Carvel quoted Olin Vanaman of Wilmington about
his excitement in purchasing 35 of the governor's decanters

during the auction, including one used at Queen Elizabeth's coronation. Vanaman said he used a slang term when describing Carvel as "a big boozer," but he did not mean that the former governor was a heavy drinker. Vanaman refers to people who collect decanters as "boozers," he explained, "the same as guys who collect cars are gear-heads." No reference to drinking or the consumption of alcohol was intended in the article.

—*News Journal* (Delaware)

An editorial in Friday's paper incorrectly stated that Florida Cresswell, a candidate for state representative in the 28th District, was convicted in 1999 of battery and stealing Tupperware. In fact he was convicted of stealing a battery from a van as well as Tupperware that was inside the van.

—*Chicago Tribune*

A Saturday Briefing item about adult filmmakers crossing over into Hollywood movies incorrectly stated that "Quinceanera" co-director Richard Glatzer had worked in the pornography industry. Glatzer, who works in independent film and reality TV, has not worked in adult films.

—*Los Angeles Times*

A story in the July 24 edition of the *Sentinel & Enterprise* incorrectly spelled Sheri Normandin's name. Also, Bobby Kincaid is not a quadriplegic. We regret the errors.

—*Sentinel & Enterprise* (Massachusetts)

CHAD SINANIAN OF DANBURY has a mild brain injury with motor coordination problems, and he is an advocate on behalf of people with mental retardation. But he is not mentally retarded, as was incorrectly stated in a story on Page 1 Sunday.

—*Hartford Courant*

❖

Richard Scott, a psychologist testifying in the kidnapping and rape trial of defendant William Thimiogianis, was mistakenly referred to in place of the defendant in a report in Thursday's Metro section.   —*St. Louis Post Dispatch*

❖

Clarification: Sonics Dance Team director Susan Hovey said she was misunderstood when she responded to a question about an eating disorder for this article. Hovey says she did not have an eating disorder, but gained personal knowledge of the disorder by watching a friend go through it.

—*Seattle Times*

❖

In an article, "I have a great sex life. Does that shock you?" page 24, G2, August 17, we mistakenly said that Liz Carr had a rare degenerative disease. She has asked us to point out that she has no such disease and is "simply a wheelchair-using disabled woman". Apologies.   —*Guardian* (UK)

❖

Darcy Crocker was not consuming cocaine the night he was sexually assaulted and choked by Dan Magda. Magda was consuming the cocaine. Incorrect information appeared in a story Oct. 19.   —*Record* (Ontario)

❖

A story in the Metro section Wednesday about a letter-reading program by the Aurora YWCA that focused on sexual assault issues, incorrectly quoted Annah Mitchell, Aurora YWCA's marketing director, as saying she was a victim of assault. —*Chicago Tribune*

✦

Misidentification: U.S. Attorney Bradley Schlozman of Kansas City, Mo., said Albert Nasser, who pleaded guilty in a pharmaceutical drug case Thursday, bought stolen drugs and sold them to secondary distributors. A story in some Friday editions incorrectly identified Schlozman, who provided details of the crime in a press release, as the person who bought the drugs.
—*Omaha World-Herald* (Nebraska)

✦

A story in Friday's Metro section mistakenly swapped the names of a Cook County state's attorney and a man charged with three homicides. Larry Countee was the person charged. During a bond hearing, Cook County prosecutor LuAnn Snow had detailed Countee's previous criminal convictions.
—*Chicago Tribune*

✦

The last sentence of a brief in some editions of Friday's Metro section confused the name of an assistant Cook County state's attorney, Mark Ertler, with that of a Chicago man sentenced to prison for two purse snatchings. The defendant, Kevin Walker, 38, of the 10300 block of South Wabash Avenue, apologized for the crime and said he was trying to support a drug habit he had had since he was 14.
—*Chicago Tribune*

✦

AN OBITUARY OF THE CIVIL RIGHTS leader James Forman yesterday misstated a word in describing his call, in 1969, for reparations to be paid by Protestant and Jewish groups for the crimes of slavery. Mr. Forman asked for $500 million for crimes perpetrated against generations of blacks, not "by" them.

—*New York Times*

✦

An article in Business Day yesterday about an effort by Richard A. Grasso, former chairman of the New York Stock Exchange, to see a report commissioned by his successor, John S. Reed, referred incorrectly to comments Mr. Reed made about the contents of the report. Mr. Reed said that the findings of the report were an embarrassment to the exchange—not that Mr. Grasso was.   —*New York Times*

✦

A story in *The Press* yesterday said a cleaning services manager at Princess Margaret and Hillmorton hospitals had won an award for "supported employment" after employing four intellectually disabled people. The staff, in fact, have physical disabilities. The error is regretted.

—*Press* (New Zealand)

PHOTO MISIDENTIFICATIONS

In an article on drug smuggling in Venezuela that began on Page 1A Monday, an incorrect photograph was used on Page 2A for jailed drug trafficking suspect Feris Farid Domínguez. The error occurred in the newsroom production process. The photo that was used was that of Leonel Fernández, president of the Dominican Republic. The *Miami Herald* regrets the error. The correct photos appear at left.

—*Miami Herald*

A photograph on page A16 yesterday misidentified former Israeli prime minister Shimon Peres as assassinated prime minister Yitzhak Rabin. Correct photos appear above.

—Ottawa Citizen

❧

Because of a reporter's error, a photograph on page B7 of the Metro section Sunday with an obituary for the Rev. Forrest G. Nees was a photo of another person, whose obituary had already been in the newspaper. The correct photo of Nees is at right. Also, Nees' first name was misspelled.

—Plain Dealer (Ohio)

❧

In using a photograph of three women pilots to illustrate a story headed How the air force kept secret watch to track down lesbians, page 3, August 22, we caused some embarrassment to one of the women in the picture and her family, for which we apologise. The photograph was taken from an archive and not intended to imply any involvement in the story of the women shown beyond their role as pilots.   *—Guardian* (UK)

❧

In *The Canberra Times* published on April 21, 2005, we illustrated an article about the conviction of Frank Patrick Barbaro, of Palmerston, with a photograph of Frank Neil Barbaro.

We made a mistake.

The Canberra Times apologises to Frank Neil Barbaro and his family for the hurt and distress caused by the use of his photograph. Frank Neil Barbaro lives at Queanbeyan and is a contractor. He is not related to the man whose criminal conviction was reported in the article.   *—Canberra Times* (Australia)

❧

A PHOTO LABELED AS PAUL MCCARTNEY on Page E4 Saturday was actually a local musician playing in a Beatles tribute band.

—Minnesota *Star Tribune*

＊

On June 5, the *Globe* published a photograph on Page B2 of a life-drawing session at a Harvard Square studio. The photograph included images of a woman model, an artist, and studio owner Duncan W. Purdy. The *Globe* learned this week that Purdy was indicted in March on charges of rape, assault, and battery on a woman at his business two years earlier. Purdy also was charged in December 2005 with maintaining a house of prostitution and deriving support from prostitution at his Cambridge business. Purdy maintains his innocence on all charges, and the cases are pending. Had the *Globe* known of the charges, it would not have taken or published the photograph.   —*Boston Globe*

＊

A story obituary and headline about Martinsburg lawyer Robert M. Steptoe in the Sunday *Gazette-Mail* wrongly said Steptoe was the chief executive officer of the law firm Steptoe & Johnson. His son, Robert M. Steptoe Jr., is the managing partner and CEO of Steptoe & Johnson. Also, the front-page photograph was of Robert Steptoe Jr., not his deceased father. We regret the error.

—*Charleston Gazette* (West Virginia)

＊

The *Daily News* on Friday ran a panel of pictures on Page 1 of homicide victims in the city in 2005. Inadvertently included was a picture of Richard Dawson, 21, who wasn't a murder victim but who stabbed to death one of seven youths who attacked him on Oct. 29 near his East Mount Airy home. Police released Dawson after concluding he acted in self-defense after being attacked by a group of gay bashers.

—*Philadelphia Daily News*

＊

A report in *The Daily Telegraph* on February 24, 2006 entitled "A bad trip for Nimbin" included a photograph of a Nimbin street. Some readers may have identified Mr Mark Richardson from the photograph and inferred that Mr Richardson was involved in drugs. Readers should note this inference is not correct.   —*Daily Telegraph* (Australia)

＊

An incorrect name was published under a photograph on Page C2 of Wednesday's *Daily News*. The photograph was of Brandon Lee Shelton, who is considered a suspect in a Walton County shooting. Instead, the shooting victim's name appeared erroneously under the photograph.

—*Northwest Florida Daily News*

＊

A photo of the wrong man accompanied a story Tuesday about Nicholas Quiles, who has been accused of molesting a neighbor boy. The photo was of another man with the same last name. Here is the correct photo of Nicholas Quiles.

—*St. Petersburg Times* (Florida)

＊

The wrong photo inadvertently ran in Thursday's Williamsburg community news section with an item about Jamestown High senior Brett Batten being named the Kiwanis Club's "Teenager of the Year." The photo showed Jamestown High School guidance counselor Bob Nilson. The corrected

item will appear June 8.   —*Daily Press* (Virginia)
IN YESTERDAY'S *Record* we published a photograph in connection with a story which reported that a policeman was accused
of stealing a WPC uniform for a bodybuilder girlfriend.

In fact the photograph purporting to be that of Agnes
Campbell was that of a woman completely unconnected to the story.

The *Daily Record* regrets the publication of the wrong photograph and unreservedly apologises to her, her husband and
family for the embarrassment which our error caused.

—*Daily Record* (Scotland)

✦

A photo caption in yesterday's *Daily News* incorrectly stated
that Donald Trump took part in Monday's LOVE Park celebration of the new advertising alliance between Monster.com and
the *Daily News* and *Inquirer*. The Monster.com mascot, which is
named Trump, was part of Monday's festivities.

—*Philadelphia Daily News*

✦

In our "Tory Tribes" feature in last week's Sunday Review we
referred to David Gold, the party's first openly gay parliamentary candidate who has been selected for Eltham. This was
illustrated with a photo of David Gold, Chairman of
Birmingham City FC and founder of Ann Summers. We apologise to both men for the error.

—*Independent* (UK)

✦

CHAPTER 9

ERRORS HEARD
ROUND THE WORLD

O N THE NIGHT OF JANUARY 3, 2006, all over the eastern part of the United States and Canada, newspapers were rolling off the presses with headlines such as "Miner Miracle" and "They're Alive!" They would land on millions of doorsteps just a few hours later. People who woke up to the rhapsodic headlines got an entirely incorrect version of reality.

At roughly 2:46 a.m. on the morning of January 4, 2006, at a time when many newspaper printing plants were churning out or bundling those editions, a woman and her two young children emerged from the Baptist church in the small mining community of Sago, West Virginia.

Clearly distraught, Lynette Roby made her way over to CNN's Anderson Cooper, who was reporting live from outside the church.

"There's only one made it out alive," she told a stunned Cooper and his international audience.

She explained that the governor of West Virginia and a mining company executive had delivered the news. Twelve of the thirteen miners trapped thousands of feet beneath the surface in a dark and airless coal mine had died.

"This is unbelievable," Cooper said.

"It's the most awful—it's unbelievable," Roby said. "It's just total—it's disgraceful. It's awful. But it needs to be known. I mean, the story needs to change to not a very—you know, it's taken a turn for . . ."

Then her young son interrupted to encapsulate the shocking turn of events: "It went from happy to sad," he said.

For the first time in nearly three hours, the media was finally reporting the truth. Within minutes, other broadcast outlets were carrying the revised story, and the Associated Press soon moved a corrected report over the wire. The wrong information had spread around the world from media source to source, and now the press had to try to get the genie back in the bottle and distribute the correct information, get the real news out just as quickly.

It would prove to be impossible.

One man emerged from the dark hole in the side of the mountain and was sped off in an ambulance. The rest had perished. That loss was the true tragedy. Sadly, however, it was eclipsed by the mistakes that had been made in the reporting and dissemination of this heartbreaking story—mistakes that were sent careening all over the globe. This compounded the grief of the families and their community.

Some newspapers literally stopped the presses and printed new front pages. The *New York Times, Boston Globe, Washington Post,* and many other leading papers on the eastern seaboard had failed to stop their full run in time, so the celebratory front-page stories had gone out into the world. The initial report that twelve of the miners were alive had spread so far over the previous three hours that it was too late to get it right.

"You hear about the fog of war," Anderson Cooper said on the air that night, "but this was not a war."

Here is what actually happened.

Two days earlier, at 6:30 a.m., an explosion tore through the coal mine in Sago, a community located in Tallmansville, West Virginia. Caught in the blast were thirteen miners. Within hours of the explosion, major media from all over the United States descended on the small mining community. Media reports streamed out. The next day, January 3, at roughly 9:30 p.m., the world received its first definitive report on the status of the miners: Rescuers had found one dead.

Then, just before midnight that evening, screams of elation and joyous singing could be heard coming from inside the church where the community had gathered to wait for information about their loved ones. The Associated Press sent a story over the wire at 11:59 p.m. with the headline, "Families Say 12 W.Va. Miners Found Alive."

It began: "Twelve miners caught in an explosion in a coal mine were found alive Tuesday night, more than 41 hours after the blast, family members said. Bells at a church where relatives had been gathering rang out as family members ran out screaming in jubilation."

On CNN, Anderson Cooper, reporting from Sago, came back from a commercial break and was reportedly the first to break the news live on air.

"Wow," he said, according to a CNN transcript. "The families, we are told, are screaming, some family members screamed that 12 people were found alive. That is—we cannot confirm that. There is a lot of hugging going on. One eyewitness is telling me right now . . ."

A man walked over to Cooper to say, "Hugging and crying and screaming 12 alive! 12 alive!"

They exchanged words, and then, after the man left, Cooper told his audience:

THAT IS INCREDIBLE NEWS. Again, if this turns out to be true, we have not been able to independently confirm this. But the family members have been told, a number of family members have been told, we're not clear on who exactly told them, but a mine official is traditionally the ones who tell them this information, that the 12 miners are alive. The governor of West Virginia, we are told, just walked out of the church, held up his thumb and said, "Believe in miracles. Believe in miracles." For the last two days, for the last 48—40 hours he has been saying miracles do happen here in West Virginia. And it appears tonight a miracle has truly happened in West Virginia.

Cooper's comments show how quickly the initial reports went from skepticism ("if this turns out to be true") to near confirmation ("it appears tonight a miracle has truly happened in West Virginia"). It was literally a matter of seconds before he made the transition. The drama of having someone from the community deliver the news live and on the fly made for great television, but it precluded any chance to confirm the report before taking it to air. This was a result of circumstance, but there was no effort to take a step back and offer a more cautionary note. Good news travels fast, especially when the stakes are so high.

With an Associated Press report on the wire and at least one major broadcaster relaying the good news, the story was off and running. The call rang out: *Twelve alive.* It was picked up all over North America and around the world. Newspaper editors on the night shift began altering their front pages to play up the "miracle." For nearly three hours after that, the mining company remained silent, neither confirming nor denying the report. In that interim, the initially cautious speculation that the miners might be alive became unambiguous confirmation that, miraculously, they were.

The mining company deserved its fair share of blame for letting the media run away with the wrong story. It had a responsibility to stand up and declare what it did or didn't know. But the media also had to accept its culpability for failing to perform the necessary due diligence to learn the truth. Instead, taking the mining company's silence as verification, they had spread what amounted to an unsubstantiated rumor as fact.

The result was one of the worst media errors of the twenty-first century. The Sago Mine mistake was an instance when all the power and technology driving today's mass media was turned against itself. Because of satellites, the Internet, and cell phones, the incorrect information was instantly passed along from one outlet to another. It eventually landed on the front pages of some of the world's largest and most respected newspapers.

Getting the news out is no challenge in today's world; correcting it, however, is an entirely different matter.

The Twenty-Four-Hour Broken Telephone

AS EVIDENCED BY THE ORAL NEWS systems of preliterate societies and the children's game of telephone (also known as "broken telephone"), information is easily distorted as it passes from one source to another. The press attempts to avoid this problem by making use of established, trusted global newswires such as the Associated Press and Reuters. Major news outlets such as the *New York Times* and the *Washington Post* have their own syndication services to spread their reporting around the globe. The press also looks to reliable sources to confirm or deny information so they can "feed the beast." This creature is insatiable, always looking for more information, fresh information. When it finds it, a call goes out to the herd and a feeding frenzy ensues.

Thanks to advanced technology, today's media can send and receive information in less than a second. It can publish it online in a matter of minutes. This causes a ripple effect because each news outlet tracks what the others are reporting. If CNN starts moving on a breaking story, everyone else will take notice and join in once there is enough information, or "official" confirmation. Reporting feeds more reporting, and the story becomes more established with each new addition. Caution eventually gives way to speculation, which begets dissemination, which in turn breeds confirmation.

Today's media is built on the instant and continuous flow of information.

"Modern newscraft, addicted to technology, worships the god of speed," wrote David Perlmutter, a professor and associate dean for graduate studies and research in the William Allen White School of Journalism and Mass Communications at the University of Kansas, after the Sago disaster. "Laptops, satellites, and cell phones make live-from-ground-zero reporting alluring. But the problems instantaneousness creates cannot be ignored."

Television news programs, and especially the twenty-four-hour cable news stations, do their best to play up the idea that they are constantly receiving the latest reports from all over the globe. It's an image consciously perpetuated by slapping a BREAKING NEWS logo on the most mundane of updates, and by designing sets that show busy workers jawing into telephones or staring at screens in the background. CNN's flagship news program, *The Situation Room*, takes this to the extreme, pulverizing viewers with images on no less than six gigantic flat-screen monitors. Wolf Blitzer leaps from story to story, coaxing out a new image or graphic to bob and weave with the torrent of incoming information.

For today's news media the priority is to get the news out first, be the one that can claim a scoop and compel the others to credit it as the source. From this initial "get," the rest of the media latches on to the story and, often within seconds or minutes, distributes it on a global scale.

The pressure to keep up with—and especially to dominate—the news cycle increases the potential for the media to get its facts wrong on a massive scale. Once something incorrect makes its way into today's powerful information current, it is swept up and carried across the world. Reeling in a misreported or incorrect item is much harder than pushing it out, and few news outlets have proved adept at the practice. While incorrect information spreads rapidly, correct information hits barriers. The result is reporting fiascos such as Sago.

Much anger was appropriately directed at the mining company, which callously withheld the truth, but the media deservedly took its hits as well. Sago stands out because of its life-and-death consequences. But it was not an anomaly. The media routinely reports, reprints, disseminates, and publishes incorrect information. It is a dangerous by-product of the twenty-four-hour global news cycle. When a single error is unleashed to multiply, it can sometimes take years before the correct information comes to light. Once ensconced in a database or cached on the Internet, mistaken information will be accessed and reprinted again and again. Journalists accessing archived reports will come across the incorrect information and publish it without a second thought, further establishing its credibility. It's a vicious cycle.

Because of this reality, the media's failure to get it right in the first place can now do more damage than ever before. The stakes are higher. It took three hours for the media to correct its reporting on the Sago Mine. This is an excruciating amount of time in today's twenty-four-hour news cycle. Yet it was respectable compared to the time it took the global media to correct the tale of Hamilton Naki, the black man with the white heart.

Too Incredible Not to Report

IN EARLY DECEMBER 1967, DENISE DARVALL, a woman in her twenties, was crossing the street in Cape Town, South Africa, when she was struck by a vehicle. Darvall was rushed to a hospital with life-threatening injuries. Doctors soon discovered that she was brain-dead, and at 9 p.m. that evening, they stopped trying to revive her.

Shortly after she passed away, doctors approached her father to ask permission to harvest her organs for use in transplants. He agreed, and soon her kidneys were given to ten-year-old Jonathan van Wyk. (This became controversial in apartheid South Africa because Darvall was white and van Wyk was black.) Then there was the matter of her healthy, twenty-four-year-old heart.

Louis Washkansky, a fifty-two-year-old South African, had experienced his third heart attack three years earlier and was still suffering from the effects. Doctors decided to do what was then a radical procedure, one that had never been successfully performed: a heart transplant. Darvall's heart was quickly delivered to a team of more than thirty medical professionals, who completed the procedure. Washkansky lived for a record eighteen days after the transplant. The operating physician, Dr. Christiaan Barnard, went into the history books as the first physician to successfully perform a heart transplant.

Many accounts of the operation commented on how large a medical team was involved; there were nurses, surgical assistants, and several doctors, and for a long time, no one who covered this major story was sure of exactly who had been in the operating theater. Only in the mid-nineties did media reports begin to emerge about a remarkable subplot to the transplant.

A black surgical assistant who performed transplants on animals, Hamilton Naki, and who normally would have been forbidden from going anywhere near a white patient, had helped prep the heart for transplant. Because of the strict apartheid laws, his role had been deliberately concealed. When Naki died on May 29, 2005, at the age of seventy-eight, the story was told and retold of how he was a man with no formal education who rose to become a skilled and admired surgical assistant and then surgeon. A truly noble and gifted man, he had remained in the shadows for decades due to the racist policies of his country.

In its obituary of Naki, the *Economist* reported how, "in one part of the operating suite, Barnard in a blaze of publicity, prepared Louis Washkansky, the world's first recipient of a transplanted human heart. Fifteen meters away, behind a glass panel, Mr Naki's skilled black hands plucked the white heart from the white corpse and, for hours, hosed every trace of blood from it, replacing it with Washkansky's. The heart, set pumping again with electrodes, was passed to the other side of the screen, and Mr Barnard became, overnight, the most celebrated doctor in the world."

As the *New York Times* noted, "There are few tales in the annals of medicine to rival the recent *obituaries* of Hamilton Naki, hailed as the unschooled and penniless black laborer who in 1967 secretly helped Dr. Christiaan N. Barnard perform the world's first heart transplant operation."

Only in the early 1990s, when apartheid was in its last throes, did the true story come out. On March 29, 1993, the Associated Press published the first article to give Naki credit. "Barnard had Naki on his heart-transplant backup team," it read. "He said the frail, 68-year-old former janitor possesses skills he does not have."

Barnard said that doctors who work with Naki "tell me that Hamilton can do all the various aspects of liver transplantation, which I can't do. So technically, he is a better surgeon than I am."

This praise, which was well deserved, was followed by the writer's statement that "when Barnard performed the first heart transplant in 1967, Naki was part of the backup team at Groote Schuur Hospital in Cape Town."

Database searches show the AP story to be the first mention of Naki in the major press. It is also the first time he was linked with the heart transplant. From this one story, the media legend of Naki grew. His participation in the surgery became well-known because it was a compelling tale of how apartheid had subjugated talented blacks and kept them from earning their rightful place in society. The global media loved it. Naki was a hero. More important, he was a symbol: In an editorial after his death, the *Sydney Morning Herald* wrote, "Most of us are so blessed by relative privilege that the story of Hamilton Naki seems like an outrageous fiction."

Unfortunately, core parts the story *were* fiction, and the media had spread it around the world for more than a decade. It took Naki's death to finally bring the truth to light. Naki's obituary was published in papers and other media outlets on nearly every continent. All of them mentioned his role in the heart transplant. The story of his part in the operation had spread and become entrenched during the more than ten years since the first AP story introduced him to the world. It was further established in his obituaries during May and June 2005.

In late August, the *Los Angeles Times* noted that "when Hamilton Naki died May 29 at the age of 78, newspapers around the world celebrated the life of the black South African, a onetime laborer who they said became adept at anesthesiology and secretly assisted in the first heart transplant surgery."

The information had been reported and re-reported so many times that no journalist or editor thought to go back and check the basic facts of the story. Professor David Dent, acting dean of the faculty of health sciences at the University of Cape Town, read the obits with great interest and began composing letters to some of the leading British medical journals. He informed them that, while Naki was a remarkable man and amazing surgeon, he had not taken part in the heart transplant. Dent's letters slowly circulated, raising questions among experts and the media. Finally, the press decided on a radical course of action: researching the facts to discover the truth.

By August, nearly three months after Naki's death, the media began backpedaling on the original tale. The *New York Times* ran an Editor's Note and a lengthy article describing the inaccuracy. "Further reporting in South Africa by *The New York Times* has discounted many details of the original account, which was based largely on earlier published reports," read the August 27, 2005, Editor's Note. "*The Times* should have attributed the account in the obituary more specifically, and should have made further efforts to verify it independently before publication. *The Times* should also have corrected its account more quickly after the initial questions were raised."

The *Times'* admissions strike at the core of how erroneous information is spread over and over again, eventually becoming accepted fact. The paper accepted other reporting without making inquiries to discover and verify its source. Then it dragged its feet in correcting the assertions because, well, everyone else had been saying the same thing. Why bother checking it now? The *Times* was not alone; it was no better or worse than hundreds of other media outlets. And that is the point. Once something has been reported and broadcast enough, no one thinks of questioning the core assumptions. It's easier and, more important, faster to run with it as is.

Every media outlet is prone to error, yet this inherent fallibility is forgotten when a good story comes over the wire. Some news organizations are of course more reputable than others. But none is immune to mistakes, and it is essential to verify incoming information before handing it off to the public as fact. This requires what is for today's press an unimaginable amount of restraint. It means not just getting it *first* but getting it *right*.

The Associated Press, whose Naki obit had run all over the world, with particularly wide distribution in North America, finally, in late August, published a correction:

> IN THE OBITUARY OF HAMILTON NAKI on June 11, The Associated Press erroneously reported that Naki helped Dr. Christiaan Barnard perform the world's first heart transplant. This was based on AP articles, including comments from Naki and Barnard, on April 4, 1993, and June 20, 2003.
>
> Doctors from the University of Cape Town say this widely reported story of his involvement in the operation has gone uncorrected since 1993 and is not true. In published letters to leading British medical journals, Prof. David Dent, acting dean of the faculty of health sciences at the University of Cape Town, said Naki was a skilled surgical assistant but was not present at the hospital when the world's first heart transplant was performed in 1967.

From that single AP story back in 1993 (note that the AP correction appears, at least according to the Nexis news database, to have cited the wrong date of its initial Naki article), the tale of Naki had grown and spread throughout the world. It became an established part of Naki's biography, a reminder of the brutal racism of apartheid.

At the core of the error was the fact that neither Naki nor Dr. Barnard made any effort to dispel the myth; certainly, their complicity in spreading the tale played a major role. But the manner in which the incorrect tale blossomed into accepted fact was due to the media's practice of accepting other outlets' reporting as fact, and republishing it without making additional efforts at confirmation. The result was an error that reached its apex more than a decade after the initial mistake, and that required corrections, apologies, and corrective articles in publications all over the world.

A few precise, dare I say scalpel-like, inquiries could have stemmed the flow of mistaken reporting, and saved the world press from embarrassment. The *Times* said as much in its article about the inaccuracies in Naki's obituary. But the *Times'*—and others'—admissions were undercut by an omission: The mea culpas did not include any statement about adopting new procedures to prevent the same thing from happening again. It's still business as usual. Corrections proliferated across the globe, some with apologies tacked on, but the issue ended there. No one looked at the Naki tale as an example of a larger problem. This problem has not begun to be solved.

The fictitious tale of Naki and the transplant was an unnecessary embellishment in his personal story; it is remarkable, if less dramatic, without it. In Naki's case, the press finally corrected its error. But other wide-ranging errors often go uncorrected. Because of this reality, a balance needs to be struck between disseminating critical news in a timely manner, and applying a proper factual test to incoming material.

A steady stream of errors flows from newspapers, the wire, and the air; these errors are then collected and disseminated by other media outlets, sending them from one medium to another, across borders and oceans. The ease and frequency with which erroneous information is spread is a serious threat to press credibility. How many Sago Mine disasters and Hamilton Nakis will the public endure before it tunes out?

Dismantling our global information networks is not the answer. The interconnectedness of the world is a tremendous advantage for society, and especially for the press. But this benefit also becomes a liability when proper standards are not enforced. Newsrooms must raise the bar for the way incoming information is published and broadcast. The Sago incident displayed how quickly erroneous information can be spread, and how difficult it is to reel it back in. The tale of Hamilton Naki exposed the flawed idea that anything already reported by a reputable news organization can be readily reprinted and repurposed without making additional inquiries.

These examples highlight the danger of our instant, twenty-four-hour news cycle, and the immediate availability of (often incorrect) archived reporting. Until the fundamental procedures for gathering, checking, and disseminating information are improved, this game of broken telephone will continue to reverberate around the globe. Fixing this critical flaw will enable the press to take full advantage of the tools at its disposal, and will save it and the public from enduring another Sago.

CHAPTER 10

THE TROUBLE WITH CORRECTIONS

WHEN BRANDI LYNCH READ the article about her family in the March 27, 2003, edition of the *New York Times*, she was surprised and more than a little amused. The story detailed the rescue of her sister, Private First Class Jessica D. Lynch, in Iraq. It described how their father "choked up as he stood on his porch here overlooking the tobacco fields and cattle pastures."

It was a touching, vivid scene. And one well suited to the cow pasture: It was pure manure.

The story was one of the many error-riddled, plagiarized, or fabricated articles produced by disgraced *Times* reporter Jayson Blair. As the paper's exhaustive report revealing his transgressions noted, "He also wrote that Private Lynch's family had a long history of military service; it does not, family members said. He wrote that their home was on a hilltop; it is in a valley. And he wrote that Ms. Lynch's brother was in the West Virginia National Guard; he is in the Army."

Brandi Lynch told the *Times* that the family joked "about the tobacco fields and the cattle" after Blair's story came out. They thought the errors were astonishing and amusing. But they never asked for a correction. "We just figured it was going to be a one-time thing," they told the *Times*.

For Blair, it was part of a campaign of fabrications, many of which went unchallenged by the people they affected. Why had so many of the people in his articles not contacted the *Times* to complain or ask for a correction?

The reasons strike at the heart of the failure of corrections as they now exist.

Many readers think the press is unlikely to correct an error, and so they don't bother to follow up. Some believe a correction is pointless and ineffectual anyway, due to its placement and length; others simply don't know how to go about getting one. Sources also decline to request corrections when they don't believe an error is significant.

As a result, if a media outlet doesn't notice a mistake on its own, an error will often remain uncorrected and, frequently, will be accessible online and in archives and databases forever. The absence of controls to prevent the error in the first place also means it's unlikely, unless a source steps forward, that the press will spot the error post publication or broadcast. As is the wont of the press, once something is printed or reported, the newsroom moves on to the next story. It doesn't go searching for errors.

In many ways, the press relies on the public and its sources to call attention to errors. While reporters are expected to report any error they notice, no matter how small or delayed, the onus is largely on those outside the newsroom to request a correction. The corrections that do appear, while better than nothing, are in fact only a small sampling compared to the true number of errors.

Of the corrections that are published, many are often too vague, or they lack the context that would enable readers to understand them and the original mistake as well. Or they're published too late or in too concealed a location to ensure that readers of the original article will discover them. Then there is the issue of databases and archives. Too few corrections are being placed within archived stories online or in news databases. This ensures that many errors are enshrined for all time, some of them destined to resurface more than once and keep compounding the original error.

In a *News Library News* article about the importance of correcting archives, Michael Jesse, the library director at the *Indianapolis Star*, emphasized the importance of correcting archival material. "Your online archive is the true final edition of your newspaper and should be corrected as such," Jesse wrote. "Now we have the Internet and it is not just the reporters seeing these stories now. It's everyone with Internet access. Every time someone comes to your online archive and plunks down $2 to buy a story from your archive, you have republished that story—containing false information which you know is there and which you insist on leaving there."

Corrections have appeared in the printed press for hundreds of years but have improved very little. One could argue that it's because they've worked well for so long, but it could simply be that no one cares enough to try to improve on them.

Corrections
A BRIEF HISTORY

WHEN THE PRACTICE OF CORRECTING an erred report emerged, around the time newspapers began publishing with a set frequency, publishers, in their effort to entice readers to buy the next issue, had to convince them that some sort of accuracy ethic was at work at their paper. If a reader raised doubts about a specific report and then didn't see those doubts acknowledged in a subsequent edition, he or she was less likely to patronize the publication again.

Benjamin Harris, who published the first newspaper in America, promised in his publisher's prospectus that "when there appears any material mistake in anything that is corrected, it shall be corrected in the next." This simple statement, made in the late seventeenth century, articulates the basic premise of correction: Any inaccuracy contained in a report would be noted in a subsequent issue or broadcast. Mistakes would be acknowledged and the correct information made known to the audience in a timely manner.

Just as the ethic of correction hasn't changed in hundreds of years, the correction format has remained largely static, with some changes coming mainly over the last thirty-five years. Advances have been made in their placement and in standardizing the language that's used, but a correction from yesterday's newspaper differs only slightly from one made long ago. From the June 12, 1852, edition of the *New York Daily Times:*

CORRECTION.—It was stated in the Times of yesterday, that Mr. Philip Smith died suddenly from the effects of intoxication, and that the Coroner's verdict was found accordingly. We are informed, however, that his death was caused by the rupture of a large blood vessel in the chest. He was a man of invariably temperate habits.

From the September 14, 2006, edition of the *Irish News*:

A COURT REPORT SUB-HEADING on page 19 yesterday incorrectly said the defendant admitted being 'happy drunk'.

As the full report made clear, Darren William Johnston (27) from Glencairn Way in Belfast, denies causing death by dangerous driving and this comment, by prosecuting counsel, referred to the deceased, Martyn Turner.

The *Times* correction was published on page 2, and the *Irish News* correction ran on page 3. While the language seems flowery and sometimes archaic in early corrections, their content and purpose is basically no different from that of their modern descendents. The date and nature of the mistake is noted, and then the correct information is given. Occasionally, a reason or explanation is offered for an error (a mistaken police report, an editing lapse, a reporting error). If the error is suitably damaging, as was the case for the late Mr. Smith, the publication will often offer some form of apology, or the classic rejoinder "We regret the error."

It's admittedly a lot of information to pack into what is usually no more than a couple of sentences. This restricted space breeds the vague and incomplete corrections that appear in the newspaper every day.

Prior to the 1970s, corrections could be found scattered in different places in different newspapers, often under different headlines within the same publication. They rarely had a dedicated editor overseeing them, and many newsrooms hadn't developed a standardized style for writing and presenting them.

Journalists and editors understood the basic idea of correction, but it wasn't encoded or written down on paper. The arts section would express a correction one way; the local news section would opt for another. From the days of Benjamin Harris, and even earlier, until well into the twentieth century, the correction remained relatively unchanged.

Birth of the Modern Correction

B Y 1973, ROUGHLY ONE PAPER out of every eight had a standard headline for its corrections; this standardization enables readers to locate corrections more easily. At larger newspapers, one in four with a circulation over one hundred thousand had a standard headline.

Change was slow in coming. But the year before the 1973 study was done, the *New York Times* began a march toward a new standard for corrections that would change the industry. The shift was led by executive editor A.M. Rosenthal.

As former *Times* assistant managing editor Allan M. Siegal wrote in the introduction to the 2002 collection of amusing *Times* corrections, *Kill Duck Before Serving*, Rosenthal told his department leaders in 1970 that "corrections or denials or amplifications don't really catch up with the original because they are not given proper display."

At the time, the *Times*, like many other publications in North America, ran its corrections throughout the paper. They would appear in every section, in different places, written in different ways, and often under different headings. If you read the initial error, the chances of your happening upon the correction were slim. It was accuracy roulette.

Two years after Rosenthal's missive, the paper anchored its corrections in one place inside the paper: on the inside of the front page. Now, the logic went, people knew where to find them every day. The industry viewed this new policy as a worthy innovation, and many papers fell into line.

Today, almost thirty-five years after Rosenthal created what many call the modern newspaper correction, you can pick up nearly any North American city daily, open it to page two, and spot one or more corrections tucked away in the bottom corner. Rosenthal gave corrections a place, a title, a format.

Rosenthal also made one other tweak to the correction. He created the "Editor's Note" for errors of a more serious nature, or those that dealt with ethical lapses. Today, the Editor's Note is a standard way for newspapers to draw readers' attention to a serious issue. They are infrequent but usually worth reading, as is this one from the *Village Voice*'s Web site, March 1, 2006:

> EARLY WEDNESDAY MORNING, the *Voice* learned that the concluding section of this week's cover story, "Do You Wanna Kiss Me?" by senior associate editor Nick Sylvester, contained fabricated material. In that section, Sylvester says he met at a New York City bar with three TV writers who had flown in from L.A. to test their updates of pickup techniques from Neil Strauss's book, *The Game*. That scene, as Sylvester now acknowledges in the statement below, never happened.
>
> We have removed the article from the Voice Web site and begun a review of the entire piece. Sylvester has been suspended.

When Rosenthal passed away, in May 2006, many of his obituaries made note of his role as the father of the modern correction. The Associated Press said he "began the paper's practice, now imitated by many others, of running corrections as a prominent daily fixture."

The *Los Angeles Times* wrote, "When the newspaper erred, he insisted that it admit its mistakes in a daily Corrections column, which he introduced in 1972. He later added the Editor's Note, which addressed flaws such as errors of omission and lapses in taste and standards."

Rosenthal's successor, Max Frankel, is credited with his own tweak on the correction. He insisted on standardizing how they are written. This is where the trail of innovation in corrections goes cold. As for the online world, its innumerable Web sites that generate articles or post stories from other sources have been compelled to begin posting online corrections, though a widely used standard for them has yet to emerge.

The placement, presentation, and preparation of a correction largely remains stuck in 1972, if not earlier. Papers that don't use the Rosenthal method, and there are many in North America, with even more in the United Kingdom and beyond, are still in the seventeenth century.

Rosenthal's innovation, while an impressive personal legacy, has been followed by more than three decades of editorial complacency in the area of corrections. Since 1972, the media landscape has evolved at an often furious pace, yet newspaper editors have failed to address the problems, old and new, that have plagued the correction.

The *Times'* most recent alteration to its corrections was to label smaller errors of fact as "For the Record," and more substantive errors as "Corrections." The paper also introduced a corrections policy for its op-ed section in 2005. The labeling makes no substantive difference to readers, while the op-ed corrections policy is beyond long overdue; its announcement, though, included an important comment from editorial page editor Gail Collins.

"These days, everything we publish is stored not only in the *Times* archives and commercially available archives, but in the files of an army of search engines," she wrote. "We don't want a college student of 2050 to come up with the wrong year for James Madison's death because of our error—particularly not when we have the means to amend the record."

The *Times* is hardly behind the curve. Rosenthal's innovation in 1972 and the paper's effective use of online corrections today have managed to keep it at or near the front of the corrections pack. Which is exactly the problem. Throughout the industry, corrections have been tweaked but not reexamined. Shuffle the *Titanic*'s deck chairs all you want; they'll still end up useless on the ocean floor.

Rosenthal's passing brought the correction into the limelight. In the process, it also revealed its stagnation and its current problems. As he is the recently enshrined father of the modern correction, it's perhaps fitting, and certainly not surprising, that his obit resulted in a few corrections of its own. In his honor, I offer this correction from the May 12, 2006, edition of the *Washington Post:*

THE OBITUARY FOR A.M. 'Abe' Rosenthal published May 11 incorrectly reported the death of *New York Times* publisher Arthur Ochs Sulzberger. He is 80.

The *Times*, as well as many other papers, has often sought to draw its reporters' attention to the importance of accuracy and errors.

"In the fall of 2000, Joseph Lelyveld, then executive editor, the highest-ranking editor at *The Times*, sent the strong message that too many mistakes were finding their way into the news pages; someone had even misspelled the publisher's surname, Sulzberger," reported the *Times* article about Jayson Blair's transgressions. "That prompted Mr. Landman to appoint an editor to investigate and tally the corrections generated by the metropolitan staff."

Landman sent staff an e-mail declaring, "Accuracy is all we have. It's what we are and what we sell."

The corrections tally, often a database operated by a newspaper's public editor or ombudsman, is another recent invention, though it has hardly attained widespread use in the industry. Many publications have no idea how many corrections they publish, what the breakdown is of types of errors, or which reporters were responsible. They often have to use an external news database such as Nexis should they want to try to gather this type of information. Most corrections are published and forgotten. They are rarely used as tools for learning or data on which to build error-prevention programs. The intelligence and insight contained in corrections goes largely unexploited.

The status quo of how to handle a mistake ensures that very few readers actually read the correct information. They can't be bothered to scan A2 every day to see whether something they read yesterday or a few days ago was incorrect. Though some papers have a toll-free number and specific e-mail address that readers can use to report errors, many publications are without even these basic measures.

After the *Times* introduced a toll-free number and e-mail address in 2000, it saw a "spurt in the number of printed corrections, as the paper learned about more of its mistakes," according to Allan M. Siegal. In 1982, a study found that the paper printed an average of one correction per day. By 2004, it was averaging close to nine.

Though it may seem surprising, the more corrections a paper prints, the more it deserves to be trusted. A paper with no corrections is simply not paying attention to accuracy; nor is it creating an environment whereby sources and readers can point out errors.

Another result of the stagnation of corrections is that too many of them fail to offer a clear explanation of the error and an adequate expression of the correct information. Errors often involve a person; ergo, a correction should be written with humanity rather than in dry stock phrases that ignore questions any reader would have. Who was the person in that photo? How did the mistake happen?

Today's corrections are often too brief, too obscure. They read like the hurried work of an editor tasked with an unpleasant chore, or in the worst examples, as the result of an effort to conceal rather than disclose. The reality is that corrections exist more to absolve a publication than to inform its readers.

The correction must evolve.

Online Corrections

THE GROWTH OF ONLINE NEWS has brought with it a requirement for the online correction. With more and more stories reprinted online and more online-specific work being created, the correction has moved from a paper-based entity to one that must now stretch to Web sites and databases. As copy flows, so should the correction. But that's not the case for many major media outlets. The technology of news is advancing past the current corrections standard.

The Internet offers the opportunity for publications to place a correction within the story itself and keep it there forever. Readers happening upon the story days or years after it was initially published can see the correction and the story in one place. The Internet is in fact a better medium for correcting errors, but it isn't yet being used to its full potential. (I offer some suggestions for improving online corrections in Chapter 14.)

At the high end of the current online standard for newspapers, both the *New York Times* and the *Washington Post*, along with others such as the *Los Angeles Times*, have settled on a similar style. They have a static corrections page linked from their home page; they link to the corrected story from this page, and they place the correction within the text of the article itself. The *Post* puts the correction at the top of the piece. The *Times* tags articles with "Correction Appended" at the top and runs the correction at the end of the piece.

Unfortunately, too many papers merely "scrub" the text of the article to eliminate the incorrect information, never advising the reader of the error or the correction. Scrubbing is a troublesome practice because it goes against the ethic of correction: The error is never acknowledged. Scrubbing is, in effect, a cover-up. It's unprincipled and disingenuous.

Even many bloggers have come to routinely correct their online errors by striking a line through the incorrect text and placing the correct information after it. The reader is thus able to see the original error in its original location. This offers a contextual correction.

Along with the scrubbing issue, an alarming number of newspapers are still without an online corrections page, let alone the commitment to place a correction within the online version of the relevant article. The *New York Post*, New York *Daily News*, *USA Today*, *San Diego Union-Tribune*, and *Detroit Free Press* are but a few of the larger American papers that run corrections in print but don't post them to the Internet on a set corrections page.

In the UK, only the *Guardian, Independent*, and *Daily Mirror* and their associated Sunday publications have dedicated online corrections pages. Other papers, such as the *Times* of London, put corrections online, but the only way to find them is to know the exact correction you're looking for, which defeats the purpose. Readers should encounter corrections as they read the article in question; they shouldn't have to go hunting. (In responding to a reader letter inquiring about its corrections policy, the *Times* noted that "a retired and much missed senior executive of *The Times* used to tell complainants that the miscreant would be hanged and the body buried in an unmarked grave, but that wasn't actually true.")

In Canada, only four newspapers—the *Globe and Mail*, the *National Post, The Gazette* (Montreal), and the *Toronto Star*—have dedicated online corrections pages.

The absence of an industry standard for online corrections is a lapse that speaks to a disturbing lack of attention to corrections and accuracy. The Internet is a medium that offers a multitude of opportunities for innovative corrections practices.

Of course, it's only fair to note that broadcast outlets are even worse when it comes to handling corrections, online or on the air.

Broadcast Corrections

A 2003 ARTICLE IN THE *American Journalism Review* quoted David McCormick, then NBC News executive producer for broadcast standards, as saying that the last correction his newscast had aired had been more than a year before. "McCormick acknowledges that the electronic media could do a better job of addressing the smaller, 'less material' mistakes that newspapers ordinarily put in a correction box and that surveys indicate contribute to the erosion of the media's credibility with the public," the article reported.

McCormick's suggestion for correcting this kind of error was to place corrections on a Web site. As of this writing, close to four years after that article was published, NBC News does place corrections on MSNBC.com. But it is in the minority.

In today's converged media world, most broadcast outlets now maintain Web sites that run wire copy and, in some cases, produce a good deal of original reporting. Yet the number of them that have taken to the print practice of corrections is disturbingly low. Not only are on-air corrections extremely rare, but the online arm of broadcasters has for the most part chosen to meet a very low standard of correction. This increases the impact of broadcast errors.

As a fundamental rule, an error should be corrected in the same place it occurred. This increases the likelihood of viewers receiving the correct information. Posting it exclusively to the Web without directing viewers to the corrections page only serves the self-interest of the broadcaster by preventing embarrassing corrections from being seen on its show. As for online corrections, Mike Sims, director of news and operations for CBSNews.com, said:

ANY POTENTIAL ERROR will be looked at and will receive either a "clarification" or a "correction" depending on what is warranted. Where the clarification or correction is carried, and how long it remains on the site, depends on the importance of the issue. "The visibility it gets depends on how serious it is," said Sims, who also noted that unless an error is caught immediately, changes are always to be noted.

This is a troubling practice. How one defines "immediately" is a serious concern. If a story with an error is online for fifteen minutes, it's still possible that hundreds, thousands, or even more people read it. The principle of corrections is to correct a factual error, no matter how small, or how briefly it was made public. Sims said that there had been talk of an online corrections page, with Sims noting that they were "trying to find the best way" to create one. As of this writing, well over a year later, CBS News does not have a corrections page.

On the positive side, CBS is rare in the United States because, in the wake of the *60 Minutes II* story about Bush's National Guard record, it created the PublicEye blog to report on the inner workings of its newsroom and answer questions from the public.

As for other broadcast outlets, NBC publishes its broadcast corrections on MSNBC.com, National Public Radio employs an ombudsman and has an online corrections page, as does the CBC, the public broadcaster in Canada (though the CBC site does not correct errors made in television or radio broadcasts; it corrects only online errors). In the United Kingdom, the BBC previously devoted an entire section of its Web site to these issues but has since scaled back.

Surprisingly, the best cross-platform corrections policy belongs to a sports broadcaster and publisher, ESPN. Not only does it have a corrections page and ombudsman online, it also publishes corrections in all of its radio, TV, print, and online products. After an error appears in the original medium, the correction is placed on the company's online corrections page.

While ESPN's practice is impressive, it should also be a source of shame for all of the so-called hard news organizations that possess neither an online corrections page nor a cross-platform policy along with procedures to back it up. One is hard-pressed to find online corrections on the Web sites of broadcasters, and the on-air correction is perhaps the rarest bird of all.

Often, the corrections that are offered by broadcasters are more puzzling than helpful. When a Utah TV station aired an incorrect photo in September 2006, it published and broadcast this correction:

> LAST NIGHT WE BROUGHT YOU the story of a Salt Lake man accused of producing child pornography.
>   We apologize we showed the wrong picture of Jonathan Cordier and would like to show the correct one now.
> FBI agents arrested Cordier earlier this week...

Clearly, this was no ordinary misidentification. But the correction fails to explain what was "wrong" about the picture. Did it broadcast a photo of an innocent person? Is it possible that the station has no idea who the person was in the picture it broadcast? Either way, the correction leaves much to be desired, as does the overall lack of standardization for acknowledging errors in television news.

Television and radio news, which still command large audiences, are just as prone to serious, harmful errors as their print counterparts. Yet they appear to have a lower standard for corrections.

The Failure of Corrections

A 1998 SURVEY BY THE American Society of Newspaper Editors found that 63 percent of newspaper readers said they "felt better" when they saw corrections in a publication. But many see more sinister or arrogant factors at play. A 2005 survey saw two-thirds of Americans express the belief that the press ignores or even covers up known errors. A survey released in 2004 found that 54 percent of Canadians believe the press tries to cover up mistakes. It's even worse among young Canadians: 68 percent of those age nineteen to twenty-five believe the news media hides its errors.

"The news profession apparently sees it differently," wrote Scott Maier, a University of Oregon journalism professor and accuracy researcher, in a report about corrections. "A separate survey of journalists found that three-fourths contend they quickly report their mistakes."

Maier used the data he and Philip Meyer collected in their accuracy-check survey of newspapers in markets all over the United States to evaluate the number of times sources requested corrections to perceived errors. Their survey asked sources who claimed to have spotted an error to explain why they did or didn't ask for a correction, and what the result was. The survey results reinforced the idea that published corrections are an inadequate representation of the actual number of errors. Given the current state of the correction, it can't be seen as a meaningful journalistic function, because a high number of errors are not corrected.

Maier wrote that the research results "[challenge] journalists' widely held belief that errors, when detected, are commonly corrected. It is sobering that errors were brought to the attention of newspapers in only 300—about 11 percent—of the 2,700 stories in which news sources identified inaccuracy."

Maier found that sources who are more media savvy—"those working in business and government and those having extensive media contact"—are more likely to request a correction, and more likely to have success in doing so. There is a barrier to entry for corrections because so many press outlets don't have a prominently displayed e-mail address or toll-free number for readers to report corrections. For television and radio programs, it's even harder to locate the proper contact information for a correction. And so, for the most part, sources don't bother to request them.

Then there is the issue of how published corrections are actually written. When reading corrections, one often gets the impression that the editor responsible for writing it is doing his or her best to get it over with in as few words as possible so as not to draw any undue attention to it. If the goal of corrections is in fact to ensure that as many people who read the incorrect information are subsequently given the correct facts, then corrections would take on an entirely new form and placement. For example, I know of only two newspapers that regularly publish corrections—regardless of content or error—on the front page. Why is this such a taboo practice in the profession?

With the exception of Web sites that keep a week's or month's worth of corrections online on a static corrections page, corrections are rarely published for more than one day, even in the most serious instances of error. Miss a day of the paper, or neglect to read the corrections box, and you'll likely never spot a correction to an article you've read.

One of the most important places for a correction to appear today is in a publication's archives and other news databases. Too often, articles are corrected in the paper and not on the outlet's Web site. Or if they are, the story is not corrected in the database version, the most accessible historical record.

Of the corrections that are published, many are confusing, inadequate, misleading, or simply useless. Such was the case with this *Seattle Times* correction:

> INFORMATION IN THIS ARTICLE, originally published May 18, [2006] has been corrected. A previous version of this story contained an error.

How thoughtful of the *Times* to acknowledge that something was amiss. Of course, it didn't explain what the incorrect information was, or what the correct information is. But it's still a correction, albeit an entirely useless one. It appeared on the paper's Web site in May 2006 and was finally later updated to include the pertinent information, noting, "Edmonton defeated San Jose to clinch an NHL playoff series. A Thursday headline on the front page of Sports promoting an inside story referred to the incorrect losing team."

Newsday, a daily newspaper in New York, did a little better when a May 10, 2007, correction informed readers that, and only that, "'Selita Ebanks' name was misspelled in a photo caption yesterday."

Never mind how it was misspelled or where the photo appeared. Just move along, dear reader, there's nothing to see here.

Corrections can be as frustrating as the error that caused them. They often raise more questions than they answer, such as this March 2005 correction from Canada's *Globe and Mail*:

> HASH BROWNIES WERE NOT CONSUMED on *The Dawn and Drew Show.* Incorrect information appeared yesterday.

So what *was* consumed? And how did the mistake occur? These are logical questions any journalist would ask, and yet the press frequently fails to provide even the most basic information in a correction. One of the vaguest corrections I've come across was published in the *Orlando Sentinel* on June 24, 2005:

> A PROMOTIONAL ITEM in the Up Next feature on Page A2 Wednesday about a couple who make clown shoes reported incorrectly when the article would be published. The article is scheduled to appear in the Life & Times section at a later date.

(But we won't tell you when.)

From the *Miami Herald* of February 11, 2007:

> A Feb. 4 story about the fundraiser Relay for Life incorrectly identified Patty Hernandez.

(But we won't tell you how.)

And this from the Florida *Times-Union* of April 11, 2007:

> ONE PERSON WAS KILLED and six were injured in a Heckscher Drive crash Monday. A headline on Page B-1 Tuesday was misleading.

(But we won't tell you why.)

Corrections are useless if they don't contain the necessary information. Of course, corrections themselves occasionally need to be corrected.

This chain of error is usually amusing to those who follow corrections, but it's highly embarrassing for the press. On October 31, 2004, the *Akron Beacon Journal* ran a front-page correction to alert readers to an error in that day's edition:

> WATCHED ANY FUTBOL AMERICANO lately? The Channels television guide in today's *Akron Beacon Journal* says you can find it at 1 and 4 p.m. today on WJW (Channel 8). Due to a production error, the listings for the Browns vs. Eagles game at 1 and the Cowboys vs. the Packers at 4 are in Spanish. The information in English is on Page 2 in today's Premier section. Lo sentemos . . .

The next day it published this correction:

> WE GIVE UP. A front-page correction Sunday about a listing in the Channels television book having been written in Spanish contained an error—in Spanish. What we meant to say was "Lo sentimos" ("We're sorry"). What we inadvertently said was "Lo sentemos," which roughly translates "We sit it down." Oi, vai!

But that pair pales in comparison to this three-peat from the *Guardian* (UK):

> THE HOME OF CHARLES DARWIN, author of "On the Origin of Species," is Down House in Kent. It was garbled in a news report on page 12 on April 11. [Corrected April 21, 1998]

> IN A CORRECTION PUBLISHED in this column yesterday, we misspelt Downe House, the home of Charles Darwin in Kent. [Corrected April 22, 1998]

> A CORRECTION TO A CORRECTION of a correction. Darwin spelled both the name of his house and the village in which it is situated, Down. The village became Downe. The house is still Down. [Corrected April 23, 1998]

One of my personal pet peeves is when a newspaper misidentifies someone in a photo and the correction fails to identify who it was. Such is the case with this December 2005 correction from AP, as published in the *Fresno Bee:*

> AN ASSOCIATED PRESS PHOTOGRAPH that ran on Page B5 of Sunday's *Bee* was not of convicted murderer Mitchell Sims.

In this particular case, the misidentified person in the photo was also labeled a murderer.

Other corrections, like this from the November 22, 2001, edition of the *Ottawa Citizen,* leave the reader wondering what kind of person writes these things:

> THE *OTTAWA CITIZEN* AND *Southam News* wish to apologize for our apology to Mark Steyn, published Oct. 22. In correcting the incorrect statements about Mr. Steyn published Oct. 15, we incorrectly published the incorrect correction. We accept and regret that our original regrets were unacceptable and we apologize to Mr. Steyn for any distress caused by our previous apology.

As Mark Steyn, a journalist and author, later explained, he had in fact dictated this correction after the previous apology failed to meet his expectations. Steyn originally complained because he felt a columnist had libeled him. After the unsatisfactory first apology failed to address his concerns, he made the subsequent one consciously convoluted so as to make the paper look stupid.

Steyn said he "dictated this apology, more or less, off the top of my head. And [the editor] said to me, 'You're joking. We're going to look like a bunch of idiots.'"

Steyn's retort to the editor was that he "should have thought about that" before giving such a pathetic first apology.

The second apology was good enough to be read out on the *Tonight Show with Jay Leno.* For the *Citizen,* it was a good lesson in getting it right the, well, second time. Though only a journalist like Steyn would know how to properly stick it to a paper that libeled him.

The Art of Correction

FOR ALL THEIR FAILINGS, CORRECTIONS have an undeniable charm. In the right hands, they can become epic feats of wit and a powerful means of communication. One of the foremost corrections *artistes* is Ian Mayes, the former reader's editor (ombudsman) of the *Guardian* (UK).

Mayes never missed an opportunity to accentuate the inherent humor of a mistake while never overshadowing the correction itself. He was also adept at finding a way, in just a few words, to convey the fact that he—and therefore the paper itself—understood the serious nature of a particularly damaging error. Whether he had just tens of words or a couple of hundred of them to work with for a correction, he would polish them to perfection; in the process, his corrections were such marvels that he made the paper's corrections column a destination for readers, which is a difficult thing to achieve. But that should be the goal of every publication.

"The principle is a simple one: news organizations that, almost by definition, constantly call others to account should be more readily accountable and open themselves, and should be seen to be so," was how Mayes described the role of the ombudsman in an article in the *British Journalism Review.*

After a decade on the job, he stepped down in March 2007 to write the latest in a series of books about the history of the *Guardian.* In recognition of his work for the paper, his departure was given four pages of coverage, undoubtedly a record for any departing ombudsman, a position that is unique in its ability to anger both readers and journalists alike. Ombudsmen are a much-maligned but entirely necessary group of journalists. Mayes was among the best of the discipline. During his tenure, he received more than ninety thousand complaints from readers and wrote fourteen thousand corrections.

"When I started, the whole of the British media was gripped in a culture of denial—a resistance to correcting," Mayes told the *Press*

Gazette. "Denying that mistakes occurred was really the name of the game. We set out to change that. It was not a tenable situation and the advent of digital media has made it less tenable. People expect to get answers from us now."

Mayes did more than provide answers and the necessary correction to erroneous reporting; he often elevated correction writing to an art. From the November 7, 2005, *Guardian* corrections column:

> IN A MISPLACED OUTBREAK of politeness, the Weatherwatch column, page 39, November 1, described average temperatures in Tromso and Bergen as being "0C and 3C respectfully".

While this correction was by no means one of Mayes's literary feats, he added a touch of humor to an otherwise banal error and correction. He again flexed his talent for humor in this August 24, 1998, correction:

> WE REFERRED TO THE £250,000 advance for Vikram Seth's prize-winning novel, "A Suitable Buy." Although undoubtedly worth every penny, the book is actually called "A Suitable Boy."

He has also been frank about the paper's frequent mistakes, often using a correction to make a point about a particular error. On August 21, 1998, he published a rather blunt correction:

> WE SPELT MORECAMBE, the town in Lancashire, wrong again on page 2, G2, yesterday. We often do.

That correction, which has become a favorite among readers, is both an admission to readers and a message to *Guardian* reporters and editors.

"People remember that [correction] in a way that has sort of surprised me," Mayes told the Associated Press. "But the intention was that it would be memorable . . . particularly to the journalists on *The Guardian* so that they would stop doing it. And I think by and large it doesn't occur in the way that it used to."

He pegged another common mistake in a June 17, 2005, correction:

> SEVEN YEARS AGO NEW LEGISLATION transformed industrial tri-
> bunals into employment tribunals and this column has
> pointed out that change on as many occasions: January 27
> 2000; March 5 2002; October 18 2002; June 23 2003;
> September 16 2003; February 27 2004; and January 22 2005.
> Nevertheless, they cling to existence, most recently in Alarm
> bells ring again at FA, page 31, June 15.

And made a subtler dig at his paper's hubris in this June 23, 2005, correction:

> IN AN ITEM, MILLIONAIRES AT SEA, about Who Wants to be a
> Millionaire Live, at a theatre in Eastbourne, page 10, G2, yes-
> terday, we note the ignorance of some of the contestants and
> say: Another doesn't know that heuvos fritos is Spanish for
> fried eggs. It isn't, but huevos fritos is.

On February 2, 1999, came the inevitable:

> THE ABSENCE OF CORRECTIONS yesterday was due to a technical
> hitch rather than any sudden onset of accuracy.

Some of these classics were collected in Mayes's 2000 book, *The Guardian Corrections and Amplifications*. Along with the *New York Times'* collection, *Kill Duck Before Serving*, it is one of only two books published by newspapers about their own corrections. These books demonstrate the newspapers' admirable willingness to laugh at themselves.

Indeed, the *Guardian* is so noted for its misspellings that the English publication *Private Eye* has taken to calling it "The Grauniad" because it's inevitable that the paper will one day get its own name wrong. And yet the *Guardian*'s dedication to corrections is unmatched in the British press, and many credit Mayes for playing a major role in making it so.

Even though UK papers are in general not as faithful in the practice of correction as their North American counterparts, there is an undeniable charm to the work of their error acknowledgments. Often, however, the colorful and reprehensible reporting that prompted the correction is the source of its humor and delight. I awarded 2006's Correction of the Year to this May 1 stunner from the *Sun*, an English tabloid:

> FOLLOWING OUR ARTICLE on Princess Eugenie's birthday celebrations, we have been asked to point out the party was closely monitored by adults throughout and while a small amount of mess was cleared away at the end of the evening, there was no damage to furniture, no revellers dived into bedrooms in search of drunken romps and to describe the house as being trashed was incorrect. We are happy to make this clear and regret any distress our report caused.

THE CORRECTION HAS ALSO BEEN USED as a means to both acknowledge an error and land one more jab at a source's expense. The phenomenon of the correction-as-weapon is both amusing and troubling. A correction should by all means read as though a human wrote it, but journalists should resist the urge to turn corrections into parlor tricks or platforms for airing personal gripes.

Editorial writer and columnist Patrick McGann of the *Lewiston Morning Tribune* in Idaho used the language of correction to append a note at the end of an October 2004 column. After a candidate for the U.S. House of Representatives whom the paper had previously praised as being "classy" chose to run what McGann deemed to be a nasty attack ad, he ended a column with this "correction":

> AN OCT. 1 EDITORIAL REFERRED to Washington state Rep. Cathy McMorris, R-Colville as a "classy candidate." This page regrets the error.

Ian Hyland, a columnist for the *Sunday Mirror* in the United Kingdom, used a factual correction on September 25, 2005, as an opportunity to deliver a swift kick in the conclusion:

> LAST SUNDAY I IMPLIED Stretch Mark Durden-Smith wouldn't be presenting ITV2's I'm A Celebrity coverage because bosses didn't want to pay for his airplane seat(s). It has since transpired it's actually because his wife is expecting twins and is busily eating for three as we speak. So lovely when couples have something in common.

The humor is undeniable, and yet it couldn't help but make sources wonder if it's better to not ask for a correction than to offer the writer another opportunity to stick the knife in. Perhaps that thought occurred to an unlucky footballer who was the subject of an August 19, 2006, correction in the *Australian:*

> AN ARTICLE IN *The Australian* yesterday ("Tarrant caught out again as rock 'n' roll lifestyle lingers", page 31) said AFL footballer Chris Tarrant was "spotted at a Jet concert, drink in one hand, cigarette in the other". This was incorrect. *The Australian* accepts that Tarrant was not at the Jet concert. As reported, Tarrant was out late and drinking the previous Saturday night.

One need not turn nasty to use a correction for humor and humility. The *North-West News* of Brisbane, Australia, added a subtle jab at itself in a November 2006 correction:

> IN LAST WEEK'S MY NORTH WEST, the caption under the photograph of dirt biker Chris Bierton referred to the BMX competition he organised as "De-caking of dirt". Although dirt bikers no doubt often get covered with mud and dirt as they tear around tracks, the competition was called "DK King of the Dirt". Now there's mud in our eye—Ed.

Bankrate.com also bowed to humor when it mixed up some super-heroes in October 2006:

> OUR STORY ABOUT THE MOST POPULAR Halloween costumes of the season, first published Oct. 14, misidentified the super-speedy The Flash and Boy Wonder superhero Robin as Marvel comics characters. In fact, they are DC Comics superheroes. We regret this error; it is against Bankrate's policy, and just plain unwise, to cause offense to superhumans and superheroes.

The use of humor also extends beyond the correction and into more serious matters of apologies. Or, rather, what I call "pseudo-apologies"—expressions of regret that would seem like true apologies if it weren't for the writer's tongue being stuck firmly in his or her cheek. Once again, the Brits take it. The sport of soccer in particular has caused several UK tabloids to reach for pseudo-apologies.

From the *Sun*:

> RECENT ARTICLES in this column may have given the impression that Mr Sven Goran Eriksson was a greedy, useless, incompetent fool. This was a misunderstanding. Mr Eriksson is in fact a footballing genius. We are happy to make this clear.

Also from the *Sun:*

> SUNSPORT WOULD LIKE TO take this opportunity to say a heartfelt SORRY to Owen Hargreaves.
>
> Over recent weeks we might have given the impression we thought he was, well, rubbish.
>
> But Owen proved against Portugal, with his all-action performance, that he was well worth his place.
> Unlike soppy Sven, we're big enough to admit we got it wrong.

From the *Daily Star:*

IN PREVIOUS ISSUES of this newspaper, we may have given the impression that the people of France were snail swallowing garlic munching surrender-monkeys whose women never bother to shave their armpits.

We now realise that the French football team can stop the Portuguese—and in particular their cheating whingeing winger Cristiano Ronaldo—from getting to the World Cup Final which we so richly deserved to do.

We apologise profusely to France and its sporting heroes like Thierry Henry and Zinedine Zidane who we now accept are skilful, brave and the most wonderful neighbours we could ever wish for.

Vive La France!

The use of humor, humility, and a definitive writing style in corrections is a welcome way to elevate the genre. If only every publication ran such artful and witty corrections it would get them the attention they deserve, but only the few that take corrections seriously are willing to support the work of true corrections artists.

It is time for corrections to evolve, be brought into the world of the Internet and databases, and be given more prominence. I believe the correction is today an inadequate means of correcting the record, and many readers agree. The press should look at the correction in a critical manner and ask if, in its current form, it is actually working.

In their current form, corrections leave much to regret.

The Corrections
STRANGE AND SUBLIME

IN OUR LAST ISSUE . . . we may have given the impression that the conduct of the Federal Bureau of Investigation in the prosecution of Timothy McVeigh had been exemplary; that the trial of the Oklahoma City bomber had followed the legal textbook to the letter ("none of the usual tales about drunk lawyers and uncalled witnesses"); and that, "barring a miracle", he would be executed on May 16th. However, the FBI having suddenly discovered 3,000-odd pages of evidence that Mr McVeigh's lawyers should have received before his trial, and his execution having thus been postponed to June 11th (at least), we now accept unreservedly that we should have always known the Bureau was bound to cock it up in the end.   —*Economist*

             +

NEIGHBOURS TOLD POLICE that murder victim Roseanne Harry did not have any affairs before her death, contrary to a report yesterday. The error is regretted.

—*Dominion Post* (New Zealand)

             +

Because of an editing error, a recipe last Wednesday for meatballs with an article about foods to serve during the Super Bowl misstated the amount of chipotle chilies in adobo to be used. It is one or two canned chilies, not one or two cans.

—*New York Times*

Term considered derogatory: A *Canadian Press* story published Tuesday made a reference to "rig pigs" as if the term were an acceptable one in the oil industry for drilling rig workers. In fact, the term is considered derogatory and outdated.

—*Canadian Press*

             +

An error in reading a shorthand note caused us to quote Phil Sawford, who is defending Kettering for Labour, as accusing his ex-colleague Brian Sedgemore as "pissing in the pool" after he had defected to the Liberal Democrats (Sedgemore bolsters Lib Dems' Iraq attack, page 4, yesterday). What Mr Sawford told our reporter was that Mr Sedgemore had "peed" in the pool. He does not use the word piss nor does he like it. Apologies.

—*Guardian* (UK)

A Japanese fish expert suggested that sushi grade tuna be stored at less than minus 20 degrees Centigrade when asked how long the fish could be safely kept before using. A page-one article Monday about an e-mail network called Foodsafe failed to include the minus.   —*Wall Street Journal*

✦

Because of an editing error, an article in Opinion Sunday incorrectly reported that Tommy James and the Shondells will appear at North Fork Theater in the next few months. No appearance for James is scheduled, and the Shondells are defunct as a group.   —*Newsday* (New York)

✦

A headline in Monday's *Daily News*, "He regrets his role in 'postal' vid," implied that Richard Marino, the subject of a YouTube video, was sorry for an incident in December at a Brooklyn post office. Marino, in fact, is not sorry. The *News* regrets the error.   —*Daily News* (New York)

✦

In Tuesday's column, Jim DeFede incorrectly stated that Miami Police Chief John Timoney was grabbing protesters and spewing profanities at them during the Free Trade Area of the America's summit. The *Herald* previously reported that Timoney only grabbed one protester by the arm and swore at one protester.   —*Miami Herald*

✦

A recipe in the Entrée section Sunday for Mr. C's Bread Pudding misstated the length of time for baking the pudding. The recipe calls for baking it for 40 minutes, not 540 minutes.
                                   —*Milwaukee Journal-Sentinel*

✦

BECAUSE OF A LAYOUT ERROR, paintings running alongside "The fake" and "The genuine article" on the front page of Tuesday's Globe Review were reversed.

—*Globe and Mail* (Canada)

✦

An item on Page 5P of Thursday's Rocky Preps football preview section said running back Devon Knight would be a key player for Horizon High this fall. Knight, however, died in an April car crash after the school's prom. The *News* apologizes for the error.   —*Rocky Mountain News* (Colorado)

✦

Country musician Buck Owens died in March. His name was inadvertently included Saturday in the list of celebrity birthdays on the Live! page.   —*Star-Telegram* (Texas)

✦

For the Record . . . In the December issue, we mistakenly ran the box cover art of the first "Swallow My Squirt" from Elegant Angel with our review of "Swallow My Squirt 2." Here's the correct box. We swallow our pride and apologize.

—*Adult Video News*

✦

The Clark and Barlow Hardware Co. at 353 W. Grand has been in business since 1876. The store was incorrectly listed under "new" hardware stores in the greater downtown area on a map that appeared in Sunday's editions with the article "Downtown Future in the Bag."   —*Chicago Sun-Times*

✦

MSNBC.com on Friday, March 17, published an Associated Press story about a Lake Geneva, Wis., high school student who was cited for disorderly conduct for wearing a dress to his prom. It was later discovered that the story was more than 10 months old.   —MSNBC.com

✦

A March 5 article about problems with MetroAccess service did not make it clear that Scott McDaniel, a MetroAccess rider, is an employee of Service Sources Inc., which operates the Woodmont Center in Arlington County. The article also misstated the nature of his disabilities. McDaniel is legally blind, and although he has other disabilities, he and his parents say he is not mentally disabled.   —*Washington Post*

✦

The *Istanbul Journal* article on Feb. 14 about "Valley of the Wolves—Iraq," a popular Turkish-made film that depicts American soldiers in Iraq as tyrannical occupiers, referred imprecisely to scenes cited by the screenwriter as "inspired by real events." While two such scenes—the killing of Iraqis by American soldiers and the mistreatment of inmates at Abu Ghraib prison—have been documented, the scene depicting an American Jewish surgeon at Abu Ghraib removing organs from Iraqi prisoners for shipment to recipients in New York, London and Israel is fictional.   —*New York Times*

✦

A quote that appeared April 19 in an article about the late Betty Steflik may have been misleading. The article referred to Jack Plimpton as a friend of the late activist and quoted Plimpton as saying naming the bridge after Steflik was like "naming a bar after an alcoholic." Plimpton was using a simile, and Steflik was not an alcoholic. Plimpton knew Steflik partly from working with her on city projects. He is not close to her family.

—*Daytona Beach News-Journal*

✦

A STORY APRIL 20 REFERRED TO the stories of the Tuskegee
Airmen from 1941–1946 in Tuskegee, Ala., as the Tuskegee
Experiment. The article should have clarified that another
Tuskegee experiment took place from 1932–1972 in Tuskegee,
Ala., in which the federal government sponsored a study that
examined the impact of syphilis among black men. The gov-
ernment withheld medical treatment from 399 men with
syphilis, who were not told they had the disease.

—*Daytona Beach News-Journal*

The Budapest story headlined "Hungary workers get shock at
bottom of rum barrel" issued on May 4 is withdrawn. Police
said the incident, reported on a police magazine Web site, happened 10 years ago. Reuters has been unable to make any further checks to substantiate the story. There will be no substitute story.   —Reuters

In the Oct. 17 Sunday Source, the 'Gatherings' story
described a Republican barbecue held to watch a presidential
debate. The item reported 'the possibly unprecedented occurrence of a young woman in a cowboy hat pretending to make
out with a poster of Dick Cheney.' The item should have
explained that the woman was asked to pose with the vice
president's picture by the photographer working for *The
Washington Post*. The woman also did not pretend to 'make
out' with the picture; at the photographer's suggestion, she
pretended to blow a kiss at it. The item should have explained
that the party was hosted in response to a request from *The
Post*, which discussed the decorations and recipes with the
host and agreed to reimburse the cost of recipe ingredients.

—*Washington Post*

Dustin Neff was cited 7:54 p.m. Sunday at the Casey's parking lot in West Burlington for urinating and defecating in public. While that was how police formally described the incident, Neff was observed only urinating.

—*Hawk Eye* (Iowa)

Megan Thomas was incorrectly identified Wednesday as a seventh-grader at Erwine Middle School. She is a ninth-grader at North Middle School. It was also incorrectly stated that the person she admires the most is her grandfather. It should have said her sister.   —*Akron Beacon Journal*

A story in Tuesday's Tropical Life section about the safety of personal-care products misstated the views of Irene Malbin of the Cosmetic, Toiletry and Fragrance Association. She did not suggest that shampoos and hair dyes might have cancer-causing ingredients.   —*Miami Herald*

In a March 2 "Culturebox," Timothy Noah described the words humbug, poppycock, tommyrot, hooey, twaddle, balderdash, claptrap, palaver, hogwash, buncombe (or "bunk"), hokum, drivel, flapdoodle, and bullpucky as adjectives. In fact, they are nouns.   —*Slate*

A story in Thursday's *News* concerning Dr. Donald Dyson's controversial speech to Cumberland Regional High School seniors on Wednesday incorrectly indicated that a second speaker participated in the program. The story indicated that, according to a parent, this second speaker reportedly had a sexually transmitted disease. In fact, there was no second speaker during Dyson's presentation.

A presentation on abstinence and STDs delivered to CRHS seniors on Tuesday was presented by a health educator, not someone suffering from an STD.

—*Bridgeton News* (New Jersey)

＊

IN A STORY SUPPLIED TO US on October 4, quotes attributed to actor Chevy Chase about Mel Gibson were actually lines taken from a script spoken by his character and not by Chevy Chase.

"These statements were made under the influence of alcohol and sleep medication," are actually quotes from the script from his upcoming episode of *Law & Order* and Chevy Chase in no way implied he was defending Mel Gibson.

We apologise for this error and any inconvenience.

—*Evening Echo* (UK)

＊

An article on Sept. 17 about the abundance of satire in American culture referred incorrectly to an episode of "South Park." In it, the character Cartman tricks another child into eating his own parents in a bowl of chili; Cartman himself does not eat them.   —*New York Times*

＊

A story Monday about Bishop O'Hara High School students' visit to Quebec City, Canada, mistakenly attributed a statement about the Quebecois having a reputation for being rude to English speakers to Carmel D'Angelo, a school official and chaperone for the trip. Mrs. D'Angelo did not express the sentiment, which was actually an observation made by the reporter.

—*Times-Tribune* (Pennsylvania)

＊

Headline referred to trailers, not residents: In some Thursday editions, a headline on a story about illegal travel trailers said "Kenner targeting 'trailer trash'." The phrase "trailer trash" was not used by anyone quoted in the story and was not intended in the headline to refer to Kenner residents living in FEMA trailers. The headline referred to the trailers themselves.

—*Times-Picayune* (New Orleans)

A Feb. 5 Names & Faces item on an Evite e-mail invitation to Michael Saylor's birthday party was based on a copy of the invitation that had been partially forged before it was sent to *The Post*. The original Evite from MicroStrategy's chief executive said the party will be "exotic, mysterious and ebullient," but it did not say "erotic." It said "Think 'Alias' (the TV show), but sexier" but did not include "much sexier," as was reported. The original also specified "cocktail dresses" but did not say "the shorter the better." And, the original did not end with—or even contain—the words "no one leaves alone." Nor was there anything in the original invitation unfit for a family newspaper. The birthday celebration involved dinner and dancing at the Ortanique restaurant for about 200 guests.

—*Washington Post*

Imaging satellites: An article in the Nov. 5 Travel section about Google Earth ["Talk About Global Outreach," Her World] called the Keyhole satellite system a fictional part of Tom Clancy novels. It is a spy satellite program by the U.S. military.

—*Los Angeles Times*

SEVERAL READERS COMPLAIN that the dancing cow illustrating Feedback, 20 January, appears to have six teats. It was of course drawn as seen by an intoxicated fellow dancer.

—*New Scientist*

In the article Therapy in Song in last week's Green Guide it was stated incorrectly that the aria Bastard, written as part of therapeutic treatment, was written about the patient's husband. In fact, it was about a doctor in a private clinic.

—*Age* (Australia)

A column in yesterday's Today section implied that the National Football League would never return the Super Bowl to Detroit. The football championship is scheduled to return to the city next year.

—*Baltimore Sun*

So Sorry
REMARKABLE APOLOGIES

ON 13 FEBRUARY WE PUBLISHED an article headed "Who bum it?" reporting that two Premiership footballers and a music industry figure had a "gay romp" in which a mobile phone was used as a "gay sex toy". On 16 February we published a picture of Mr Cole and his fiancee headed 'Ashley's got a good taste in rings'. Some readers have understood that Mr Cole was one of the two Premiership players involved in the gay sex and that Choice FM DJ, Masterstepz, was the music industry figure.

We are happy to make clear that Mr Cole and Masterstepz were not involved in any such activities. We apologise to them for any distress caused and we are paying them each a sum by way of damages. *The Sun* wishes Ashley all the best for next Saturday's World Cup quarter-final.

—*Sun* (UK)

❖

On Monday, February 27, 2006 in a report under the headlines: "Rats Trapped" "Bungling gang gets stuck in lift", we
stated that eight people who were trapped in a lift at Dundalk
Greyhound Stadium were criminally involved in a botched raid
on the stadium on Saturday, February 25 last.

We fully accept that the above-recited allegations made
about these persons were totally false and without foundation.
We wish to retract the entirety of the false statements made
concerning them.

We accept that although they were not named or pictured,
some readers would have understood the article as referring to
the eight persons named above and we accept that the article
was defamatory of them.

Accordingly we apologise to each of them for the
embarrassment and hurt caused to them by the publication
of our report.

We have agreed to pay a sum in damages to each of them
and their appropriate legal costs.

—*Daily Mirror* (UK)

❖

In a diary item, page 31, on Wednesday October 19, we attributed
remarks and actions to Andy Trotter, deputy chief constable of the
British Transport Police, which we now fully accept were not
made by him. We did not discuss the contents of the diary item
with Mr Trotter prior to publication, nor did we make any attempt
to do so, and indeed had no evidence to support them. We regret
publication of this item and are happy to be able to correct this
matter now. We apologise to Mr Trotter for any distress caused.

—*Guardian* (UK)

❖

Following the publication of an interview with Glenda Gilson on 11 September 2006, Ms Gilson contacted us to state that the words published on the front page: 'I haven't had sex for four months' were not words used by her.

While we accept that these precise words were not used by Ms Gilson we believe that they conveyed the sense of what was said in part of the article published on pages eight and nine to which the readers' attention was expressly drawn.

We acknowledge that Glenda Gilson was offended by the words in question and we wish to express our regret for any offence caused to her and her family.   —*Daily Mirror* (UK)

A BACK-PAGE HEADLINE in yesterday's *Daily Telegraph* ("Can't Bat, Can Bowl") may have inferred that Australian cricketer Andrew Symonds' success with the ball was a one-off in an otherwise fading Test career.

After watching Symonds blast South Africa yesterday with the bat—including a record six sixes in an innings at the MCG—*The Daily Telegraph* concedes it was wrong and apologises unreservedly for any hurt and embarrassment caused.

With each of the Queensland all-rounder's big hits, the paper went a deeper shade of red.

And by the time Symonds had helped rip through the South Africans in the second innings, the *Telegraph* would have eaten its hat if it had one.

It is now accepted Symonds is indeed a quality Test cricketer after scoring 72 and taking 2-6, and he will be warmly welcomed by Sydneysiders when he plays at the SCG.

—*Daily Telegraph* (Australia)

On May 20 and May 27, 2007, *The Mail on Sunday* published stories claiming that TV news presenter Jon Snow had an affair with a writer called Precious Williams, and that they smoked cannabis together. There is no truth in these allegations.

We accept that in fact Mr Snow never had any relationship with Miss Williams, and that the allegation of drug-taking was unfounded.

We are happy to set the record straight, and we apologise for the embarrassment caused.   —*Daily Mail* (UK)

＊

An item on 2 August last year "Telly Teri's Romps in Van" stated that actress Teri Hatcher had sex romps in her VW camper van at her home.

Although published in good faith, we now accept that the article was totally incorrect and we apologise to Ms Hatcher for the embarrassment caused.   —*Sun* (UK)

＊

In our March 25 article "Countdown to disaster", we alleged that Carol Vorderman made the job of Countdown's production crew difficult because she was so demanding. We now realise this is completely without foundation. We accept that Ms Vorderman has had an excellent, extremely close working relationship with the programme's production team for more than 23 years.

We also accept that the caption to our accompanying front page photograph of Ms Vorderman "Has TV Carol become a hate figure?" was unwarranted and caused offence to Ms Vorderman. We apologise sincerely to Ms Vorderman for the hurt and distress caused.   —*Daily Express* (UK)

＊

In two articles published last year ("Cyanide fear triggered terror raid" and "Bomb suspect 'shot without warning'", June 4) we stated that government officials had said Abul Koyair, the brother of Abdul Kahar (who was shot by police when they raided the family home on June 2) had a number of criminal convictions and that their parents had gone on a planned holiday despite what had happened to their sons. We now understand, and accept, that that information was not true, that the decision to raid the family's home was based on false intelligence and that the family have never been involved in terrorism. We apologise for any embarrassment caused.

—*Times* (UK)

On 12 August we named Amjad Sarwar (pictured above) as one of the suspects who had been arrested in the recent terrorist plots to blow up numerous passenger aircraft, and also published his photograph.

We wish to make clear that this suggestion was false, and Mr Sarwar has not been arrested nor questioned in connection with the terrorist plots.

We apologise to Mr Sarwar for the distress and embarrassment caused to him by our publication of these false allegations.

—*Daily Mirror* (UK)

On 26 April 2006 we reported that Euan Blair was drunk and tried to set fire to a table in a bar in Washington. We now accept that this was untrue and apologise for any embarrassment caused to Euan Blair by the publication.

—*Daily Mirror* (UK)

A feature article (*Yorkshire Post*, 1 June 2006 and on www.yorkshiretoday.co.uk) entitled "Nudes and Prudes—time we face the naked truth" reported that Morien Jones had filmed his neighbour, Lynette Burgess, while she was sunbathing naked in her back garden, and that he had reported this to the police, resulting in Ms Burgess' prosecution for indecent exposure (of which she was subsequently acquitted). Our article, which was based on an agency report, suggested that Mr Jones was a voyeur. In fact, Ms Burgess was filmed because she decided to walk naked on Mr

Jones' driveway at the front of his house. She was not filmed on her own property, and it was not even Mr Jones who did the filming. The filming took place as part of a process of gathering evidence against Ms Burgess in the context of a possible court action against her for ongoing acts of harassment, an exercise which was carred [sic] out on police advice. We apologise unreservedly to Mr Jones for the distress and embarrassment caused to him by our publication of these false allegations. As a mark of our regret we have agreed to pay him damages and his legal costs.

—*Yorkshire Post* (UK)

＊

A review in the Book Review on June 18 about "Sex Collectors: The Secret World of Consumers, Connoisseurs, Curators, Creators, Dealers, Bibliographers, and Accumulators of 'Erotica,'" by Geoff Nicholson, referred to one collector, Naomi Wilzig, as "foul mouthed." The book, however, does not describe her as such, and the one mild vulgarism it attributes to her did not merit the adjective. The Book Review regrets the misrepresentation. —*New York Times*

＊

On 16 April we reported on an interview given by Bryan Ferry to a German newspaper. Our article was headed "The Nazis were so amazing" and claimed that Mr Ferry had been "singing the praises of the Nazis". We now accept this was not true. In fact, Mr Ferry had spoken only of his admiration from an artistic point of view for some aspects of German art, architecture and presentation which were associated with the Nazi regime. He made no mention of the Nazi regime nor did he use the word "Nazi". We accept that Mr Ferry abhors the Nazi regime and all it stood for.

We apologise to Mr Ferry for the offence caused by our report and are happy to set the record straight.

—*Daily Mirror* (UK)

IN A REPORT ABOUT THE SCOTTISH ELECTIONS, an editing error led to us wrongly suggesting that John Swinburne of the Scottish Senior Citizens' Unity Party had been accused of allegedly causing a breach of the peace by running amok in a polling station with a golf club (Recrimination follows chaos over new Scots voting procedures, page 5, May 5). We apologise to Mr Swinburne for any embarrassment or distress caused.

—*Guardian* (UK)

IN WIMBLEDON DIARY, page 35, June 23, we incorrectly reported that Brian Lara had been thrown out of the press box on Court two at Wimbledon. Mr Lara and his longstanding partner were not thrown out and left before the end of the match when their transport arrived. We apologise for any embarrassment and upset caused to Mr Lara and his partner.

—*Guardian* (UK)

The Nov. 29 comic Schizophrenic Bosnian depicted a character calling the crane the "gayest-looking of all birds." *The Cavalier Daily* regrets printing this comic and deeply apologizes to those who were offended.

—*Cavalier Daily* (University of Virginia)

A story titled "Church silence deepens AIDS crisis, says bishop", published on October 27, said Mr Carlos Perera was HIV-positive.

Mr Perera says he is not HIV-positive. *The New Zealand Herald* accepts this and apologises to Mr Perera for the misstatement.   —*New Zealand Herald*

CHAPTER 11

THE DISAPPEARANCE OF NEWSPAPER PROOFREADING

U P UNTIL AROUND THE 1970s, when computers began making serious inroads into the editorial and printing processes of newspapers, one could expect to enter the headquarters of a newspaper and be led into a room filled with a row of (mostly) men wearing green visors and staring at the galleys of the next day's edition. Separate from the floors where writing, editing, printing, ad sales, and distribution took place, this was the den of the proofreader. They often found themselves in a room close to the cranking, almost rhythmic noise that shouted from the Linotype machines used to set the newspaper's stories into small bricks of lead type suitable for the printing press. As each row of words was entered into the machine and then spat out as freshly hardened type, they were placed together to form whole stories and entire pages. With the quick application of some ink and paper, a story would be printed as a one-off proof, or galley, and taken next door to the proofreaders.

Proofreaders were the final line of defense against typos, grammatical errors, factual errors, and other mistakes. They were among the last people to see the paper and give it its final review before it was sent off for printing. Proofreaders were "the best-educated of craft workers, and their incidental discoveries rescued many a writer's reputation," wrote Allan M. Siegal, who retired as the standards editor of the *New York Times* in 2006, in the introduction of the corrections compilation *Kill Duck Before Serving*. Siegal described proofreaders as "those artisans in green eyeshades who pored over the printer's galley letter by letter alongside the writer's manuscript."

Carl Schlesinger, 81, started at the *Times* in 1953 and worked as both a proofreader and Linotype operator until his retirement in 1990. For him, the composing room—where the Linotype operators, proofreaders, and others worked—was an almost musical place. "You'd turn on 10 Linotype machines and hear the humming, clicking and smashing," he told me. "You couldn't talk over the noise. When we got to the last minute of the nine o'clock [p.m. deadline] crescendo you could hear the humming and banging. . . . It had all the sounds of a symphony and all the drama that goes along with it."

The proofreading room was home to its own soundscape. One of the main responsibilities of a proofreader was to ensure that the type version of a story matched the original copy written and edited by the news team. Proofreaders checked grammar, spelling, and facts and ensured that the spacing and hyphenation were correct. A proofreader would check the original manuscript against a proof of the type produced by the Linotype operators. Rather than compare one against the other on their own, proofers often had an assistant read out the original copy while they inspected the type version. This relationship gave rise to a unique language of sounds and actions.

"For any statistical table [like stocks] we used to have symbols which involved hands and feet," he told me. "To indicate a period [the assistants] would hit their foot on the ground. For the end of a regular paragraph of type you would just touch your foot on the ground. And at the end of a sentence you would lower your voice."

The assistant would also slap his or her hand on the table to indicate if the first letter of a word was capitalized. "Hands and feet were going just as much as mouths," Schlesinger said. "It was part of the lore of printing."

"Farewell, Etaoin Shrdlu"

SCHLESINGER WAS THE PRODUCER and narrator of *Farewell, Etaoin Shrdlu*, a documentary made about the last night of "hot type" typesetting at the *Times*. He also composed a poem and song of the same name. The film is a snapshot of July 2, 1978, the very day when computers killed off the Linotype operators and proofreaders at one of the world's largest newspapers. After that, Schlesinger stayed on and would eventually train roughly 125 former Linotype operators and others to use the new computerized systems before he retired in 1990. "During that period there was a great sense of loneliness and blues," he told me. "People felt as if they were missing their favorite pet."

The film was directed by David Loeb Weiss, a longtime proofreader at the paper, and found its title from a structure of letters unique to the Linotype machine. "Etaoin shrdlu" are "the 'words' formed by striking the first 12 keys, in two vertical rows, at the left of the Linotype keyboard," explained the *Times* obituary of Weiss, after he passed away in 2005. "A compositor would strike those keys to fill out a garbled line of type, indicating that it should be discarded. On occasion, the offending line found its way into the paper, 'etaoin shrdlu' and all. With the advent of computerized typesetting, 'etaoin shrdlu' disappeared from the paper forever."

So did the proofreaders.

Proofreaders didn't assign or write stories, and their names were absent from the masthead. Few ever earned a byline—and few aspired to one. They were a unique—but by no means a homogenous—breed of newspaper professional, able to recite the paper's stylebook backward and forward, spot an errant comma with aplomb, and realize when a particular word's misuse could bring profound embarrassment to the newspaper and the writer. Schlesinger calls the best of the breed "Renaissance men."

"Proofreaders were," in the words of David House, now the reader advocate for the Fort Worth *Star-Telegram*, "those wonderful thinkers, grammarians, spellers and widely read all-around trivia experts from yesteryear."

Proofreaders were the jewels of the newsroom, the thin pencil line that protected editors and reporters from humiliation and lawsuits. Their disappearance was the result of advances in printing technology and desktop publishing that enabled newspapers to eliminate the need for a final "proof." Edits and layout could be performed on a computer screen, and suddenly there was no need for a roomful of proofers; and when the galleys ceased to exist, they soon vanished too. By the end of the 1980s, the proofreader was all but an extinct newsroom species.

The Demise of Newspaper Proofreaders

TODAY, REFERENCES TO PROOFREADERS are often in the form of nostalgic laments, usually found in the column of a newspaper's ombudsman or reader's advocate who is duty bound to explain why the level of accuracy and quality of the language in the paper isn't what it used to be. Some papers or magazines still employ people with the title of proofreader, but they are more accurately called copy editors. It's a different job. The loss of the proofreader eliminated a layer of checking that has never been fully replaced.

"Their roles were absorbed by technology and loaded onto copy editors, and we've paid the price in inaccuracies ever since," noted House in his *Star-Telegram* column. "Probably the worst idea to hit the newspaper industry (other than public ownership) was the elimination of proofreaders."

Today's copy editors still check for conformity of style, and scour the copy for grammatical and factual errors. But they are also often charged with page layout, and writing the captions for photos. The pure breed of proofreader is gone, and with it went the higher level of scrutiny, the loss of which many journalists and readers bemoan to this day.

"Back in the day, newspapers had proofreaders who reviewed stories, headlines and entire pages, and corrected mistakes," wrote Wayne Ezell, the reader advocate of the *Florida Times-Union*, in a November 2006 column. Like House, he was responding to a flurry of e-mails from readers complaining about poor grammar and rampant typos in the paper. One reader reminded the editors that the paper is provided to classrooms as an educational tool, and asked, "What sort of learning experience is provided when the newspaper personnel cannot spell 'BOLOGNA'?" In fact, the paper had referred to "bolonga sandwiches" two days in a row on the front page.

Ezell offered an explanation of the current state of the proofreaderless newsroom.

"Now most pages are 'proofed' by an editor, usually after one or more other editors have edited stories, written headlines and placed them on a page," he wrote. "The second or third set of eyes is supposed to see every page, but when deadlines loom or editors are in a hurry, pages don't get a careful review. At other times, bleary-eyed copy editors miss stuff—or fail to use spell check." He also admitted what many language buffs already know. "Too many newspapers are not the standard-bearers they once were when it comes to handling the language."

The decline of good grammar and language in newspapers is a frequent complaint of readers, some of whom make a point of noting the errors of their local sheet. A few even keep records, like Benedict Nixon, a retired computer scientist in England. He tracks homophone-related errors in the *Guardian* and other published material. (A homophone is a word that sounds the same as another but has a different meaning. Think "hoards" and "hordes," for example.) Nixon wrote the *Guardian*'s reader's editor to note his disapproval.

"I am concerned about what seems to me to be the creeping deliquescence of literary English by way of illiterate confusion of near homophones," he said. "*The Guardian* is by no means the only culprit; the decay of the profession of publisher's reader (and, I must suppose, of that of newspaper proof-reader) has given rise to an epidemic of such howlers throughout the world of books and journals as well as that of newspapers."

It sometimes seems as though the decline of the newspaper proofreader has led to the rise of the proofreading reader. In addition to their letters of complaint about the existence of typos and poor language, readers, like editors, also note the perils of spell-checkers, the automated feature contained in word-processing programs. It's a case of technology being used to replace a role once performed by human beings. As a proofreader, the spell-checker is woefully inadequate.

One *Times-Union* reader, a reference librarian, noted that in a story about a retired firefighter, "The gentleman recommended that one should eat 'collared' greens. I'm sure [the writer] knows about 'collard' greens; I suspect spellcheck may not be [aware of] the Southern version!"

Overworked copy editors and the increasing reliance on spell-checkers are lowering the quality of newspapers, not to mention angering and alienating readers. This is not a point of argument in newsrooms; many journalists and newsroom managers have the same complaint, but they are quick to explain that budgets don't allow for more bodies and the careful eyes and encyclopedic brains that come along with them. With no solution in sight, on a regular basis ombudsmen's columns appear that commiserate with unhappy readers, pointing to the loss of proofreaders and other constraints. In drawing attention to their own failings, newspapers occasionally have some fun with the shortcomings of computerized spell-checkers. They were the subject of a colorful, homophone-filled comment piece in the *Ventura County Star* of California, in 1997.

"I have a friend who was a newspaper proofreader," it began. "Each knight, he wood read a pre-edition copy to correct errors."

The point is of course that spell-checkers can't recognize the context of a word. "Knight" is spelled correctly, but it has no place in a sentence about nocturnal activities, unless they involve a jousting match or damsel in distress. "Our *Star*, and possibly most papers, now spell-Czech by computer," continued Harold Simon in his ode to the dangers of computerized spell checking. "It is very fast and does knot make mistakes. If an author has an arrangement of alphabetic cymbals that exactly match the data base dictionary, it is ignored."

Reuters, the global news service, has suffered hilariously at the hands of spell-checkers. In November 2005, it sent a report over the wire noting that "Quaker Maid Meats Inc. on Tuesday said it would

ABC.com was just one of many Web sites that published a Reuters story about the recall of "beef panties" in November 2005.

voluntarily recall 94,400 pounds of frozen ground beef *panties*" (emphasis added).

Nearly a year later, in a story about honeybees, it reported "Queen Elizabeth has 10 times the lifespan of workers and lays 2,000 eggs per day." A spell-checker had morphed the queen bee into Queen Elizabeth, much to the dismay of the royal family and the growing ranks of former proofreaders now employed by the great newspaper in the sky.

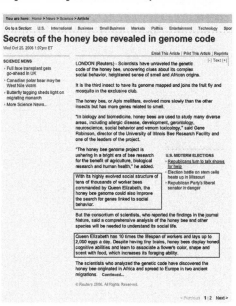

The demise of the newsroom proofreader is now entering its corporeal stage: the death of the proofreaders themselves. I asked Carl Schlesinger, the former proofreader at the *New York Times*, if he could put me in touch with any former colleagues.

In October 2006, Reuters again fell victim to the spell-checker.

"You would have to dig them up," he said. Schlesinger was right. In searching for retired newspaper proofreaders to interview, I landed primarily on their obituaries. One stood out:

Audrey Stubbart, a woman who spent nearly forty years on the job with the *Examiner* in Independence, Missouri, was one of the most celebrated American newspaper proofreaders. Prior to her newspaper job, she filled a similar role at a book publisher; before that she was a teacher. It was only when she turned sixty-five and was forced to retire from her job in publishing that she found her way into the newsroom. She died in 2000, roughly a month shy of her 105th birthday. Stubbart was one of the oldest working people in North America at the time. When asked about the secret of her longevity, she said, "I never smoked, I never drank and I tried to never tell a lie. That last one is the hardest."

She also had the proofreader's eye for spelling, grammar, and facts, and a love for hunting down an error. "I love to find mistakes," she said. "It makes me feel like I've done my job."

She joined the paper in 1961 as a proofreader and also wrote a weekly column. Much to her chagrin, she later had to work with a computer—the device that had cost many proofreaders their jobs. It's not that she had trouble using her PC; she just thought computers made people lazy and were "disintegrating" the minds of kids.

"She was an inspiration to all of us in the profession for her ability to still find the slightest error at the age of 105 that might have slipped by many of us much younger," Dale Brendel, executive editor of the *Examiner*, said after her death. "She had a way with the English language and knew the meaning and spelling of every word and their proper usage. Many an editor and reporter had challenged her over the years over usages and the correct way of using words, only to have her go to a dictionary to prove she was right."

Stubbart liked being right, but she didn't lord it over reporters. "When they make consistent mistakes, I like to point it out to them," she said. "I think they appreciate it. I don't [correct them] in a demeaning or insulting way. They just know I'm an old schoolteacher."

It seems fitting that one of the oldest working people in North America, at the time of her death, was holding down a job that was nearly extinct. She was a centenarian in an occupation that had been sacrificed in the name of efficiency and the computer age. Stubbart had tried to warn us.

"We think that whatever's been hard for us, machinery will do it," she said in 1999. "And that is just too bad, when we get to leaning on machines."

Though few ever accused a proofreader of being a glory hound, the job was made famous during its prime in a 1950s NBC television series based on *Adventures of Hiram Holliday*, a series of stories by author Paul Gallico.

A mild-mannered newspaper proofreader, Hiram Holliday managed to save his newspaper, the fictitious *New York Sentinel*, by inserting what came to be known as the "$500,000 comma," the amount Holliday's correction later saved the publisher in a libel suit.

"When the original copy was exhumed and examined during the trial, it was found that no comma had existed there when the story first arrived at the copy desk, but that a large, fat, and pointed one had been inserted with a firm stroke of the pencil by the hand of Hiram Holliday," wrote Gallico in the first story. (Holliday is referred to as a "copyreader" in the books and as a "proofreader" in the television series.)

As a reward for his valuable contribution, the publisher gives Holliday a bonus of $8,000 and a month's paid vacation. Holliday sets out to travel the world with Joel Smith, a reporter from the paper. Smith is instructed to file stories about their trip, and he hopes to make his name with a big scoop from abroad. Smith expects to take the lead, but it's Holliday's careful attention, meticulous nature, and encyclopedic knowledge of, well, everything, that inevitably saves Smith's bacon in every episode.

In the first television episode alone, Holliday demonstrates a familiarity with the Chinese language and a vast amount of knowledge about the rare indigenous sea cucumber. He later disarms a bomb and details the trials of its developer, defeats two villains in a swordfight armed only with his trusty umbrella, and also displays admirable dancing skills. Portrayed by Wally Cox of *Mr. Peepers* fame, Holliday dresses in plain black suits and speaks with a slightly nasal tone that matches his Coke-bottle glasses and skeletal frame. You half expect him to die from a common cold, only to suddenly see him thwarting Nazis in the name of a distressed princess, or saving the entire American naval fleet while searching for the lost consonant of the Hawaiian Islands.

Many a proofreader was a hero, thanks to his or her careful eye and unique knowledge base, but Gallico and NBC managed to create one that America—and then Britain—watched, beginning in 1956.

The $500,000 comma that launched Holliday's adventure remained a work of fiction and drama until 2006, when Gallico's clever plot construction made its way into the press. This time, however, the story was real.

That year, two major Canadian telecommunications companies appealed to government regulators over a contract dispute that centered on, yes, a single comma. Unlike Holliday's comma, this one was worth just over $2 million in Canadian funds. The *Globe and Mail,* which broke the story in August 2006, noted, "It could be the most costly piece of punctuation in Canada."

One company thought it had locked the other into a five-year deal. But a misplaced comma allowed the other party to slip out sooner. The contract stated that the agreement "shall continue in force for a period of five years from the date it is made, and thereafter for successive five year terms, unless and until terminated by one year prior notice in writing by either party." According to regulators (and language buffs), the placement of the second comma in the sentence enabled the contract to be canceled at any time upon one year's written notice. This was supposed to apply only after the initial five-year deal.

"The controversial comma sent lawyers and telecommunications regulators scrambling for their English textbooks in a bitter 18-month dispute that serves as an expensive reminder of the importance of punctuation," wrote the *Globe*'s Grant Robertson.

Much like how the proofreaders of old might catch many of the spell-checker-created errors of today, lawyers from another time might have been more prepared to catch that costly comma, according to one expert. "In olden times, lawyers would have acquired (an approximation to) these skills in the course of learning dead languages," wrote University of Pennsylvania phonetics professor Mark Liberman. "These days, I suppose that few of them get any educational help at all in such matters, and have to fall back on their native wit, such as it may be."

Substitute "educational help" for the assistance of proofreaders and it's a sentiment that could just as easily apply to the newspaper journalists of today. Proofreaders are long gone, but their absence is felt—and read—on a daily basis, thanks to the onslaught of errors and typos present in daily newspapers.

CHAPTER 12

THE BIRTH
(AND SLOW DEATH) OF
MAGAZINE FACT CHECKING

AFTER ITS FOUNDING IN 1923, *Time* magazine began employ-ing a group of women—and *only* women—to check the facts in the magazine. "A number of early research departments, including that of *Reader's Digest*, were markedly discriminatory," according to Sarah Harrison Smith in her 2004 book, *The Fact Checker's Bible*. "Fact-check-ing was considered women's work."

These female checkers are considered the first fact-checkers in the publishing industry, and they, along with the staffers who started checking at the *New Yorker* in 1927, helped establish fact checking as a practice within major North American magazines. The concept of fact checking as "women's work" would persist for decades. "The checker, or researcher, is usually a girl in her twenties, usually from some Eastern college, pleasant-looking but not a *femme fatale*," wrote Otto Friedrich in a 1964 feature about fact checking at newsweeklies for *Harper's* maga-zine. "She came from college unqualified for anything, but looking for an 'interesting' job. After a few years, she usually feels, bitterly and rightly, that nobody appreciates her work."

The job itself is straightforward: fact-checkers take the notes, inter-views, and sources used by a reporter and combine them with research, using credible outside sources to verify every fact, statistic, and quote in an article prior to its publication. Checkers look at names, dates, num-bers, quotes, descriptions—anything and everything that is verifiable and not opinion. "The theory of fact checkers is that even the tiniest details are part of the larger whole, like bricks in a building," said a 1998 article in the *New Republic*. "For the sake of credibility—a term fact checkers invoke with reverence—*all* the facts have to be right . . . if one brick crumbles, the whole structure is weakened."

Like that of the proofreaders of the past, the goal of magazine fact-checkers is to deliver that last line of verification before something makes it into print. Also like the proofreaders of yore, fact-checkers toil in obscurity and have a spotlight shone on them only when something goes terribly wrong.

In the early days of checking at *Time*, editor Edward Kennedy prepared an informative memo for the women of his checking department, though one has to get past his sexist view of the position to appreciate his words:

> CHECKING IS . . . sometimes regarded as a dull and tedious occupation, but such a conception of this position is extremely erroneous. Any bright girl who really applies herself to the han-dling of the checking problem can have a very pleasant time with it and fill the week with happy moments and memorable occasions. The most important point to remember in checking is that the writer is your natural enemy. He is trying to see how much he can get away with. Remember that when people write letters about mistakes, it is you who will be screeched at. So protect yourself.

Kennedy's memo highlights some of the eternal truths about fact checking: the work rarely earns outside recognition unless a mistake occurs; fact-checkers will often unfairly suffer from a lack of respect; there is some joy and much honor to be found in checking; and, finally, writers make mistakes. The idea of a writer and checker being "natural enemies" is perhaps a bit too dramatic, though a healthy adversarial relationship is often required.

In the end, fact-checkers exist to make the writer and the magazine look good and to protect them from embarrassment or legal action. To do this, they must take nothing at face value and blind themselves to any preconceived notions about the article or its author. Many begin a check by assuming everything in an article is wrong.

"Pound for pound, the most mistake-packed article I have ever checked was written by a Pulitzer Prize winner," wrote Ariel Hart, a freelance fact-checker at the *Columbia Journalism Review*, in a special report after the Jayson Blair scandal at the *New York Times*. "As I approached the job, I felt I was on a futile mission. The piece seemed fine, the facts made sense, and most important, the narrative voice spoke with total authority. I could not imagine finding any mistakes here, but I'm paid by the hour so I set to work. Immediately, I found a significant error in the lead, then a cascade."

Hart noted that the writer "moved from impatience to outright anger" at being asked for backup material. But, as is often the case, after being delivered corrections to the piece, the author ended up offering "gracious cooperation." The writer's reputation as a Pulitzer Prize winner had been safeguarded.

It's not known if one specific inaccurate article in *Time* was what caused its editors to recruit their cadre of female checkers, but it is believed that a single particularly flawed story led to the creation of a fact-checking department at the *New Yorker*, in 1927. The magazine is now sometimes referred to as "the Vatican" of fact checking—but it took a measure of embarrassment to get it to that standing.

The February 12, 1927, issue of the magazine carried a profile of poet Edna St. Vincent Millay written by Griffin Barry. It began, "Edna Millay's father was a stevedore on the wharves at Rockland, Maine. So was his father." In the same paragraph, the story noted that Millay's mother "appears to remember little of her own biography."

In fact, her mother's recollection was quite good. Under the headline "WE STAND CORRECTED," the magazine subsequently printed a letter from Mrs. Cora B. Millay that proceeded to list several inaccuracies in the piece and chastise the writer for not contacting her or her husband, especially since "both of these parents are living, and in full possession of their faculties." Mother was not pleased.

Mrs. Millay began her dissection of the article by noting that, contrary to the opening sentence of the piece, her husband was not a stevedore and neither was his father. "Henry T. Millay, the father of my daughters, was in his younger days a schoolteacher," she wrote, and then continued on with several more corrections. In fact, the letter was the result of a compromise in order to avoid a lawsuit after "the poet's mother stormed into the magazine's offices and threatened to sue if an extensive correction was not run," Harrison quotes Ben Yagoda in his book, *About Town: The New Yorker and the World It Made*.

This embarrassing incident was compounded by the magazine's tendency to point out the errors, awkward language, and amusing gaffes in other publications. In the issue that carried the Millay letter, for example, the magazine had reprinted this advertisement from the *Fremont Eagle* of Indiana: "Don't divorce your wife if she can't cook—eat at the Hotel Fremont and keep her for a pet." The magazine commented underneath, "But suppose she can't pet either?" *New Yorker* founder Harold Ross saw that, thanks to its treatment of other publications, his magazine was likely to come under extra scrutiny. In 1927 he sent a memo to staff that set out a high standard for the magazine. "What with our making fun of other publications and what with the nature of the magazine, 'The New Yorker' ought to be freer from typographical errors than any other publication. . . . A SPECIAL EFFORT SHOULD BE MADE TO AVOID MISTAKES IN 'THE NEW YORKER.'"

That memo and the Millay debacle set the magazine on a path to a place among the publications most respected for their accuracy. (Millay earned another distinguished place in the annals of corrections when an embarrassing typo in an ad for a collection of her love sonnets referred to it as "Immoral Poetry" instead of "Immortal Poetry." The ad appeared in the *New York Times* on July 28, 1931, and caused Adolph S. Ochs, the owner of the paper, to write his business manager, "I regret to say that I think the error was to their advantage." Seeing as it was the paper's mistake, Ochs said a correction would make "an interesting item besides being an act of justice." And so one was published.)

Thomas Teal, who worked as a checker at the *New Yorker*, once estimated in the late 1980s that the magazine's checking department had eliminated a thousand errors in a single issue. In addition to the rigorous checking applied to written work, including fiction, the cartoons are also fact-checked, according to Erin Overbey, one of two head librarians at the magazine. "Every cartoon is fact-checked for accuracy and also checked against the library's archive to make sure that a similar cartoon has not run previously in the magazine," she said. "If a drawing of the White House has the wrong number of columns on it or if a man's coat is buttoned on the wrong side, then the fact-checking department informs the cartoon department of the discrepancy. . . . In addition, if a cartoon caption gets a proper name wrong or, say, locates the Nôtre Dame in Bangkok, the fact-checking department will point out these inaccuracies. The cartoonists have learned that even a detail as small as the number on a taxicab will be checked to make sure it does not represent an actual cab number."

If it all sounds a bit too pedantic, that's the point. Checkers must revel in the finest of details, be willing to make phone call after phone call to confirm the smallest fact, and do it all knowing that if any recognition for their work is forthcoming it will likely be for a mistake they made. It's a job that requires a special kind of person.

Anatomy of the Checker

ASK A FACT-CHECKER or the head of a fact-checking department what makes a good checker and you are likely to hear a list of psychological conditions including obsessive-compulsive disorder and split personality. Anne "Dusty" Mortimer-Maddox, who worked as a checker at the *New Yorker* and several magazines in Canada, told me that when it comes to the job, "OCD is the whole ball game."

I also asked Robert Scheffler, the research editor at *Esquire,* what made him suited to the job.

"I'm German," he offered with a smile. "Something in me just really loves to dissect a piece, tear it apart and figure it all out."

Being able to deal with writers and outside sources requires a certain level of tact. A checker will encounter resistance, outright hostility, grudging cooperation, and immense gratitude, often while checking the same article or single fact. The range of emotions can be wide, but checkers have come to expect a certain progression with writers who are new to the process, or are surprised by their own fallibility. In general, the more a writer deals with fact-checkers, the more he or she comes to appreciate them, though some famous writers choose to avoid checkers altogether: "Fact checkers at *Esquire* aren't allowed to talk to Norman Mailer," reported the *New Republic* in 1988. "Gore Vidal is also said to be hard to check. 'They think we're tinkering with the muse,'" said one checker at the time.

Fact-checkers often possess surprising skills and characteristics. The *New Yorker's* current head of fact checking, Peter Canby, told a reporter in 1998 that he wanted checkers with "split minds," meaning "the education and interests of a generalist, the surgeon's focus on detail." In the same article, the department head at *Vanity Fair* revealed a preference for "terrier-like" checkers.

Canby declined to conduct an interview with me, but did respond by e-mail. "It's not that we don't make mistakes of course: we aspire to no mistakes but find that goal continually elusive," he wrote. "Nor is there anything particularly magical about our procedures—we just take the pursuit of accuracy seriously and work hard to approximate it."

Checkers are often hired based on certain areas of expertise. Depending on the focus of the magazine, the team must have a mix of those with facility in pop culture, politics, the arts, sports, fashion, and other categories. At the *New Yorker*, fluency in a foreign language is reportedly valued. "Their prowess for languages may be what separates them from other fact-checking departments; Farsi, Sinhalese, Spanish, French, and Italian are all spoken there," noted a spring 2002 article in the *New York Review of Magazines*.

Cynthia Brouse, a Canadian journalist and editor with more than fifteen years of fact-checking experience, teaches a fact-checking course in the journalism department at Ryerson University in Toronto. She said one of her best attributes as a checker is her degree in the psychology of linguistics because it helps her spot errors that others often don't pick up on.

What one doesn't frequently hear, however, is that good checkers should be aspiring writers or reporters. Having excellent reporting skills is always appreciated, but few major magazines with full-time checking departments will want someone whose ultimate goal is writing. (And here is another truth about fact-checkers: In North America they exist primarily at large-circulation magazines. Smaller publications can't afford them, and elsewhere in the world, the practice itself is not common. For example, one British expert's response to my inquiry about magazine fact checking in the United Kingdom was a hearty laugh.)

Of all the attributes of a checker, doggedness is the most valued. A checker who gives up after finding one seemingly reliable source won't last long. And, of course, a checker who makes mistakes won't last, period. A checker was dismissed from the *New Yorker* after making five mistakes in a January 24, 1994, Talk of the Town article. "There were five errors in two and a half columns of copy, and I just was not comfortable with going ahead with the next piece with that checker," managing editor Pamela Maffei McCarthy told the Columbia Journalism Review in 1994. In an ironic twist to the tail, the article dealt with Court TV, a channel owned by Stephen Brill, a journalist, author, and entrepreneur. When he was editor in chief of *American Lawyer*, he had distinguished himself in the history of fact checking by making a habit of inserting errors in the articles. It was his way of checking up on the checkers.

Since for checkers failure is not an option, there are numerous stories about them going far beyond the call of duty. Even the fiction in the *New Yorker* has produced its share of checking tales. One short story about sailing on the Indian Ocean caused Thomas Teal, a checker, to plot the vessel's fictional course. He realized that the purported path of the boat was impossible, so he created a new course and passed it by the author. "I knew nobody would notice the difference," Teal said later. "But there's a certain aesthetic pleasure in just knowing it's correct."

There is also the tale of a stringer (freelancer) employed by an unnamed newsweekly who, in 1953, was asked to confirm some details about General Muhammad Naguib, who had just been elected Egypt's first president. The writer of the piece sought to convey Naguib's modesty by noting that his name didn't appear among "the 000 people listed in *Who's Who in the Middle East*." He was also said to shun luxury and "had refused to live in the royal palace, surrounded by an oo-foot-high wall," according to Friedrich's retelling in *Harper's*. The stringer was asked to fill in the "oo"s with the correct numbers.

The deadline for the information came and went with no word from the stringer, so the publication reworked the article to exclude the missing numbers. It later received a telegram that was approximated by Friedrich to read, "I am in jail and allowed send only one cable since was arrested while measuring fifteen foot wall outside palace and have just finished counting thirty eight thousand five hundred twenty two names Whos Who in Mideast."

The doggedness of a checker can also sometimes inspire others to join in the hunt. Davin Coburn, the head fact-checker at *Popular Mechanics* magazine, recalled trying to locate the identity of a football player who was in the background of an illustration of a famous play that occurred in the 1960s. Coburn clearly had the checking bug early on; at the time he was only an intern at *Sports Illustrated for Kids*. "I'm hazy on the 17 phone calls I made until ending up with some one-hit-wonder documentary director with B-roll in his basement [of the original play]," he told me. "He watched the thing while I was on the phone so he could pluck a last name from the jersey."

People aren't always so cooperative. In July 1980, *Esquire* ran an article about the invention of the vibrator and interviewed its inventor, Tex Williams. He said he had come up with the vibrator because his wife at the time had trouble reaching orgasm. Ava Plakins, the checker working on the piece, called Williams's ex-wife to confirm the tale. "That son of a bitch!" the woman exclaimed. "Did he tell you that the reason I couldn't have an orgasm was because he was a premature ejaculator?" Plakins ended up getting the former couple to speak and resolve their issues. The published story included both of their points of view.

The often invisible job of fact checking received a measure of notoriety when Jay McInerney made the main character of his best selling novel, *Bright Lights, Big City*, a fact-checker at a big New York magazine. The book was later made into a film starring Michael J. Fox, who studied for the part by spending time in the fact-checking department at *Esquire*. One of his checking tasks involved verifying a recipe for blueberry pie. Fox called a local bakery to verify its contents. "The baker got very irate and said, 'Young man, I don't know who the hell you are, but that pie is going to explode if you don't poke some holes in the top,'" recalled former *Esquire* research editor Larkin Warren. Fox was so enthralled by his discovery of an important omission that he rushed into Warren's office "screaming that he'd saved America." Call it the thrill of the fact.

Fact-checkers often encounter people, even some who have had a lot of media coverage, who have never before received a call from someone like them. For these sources, the ritual of having every detail about themselves confirmed and every quote paraphrased back is a curious but enjoyable procedure. Some, of course, try to dispute material or quotes that might reflect poorly on them, and that's when the checker must work with the editor and writer to see what they have on tape or from reliable outside sources. It's this kind of judgment call that presents the checkers with some of their bigger problems. For interviews, a recording can provide the essential evidence, but reporters don't record everything. In such cases the checker must rely on the writer's notes. The stark reality of checking notes surfaced in the case of Stephen Glass, a writer for the *New Republic* who in 1998 was revealed to have fabricated at least thirty-five stories for it and other publications. (It was a dose of irony, considering that an amusing 1988 *New Republic* article about fact checking concluded that "facts aren't really that important. A few factual errors don't undermine the crucial essence of a story.")

Glass's story was later turned into a film starring Hayden Christensen in the lead role. In one scene, Glass returns to his old school to speak to a class about being a reporter. "There is a hole in the fact-checking system," he tells the kids. A montage of scenes showing how a story is edited, checked, reedited, rechecked, and on and on, reveals the supposed inner workings of the magazine's process. The fictional Glass then explains that, in some cases, all the checker has to go on are the writer's notes.

The real Stephen Glass had in fact forged his notes for the checkers. Everything was there on paper to compare to his reporting, but the notes were pure fiction.

"I knew how the system worked," Glass told *60 Minutes* in a segment that aired in August 2003. "And I made it so that my stories could get through. I invented fake notes. I later would invent a series of voice mailboxes and business cards. I invented newsletters. I invented a Web site," says Glass. "For every lie I told in the magazine, there was a series of lies behind that lie that I told—in order to get it to be published."

Glass's willful deception is rare, especially his brazen (and successful) attempts to subvert the fact-checking process. It took Adam Penenberg, a reporter for *Forbes*'s online operation, to expose one of Glass's fabrications, and then his whole house of cards came down. Glass later wrote a novel, *The Fabulist*, about a journalist who lies. Glass's exploits demonstrate that no fact-checking system is impervious to the depradations of a malicious reporter.

Everybody Has a System

BECAUSE FACT CHECKING PULLS APART an entire piece fact by fact and then puts it back together, keeping track of what has and hasn't been checked, and noting the sources and changes, requires a clear system. Checkers can't get lost in the course of their work, or else they might have to start over. As a result, experienced checkers have their own systems, and though there are certain similarities in how one person or publication does a check, it's often a very individual process.

One thing that's consistent: Nobody fact-checks on a computer screen. They print out the story and work it over on the page. Apart from that, systems vary, and I discovered that not everyone likes to share.

"Can you show me?" I asked David Cohen, the research editor at *Playboy*, hoping to see an example of a story he had marked up. "Is it a secret recipe?"

"It's not a secret," he said after five seconds of silence. "Let's just say it involves multicolored markers. It's pretty on the page.

"When I hire somebody I have them mark up a story the way they do it," Cohen told me. "And then I say, 'Let me show you how it's done.'"

Other examples I had seen used various markings: slashes through every word that did not contain a fact, underlines, circles, and arrows. Phone numbers were linked to source names by a pencil line to the margins, and questions were written all over the page and linked back to sentences. A printout of a story going through a check tends to look as if someone had written a musical score over, below, and above the text, often in multiple colors. Some checkers swear by pencil while others require highlighters or a combination of both.

Prior to meeting Cohen, I had interviewed Robert Scheffler, the research editor at *Esquire.* While he also declined to share a sample check, he referred me to Davin Coburn at *Popular Mechanics,* who had taken it upon himself to prepare a research guide for fact-checkers. Coburn said he had been introduced to the "black check, red check" system while at Time Inc.: A fact or quote that has been verified by a primary source—the person interviewed, an original document or authoritative report, for example—is marked on the page with a red check. It's solid. Facts that don't have a primary source get a black check, and a certain number of black checks are required to equal a red check. "By the time you are done you can hardly read the text," he said.

For fact-checkers, the Internet in particular has become both a boon and a scourge. "The Internet has revolutionized this game, but it also presents all sorts of interesting problems," says Coburn of *Popular Mechanics.* "One of the things we emphasize is that, regardless of how good you are with Google, the job [of fact checking] is done on the phone."

Checkers are often sent background material by writers that consists of links to Web sites, but just because something is published online—or anywhere else, for that matter—doesn't mean it's authoritative. While a newspaper article or Web site might be helpful in the initial search for checking materials, they are not considered authoritative sources. Ideally, they can lead a checker to someone who is an expert in a certain field, or to an original report from a government body or other definitive source.

"However their accuracy may vary, newspapers are invaluable to fact checkers, particularly when checking news stories," wrote Sarah Harrison Smith. "The trick is to remember that they are fallible and never to rely on newspapers to check anything that you could check with a better source, such as a reliable reference book or a scholar."

Most checking departments hold on to their materials for at least a few years (*Esquire* does it for three), just in case there's a lawsuit or request for correction. The potential for legal action as a result of an error is one of the driving forces behind fact checking. As a result, some magazines make the legal department part of the checking process. Legal is perhaps nowhere more involved than at *Playboy*, where David Cohen is responsible for sending a daily fax to the magazine's legal counsel with the latest checked material.

"Things are a little different in the world of *Playboy*," he said. "I tell my assistant that that fax is the most important thing that we do. The lawyer reads everything and it is faxed back [with comments]."

Cohen says the content of the magazine and its high profile and circulation necessitate the extra oversight. "We feature comely young women, for example, so we have to deal with identifiability/stalker issues," he said. "Also, rightly or wrongly, people assume *Playboy* has deeper pockets than some [publishing companies] so it would make [some people's] day to give them a lawsuit.

"There is a system of checks and balances of which I'm a part," he continued, "and I have faith in that system."

Death by a Thousand Cuts

WHEN TIME INC. ANNOUNCED A LARGE round of layoffs in January 2007, one needed only look at the editorial positions being cut to see how far fact checking has fallen over the last couple of decades. Though some major magazines are holding fast to the checking ethic, many others are watering it down, or simply getting rid of fact-checkers.

Time magazine, as well as *Newsweek*, eliminated its research department in the fall of 1996 to create the reporter-researcher role and rely on an "author-checked" system. Pure fact checking was abandoned and fact-checkers displaced in favor of hybrid multitaskers who could check parts of stories while also reporting, and occasionally writing. Like the merging of some proofreading functions with the duties of newspaper copy editors, the switch to reporter-researchers diminished the overall effectiveness of quality control.

At the time, *Newsweek*'s assistant managing editor said the decision to offer its checkers a buyout or a job change to the hybrid position wasn't for budget reasons. "The people who used to be fact-checking are happier in their new jobs, and now we have more reporters." Tellingly, not long after the change, in early May 1997, *Newsweek* suffered one of the most serious reporting errors in its history when a special issue, "Your Child," told readers that infants—even as young as five months old—could safely feed themselves zwiebacks and chunks of raw carrot. This error could have resulted in a fatal choking incident, so the magazine recalled several hundred thousand copies and rushed corrected versions to newsstands, hospitals, and doctors' offices.

It ran a correction on page 10 of its May 12 issue that read,

> A CHART ENTITLED "Building Healthy Habits" on page 58 contained a serious error. Five-month-old babies should not be fed zwiebacks or raw carrot chunks. Though many infants are ready to try pureed solids between 4 to 6 months, raw carrots and other hard foods could cause choking.

"We are very sorry about this mistake," *Newsweek* editor in chief and president Richard M. Smith said in the correction. "And we are taking extraordinary measures to correct it."

According to the magazine's spokesperson, a copy editor who was editing two articles at the same time introduced the error.

Just as *Newsweek*'s lack of checking quickly came back to haunt it, *Time* also felt the loss. By the summer of 1997, Marta Dorin, then *Time*'s chief of reporters, admitted to the *Columbia Journalism Review* just a few months after the change that already "there have been some bad errors that wouldn't have happened under the old-fashioned system." She said the decision to cut back on checking was "entirely budgetary. These systems cost money."

Also in 1997, *Fortune* eliminated its checking department and performed checks only on rushed stories or those written by new writers. "Eighty percent of the fact-checking we did was redundant," the executive editor said at the time. During the same period, the *Columbia Journalism Review* also reported cutbacks at *Vogue* and the *Village Voice*.

The Time Inc. layoffs of January 18, 2007, eliminated 289 positions, with 172 coming from the editorial side. Though the reporter-researchers who had replaced the fact-checkers a little over a decade before were by no means the largest group eliminated, their ranks were culled at *Time*, *Sports Illustrated*, and other marquee publications. The resulting effect on overall quality was unknown at the time, though the loss could only hurt the publications.

"In the past, every piece of copy published in *Time* was researched and fact checked," wrote Sarah Harrison Smith, author of *The Fact Checker's Bible*. "Now about 50 percent of the pieces are fact checked by the writers themselves, and some writers do not even use reporters to help with their preliminary research. Whether a piece is checked by a reporter seems to depend upon the length of the story—longer pieces generally requiring more checking—and the amount of time the writer had to research and write the story."

Bastions of checking such as the *New Yorker* and *Vanity Fair* continue to maintain their fact-checking departments, but the reality of the industry is that they are either slowly shrinking or being decimated and their work farmed out to freelancers, or they are increasingly populated by green interns trying to make their way up the editorial ladder—and that's if the departments aren't eliminated entirely. Both *Playboy* and *Esquire*, two magazines that still perform a rigorous check on everything in the magazine, have fewer full-time checkers on staff than they used to.

Layoffs have thinned the ranks of full-time checkers and the pseudo-checkers at *Time* and other publications, many of which now turn to freelance checkers to fill the gaps.

Many high-profile Canadian magazines have introduced what some call the "light check." Rather than have checkers examine every part of every story, reporters and writers are expected to check their own work. Checkers are brought in on particularly complicated, long, or controversial pieces, and even then they might not perform a full check. It's a model much more akin to that of a daily newspaper, and the excuse for this practice at newspapers is the rigor of a daily publishing schedule that leaves little time for checking.

"It is clear that fact checking is allotted less time than it was a decade ago and is becoming less an integral part of the everyday operation of the general-interest magazine—despite an increasingly litigious environment and a public justifiably suspicious of journalism," reported Leslie Lucas in the *Ryerson Review of Journalism* in 1999. Lucas tracked the decline of checkers and/or the introduction of light checking at some of the country's largest magazines, including *Maclean's*, *Canadian Business*, *Chatelaine* (the country's largest women's title), and *Toronto Life*, a city magazine that consistently fares well at the National Magazine Awards.

In September 1997, *Canadian Business* moved from a monthly schedule to publishing every two weeks. With its increased frequency, the magazine attempted to introduce a light check: Only things such as names and dates would be checked in every piece. The light check lasted only a few weeks before the magazine went back to the old system.

"They had this really stupid idea," Pat Ireland, an experienced copy editor and checker at *Canadian Business*, said after the episode. "The editors would supposedly go over what needed checking and they'd mark it for you. Well, they never did, and editors, in my experience, don't have any idea of what should be checked. You check everything. You never know what you're leaving out."

The magazine's decision to bring back a full fact-check paid dividends at the 2006 Canadian National Magazine Awards. "I want to take a moment to acknowledge some people in the business who don't get enough credit," said *Canadian Business* staffer Matthew McClearn as he stood onstage to accept his gold medal for investigative reporting. "We call them associate editors at *Canadian Business*. You probably know them as fact checkers."

A year earlier, in June 2005, the checking department at *Maclean's*, one of the country's oldest and most respected magazines, went from eight full-time staff checkers to two. The positions were eliminated in favor of hiring more writers, according to the magazine's recently installed publisher and editor, Kenneth Whyte. He had also been the new editor of *Saturday Night*, an influential but now-defunct national magazine, when the magazine cut its fact-checking budget in half in 1994.

"It has allowed us to be a lot more current and make changes later in the week, do more updates, push more things through closer to deadline," said Whyte of the changes at *Maclean's*. The irony that eliminating fact checking allowed his magazine to engage in the error-prone newspaper-like rush to deadline was apparently lost on him. Whyte didn't think anyone would notice a change in quality. "I don't think there's any indication that the readers have noticed any difference, nor do I think they should have," he said. "I don't believe there are any more errors getting into the magazine as a result of the changes."

It begs the question: If fact-checkers were always so disposable and ineffectual, then why were they ever there in the first place? Magazines that cut back on checking understandably don't want to publicize their diminished quality, but it's disingenuous and perhaps even insulting for editors to argue that no change will occur when an entire magazine department is eliminated or downsized. Some argue that magazine writers and editors can become lazy when they know a fact-checker is there to catch any mistakes and fill in the holes. Removing the safety net, they argue, simply makes reporters more careful in their work because they will have only themselves to blame for errors. This would be a more effective argument if magazines didn't make so many protestations about the quality of their content versus that of deadline-driven daily newspapers. Because of these claims, readers have come to expect a higher standard from serious magazines.

"Readers have a feeling that magazines are going to be better [than newspapers] and they don't really know why," said Brouse. "They look nicer, they are glossy and colorful...Readers know that it takes longer to put together the issue so they have higher expectations of magazine [quality]."

In addition, the oft-cited work done by checkers at places such as the *New Yorker* rubs off on other magazines. Over the years, a perception has been cultivated that magazines meet a higher standard of accuracy than do other forms of media. While some publications continue to earn this distinction, others are trading on that perception without informing readers of their decreased commitment to it. Even those with strong checking departments still publish errors, sometimes significant ones. But it's only a matter of time before a checker-less publication suffers a serious lapse that reveals the diminished reality.

In my interviews with fact-checkers, they all made the distinction that newspaper articles were not considered a reliable source of facts on their own. Yet top magazine editors appear to be embracing the check-it-yourself model of daily papers. Adding to the blurring of the lines is the push by many newspapers toward more lengthy magazine-esque features and service journalism, without adding magazine-level checking. It's a disconcerting race to the bottom. *Newsweek*'s experience with its "Your Child" debacle serves as an illustrative example.

"I can't see how you can put out a decent magazine without fact checking," said David Zimmer, editor of Canada's *Cottage Life*. (Though the magazine's focus might seem casual, it follows a rigorous checking procedure.) "It's the one thing that makes it different from a newspaper or TV. Magazines are one of the last bastions of journalism where you can get the straight dope, and really trust what you read."

Magazines have always billed themselves as an authoritative voice. These days, that kind of quality is even more important, if only to cut through the massive daily assault of information and misinformation: infomercials, instant and unedited Internet news, and advertising supplements masquerading as editorial content. If magazines do manage to hang on to rigorous fact checking, despite the time and expense involved, they'll have a fighting chance of providing that voice. Readers, who show an almost filial loyalty to their favorite mags, deserve no less.

In today's media environment it seems almost negligent for a magazine to eliminate its fact-checking department. *Newsweek*'s "Your Child" error, which led to the first recall in the publication's history, was reported by the Associated Press, the *New York Times*, and other publications. That kind of coverage in 1997 would pale in comparison to what would happen today after such a significant error. It would become fodder for the numerous media watchdog Web sites, press blogs, columnists, and twenty-four-hour news networks. The magazine would have to spend much more time explaining its error and attempting to defend its overall credibility. Errors of that nature, even smaller ones, exact a much higher toll today than ever before.

To see the difference one need only point to *Newsweek*'s now-famous 2005 report claiming that U.S. interrogators had flushed a Koran down the toilet. While the topic of the article and error was much more controversial than "Your Child," and came during a time of war from a source who later admitted making the error, the weeks of coverage and cacophony of criticism (mine included) caused *Newsweek* to pay a much higher price and devote significantly more resources to damage control. This heightened scrutiny is the norm today, and it makes fact-checkers more essential than ever. The great fear is that, like proofreaders, they might one day be reduced to the subject of dewy-eyed reminiscences about the good old days when now-extinct fact-checkers roamed the office. That time seems to be approaching at an alarming pace.

CHAPTER 13

WATCHING THE DETECTIVES: THE RISE OF EXTERNAL FACT CHECKING

A S THE SUN SETS ON THE PROOFREADER and seemingly begins to descend on the magazine fact-checker, there is a new class of checkers rising—a motivated, opinionated, public cadre of checkers who exist outside the press.

You would be hard-pressed to believe, after you'd visited a newsroom, that there's an unprecedented amount of fact checking going on—though it doesn't follow that there's a high level of accuracy.

Today facts are gathered to be wielded like weapons, like artillery shells in the battle of ideas and ideologies. Some of the "new checkers," as I'll call them, try to discover true facts; others use fake facts to push their cause.

This culture of checking that has emerged primarily online in recent years focuses largely on holding the press to account and pointing out its errors. Fact checking—once exclusively the province of magazines such as the *New Yorker*—is now an industry of NGOs, a hobby for engaged citizens, and standard operating procedure for bloggers. At times, though, it's also a blood sport.

Facts are used to expose the perceived bias and inaccuracy of journalists and media outlets, to reveal the incompetence of organizations, to cut people down. In some hands, fact checking in pursuit of the truth has become weaponized; spotting a factual error is proof of your enemy's folly, ammunition for partisan hackery, and fodder for blogs (I plead guilty), columns, and books (again). We have a culture that is pulsating with warring facts: facts from different sources; facts from endless polls, surveys, NGOs, experts, studies, political parties.

Prior to the American invasion of Iraq, Ambassador Joe Wilson went on a fact-finding mission to Niger to see about some yellow cake uranium for the CIA, the agency that publishes the famous *World Fact Book*. He would later feel that the Oval Office had twisted the facts he found, so he took to the op-ed page of the *New York Times* to set the record straight. The facts in his op-ed piece then came under intense scrutiny, and on and on it went.

The current obsession with facts has not necessarily elevated the level of truth or accuracy, though evidence of the power and skill of the new checkers to do so occurs on a regular basis. They have had many remarkable successes. At the core of this new upsurge of checking is the fact that, through Internet searches, information databases, and their own individual expertise, members of the public as well as organizations can gather information from a wide variety of sources and easily question what they read and see in the press. They can then share what they've learned with others via comment postings on blogs and news Web sites, or through their own Web sites, blogs, and social networks. As a result, news stories never die. They fork and fragment. They spark new narratives. The conversation continues outside the realm of the press, and is frequently about the press itself.

There is also a growing list of media-monitoring organizations whose sole purpose is to check up on the press. For example, Media Matters for America checks the facts for the Left, while Accuracy in Media checks them for the Right. FactCheck.org checks the facts of major political players, while the Committee for Accuracy in Middle East Reporting in America (CAMERA) and Honest Reporting check the facts on reporting about Israel. The Media Research Center, a conservative organization, funds a Web site called Newsbusters.org, a name that speaks for itself.

Nonpartisan Web sites such as NewsTrust.net have also emerged to enable readers to rate the accuracy and authority of a given news article. Another, called StinkyJournalism.org, enables readers to send comments and requests for correction to news outlets, and to rate the perceived "stinkiness" of a particular story.

"We start with the facts instead of starting with the assumption that the story is inherently biased," said Jeremy Miller, the editor of the site. "We are interested in factual errors and how they contribute to the thesis of an article being skewed."

In conjunction with these organizations, readers themselves have become more active, more demanding of the press. Feedback is no longer ghettoized in the letters page of newspapers. It explodes onto the Internet on blogs, message boards, and Web sites belonging to news organizations. Journalists can't just publish and then move on without another thought to yesterday's news. They must engage and, frequently, defend themselves and their work.

This culture of checking can at times be personal and vindictive, but it can also be revelatory, impassioned, and highly effective. Most of all, it simply cannot be ignored by the press.

"For a writer, this huge, suddenly vocal audience has some significant advantages," wrote Gary Kamiya in an essay for Salon.com. "For one thing, it serves as an enormous fact-checker. If you make a mistake in a piece, some eagle-eyed reader will let you know, often within minutes. But a far more important effect of the reader revolution is that it has forced writers to immediately deal with substantive arguments and critique."

When I accessed Kamiya's article in early June 2007, six months after it was first published, *Salon*'s own metrics showed that it had generated more than three hundred letters from readers, and 120 posts on different blogs.

"A writer privileged enough to publish has to be thick-skinned to accept fair criticism, no matter how harsh," wrote Kamiya. He went on:

BLOGGERS' DENUNCIATION OF the "imperial media" can be overblown and paranoid, but it's legitimate to expect journalists to accept criticism. Once you write something and send it out into the world, you don't own it anymore: You offered it to the reader, and the reader has the right to respond as he or she wants. Before the Internet, it was easy for a journalist to behave like a sniper, rising furtively out of a foxhole, firing off a shot, then ducking back down to safety. Now, people are shooting back, and it's a bit much for the sniper to complain.

At their worst, this new breed of checker can be blinded by ide-
ology and fail to stick to the facts; at their best, however, they are
forcing the press to engage with the public more than ever before, to
meet a higher standard of accuracy, and to put an end to what one
U.S. newspaper editor called the "fortress newsroom." It has also
given rise to "citizen journalism," the product of an informal body of
readers who have become reporters, fact-checkers, and contributors in
all forms of media.

"Fortress newsroom was the walled enclave where journalists practiced their craft in a 'just the facts' environment, using selective notions of
objectivity and artificial forms of balance to shield themselves from many
consequences of their work," wrote Steven A. Smith, the editor of the
Spokane *Spokesman-Review*, in a commentary published on PressThink,
the influential blog operated by New York University journalism professor
Jay Rosen. "In fortress newsroom, readers are something of a necessary
inconvenience. We need their business, but not their ideas. In fortress
newsroom, objectivity means independence defined by *separation from*."

Smith's paper bulldozed its fortress by inviting members of the
public to attend its daily news meeting. It gave blogs to active citizens to
have them write about their areas of interest and expertise, and it began
Web casting its news meetings and inviting readers to watch and join
the conversation in chat rooms. His paper, the *Spokesman-Review*, has
opened up to the public and asked them to be involved.

There are today many outside forces banging at the fortress gate,
demanding to be let in. Often, their weapon of choice is facts, or claims
of error. In this, the age of the fact-checking reader and well-funded
media monitor, press outlets that do not dedicate themselves to a high
level of accuracy can expect to be called to account.

Distributed Fact Checking
RATHERGATE

I N A NOW FAMOUS AND INFAMOUS *60 Minutes II* report aired on
September 8, 2004, Dan Rather detailed what he and his team of producers believed to be important evidence regarding the National Guard

record of U.S. president George W. Bush. The report aired just two months before the presidential election, and Rather said the piece was based on "new documents and new information on the President's military service."

It relied primarily on six documents relating to Bush's service that were provided by Lieutenant Colonel Bill Burkett, a former Texas Air National Guard officer. They apparently showed that Bush was given preferential treatment while in the Guard, and that his commanding officer had recommended he be suspended, among other seemingly damaging information. The documents were said to have been written by the late Lieutenant Colonel Jerry B. Killian, who had been Bush's commander when he was in the Texas Air National Guard during the 1970s.

The story also relied on comments by Ben Barnes, a man actively raising money for Bush's opponent, who said he had helped land Bush a cushy placement in the National Guard to keep him from going to Vietnam. In the story, a spokesperson for Bush was given airtime to deny the charges as being totally false.

It was a big story, big enough to potentially impact the results of the upcoming election. As soon as it aired, other media outlets picked up on its claims. But so too did many right-leaning blogs and Web sites including FreeRepublic.com, PowerLine.com, and LittleGreenFootballs.com.

Commenters and writers questioned the authenticity of the documents, the research done by CBS News, and the overall claims of the story. They were at first driven by their political views, but soon they began to delve into the story's facts and background.

The day after the report, Power Line published a post, "The Sixty-first Minute," that initially passed on some of the questions raised in comments posted on Free Republic. But as the day progressed, the Power Line post was updated with more information from readers, other bloggers, and experts who stepped forward to add elements to the story. People from all over were engaging in a form of distributed fact checking. Each dug in different areas—evaluating the authenticity of the documents, revealing background on the sources—until a clearer, more troubling picture began to emerge.

One Power Line reader identified himself as a "clerk/typist for the US Navy at the Naval Underwater Systems Center (NUSC) in Newport RI for my summer job in 1971" and proceeded to list several points backing up why the memos had to have been forged.

"From 1973 until late 1982 I was a repairman for the Office Products Division of IBM," wrote in another reader, offering his expertise. Questions about the type and lettering style on the CBS documents abounded.

As the blogosphere cranked up the heat on CBS and its story, the mainstream press worked to stay on top of it, but it seemed as though the blogs were one step ahead of them, driving the narrative and turning up new evidence.

By the end of the day, on September 9, less than twenty-four hours after the story had aired, CBS felt compelled to issue a series of statements to defend its reporting. The first read,

> As is standard practice at CBS News, each of the documents broadcast on *60 Minutes* was thoroughly investigated by independent experts and we are convinced of their authenticity. In addition to analysis of the documents themselves, CBS verified the authenticity of the documents by talking to individuals who had seen the documents at the time they were written. These individuals were close associates of Colonel Jerry Killian and confirm that the documents reflect his opinions at the time the documents were written.

It was later changed to:

> As is standard practice at CBS News, the documents in the *60 Minutes* report were thoroughly examined and their authenticity vouched for by independent experts. As importantly, *60 Minutes* also interviewed close associates of Colonel Jerry Killian. They confirm that the documents reflect his opinions and actions at the time.

The major shift was that the story was being driven by blogs and average citizens, and not by the mainstream media. Commenters and writers from Free Republic, Power Line, and other blogs raised questions about whether a typewriter made in the 1970s could have produced the documents used by CBS. Two days after the story aired, news organizations had taken up the charge and found world-renowned typewriter experts to comment on the documents. This added a layer of professional authenticity to the fact checking, but it was in large part just a follow-up to the story being dug up by the blogs. The new checkers were leading the field.

For more than a week, CBS News stood behind its reporting. In the meantime, the media began to pick up the trail of the bloggers and readers who had seemingly broken the story wide open. As journalists worked to unpack the series of events that led to the questioning of the documents, they keyed in on one person who went by the name "Buckhead" and had posted a comment on Free Republic at 11:59 p.m. on the evening of the *60 Minutes II* broadcast.

He appeared to be patient zero of the fact-checking epidemic.

His post was lengthy and seemed to imply a high level of technical expertise. "I am saying these documents are forgeries, run through a copier for 15 generations to make them look old," he concluded. "This should be pursued aggressively." From there, it was.

Power Line put the comment up on its Web site the next morning, and soon former naval officers, typewriter mechanics, and others began weighing in. They were like a group of reporters pursuing a hot story— except that they weren't, at least not professionally trained ones.

Later that day, September 9, Little Green Footballs compared the CBS documents to one prepared on a basic word processor and marveled at the seeming similarities. For Matt Drudge, that was enough. Just before 3 p.m. on that day he updated his hugely trafficked Web site to read,

'60 MINUTES' DOCUMENTS ON BUSH MIGHT BE FAKE
32-year-old documents produced Wednesday by CBSNEWS 60 MINS on Bush's Guard service may have been forged using a current word processing program typed using a proportional

font, not common at that time, and they used a superscript font
feature found in today's Microsoft Word program, Internet
reports claim . . . Developing . . .

That led CBS to issue its statements supporting its story. It also
brought an even larger audience to the blogs.

"The server hosting Power Line crashed as hundreds of thousands
of Drudge readers tried to learn about the 60 Minutes scandal," reported
the *Weekly Standard*. "By 5:00 P.M., CBS was spooked enough to release
a statement saying the memos were 'thoroughly investigated by independent experts, and we are convinced of their authenticity.'"

Not all of the action was happening on the right-leaning blogs. Liberal
sites such as Daily Kos were also looking at the documents. A writer named
"Hunter" did a point-by-point takedown of the claims on the other blogs.
In a follow-up post to his first entry, Hunter wrote, "My point . . . was
simply to prove that the argument being proposed and propagated—that
MS Word and original version of the documents were 'mostly identical'—
was a red herring, and that the denizens of LittleGreenFootballs are
intellectual half-wits in a very large pond of right-wing half-wits."

There's no denying that the fact checking taking place on various
blogs was largely ideologically driven. And yet the warring posters
attempted to do battle with facts. They dug and researched like any journalist would, and they turned up reams of evidence. Some worked to
confirm the documents; others worked to debunk them. Aside from the
occasional sniping at each other, they chose to pursue their respective
agendas by fact-checking CBS and each other.

Charles Johnson of Little Green Footballs later said the success was
all due to "open-source intelligence gathering."

He told the *Washington Post*, "We've got a huge pool of highly motivated people who go out there and use the tools to find stuff. We've got
an army of citizen journalists out there."

Howard Kurtz, the *Post*'s respected media writer, noted, "Many sites
are seething with partisan passion, often directed at the media." And yet
he couldn't help but acknowledge that "they are also two-way portals for
retired military officers, computer techies, former IBM Selectric sales-

people and just about anyone else to challenge and fact-check media claims."

By September 20, the pressure finally got to CBS's main source, Bill Burkett. That day, CBS reported, he admitted "that he deliberately misled the CBS News producer working on the report, giving her a false account of the documents' origins to protect a promise of confidentiality to the actual source."

CBS president Andrew Heyward released a statement. "Based on what we now know, CBS News cannot prove that the documents are authentic, which is the only acceptable journalistic standard to justify using them in the report. We should not have used them. That was a mistake, which we deeply regret."

That evening, Dan Rather gave an on-air apology:

I NO LONGER HAVE THE CONFIDENCE in these documents that would allow us to continue vouching for them journalistically. I find we have been misled on the key question of how our source for the documents came into possession of these papers. That, combined with some of the questions that have been raised in public and in the press, leads me to a point where—if I knew then what I know now—I would not have gone ahead with the story as it was aired, and I certainly would not have used the documents in question.

But we did use the documents. We made a mistake in judgment, and for that I am sorry.

RatherGate, as many have come to call this episode, is today seen as a watershed for the power of blogs and the potential for average citizens to take part in reporting and acting as external fact-checkers on the press.

It should be noted that the documents themselves remain in dispute, which supports the idea that they shouldn't have been presented as totally reliable evidence. Mary Mapes, the top producer on the story, who was fired by CBS, later wrote a book that laid out her case for why they are genuine. Today, most believe that the documents are not trustworthy. The bottom line is that, in the end, there are too many questions and uncertainties about the documents' authenticity to make them the basis for any reporting.

In the years that have passed since RatherGate, more and more blogs have engaged in "distributed fact checking" by encouraging readers to hunt for information and facts to support or debunk a story or theory.

Talking Points Memo, a left-leaning blog operated by Joshua Micah Marshall, is credited with breaking the story about the questionable firings of U.S. prosecutors by the Bush administration in 2007. When the mainstream media failed to pursue the issue, he and his readers and contributors kept digging and eventually blew it wide open. Resignations and Senate hearings followed their work.

In 2006, Charles Johnson of Little Green Footballs raised doubts about photos taken by Reuters contributing photographer Adnan Hajj. He said they had been manipulated, and it turned out he was right. Hajj was then fired by Reuters.

In October 2006, I was introduced to one dedicated independent fact-checker via e-mail. The subject line of the message seemed spam-like enough: "Perhaps the most important inquiry you could get." I came close to deleting it before having a quick read.

"I'm just getting familiar with your site," it read. "Bravo for high-lighting the errors, egregious and/or just silly, that big papers make *and admit*. But at my first glance, you don't seem to deal in a yet-more-important issue: the *uncorrected* errors constantly and permanently disinforming the public."

The writer, Mark Powell, then outlined his months of work fact checking one U.S. newspaper. His conclusion was

THIS IS THE BIGGEST UN-/UNDERREPORTED SCANDAL IN U.S. JOURNALISM. While the chattering class ever harps on so-and-so's political bias, real and imagined, sheer topical and journalistic INCOMPETENCE is destroying print's last hope in the electronic age, viz. acknowledged credibility/ authority superiority.

Powell lives in Virginia and his paper of choice is the *Washington Post*. As far as he is concerned, the paper's corrections "represent a very tiny fraction of the paper's 'correctable' errors. Fact is nearly none of the thousand-odd errors I've cataloged—probably less than 2 percent— were ever corrected."

While most people might scoff at someone claiming to have cataloged roughly a thousand uncorrected errors in a single newspaper, I had to admit that if I could spend countless hours reading tens of thousands of corrections over the past couple of years, chances were good that my uncorrected-errors doppelgänger existed somewhere in the world.

Powell is a writer who has been published in many different U.S. newspapers. He had taken it upon himself to track the number of errors he could spot in each day's edition of the *Post*. He was in the process of looking for a publication that would publish his reams of daily and monthly reports about what he perceived to be the *Post*'s litany of errors. (Powell had applied for a job as a copy editor at the *Post* and had been rebuffed.) He was as focused and dedicated an external fact-checker as I've come across, and no doubt a thorn in the *Post*'s side since he regularly e-mailed editors with his findings. I told him he struck me as the kind of person who would have been well suited to the job of proof-reader. Too bad it no longer exists.

The examples of blogs and individual citizens engaged in fact checking the press are now legion. It has become routine, expected. Even before RatherGate, many in the press and the online world saw it coming.

"Keep an eye on bloggers," suggested a *U.S. News & World Report* article in 2002. "The main arena for media criticism is not going to be books, columns, or panel discussions, and it certainly won't be journalism schools. It will be the Internet."

"Web diarists are calling the print media's bluff," concluded the writer.

In a post about the *U.S. News & World Report* story on his personal blog, Nick Denton, a former journalist turned successful blog publisher, noted, "I have a friend who is doing a piece on weblogs for New York Magazine. She's terrified. Good."

Some in the profession see this new level of press scrutiny as troublesome. They view bloggers and the other new checkers as nothing more than amateur partisan critics hammering away at stories they don't like. But examples such as RatherGate and the Reuters photo-manipulation scandal demonstrate the public's newfound ability to participate in the reporting process and hold the press to account. It has also raised the stakes for press mistakes.

Errors are being turned up more frequently than ever before. Specific reporters are facing increased, and sometimes unfair, scrutiny. New pressure is being exerted on the press, and though bias is usually the charge that follows an error, the error frequently relates to accuracy. Get something wrong or report something questionable and, as Ken Layne put it in a widely quoted blog post from 2002, "This is the Internet, and we can fact check your ass."

This makes accuracy within newsrooms all the more important and urgent. If journalists don't find and eliminate errors, there are plenty of outside citizens and organizations itching for the chance to do so.

News organizations such as the *Spokesman-Review* that embrace the power and wisdom of the crowd can leverage this new environment of checking and reader engagement to forge a stronger connection with their community. It can open doors to new stories and add expertise to reportorial work that can improve overall accuracy.

Press outlets that continue to fortify their crumbling fortress walls will continue to be checked and prodded. Their errors will be held up as examples of their arrogance and incompetence.

The best solution for the press today is to raise its level of accuracy and embrace the legions of checkers and citizen reporters clamoring to take part in the news process. Improve the quality of reporting, and there will be less of a need for bloggers to act as fact-checkers. Better yet, invite them into the news process and harness their expertise to do better reporting. The new checkers represent a threat, but they are, more than anything else, an opportunity. They are passionate about the news; all they ask is that they be able to participate in a meaningful way and not be shut out or ignored.

Media-Monitoring Organizations

IN 1969, REED IRVINE, AN ECONOMIST with the U.S. Federal Reserve Board, approached Arthur Krock, the legendary retired Washington bureau chief and columnist for the *New York Times*, to see if he was interested in a collaboration.

Irvine wanted Krock to be the chairman of a new organization, Accuracy in Media, or AIM. The idea was to create an organization that could monitor the mainstream press for inaccuracy and bias, and provide an external conservative voice for media accountability. Krock declined the offer, citing his long-time relationship with the *Times*.

According to a passage from Irvine's book *Media Mischief and Misdeeds*, quoted in an article in the *Nation*, this led him to believe "that the type of organization I had in mind would have to be representative of and run by consumers of the journalistic product, not by the producers. . . . We created Accuracy in Media with the deliberate policy of not involving active journalists in its work or direction."

AIM was among the earliest of the external media-monitoring organizations. Today, the ranks of these groups have swelled. Monitoring the press for errors and bias is now an industry unto itself.

Some of these groups focus on a single issue (such as reporting about Israel, or business), while others work to combat ideological bias and inaccuracy in the press as a whole. AIM and the Media Research Center are two of the most prominent right-leaning monitors. On the left, Media Matters for America is one of the largest.

There are other groups such as Fairness and Accuracy in Reporting (FAIR), which positions itself as a "progressive" anticensorship organization that is "advocating for greater diversity in the press and . . . scrutinizing media practices that marginalize public interest, minority and dissenting viewpoints." (Most of the other monitoring groups place them on the left end of the spectrum.)

These groups publish their own critiques of the media, hunt for bias and inaccuracies, and contact press outlets to raise their concerns. They will often ask for corrections or seek to get a particular news organization to rethink its coverage on a certain issue. They are organized and often well funded, and many journalists are aware of their presence, if only because they or their colleagues have been put in their crosshairs.

Media monitors are another layer of external checking on the press, though their constant critiques and accusations of bias frustrate many journalists.

Cliff Kincaid, the editor of the *AIM Report*, says Irvine was, among other things, concerned about the failure of news organizations to offer proper corrections for incorrect reporting.

"He was always concerned about the media and, in particular, the *New York Times* not making prominent corrections and not giving readers enough context to make it clear what the error was," he told me.

Kincaid says the goal of AIM is to "create a healthy skepticism about what people see, read, and hear in the press."

Eric Boehlert, a former writer for *Rolling Stone* and Salon.com, is now a senior fellow at Media Matters for America. David Brock founded it in 2004 with the aim of "monitoring, analyzing, and correcting conservative misinformation in the U.S. media."

When asked to describe his group's work, he is quick to point to its emphasis on hard facts, rather than issues of bias. "We don't pretend to read the minds of journalists the way the conservative groups do," he told me. "We are much more of a fact-driven organization. Our Web site is full of transcripts and audio and video."

Those on the left see AIM and the Media Research Center as rabid conservative groups pushing a political agenda. But the same can be said for how those on the right see groups such as Media Matters and its liberal leanings. Caught in between is the press.

An old adage in journalism holds that if both sides of a story are mad at you, then you probably got it right. But that's a myopic view. It can sometimes be cited to avoid discussion with sources, or even as justification for not offering a correction.

The most effective of these groups focus on using facts—or errors—to make their case, because they recognize the power of accuracy and the press's desire to achieve it. Debates about perceived bias of coverage or sins of omission are also healthy and necessary; journalists have them with one another all the time. The public and interested parties should also be free to engage in this discussion, and, most of all, they should be heard.

These groups constitute another force that is driving the press to open up and be more transparent about how it works, and more conscientious about admitting and effectively correcting mistakes. The overall effect is a positive one as long as the debate and discussion don't degenerate into empty claims of bias and unprofessionalism. This is the tightrope these organizations must walk in order to be seen as genuine monitors, rather than partisan attack dogs.

In many ways, the best of them attempt to operate as their own accuracy news service. They publish, report, and research. But just like the press, they are prone to their own mistakes. Everyone is fallible, but a higher standard of reporting and public discourse can be achieved when various parties act as checks and balances on one another. The press is supposed to act as a check and balance on the major institutions of society, and as the faithful agent of free speech and public discourse. These organizations, and the new checkers, attempt to act as media watchdogs, but they are also prone to checking on one another.

During my interview with Kincaid, he spent a good deal of time talking about the faults of Media Matters for America, in addition to citing problems with various news organizations and the press in general.

When I mentioned this to Boehlert, he laughed. Then, a few days after we spoke, he sent me an e-mail message with a link to a post on NewsBusters.org in order to drive home a point about the difference between his organization and what he called "conservative 'fact-checkers.'" A week later, he offered another example of an agenda-driven error by the Media Research Center. It's not surprising that these monitoring groups often can't help but monitor one another.

In pointing out the differences between his organization and others such as the Media Research Center, Boehlert said that liberal media critics "want the press to get better and be more responsible. I write about the press as someone who loves it and I am saddened when it doesn't do a better job. In terms of conservative critics, their only real beef with the press is that it exists."

Kincaid said one of the faults of Media Matters is that "it is too quick to favor government regulation [of the press]." He was frank in saying that some of the newer watchdog groups "should be watched" as well as the press itself, but his larger point was directed at today's readers: "Become your own media watchdog. . . . what you have to do is compare and contrast and get multiple sources and investigate for yourself. You cannot assume anything out there is the gospel."

Even with the understandable competition and animosity that exists between the right- and left-leaning monitoring groups, they do for the most part manage to stay focused on the press. They have no shortage of issues to raise, reports to correct, coverage to question. Some of it is of course a matter of opinion, but often they do a good job of sticking to the facts, even if they use the facts to stick it to a particular political point of view.

For the press, these organizations are difficult to ignore. They are often staffed by former journalists who know how to navigate their way up the editorial chain, or how to formulate a compelling complaint or request for correction. The members and followers of these organizations are also often organized to send in letters to the editor or requests for correction to create what appears to be a groundswell of support and communication.

Unfortunately for these organizations, members sometimes neglect to write their own individual letters, so a newspaper is inundated with dozens or hundreds of letters that largely read the same, and are therefore easily dismissed as part of a campaign. This practice of manufacturing a "grassroots" reaction is called "Astroturfing," as in fake grassroots. Newspaper ombudsmen and letters-page editors are all too familiar with it these days. In truth, it hurts the credibility of the organization behind it, but it's an example of another level of pressure that is being applied to the press, albeit a frustrating one.

This age of fact-checking readers, blogs, media-monitoring organizations, and other groups and individuals who watch the press is bringing a new sense of urgency to the issue of accuracy. Facts are flying fast and furious. Campaigns are being orchestrated to request corrections, and specific reporters and news outlets are dealing with an unheard-of level of scrutiny. This is forcing the press to open up and be more communicative about how it operates, and to admit mistakes when they occur.

Regardless of whether they are presented by a partisan group or an individual (and aren't we all partisan in the end?), facts are meant to be revered by the press. They are the building blocks of journalism. But journalists are no longer the owners and distributors of the facts. They have competition. People are looking over their shoulders, banging on the fortress gate. In the end, the press will benefit by letting them in, and being more open and frank about how it goes about doing its work.

Journalists used to have a kind of monopoly on the news. Every morning a newspaper would hit your doorstep and tell you what you were supposed to know. Radio would fill you in during the day, and TV would wrap it all up in a nice package at night. Then you could turn to a magazine or book for a more focused or long-term view on the news. It was a nice little ecosystem of information, and the average person largely picked from a menu of options determined by the media itself. That's no longer the case.

The new checkers are helping to create a new ecosystem of news, and they are doing it by attacking error and demanding accuracy and honesty from the press. In the process, they are creating a media environment in which errors are more costly and damaging than ever before. They are pushing the press to a higher standard, one fact, one correction, at a time.

CHAPTER 14

THE BIG NEWSPAPER
IN THE SKY

THERE IS GOOD NEWS TO REPORT. Pockets of innovation exist within the press, and many dedicated journalists, editors, and organizations are pushing accuracy and corrections forward.

The *Telegraph Herald*, a daily newspaper in Iowa, has for years been publishing its corrections on the front page—regardless of how big or small the error. The *Star-Telegram* in Texas is using a plagiarism detection service to spot-check work for theft. Online news operations such as Slate.com have turned the correction into a useful part of a story, while the *New York Times* is working to apply corrections to breaking news online. The *San Francisco Chronicle* has taken its corrections and reader feedback and turned them into a podcast. Journalism organizations have devised accuracy training programs and initiatives, and ombudsmen are agitating for better handling of corrections online and in databases.

These initiatives from within the profession combine with outside pressure from blogs, media-monitoring organizations, and increasingly media-savvy readers to give the impression that things are slowly beginning to change.

It has become fashionable—and in many ways valid—to point to the declining readership and circulation of daily newspapers and the shrinking audiences for network newscasts as the factors that are forcing journalism to evolve. But journalists themselves also want to see the news industry take advantage of technologies that are creating new ways of reporting, verifying, and disseminating news.

In every interview I've conducted about accuracy and corrections, on the issue of resources, journalists ask, How can we afford to focus on this issue and put resources into developing new processes and new verification techniques when we're simply trying to publish or broadcast in a difficult staffing and economic environment? A glib answer would be, How can you afford not to?

Improving accuracy levels is, in and of itself, not an expensive undertaking; it begins with a commitment and flows from there into policies, practices, and technologies. Training journalists to spend ten minutes checking their work before they send it to an editor—and giving them the tools to do it effectively—is not a major drain on a news organization. Neither is assigning an editor to do random fact checking on just a few of the stories for that night's newscast or the next day's paper. While antiplagiarism services are currently too expensive for most news organizations to use on every story, they could become more affordable if the industry came together to negotiate group pricing.

Creating an online corrections page and style is not going to cost huge amounts of money, nor is devising a standard for how corrections are written and presented. If ESPN, a sports network, can develop a corrections policy that covers its television, radio, print, and online properties, so too can other broadcasters and publishers. (In fact, ESPN benefited from the free advice offered by the Poynter Institute, a nonprofit organization that helps guide news organizations in issues such as these. Their expertise and resources should be called upon by more news organizations.)

There is too much emphasis on the reasons why accuracy is difficult to achieve, and why the human and economic resources aren't there to deliver it. Journalists think that smaller initiatives don't matter, and that's absolutely not the case. The only thing costly about accuracy is what happens to journalism when we don't pay attention to it.

Along with a renewed sense of commitment and the realization that accuracy can be improved with inexpensive initiatives, there also needs to be a shift in how news organizations view their work.

As Jeff Jarvis notes in the foreword of this book, news must be seen as a process, not a product. Just as computer manufacturers realize they must provide a certain level of postpurchase service to customers, journalists must understand that the reporting they produce does not end with its publication or broadcast. Stories must be maintained, updated, and, of course, corrected. Part of the job of being a journalist is to heed feedback from readers, and engage them in conversation. A correction can be one result of this conversation; a new story or important insight could be another.

In today's media environment, a story never dies. The act of publication or broadcast merely delivers the story to the world. From there it is archived, cached, linked, quoted, and blogged. Readers, critics, other news organizations, and the public at large take hold of it and, for better or worse, turn it into something new. This makes the correction more important now than it has ever been before. It must be woven into the fabric of news. Corrections must exist wherever journalism exists. Readers should be given new tools to help them report and track corrections and errors. To help journalists attain a higher level of accuracy, the collective knowledge of readers everywhere should be welcomed and brought to bear on news coverage.

In this media era, people expect stories and information to be constantly updated; the correction is, in essence, a form of update, albeit one that addresses past error rather than breaking news. Corrections must not be ghettoized or hidden or perceived as punishment; rather, they should be part of the job of reporting and editing. Corrections are acceptable when a news organization has taken all necessary steps to prevent errors in the first place, but the current level of error in the press is unacceptable. Perhaps even more important, most errors go uncorrected.

To stop the pollution of the information stream, the press must attack uncorrected errors—detect them before they are published, and build and strengthen mechanisms to locate and correct errors that had not previously come to light.

"The public expects more than just talk about accuracy; they want to know that efforts are in place to try to be more accurate," said a report from the American Society of Newspaper Editors. "Besides the obvious (correct grammar and spelling), they expect journalists to get the facts right, to have the right facts, and to correct the record when they err. In short, errors can be forgiven, but confession is required first."

It might sound contradictory, but to have fewer errors we will need to have a period of more corrections. This doesn't mean ignoring error-prevention initiatives; they can be bolstered by useful error data: How many errors are being made? What are they? Where do they occur? What caused them? This kind of analysis is essential for devising a prevention program, and yet too many media outlets don't collect the data or put enough effort into encouraging sources, the public, and their own staffs to report errors.

No journalist will argue that accuracy isn't important, yet it is not an area of investment or innovation. Journalism talks about itself in very lofty terms: It asks the public to trust and support it, and asks political, business, and social leaders to provide access, answer questions, and stand up to be scrutinized. But how can the press expect to maintain its important position if it does not meet one of the fundamental values it espouses—accuracy?

The areas for improvement and innovation to raise accuracy levels are many. Herewith, I suggest some of the better accuracy ideas and initiatives I've collected, and present them as a menu of options for the press and the public. This is by no means a definitive list. I only hope that the best of these examples that are already in use come into wider practice, and that the profession will consider some of my recommendations.

There is no single silver bullet for achieving greater accuracy, but there are many very-high-caliber practices and initiatives that will deliver demonstrable results.

Accuracy Training

ORGANIZATIONS SUCH AS THE POYNTER INSTITUTE and the American Press Institute have established accuracy training programs, or at the very least have experts who can offer advice free of charge to newsrooms. Newspapers such as the *Chicago Tribune* have devised their own accuracy training and tracking programs. Innovations are taking place within news organizations, but knowledge is not being shared and the industry has not come together to set broad new standards for accuracy and corrections. One of the key ways to provide better accuracy training for journalists and editors is to collect this dispersed knowledge and turn it into a single program that can be adapted to newsrooms large and small.

Journalism schools should develop ways to put even more emphasis on the issue of accuracy. At Concordia University, where I studied journalism, students would lose a letter grade on their work if they misspelled a name in a piece of class writing. Some schools offer more serious punishment for the offense, while others don't even have accuracy-related requirements. Aside from using these punitive measures to emphasize the importance of accuracy in journalism, schools could use accuracy-specific courses and programs to help train young journalists to develop good habits early on. They should be required in every program.

According to the American Press Institute's accuracy program, journalistic accuracy boils down to several key issues:

- Asking effective questions
- Taking accurate notes
- Gathering source documents
- Questioning information
- Verifying information
- Fact-checking your story

It then explores these specific areas to offer advice. Interns and new reporters should be required to do some sort of accuracy training when they start, and existing staff should be given refresher courses on a regular basis.

Training programs of this kind need to be kept alive and fresh in the minds of journalists through regular conversations about accuracy. As a specific measure, for example, corrections could be compiled at least monthly and sent to section editors so they could spot reporting weaknesses. If a reporter has a specific problem with, say, spelling names, or handling numbers, instead of simply being reprimanded, he or she should be encouraged to take a course of training, or use an accuracy checklist.

An accuracy checklist is a document used by some newsrooms as a guide for reporters to use before they file their stories. It's just what it sounds like: a list of specific facts to check before completing a story.

Verifying names, dates, figures, and other basic information is supposed to be a standard practice for reporters, but often, especially on deadline, they forget, or just rely on memory. A checklist gives them a concrete tool they can go through when they've finished writing every story. Checklists can also be useful for story editors, both print and broadcast.

In addition to training and tools, accuracy should be made part of the newsroom culture, which means errors must be destigmatized. They are not the exclusive province of sloppy or bad journalists. They happen to everyone. This is because of how our brains work, the technologies we use every day (think spell-checkers), and the nature of journalism itself. Getting journalists to acknowledge that errors, while unacceptable, are a part of journalism, helps to remove some of their stigma. The challenge then is to get people excited and passionate about preventing and correcting them.

News outlets should consider having error or correction competitions to reward reporters and editors who produce error-free copy. Along with rewards for good work, there should also be clear procedures and penalties for inaccurate or unethical reporting practices. Training can help turn a sloppy journalist into a careful, accurate one. People who cannot be trained to be accurate simply don't belong in journalism.

Ombudsmen as Error Trackers

AT A DAILY NEWSPAPER, an ombudsman or public editor is largely tasked with responding to reader questions and complaints, typically writing a weekly or twice-monthly column that addresses issues in their paper. Broadcast and other media also have editors who deal with reporting issues that concern their audience. Ombudsmen and public editors often, but not always, are also in charge of the news outlet's corrections.

An additional role of the public editor or ombudsman should be to oversee the tracking and analysis of his or her outlet's errors. Errors should be cataloged according to their severity (low, medium, high, or something similar); the nature of the error (misspelling, misattribution, incorrect statistic, and so on); the cause of the error (reporter error, editing error, source error); how the error was discovered (by the source, by a reader, by the reporter); and the author of the article, the section it appeared in, and the date the article ran.

Using a simple database program with decent reporting features, a publication or outlet will be able to see the number and types of errors along with their causes to get a clear picture of the news organization's level of accuracy.

This may sound like an intensive process, but once it's up and running it requires only a bit of work each day to gather the details of that day's errors and input them. It's well worth it.

Papers such as the *Rocky Mountain News*, *Boston Globe*, and a handful of others have tracking systems in place. For those papers that feel they can't afford to build a system, organizations such as the American Society of Newspaper Editors should consider creating a free Web-based system that will enable any newspaper to input and track its errors. This data would remain private to the specific publication but could potentially be anonymized and used to produce an industry-wide accuracy report that could inform larger initiatives.

Instant Source Surveys

SOME PUBLICATIONS CURRENTLY USE a postpublication survey to gauge the accuracy of their reporting. Forms are mailed to sources quoted in specific articles so the paper can gather feedback on the accuracy of the article. This is a good practice, but research has shown that when the survey comes from the paper itself, sources tend to complete and return a lower percentage of error reports. A survey form that is sent weeks or months after an article is published can further decrease the return rate.

The postpublication survey should be made available online immediately after publication of the article. Using an online form could also speed up the error tracking and correction process. Much like the error database, this system could be created as an industry-wide initiative that would spare individual news outlets the costs of having to produce their own technology.

The Corrections

Wᴵᴛʜ ɴᴇᴡsᴘᴀᴘᴇʀs, ᴍᴀɢᴀᴢɪɴᴇs, and broadcast organizations now largely running both print and online operations,
more thought needs to be given to how each of these media requires a
unique approach to corrections.

UPDATES AND MISTAKES

Iɴ ᴘʀɪɴᴛ, ᴄᴏʀʀᴇᴄᴛɪᴏɴs sʜᴏᴜʟᴅ ʙᴇ ɢɪᴠᴇɴ more prominence. The best
way to achieve this is to print a few of them on the front page and
continue them inside the paper. This is of course the most valued
real estate in a newspaper, and I understand editors' hesitation to
use it to deal with issues relating to previous reporting. As a compromise, I propose that publications create a small "Updates and
Mistakes" box for the front page, which would be part of the
existing story index. The idea is to give readers an easy way to
locate articles from recent editions that have been updated with
new information or a correction. The box would simply list the
headlines of the relevant articles or corrections and direct readers
to their location in the paper.

A front-page box ensures a higher level of recognition for corrected articles. It connects the story to the correction, a link that
doesn't exist in today's print editions. The updates also are a way to
keep articles "alive." Not all articles can be followed, and not all
need to be corrected. But new information often arises. Online,
updates and corrections can be added to an article or easily
uploaded as wire copy. But in the print version, space is at a premium, so full updates would not always be possible. The print
updates, however, could offer basic identifying information and also
direct readers to the Web site for a more comprehensive approach.
It keeps the stories alive and offers a better way of directing readers
to relevant corrections. Here is a simple representation of what it
could look like:

Updates and Mistakes

Corrected Articles

Headline, date published . . . A2

Headline, date published . . . A2

Updated Articles

Headline, date published . . . E4

Headline, date published . . . B12

This box could also be reproduced on a news organization's Web site; just as many of them now have listings of "Most Read" and "Most E-mailed" articles, they could add an "Updates and Mistakes" tab and give readers a way to see if recent stories they've read have been corrected or updated.

In addition, outlets in all media must ensure that they have a specific editor who handles corrections and that the editor's contact information is easily found by readers. Corrections that do appear must cite the headline of the original article and the date of its airing or publication, list what the incorrect information was, provide the correct information, and also explain why the error occurred. These are the most basic requirements for a correction.

For broadcasters, the correction should appear in the medium in which the error originated; an online correction for a radio or television report is simply not doing enough to ensure that the audience will find it. Placing it online on a set page, and within the article's text, is also essential.

ONLINE CORRECTIONS

THERE ARE SIMILARITIES IN HOW some of the larger American newspapers are handling corrections online. Both the *New York Times* and the *Washington Post* have a static corrections page linked from their home page; the corrections page links to the corrected story and places the correction within the text of the article itself. The *Post* puts its corrections at the top of the piece, while the *Times* tags articles with "Correction Appended" at the top and runs the correction at the end.

The first rule of online corrections and errors is: Never "scrub." If an article containing an error is published, once the error is discovered it must be updated with a correction. Newspapers and every other news organization with an online presence should have an online corrections page linked from its home page, and all corrections must also be clearly placed within the text of the story. Corrections also apply to breaking news published online. (Again, this is a place where an "Updates and Mistakes" tab can be of use. It helps readers track breaking stories.)

The *New York Times* has dedicated itself to correcting breaking stories from its Continuous News Desk. This desk's reporters write stories for the Web, often about breaking events, so yes, their reports are continuously replaced by updated reports. In the past, errors would be corrected in subsequent drafts—but not noted. Now the paper is placing a correction notice at the bottom of its continuous reports. One example from the bottom of a December 12, 2006, story:

> EARLIER VERSIONS OF THIS ARTICLE gave an incorrect street address for the BMW of Manhattan showroom on Wall Street.

Slate.com also deserves recognition for creating an entirely new way to present corrections online. In articles that have an error, *Slate's* editors place an asterisk at the end of the corrected sentence. Clicking on this asterisk takes the reader to the correction at the bottom of the article. (*Slate* doesn't note at the top of the piece that the article has been corrected; its editors might consider adding this feature.) *Slate* also has a static corrections page for the week's corrections.

The asterisk feature helps show the reader exactly where the error occurred, and it then links this location with the resulting correction. It's a lovely bit of context, especially since corrections in general are often written in a confusing style. The hyperlinked asterisk makes great use of the medium.

Another advancement at *Slate* is that it offers an RSS (Really Simple Syndication) feed for corrections. Very few papers currently offer this feature. If columnists and sections get their own RSS feed, then shouldn't corrections warrant one? They do. And more should be done with corrections feeds in general.

Many news organizations' Web sites now enable readers to sign up to receive notification by e-mail when a specific journalist has published an article. Readers can also sign up to track certain topics, personalities, or sections. RSS feeds and e-mail alerts should be set up for corrections as well. Readers should be able to be notified if a particular article they read has been corrected. This is a simple matter of adding a sign-up box under the existing notification box that will enable readers to enter their e-mail addresses and be contacted if a correction is issued for that given article. Some Web sites, such as the *Toronto Star*'s, already have a button on every article that readers can click on to report a typo or error. This is another good way to make it easier for readers to report errors.

Overall, readers should have more options and tools to report and receive corrections.

The *Wall Street Journal* is pursuing another minor corrections innovation. The paper has a corrections-only search box on its online corrections page. This offers readers easy access to previously corrected material. Of course, viewing corrections that are more than ninety days old will cost $2.95 each, but at least readers can search to see if a particular topic has warranted recent and past corrections.

The Internet has created an opportunity for a new form of correction: one that is fluid, linkable, interactive, and more trackable than ever before. Some news organizations are working toward this goal; most, unfortunately, have a long way to go.

One way to raise the corrections standard industry-wide would be for professional journalism organizations to work together to set a baseline standard for online corrections. This step would help the news industry demonstrate that it does care about correcting its errors in the online world.

Fact Checking and
Plagiarism Detection

DAILY AND ONLINE NEWS OPERATIONS largely view fact checking as a nonstarter. Because they don't have the time or resources to pursue the kind of painstaking checking done by top magazines, they simply say it's not possible. But fact checking can take many forms. Just because the magazine model won't work for newspapers and online operations doesn't mean there isn't another type of checking that can.

As it stands today, reporters in daily or 24/7 news operations are expected to check their own work. Copy editors then spot any obvious factual errors and fix any misspellings or incorrect language. But some newspapers, such as the *Star-Telegram* in Texas, have gone a step further and introduced a form of postpublication fact checking. David House, the paper's reader advocate, will randomly select an article from a recent edition and do a thorough fact-check on it, as well as run it through the iThenticate plagiarism detection service. This is admittedly a very small sampling of the paper, but House feels that it has been effective. It acts as a deterrent to would-be plagiarists and sloppy reporters, and it also helps reinforce the quality of the paper's work because, after "a few dozen" random checks, he had yet to find any serious errors.

"It's just a great reassurance of our staff's competence and our commitment to good work," he told me.

This kind of random postpublication fact checking is not especially time-consuming, and it can be both an effective deterrent and a badge of honor for the staff. But a checking program need not end there. Prevention is of course extremely important. News organizations should consider assigning one copy editor per section to perform a random fact-check on a single story in each day's edition or broadcast. He or she would gather all of the source material from the reporter and double-check it for accuracy: names, dates, and statistics—all the basic factual information. This would occupy perhaps thirty minutes or an hour of the copy editor's time, and the job would be rotated on a daily basis. It's an easy, effective, and inexpensive way to bring a level of checking into a fast-paced news environment. It also puts reporters on notice.

The second aspect of House's program is also something other news-rooms should consider. Currently, most news outlets see services such as iThenticate and MyDropBox as too expensive to be used regularly. Indeed, House's paper had to trade its preferred service, iThenticate, for MyDropBox due to budget cuts. (The funding was later restored and his program now continues with iThenticate.) The cost of checking every article for plagiarism would be too high for almost every newspaper and online news operation in existence. But just as fact checking can be done on a daily random basis, so too could plagiarism checks. Running between five and fifteen stories through these services on a daily basis would not create a significant expense. If the major publishers banded together to negotiate special pricing from the providers, the cost would drop even lower.

All it requires is the will of the industry to find an affordable, acceptable solution. There's no question that one exists.

"My great dream is that iThenticate becomes for the editing process what spell-check is for the writing process," House told me, though he was quick to note some of the failings of spell-checkers. The point is that nothing, especially in terms of technological solutions, is perfect. But technology can deliver results. "It would be wonderful if programs like that could be so affordable that they become a regular part of the process," he said.

He also emphasized that "you don't have to do much very often" to have an impact on accuracy.

"We may not be able to use plagiarism deterrents and [fact checking] as often as we would like, but the staff knows that we do them," he said. "And it's a wonderful reminder and motivator for them to know that they're working for a newspaper that expects professionalism and detests plagiarism. You don't have to do many of these things to keep the issue fresh and top of mind for staff."

Another practice House is proud of is that the paper publishes its corrections on the front page of the section in which the error occurred. Sports errors are corrected on the front page of the sports section; errors from the front section are corrected on the front page.

Rising concerns about photo manipulation and Photoshopping are also requiring photojournalists to look for ways to ensure the quality and accuracy of their work. After it suffered criticism for the dishonest work of contributing photographer Adnan Hajj, Reuters decided to work on a technological solution that could help enforce its policy against the alteration of news photos.

"As a geek myself, I searched for a technical solution that would prevent digital manipulation," said Tom Glocer, the CEO of Reuters, in a speech after the Hajj episode. "We are working with Adobe and Canon to create a solution that enables photo editors to view an audit trail of changes to a digital image, which is permanently embedded in the photograph, ensuring the accuracy of the image. We are still working through the details and hope this will be a new standard for Reuters and I believe should be the new industry standard."

Glocer emphasized that the search for a technological solution was "not because we don't trust our photographers. . . . No, we sought a technical solution so that we had total and full transparency of our work."

Technology isn't the whole answer, but it can play a major role and even help deliver automation that saves newsrooms time and money.

Embracing the Lighter Side of Accuracy

WHEN WAYNE EZELL, reader advocate of the *Florida Times-Union*, wrote a column in November 2006 pointing out some of the more amusing recent errors readers had found in the paper, he decided to issue a fun challenge. He offered any reader who spotted an error in that day's edition a reward: a *Times-Union* umbrella.

"Perhaps this will help rivet attention on what many see as a serious problem, a decline in standards," he wrote.

He later told me the paper "heard from roughly 80 readers and about 35 mistakes were identified. The most frequently cited one was in the lead paragraph of a sports story about off-field behavior of football players."

The paper had printed the word "persay" instead of "per se." And the reader calls and e-mails flooded in.

Why can't every news organization embrace the idea of the fact-checking reader and offer rewards or even an ongoing contest for eagle-eyed subscribers? Why not enable them to create an account on the Web site and easily submit errors they spot in the paper, online, or in a broadcast? A leaderboard of the best proofreading readers and viewers could be a source of healthy competition and serve the immediate need of eliminating uncorrected errors by correcting as many errors as possible. Especially given the current enthusiasm for fact-checking, news organizations should be harnessing the collective knowledge of the public, and acknowledging and rewarding them for it. Error spotting is one way to do this, and Ezell is considering holding another contest soon.

Another example in humility and reader interaction is a project by Reuters. It now has a blog called "The Good, the Bad, & the Ugly" on its main Web site. This is where editors respond to feedback (usually complaints or requests for correction) from readers. It's often akin to a friendly café where Reuters serves itself some humble pie and readers get to enjoy watching editors eat it. It's about conversation and pulling back the veil on how the news operation works (and occasionally doesn't). The comments and complaints from readers are often very frank, even harsh, and the replies from editors are equally forthright, albeit sometimes brief.

It's a great experiment in corrections as conversation because readers get meaningful responses in a public forum and Reuters demonstrates that it does pay attention to reader comments and calls for correction.

"[The Good, the Bad & the Ugly] openly admits to readers that a lot of other people also objected to a particular headline or style or approach to a story," Robert Basler, the blog's editor, said in an interview. "It admits that some of our content didn't meet our high standards. It allows for very public interactive debate about perceived biases, agendas, etc. GBU makes us accessible and accountable, and that's what readers expect these days."

This is a great way to open up the conversation about errors, and readers feel it's appreciated when they take the time to point them out.

One of the most amusing and inventive uses of corrections I've seen in recent years is at the *San Francisco Chronicle*. In January 2007, it launched "Correct Me If I'm Wrong," a regular podcast that features selected voice-mail corrections and comments left by readers.

"Almost every day, The *Chronicle* hears from readers (and some non-readers)," the paper wrote in launching the feature. "Most of these comments—voicemail, email and letters—don't make it into our letters column. But they can be unusually passionate, irate, confounding and creative."

The acknowledgment that so many pieces of reader communication—voice mail, e-mail, and letters—end up going unacknowledged or unprinted is key. This is a way to give them new life.

The first installment of the paper's podcast was nothing short of hilarious, and it was a valid correction. The reader, who gets more than a little enraged, pointed out repeatedly in a voice-mail message that the paper referred to a "pilotless drone," which is of course redundant. Drones are by definition unmanned aircraft.

This was a fantastic update of the correction for the online world, though the paper shouldn't choose only the most irate or humorous reader voice-mail corrections and comments. By all means, offer the choice messages that give the public a sense of the kind of abuse journalists sometimes face. But if the paper ignores some of the more sincere, less histrionic offerings, the danger is that this feature could turn into something that mocks readers.

"This is about listening to your readers," Phil Bronstein, the paper's editor, told the *New York Times*. "Newspapers used to be a lot more lively than they are now, and they could definitely stand some of that." If readers respond well, he added, the paper might add "dramatic readings" of some of the letters that come in. Brilliant.

Many errors and resulting corrections are undeniably humorous. There's nothing wrong with embracing the lighter side of this content, as long the necessary prevention and correction measures are being undertaken and communicated to readers. Readers appreciate a news outlet that can laugh at itself, and errors and corrections provide ample opportunity for this. Corrections also have the type of content that can be used to encourage reader contribution and interaction in fun, useful ways.

For Readers

WHEN JACK SHAFER, THE PRESS CRITIC for Slate.com, received an e-mail request for correction from a reader using the alias "Auros," on February 27, 2007, he took the issue to two other editors at the online magazine.

"When I brought Auros' name up with *Slate* staffers June Thomas and David Plotz, both immediately recognized him— Thomas because she's the Corrections editor and Plotz because Auros e-mails him frequently to comment on his Bible blogging," Shafer wrote in a column. "After quick consultation with them, I realized that *Slate* does have a fact-check department, it works for nothing, and its name is Auros."

Shafer dedicated an entire column to the diligence of R.M. "Auros" Harman, a regular reader who makes a habit of pointing out errors in *Slate* articles. Rather than a damning portrait of a meddlesome reader, Shafer penned an ode to Auros and the way he assists *Slate* in catching and correcting errors. The secret was in the way Auros chose to express himself.

"Auros calls *Slate* editors collegial, but I'd give him most of the credit for the magazine's graciousness: His polymathic challenges are direct and respectful," wrote Shafer. "What more could a publication want?" Exactly.

HOW TO REQUEST A CORRECTION

THE MANNER IN WHICH YOU REQUEST a correction is just as important as the error itself. I've been copied on e-mails sent by people to different publications in which they dedicate paragraphs to the incompetence and idiocy of a particular reporter or publication due to a single error. Frustration can set in if a response is not acknowledged or if the error is repeated, but beginning a request for correction with insults or anger rarely serves the purpose.

One of the best examples of this type of correction was in fact the reader voice mail used in the *San Francisco Chronicle*'s first corrections podcast. The message from the reader was, in part:

> MR. HOWE. I'M LOOKING AT the Monday issue, August twenty-ninth, page E6, the article on civilian spy planes. . . . The subhead says "pilots begin testing pilotless drones". Mr. Howe! Is there any other kind of drone? You tell me, right now, is there any other kind of drone?! Other than a pilotless drone? Isn't that what a drone is—an unmanned aircraft?! Don't you check these things? Don't you supervise the subeditors who write these headlines?! Don't you do your job?! Aren't you there to ensure the English language is not *pissed on*. . . . Is it sinking into your thick skull, you high school dropout!?

Perhaps the reader was connected to the drone industry and is constantly working to eradicate talk of pilotless drones, but it's safe to assume that the sound of his voice will now be unwelcome on that particular editor's phone.

The difference between an appreciated checking reader and a detested one often comes down to how the person chooses to bring errors to light, and, of course, how willing the editorial staff is to accept a correction. Readers should think of themselves as offering assistance rather than condemnation, and should try to be as specific as possible about the nature of the error and the correct information. If the media outlet in question does not have a single contact person, phone number, or e-mail address for requests for correction, I recommend e-mailing the reporter who prepared the story as well as the editor of the section in which it appeared. For broadcast outlets, often the best way to request a correction is to call up the station if it's local, or submit an e-mail to its feedback or letters contact on its Web site.

And if you find it difficult to locate the correct person, be sure to note that politely in your communication and suggest that the news outlet offer a centralized phone number and contact person for readers.

ENSURING ACCURACY WHEN INTERVIEWED

WHEN I LEFT JOURNALISM and spent three years working full-time in the communications department for a software company, one of the things we prepared was a standard "fact-checking" e-mail that would be sent to the reporter after an interview was conducted with someone at the company.

It included the correct spelling of the interviewee's name and title, as well as important details such as the person's age, professional background, and other facts such as the spelling of the company name, the date the company was founded, and so on. The idea was to offer the reporter all the basic fact-checking information he or she needed for the story. It wasn't spin or a message document meant to drive home a point of view—it was just the facts, and journalists appreciated it.

Members of the public who are regularly interviewed by the press should create their own personal fact-checking document and provide it to every journalist they speak with. If you have a Web site, create a special FAQ for journalists and include only purely factual information.

While it is the journalists' obligation to get the facts straight, there is no reason why a source shouldn't help them. As long as you present the information in a friendly and helpful manner, and don't try to insert spin or rhetoric in your presentation, every journalist will appreciate it.

The Way Forward

THESE ACCURACY SUGGESTIONS and examples can succeed only when there is an intense, sincere passion for accuracy within newsrooms and among the public. Without a commitment to the issue, without the belief that errors can be prevented, along with a strong dedication to correcting those that do occur, there is no chance for change.

Perhaps the most important aspect of this commitment is the willingness of the press to become more open and honest about the issue of accuracy, and to offer the public a more realistic expression of what they can and should expect from their favored publications and broadcasts. The public has a demonstrated capacity for forgiving journalists' errors—they've been doing it for hundreds of years. What they won't tolerate is hubris and dishonesty.

The best expression of journalistic honesty I know of came in a speech by Pulitzer Prize–winning *Washington Post* reporter David Broder. In an address to the Pulitzer Prize winners of 1979, he explained how a more realistic portrayal of accuracy could better serve the press and the public. Rather than invoking a slogan such as the *New York Times'* "All the News That's Fit to Print," or some other self-aggrandizing maxim, he called for a truer expression of the nature and limitations of news reporting:

> I WOULD LIKE TO SEE US SAY—over and over, until the point has been made—that the newspaper that drops on your doorstep is a partial, hasty, incomplete, inevitably somewhat flawed and inaccurate rendering of some of the things we have heard about in the past 24 hours—distorted, despite our best efforts to eliminate gross bias, by the very process of compression that makes it possible for you to lift it from the doorstep and read it in about an hour. If we labeled the paper accurately, then we would immediately add: But it's the best we could do under the circumstances, and we will be back tomorrow with a corrected and updated version.

Broder's speech wasn't exactly well received. He later wrote that his fellow journalists accused him of "telling tales out of school" for being so frank. But it's exactly the kind of straight talk that's needed from journalists. We are not infallible gods. The news will never be perfect. Why not explain that clearly and stop raising expectations to unattainable levels?

Broder said that this more honest type of communication would make the press "feel less inhibited about correcting and updating our own stories." And in an incredibly prophetic wish, he spoke about "encourag[ing] readers to contribute their own information and understanding to the process.

"We might even find ourselves acknowledging something most of us find hard to accept: that they have something to tell us, as well as to hear from us," he said.

Boasting about accuracy doesn't make it a reality. This was proved in the earliest days of newspapers, and it is just as true of our current global media infrastructure. A more honest expression of the fallible nature of news is an essential ingredient in a renewed pursuit of accuracy. Once some of the stigma about errors has been removed and the press treats mistakes as an issue of quality control the way a manufacturer seeks ways to improve its processes to bolster a product, then perhaps journalists will feel freer to examine their own work as well as the policies, procedures, and technologies they deal with every day. From there, a renewed passion for accuracy can emerge.

Much of the work of journalism is done by people interacting with other people. We have to recognize the element of human error in this process, but that does not mean we have to resign ourselves to it. Outdated technologies such as the spell-checker that introduce errors should be improved. New services like those that can detect plagiarism should be adapted for the newsroom. The editing and reporting process should be broken down and analyzed to identify the weak points that lead to mistakes, and these failings should be addressed.

Other industries have recognized the importance of quality control and have compensated for human error with better processes and technology. The press has thus far failed to make a concerted effort to do so, and so today faces declining trust and, in some cases, economic uncertainty.

In many places in this book I have written about the new culture of scrutiny that today's media operates in. The press can no longer hide its mistakes and errors, and journalists can no longer go about their daily work sequestered from their readers and the public at large. In a time of unprecedented news options for consumers, they will inevitably flock toward the sources they feel are the most trustworthy, the most accurate.

The press cannot indefinitely defer the problem of accuracy on the grounds that solving it would be a cost and a resource drain, or claim that sporadic newsroom-wide e-mails reminding staff to avoid mistakes are doing the job. The principle of accuracy all journalists venerate is hollow unless the press acts on it—embraces it as its core function and integrates it into every aspect of its operations. Accuracy is in fact an enabler of journalism. When the facts and details are correct, when the reporting is factually sound, journalists are able to push and dig for the kinds of investigative, enterprising stories that demonstrate the critical role the press plays in a democracy.

Accuracy, in the end, is not just one of the central tenets of the profession. It is the very substance of the product of journalism—sound reporting and perspectives that inform and enlighten the public.

For hundreds of years, the press has been promising the public accuracy. Now it's time for the press to realize that promise for itself as well.

Otherwise, I fear there will be more to correct, and much to regret.

Afterword

MUCH LIKE THE *LEXINGTON Herald-Leader* when it published its decades-old apology for neglecting to cover the civil rights movement, I am obliged to acknowledge my own past failings.

I am painfully, frightfully aware that by writing a book that exposes the confounding lack of accuracy in the press and its consequences, I have painted a gigantic bull's-eye on my chest and fixed a sign to my back that says, CORRECT ME.

I take some solace in the fact that the irony of finding errors in this book will bring joy to some of my readers, but every error I have made in my more than eleven years of published writing has stuck with me, and, as is the case for most journalists, they rattle in my brain and renew my sense of horror every time I recall them. So as I've fixed on the errors of others throughout this book, I feel it necessary, and perhaps cathartic, for me to lay out for you here all of my own journalistic mistakes in all their idiotic, incompetent, lazy, arrogant lack of glory.

I kneel before you and ask—not for forgiveness, but for understanding; first for me, and then for my fellow journalists. This book is not another vitriolic rant against the mainstream media. Nor is it a condemnation of the profession of journalism. While I have certainly aired the dirty laundry of the profession—laundry that, to stretch the metaphor, has piled up for centuries largely away from the public eye— I have done so in the hope of also offering the means to cleanse our craft and make journalism better. On my Web site, and in this book, my purpose is to offer journalism ways to succeed in a world of online news, blogs, media-monitoring organizations, partisan hackery, and the other elements that exert a new level of pressure and fact checking on the press, particularly when it comes to errors and accuracy.

With this in mind, I offer you a litany of my own incompetence.

My first correction—and like other things in life—journalists always remember their first, filled me with fear. It was also the worst correction a journalist can have to make—one that never actually appears, or is published too late to matter. My fear wasn't like the fear I felt the first time I was threatened with a lawsuit; rather, it was a very specific kind of fear engendered by the circumstances. It all started with a *shish taouk* sandwich.

In 1998, I was a second-year journalism student at Concordia University in Montreal. I had walked over to a Lebanese restaurant to have a cheap *shish taouk* sandwich for dinner, and I was eating the sandwich and flipping through the local weeklies while exercising my eavesdropping skills. From a table nearby, I overheard a man talking to a woman about a corset he was making for someone. As they were walking out of the restaurant, I approached the man and asked him whether I could go along and watch him make the corset, and write about it for the student newspaper. He said okay.

A few days later, I went to his apartment—a well-kept place filled with medieval swords, fetish gear, and noxious chemicals—and watched him and his business partner encase a very tall, pale man in a cast that would later be a shiny Lucite corset. Perfect for fetish night at a local club.

I took note of their faces, their mannerisms. I recorded everything I saw and heard. This, I felt, would be the best story I had ever done, and I had found it all on my own. I was excited. I took my own pictures and wrote it up. After it ran in the student paper, the story was put over the national student newswire. My first wire story!

A few days later I got a phone call from the corset maker thanking me for the article and asking me to correct a couple of small factual errors. We ran a correction in the paper, but I neglected to send one out for the wire version. The article, errors intact, was picked up by another local student newspaper, at whose office the man in the article promptly turned up to complain. Correction: a very irate version of the man in the article.

As you might imagine, the young college students in the newsroom were somewhat alarmed by the angry presence of a man whose profession was molding S and M fetish corsets, and who had been described in my article as being an avid practitioner of branding (burning designs into his body). For days I was in fear that he'd come by our offices, though we were lucky, and he never did. Finally, I made the correction in the wire story that, undoubtedly, I had hesitated to make earlier

because I felt it would make me look bad in front of other student journalists across the country. I put my pride before journalistic accuracy
and, rightfully, paid the price.

My second error came roughly a year later, when I was working as
a freelance writer for the *Coast*, a weekly paper in my hometown of
Halifax, Nova Scotia. I'd spent a summer there as an intern, and I
returned the following summer to begin regularly contributing articles. At one point, the music editor handed me a cassette tape of a local
hip-hop artist and asked me to review it. I did, and gave it a favorable
review. But I made a serious error: I mistook the rapper for a producer
who had worked on several of the songs. I thought it was the producer's album, and I reviewed it as such. Basically, I credited the wrong
person and proved my ignorance. This resulted in another angry visit
to a newsroom—mine—and another correction. I was slowly learning
to check my work more carefully, lest I come face-to-face with the victims of my errors.

My work must have improved, because the next published error I
can recall didn't come until more than five years later, roughly a week
after I launched RegretTheError.com in 2004. By this time I was a full-
time freelance writer with a weekly column in Montreal's *Hour*
magazine. In a column about the Olympic Stadium in Montreal, known
locally as the "Big O," or the "Big Owe," due to its massive debt, I wrongly
stated that the tower on the stadium was completed twenty years after the
1976 Olympics were held. It was in fact completed in 1987.

I made another error in an article I wrote for the summer 2005
issue of the *NewCanadian*, a magazine where I worked on contract. In
the article, about how some consumer products are linked to the idea of
Canadian identity, I mistakenly located an Edmonton retail store in
Winnipeg. (By the time the error was revealed, the magazine had gone
out of business.)

I made my next error in August 2006 in an article I wrote for the
New York Times about LibriVox.org and other projects that create and
offer free online audio books. Soon after its publication, the editor on
the piece forwarded me an e-mail from a woman saying I had incorrectly said that she is based in New York. In fact she lives in California.

This mistake was particularly disappointing because I had spent extra time checking the article and confirming facts. Not only had I made an error; I'd done it in a high-profile publication, the *Times*.

How, I wondered, had my checking procedure failed me? I looked back at my source of the facts about her: I had quoted a post from her blog, and I had looked at her resume on her professional Web site, which said that she was currently employed by an organization based in Brooklyn. Overlooking the fact that many people telecommute, I had wrongly assumed that *she* was therefore based in New York. If I had looked elsewhere on the site I would have seen that she resides in California. So even though I made the effort to double-check my facts, I had not been thorough enough; she did work for a Brooklyn-based company, but she resided in California. I recalled that before I submitted the piece I thought that I should e-mail her just to verify some details, but then I didn't bother. This extra effort, which would have taken maybe a few minutes of my time, could have saved me from my mistake. Instead, I took the easy route, and I paid the price. This is a common failing among journalists.

The *Times* published this correction on August 30, 2006:

> AN ARTICLE IN WEEKEND ON FRIDAY about free online audio books of works in the public domain referred incorrectly to Arlene Goldbard, a writer who discussed on her blog her first experience with such recordings. She is based in Richmond, Calif., not New York.

I finally got around to e-mailing her—this time to apologize.

These are my print errors of memory, but I also regularly run corrections for my mistakes on the Regret the Error site, and they can be viewed there.

I feel strongly that this personal history of error is an important element of this book. It is a way for you to judge my level of accuracy and, at the same time, to realize that every journalist will fall victim to errors and oversights. By cataloging my own errors, I have been able to diagnose the areas where I am prone to failure. I believe other journalists could also benefit from this process of self-criticism.

Acknowledgments

WRITING IS A SOLITARY ACT, but it is possible only because of the people who enable me to find the time, inspiration, and encouragement to do it. Family, loved ones, friends, agents, editors, colleagues, bartenders . . . they all have been indispensable. I can't name them all, but I'm going to name a few. Those I forget can rest assured, the next round is on me.

I offer my profound gratitude to Sarah Carney for her love, support, and encouragement. She has been a blessing to this book, and to my life.

My family members are the biggest fans of my writing, and that was never more the case than with this book. My mother, father, and sister have always been there for me, and I take great comfort in knowing that they always will be. Vangie Sadler has also been a source of encouragement, not to mention many interesting discussions about the media.

I want to make special mention of Julius and Sara Silverman, my beloved departed grandparents, who have been so important in my life. They were inspiring people and wonderful grandparents. I will love and miss them always.

This book would not have come to fruition without the tireless work of Don Sedgwick and Shaun Bradley, my agents at Transatlantic Literary Agency. They have gone above and beyond merely being excellent literary agents; they are good friends and a valuable sounding board for ideas and writing. I'm lucky to work with them.

I also want to thank my good friend Max Lenderman, who was instrumental in putting me together with Shaun and Don, and who is a great friend.

My editors at Union Square Press and Penguin Canada have been a pleasure to work with. I feel truly lucky to be associated with them. Philip Turner was one of the first to see the potential for this work and has been a valued champion and wonderful editor. Doris Cross did much of the heavy lifting on the manuscript and was a delight to work with, even when she toiled through the Fourth of July holiday to ensure that we met our deadline. Iris Blasi also gave valuable assistance, and more than once managed to find a worthy correction that I had missed. Helen Reeves at Penguin Canada offered unrelenting encouragement and guidance for the Canadian edition.

My colleagues at *Hour*—Jamie O'Meara, Richard Burnett, Isa Tousignant, Melora Koepke, Meg Hewings—have always given great support and friendship. So too have current and former editors, colleagues, bosses, and forever friends such as MJ Milloy, Lyle Stewart, Martin Patriquin, Dov Smith, Cathy Stojak, Austin Hill, Hamnett Hill, Hammie Hill, Pat Lynch, and Kevin Siu. Jamie Reynolds did me a great favor by offering me a place to stay while working in New York, and by helping connect me with sources while there. James Fitz-Morris produced valuable research about public attitudes toward the press. I wish I could have used more of it.

I offer my thanks to Carlos and the staff and patrons of the Copacabana in Montreal. Their continued delivery of sustenance and humor has enabled, and occasionally prevented, this work. The members of the Crackbeat Society deserve special mention for their endless supply of wisdom and camaraderie. Gentlemen, I salute you.

I also want to thank the many people who gave interviews, provided me with research and information, and offered other important support. In particular, Scott Maier, a leading press-accuracy researcher and professor of journalism at the University of Oregon, shared his research and time with me. It was also a thrill and honor to have Jeff Jarvis offer his words to this book. His foreword is a fantastic addition. I am grateful to all of them, and to the many others who have helped me.

Finally, my work on RegretTheError.com, and this book, has been made possible and better by the many people—journalists and not—who supply me with corrections and errors, and who are always reliable in helping me catch and prevent my own. I am in their debt. I can only hope they continue to contribute and, in the process, keep me—and the press as a whole—honest and accurate.

Craig Silverman
Montreal, July 2007

Notes

INTRODUCTION

page 1   "They catered to the white citizenry": Linda Blackford and Linda Minch, "Front-Page News, Back-Page Coverage: The Struggle for Civil Rights in Lexington," *Lexington Herald-Leader*, July 4, 2004.

page 3   "more than 20 years": *The State of the News Media 2007*, Project for Excellence in Journalism, http://www.stateofthenewsmedia.org/2007/narrative_overview_publicattitudes.asp?cat=8&media=1.

page 3   "Despite the relative popularity": Ibid.

page 3   In 1985, 84 percent: *Public More Critical of Press, but Goodwill Persists*, Pew Research Center for the People and the Press, conducted in association with the Project for Excellence in Journalism, June 26, 2005, The Pew Research Center for the People and the Press, http://people-press.org/reports/display.php3?ReportID=248.

page 3   A Pew survey in 2002: *News Media's Improved Image Proves Short-Lived*, Pew Research Center for the People and the Press, conducted in association with the Project for Excellence in Journalism, August 4, 2002, http://people-press.org/reports/display.php3?ReportID=159.

page 3   In Canada, a 2007 poll: "Most Trusted Professionals: The Firefighters, not the CEO," *Globe and Mail*, January 22, 2007.

page 4   "In the 1999 ASNE Credibility Study": Robert J. Haiman, *Best Practices for Newspaper Journalists*, Freedom Forum Free Press/Fair Press Project, 2000, http://www.freedomforum.org/templates/document.asp?documentID=12828.

page 5   "beyond the thick walls of the *Times* building": Gay Talese, *The Kingdom and the Power* (New York: Random House, 1969), 24.

page 5   Talese speculated that: Ibid.

page 7   Writing in *Forbes* magazine: Rupert Murdoch, "Mixed Media," *Forbes*, May 2007.

page 10   "Although many journalists may think": Haiman, *Best Practices*, 9.

page 10   A 1988 paper in *Journalism Quarterly*: Cecilie Gaziano, "How Credible Is the Credibility Crisis?" *Journalism Quarterly* 65, 2 (Summer 1988).

page 10   As Howard Tyner: Haiman, *Best Practices*, 15.

page 11   When Philip Meyer, one of: Philip Meyer, *The Vanishing Newspaper: Saving Journalism in the Information Age* (Columbia : University of Missouri Press, 2004), 44.

page 11   Meyer's research revealed two links: Philip Meyer and Yuan Zhang, "Anatomy of a Death Spiral: Newspapers and Their Credibility" (paper delivered to the Media Management and Economics Division, Association for Education in Journalism and Mass Communication, Miami Beach, Fla., August 10, 2002).

page 11   Another Meyer study revealed: Philip Meyer and Joe Bob Hester, "Trust and the Value of Advertising: A Test of the Influence Model" (paper delivered to the American Association for Public Opinion Research, Nashville, Tenn., May 17, 2003).

page 11   "If you are trusted you retain": Philip Meyer (Knight Chair in journalism at the University of North Carolina and author of *The Vanishing Newspaper*), telephone conversation with the author, March 20, 2007.

page 13   "You must grant my claim": Upton Sinclair, *The Brass Check: A Study of American Journalism* (Champaign: University of Illinois Press, 2002), 10.

CHAPTER 1

page 15   The oldest surviving: Mitchell Stephens, "History of Newspapers," *Collier's Encyclopedia*, http://www.nyu.edu/classes/stephens/Collier's%20page.htm.

page 16   "Human beings exchanged": Ibid.

page 16   The Chinese philosopher Confucius: Onora O'Neill, "Spreading Suspicion" (2002 BBC Reith Lecture, http://www.bbc.co.uk/radio4/reith2002/lecture1.shtml).

page 16   The change over time: Stephens, *A History of News*, 212.

page 17   "About 80 years ago": Stephen J.A. Ward, *The Invention of Journalism Ethics* (Montreal: McGill-Queens University Press, 2004), 10.

page 18   "A Bedouin scout's report": Stephens, *A History of News*, 29.

page 19   "With regard to my factual": Bill Kovach and Tom Rosenstiel, *The Elements of Journalism: What Newspeople Should Know and the Public Should Expect* (New York: Three Rivers Press, 2001), 70.

page 19   though a 2006 discovery: "New Evidence Suggests Longer Paper Making History in China," Xinhua News Agency, August 9, 2006.

page 20   "I shall never admit": Stephens, *A History of News*, 248.

page 21   "passing by what's past": Ibid., 110–111.

page 21   "certifie the truth": Joseph Frank, *The Beginnings of the English Newspaper, 1620–1660* (Cambridge, Mass.: Harvard University Press, 1961), 302.

page 22   "without any reflection": Stephens, *A History of News*, 114.

page 22   Scientists were joined with: The stipulation of a "matter of fact" is integral to the early emergence of accuracy as a value in the press. The idea of facts as a cornerstone of the press likely finds its origins in fifteenth- and six-teenth-century England, when the principles of common law were built upon the concept of factual determination in proceedings.

page 22   "to encounter falsehood with the sword of truth": Ward, *The Invention of Journalism Ethics*, 106.

page 22   "Truth is the daughter": Ibid., 107.

page 23   "Truth impartially related": Stephens, *A History of News*, 248.

page 23   "from the beginning": Joseph Frank, "Mercurius Melancholicus," *University of Rochester Library Bulletin* 12, 3 (Spring 1957), http://www.lib.rochester.edu/index.cfm?PAGE=3444.

page 23   "In one [1624] issue": Ward, *The Invention of Journalism Ethics*, 109.

page 23   "In our laste newes": Stephens, *A History of News*, 161.

page 24   "In one thing I yield not": Ward, *The Invention of Journalism Ethics*, 124.

page 24   "nothing shall be entered": Walter Lippmann, *Liberty and the News* (Vancouver: University of British Columbia Press, 1995), 8.

page 24   "trace any such False report": Ibid.

page 24   "sundry doubtful and uncertain Reports": Frank Luther Mott, *American Journalism* (New York: Macmillan, 1962), 9.

page 25   American journalism historian: Ibid., 9.

page 25   In 1709, London was home: Peter Burke, *A Social History of Knowledge* (Boston: Polity Press, 2000), 47.

page 25   Germany's first regularly published: Mott, *American Journalism*, 116.

page 25   The Unites States saw: Mott, *American Journalism*, 115.

page 25   One journalist of that century: Stephens, *A History of News*, 214.

page 25   "The chance of making": Ward, *The Invention of Journalism Ethics*, 131.

page 26   "[Publishers] started producing": Stephen Ward (director and associate pro-
          fessor of journalism ethics at the University of British Columbia), telephone
          conversation with the author, January 17, 2007.

page 26   When asked if: Stephens, *A History of News*, 227.

page 26   "They covered a wide": Ward, *The Invention of Journalism Ethics*, 149.

page 27   John Walters I founded: Ibid., 150.

page 27   "The lack of a proper system": Mott, *American Journalism*, 155.

page 27   "We are informed": Ibid., 155.

page 28   Edmund Burke, as later reported: Thomas Carlyle, *On Heroes, Hero Worship,
          and the Heroic in History* (London: Wiley and Halsted, 1859), 147.

page 28   "The embryonic journalism": Ward, *The Invention of Journalism Ethics*, 173.

page 29   "These journalists were interested": Stephens, *A History of News*, 217.

page 29   "When, in the early nineteenth century": Nicholas Lemann, "Amateur
          Hour," *New Yorker*, August 7, 2006.

page 29   As the London *Times* informed: Stephens, *A History of News*, 249.

CHAPTER 2

page 30   I am indebted to Alex Boese, an author and the proprietor of
          MuseumofHoaxes.com, for providing me with a copy of the *Sun*'s moon
          series, which can be viewed at http://www.museumofhoaxes.com/moon-
          hoax1.html. Through his unfinished but well-researched dissertation, "The
          Great Moon Hoax of 1835: Truth, the Public, and the Mass Media in
          Antebellum America," he also provided me with many other clippings from
          the *Sun* and its competitors, which provide important information
          throughout this chapter.

page 32   "*The Sun* editors sometimes abused": Susan Thompson,. "Rising and
          Shining: Benjamin Day and His New York *Sun* Before 1836" (paper sub-
          mitted to the 2001 convention of the Association for Education in Journalism
          and Mass Communication, Washington, D.C., August 4–8, 2001).

page 36   "The New York *Sun*'s army of loudmouthed": Vicky Hallett, "Extra! Extra!
          Life on Moon! The New York Sun Made Up a Scoop—And Remade
          Journalism," *US News & World Report*, August 26, 2002.

page 38   "There was a huge amount of skepticism": Alex Boese (founder of
          MuseaumofHoaxes.com and author), telephone conversation with the
          author, June 8, 2005.

page 39   Hearst famously replied: W. Joseph Campbell, *The Year That Defined
          American Journalism: 1897 and the Clash of Paradigms* (New York: Routledge,
          2006), 137.

page 40   Campbell wrote that Hearst: Ibid., 5.

page 40   The *Journal* itself outlined: Ibid., 42.

page 40   On February 18, 1898: Mitchell Stephens, *A History of News* (New York:
          Harcourt Brace, 1997), 254.

page 41   Behind the slogan was Ochs's plan: Campbell, *The Year That Defined
          American Journalism*. 70.

page 41   He spoke of a: Schudson, *Discovering the News*, 110.

page 42   Michael Schudson wrote in his 1978 book: Ibid., 106.

page 42   Edwin L. Shuman wrote a handbook: Ibid., 79.
page 42   Ochs's paper accused the *Journal*: Campbell, *The Year That Defined American Journalism*, 9.
page 42   Near the end of the century: Stephens, *A History of News*, 110.
page 43   The *Journal*'s front-page headline read: Schudson, *Discovering the News*, 62.
page 43   After the *World* learned: Ibid., 63.
page 43   Given this environment: Campbell, *The Year That Defined American Journalism*, 25.
page 44   "As the century progressed": Stephens, *A History of News*, 245.
page 45   In 1913, due to his recognition: Cassandra Tate, "What Do Ombudsmen Do?" *Columbia Journalism Review* (May–June 1984), 37–41.
page 45   By 1915 there were well over: Stephens, *A History of News*, 202
page 46   "Our Republic and its press": Seymour Topping, "Joseph Pulitzer and the Pulitzer Prizes," The Pulitzer Prizes, http://www.pulitzer.org.
page 46   Many more would follow: Paul S. Voakes, "The Newspaper Journalists of the '90s," American Society of Newspaper Editors, 1997, http://www.asne.org/index.cfm?ID=2480.
page 46   "It was a major gaffe": Billy G. Ferguson (author of *Unipress: United Press International Covering the 20th Century*), telephone conversation with the author, February 28, 2007.
page 47   "I have no thought of saying": Associated Press, "Statement of News Values," The American Society of Newspaper Editors, http://www.asne.org/index.cfm?ID=6120.
page 47   Its current version, called: American Society of Newspaper Editors, "Statement of Principles," http://www.asne.org/kiosk/archive/principl.htm.
page 48   By the 1930s, the ethics: Ward, *The Invention of Journalism Ethics*, 191.

CHAPTER 3

page 49   The crowds waiting to greet him: "Oral History Interview with David H. Stowe," July 24, 1980, Harry S. Truman Library, Independence, Missouri.
page 49   In the end, he traveled: "Presidential Campaign of 1948," Harry S. Truman Library, Independence, Missouri.
page 50   Members of the powerful: "After 17 Months," *Time*, April 25, 1949.
page 50   "The printers promised 24-hour-a-day": "Chicago Showdown," *Time*, December 1, 1947.
page 50   "A call was made to the paper's": Charles Leroux. "7 Blunders of Chicago," *Chicago Tribune*, March 9, 2006.
page 50   The first edition of the paper: Ralph Kovel and Terry Kovel, "Erroneous Headline Ensures Value," *Chicago Tribune*, December 25, 1994.
page 51   In the 1876 race: Michael Stroh, "Election Edition Goofs Are Prized," *The Record* (Bergen County, NJ), November 12, 2000.
page 51   In 1916, the *San Francisco Examiner*: Ibid.
page 51   "So call it 'Dewey Defeats Truman,'": "We Got It Wrong," *New York Post*, July 7, 2004.
page 52   "Thousands of St. Louisians": Anthony Leviero, "Truman Bars Third Term, Say Aids on Victory Train," *New York Times*, November 4, 1948.
page 52   "Several times the president": Ibid.
page 52   Many photographers got a shot: Harry Levins, "Globe Photographer Took 'Dewey Defeats Truman' Shot," *St. Louis Post-Dispatch*, November 2, 1998.

page 53   "The front page was done": Rick Brown, telephone conversation with the author, June 10, 2007.

page 54   "We were dim on Dewey": "Never Again, We Hope," *Chicago Daily Tribune*, November 4, 1948.

page 54   "Having been bitten": Ibid.

page 54   Reason, who is now: Renee Lertzman, "From Absent Minded to Error Wise: A Conversation with James Reason," Safer Health Care, http://saferhealth care.co.uk, January 3, 2006.

page 54   As with his food-in-the-teapot: Norman Swan,. "Absent-mindedness/Risk Management—Radio National Summer," *Health Report*, Australian Broadcasting Corporation, May 16, 2005.

page 56   "The strong link between inadequate": Kim Vicente, *The Human Factor: Revolutionizing the Way People Live with Technology* (Toronto: Knopf Canada, 2003), 74.

page 56   "At Chernobyl, for example": James Reason, "Human Error: Models and Management," *British Medical Journal* 320 (March 18, 2000): 768–770.

page 57   "We concluded that the public": Peter Harbison, "Why Safety Is Like Swiss Cheese," *Herald Sun* (Australia), March 9, 2007.

page 58   "There are as many reasons": *Newspaper Credibility Handbook*, American Society of Newspaper Editors, Reston, Va., 2001, http://www.asne.org/ credibilityhandbook/contents.htm

page 59   "By focusing on the individual": Reason, "Human error," 769.

page 59   "The presence of holes": Ibid., 769.

page 60   "The headline on the lead article": Joe Hiett, "I Apologize for Shoddy Journalism," *Daily Tribune*, March 27, 2007.

page 61   Donald Norman wrote that: Donald A. Norman, *The Design of Everyday Things* (New York: Basic Books, 1988), 106.

page 61   Slips occur because of what a: Robert J. Haiman, *Best Practices for Newspaper Journalists*, Freedom Forum Free Press/Fair Press Project, 2000, 14, http://www.freedomforum.org/templates/document.asp?documentID=12828.

page 62   After the *Tribune* instituted: Ibid., 14.

page 62   "Mistakes result from the choice": Norman, *The Design of Everyday Things*, 114.

page 62   "We make decisions based": Ibid.

CHAPTER 4

page 65   "As common as the layman's": Mitchell V. Charnley, "Preliminary Notes on a Study of Newspaper Accuracy," *Journalism Quarterly* 13 (December 1936), 394.

page 66   He chose stories: Ibid., 395.

page 66   Charnley also noted that 14.5 percent: Ibid., 399.

page 67   "Among academic studies": Scott R. Maier, "Accuracy Matters: A Cross-Market Assessment of Newspaper Error and Credibility," *Journalism and Mass Communication Quarterly* 82, 3 (Autumn 2005), 534.

page 67   "In my early years as a reporter": Scott B. Maier (associate professor of journalism at the University of Oregon), telephone conversation with the author, October 27, 2006.

page 67   Maier's comprehensive 2005 study: Maier, "Accuracy Matters," 533.

page 67   "With all the attention given to accuracy": Maier interview.

page 67   In an article outlining the research: Maier, "Accuracy Matters," 545.

page 68   Aside from the high number of factual errors: Ibid., 545.
page 68   Categories of subjective errors: Philip Meyer, *The Vanishing Newspaper*
          (Columbia, University of Missouri Press, 2004), 88.
page 68   In *The Vanishing Newspaper*: Ibid., 89.
page 68   "Here is a fact": Dan Gillmor, "Interviews, E-mail or Live," Center for
          Citizen Media, http://www.citmedia.org, April 24, 2007.
page 68   A 1982 study by William Tillinghast: William Tillinghast, "Newspaper
          Errors: Reporters Dispute Most Source Claims," *Newspaper Research Journal*
          (July 1982), 15–23.
page 69   "The difference in result was striking": George Kennedy, "Newspaper
          Accuracy: A New Approach," *Newspaper Research Journal* (Winter 1994),
          http://findarticles.com/p/articles/mi_qa3677/is_199401/ai_n8726405.
page 69   "In a review of 24 dailies": Scott Maier, "Getting It Right: Newsmaker
          Perceptions of Accuracy and Credibility" (paper presented at the annual con-
          vention of the Association for Education in Journalism and Mass
          Communication, New Orleans, August 4–7, 1999).
page 69   "The flaw with the [source survey]": Philip A. Meyer, telephone interview
          with the author, March 20, 2007.
page 69   The result was a finding that: Philip Meyer, "A Workable Measure of
          Auditing Accuracy in Newspapers," *Newspaper Research Journal* (Fall 1988):
          39–51.
page 69   A 1965 study, which received: Maier, "Accuracy Matters."
page 70   A 1985 study by Larry L. Burriss: Larry L. Burriss, "Accuracy of News
          Magazines as Perceived by News Sources," *Journalism Quarterly* (Winter
          1985), 14.
page 70   "There were several surprising things": Guy J. Kewney, "Really, What
          Matters Is That the BBC Doesn't Look Stupid," NewsWireless,
          newswireless.net, May 10, 2006.
page 71   "Guy Kewney is the editor": BBC interview with Guy Goma,
          http://img.dailymail.co.uk/video/cabbie.wmv.
page 72   Suddenly, two men appeared: Craig Silverman, "F-fired!" Regret the Error,
          http://www.regrettheerror.com, May 20, 2005.
page 72   In early 2007, a CNN report: "CNN Apologizes for Osama-Obama Headline
          Mistake," Associated Press, January 2, 2007.
page 73   "Television is much more fleeting": John D. Solomon, "Errors on Air,"
          American Journalism Review (August–September 2003),
          http://www.ajr.org/article.asp?id=3094.
page 73   "While newspapers often run": Andrea Miller, "Television Breaking News
          and the Invalid Application of a Utilitarian Justification" (paper presented
          at the Association for Education in Journalism and Mass Communication
          conference, Miami Beach, August 7–10, 2002).
page 73   "Despite one study's finding that": Ibid.
page 74   "sources were generally pleased": Gary Hanson, "Measuring Accuracy: A
          Survey of Television News Managers' Attitudes" (paper presented at the
          Association for Education in Journalism and Mass Communication confer-
          ence, Kansas City, Mo., July 29–August 2, 2003),
          http://findarticles.com/p/articles/mi_qa3677/is_199401/ai_n8726405.
page 74   A 2004 study: Gary Hanson and Stan Wearden, "Developing a New
          Measurement for Television News Accuracy" (paper presented at the

Association for Education in Journalism and Mass Communication Convention, Toronto, Canada, August 4–7, 2004).

page 74   "The answer in one word: spelling": Hanson, "Measuring Accuracy."

page 75   Twenty-seven percent said errors: Ibid.

page 75   According to Linda Mason: Vaughn Ververs, "E-Mailbag: How Does CBS News Handle Corrections?" March 29, 2006, CBS PublicEye blog, http://www.cbsnews.com/sections/publiceye/main500486.shtml.

page 75   "In most cases the scripts are read": Hanson, "Measuring Accuracy."

page 76   For example, the *Boston Globe:* Richard Chacón, "The *Globe* Stands Corrected," *Boston Globe*, January 15, 2006.

page 77   Based on circulation, the *Globe:* Audit Bureau of Circulation's FAS-FAX circulation data ending September 30, 2006.

page 77   "There are mistakes that go unnoticed": Chacón, "The *Globe* Stands Corrected."

page 78   "Years ago, the *Wall Street Journal*": Philip Meyer (Knight Chair in journalism at the University of North Carolina and author of *The Vanishing Newspaper*), telephone conversation with the author, March 20, 2007.

page 78   "Like a factory on a river": John S. Carroll, "The Wolf in Reporter's Clothing: The Rise of Pseudo-Journalism in America" (Ruhl Lecture on Ethics, University of Oregon, Eugene, OR, May 6, 2004).

page 79   In March 2003, the United Kingdom's: Elizabeth Day and Chris Hastings, "Hot Cross Banned: Councils Decree Buns Could Be 'Offensive' to Non-Christians," *Sunday Telegraph*, March 15, 2003.

page 79   "We are moving away from a religious": Ibid.

page 79   "It was a figment of the reporters' imaginations": Roy Greenslade, "Why I'm So Cross with the *Sunday Telegraph*," *Guardian*, April 10, 2007.

page 79   In 2007, it was the *Cayman Net News*: Barbara Currie Dailey, "Easter in Cayman Means BUN Not Bunnies!" *Cayman Net News*, March 24, 2007.

page 79   This caused one of the London: "Borough Bosses Bemused by Bun Ban Banter," *East London Advertiser*, April 5, 2007.

page 80   "When we were alerted to the misspelling": Greg Brock, e-mail message to the author, March 28, 2007.

page 80   "The historical error can be": Nora Krug, "The Corrections," *New York Times Book Review*, September 25, 2005.

page 81   A 1999 survey by the American Society of Newspaper Editors: American Society of Newspaper Editors, "Examining Our Credibility: Perspectives of the Public and the Press," 1999.

page 81   Said one respondent: Ibid.

page 81   "Nothing is more crucial: Stephen Hess, "Credibility: Does It Drive the Bottom Line?" *Presstime*, July–August 1998.

page 82   At noon on October 25, 1973: Alicia C. Shepard, *Woodward and Bernstein: Life in the Shadow of Watergate* (New York: Wiley, 2007), 61.

page 83   "It was the worst day emotionally": Ibid., 62.

page 83   As Woodward and Bernstein would later write: Carl Bernstein and Bob Woodward, *All The President's Men* (New York: Simon and Schuster, 1974), 111.

page 83   "I don't respect the type of shabby": Ibid., 186.

page 84   "We took a giant step backwards": Shepard, *Woodward and Bernstein*, 62.

page 84   They were "tired, frightened and confused": Bernstein and Woodward, *All the President's Men*, 187.

page 84   In the meantime, Bradlee had bought: Bernstein and Woodward, *All the President's Men*, 192.

page 84   Bradlee is quoted in a footnote: Ibid., 192.

page 86   "A newspaper with a zero level": Meyer, *The Vanishing Newspaper*, 89.

CHAPTER 5

page 91   John Temple, the editor of: John Temple, "Once in Print, There Are No Mulligans," *Rocky Mountain News*, January 14, 2006.

page 91   "At the *Rocky*, our policy": Ibid.

page 92   The reader's representative: Kate Parry, "Some Precise Advice on Accuracy," *Star Tribune*, January 18, 2007.

page 93   Jackson Pollock was Jackson Pollack: Linda Amster and Dylan Loeb McClain, *Kill Duck Before Serving: Red Faces at the New York Times* (New York: St. Martin's Griffin, 2002), 94–96.

page 93   After I saw a string of corrections: Craig Silverman, "That's Edgar *Allan* Poe," July 3, 2006, Regret the Error, http://www.regrettheerror.com.

page 94   Looking through the Nexis news: Craig Silverman, "Attention Journalists Everywhere: James Dobson Is *Not* a Minister," May 19, 2006, Regret the Error, http://www.regrettheerror.com.

page 95   "A page on the governor's Web site": "After Web Typo, Florida Newspapers Refer to Governor Crist as 'Christ,'" Associated Press, January 12, 2007.

page 96   *The Virginian-Pilot* put a positive spin: Corrected September 26, 2006.

page 97   *The Washington Post* joined in: Corrected July 12, 2006.

page 102 One of the more celebrated: Lloyd Grove, "The Reliable Source," *Washington Post*, April 24, 2003.

page 103 The mistake was later acknowledged: Ibid.

page 103 It's difficult to know exactly when: Paula LaRocque, "Corrections, However Painful or Funny, Needed for Credibility," *Quill*, April 1, 2005.

page 103 Some recent honored candidates include: Craig Silverman, "Crunks '05: The Year in Media Errors and Corrections," December 13 2005, Regret the Error, http://www.regrettheerror.com.

page 103 a Liverpool newspaper changing the Welsh: Ibid.

page 104 The Jews turned up again: Craig Silverman, "Jews Do the Darndest Things," May 19, 2006, Regret the Error, http://www.regrettheerror.com.

page 105 A 1999 survey revealed: "Examining Our Credibility: Perspectives of the Public and the Press," American Society of Newspaper Editors, August 3, 1999, http://www.asne.org/index.cfm?id=2632.

page 105 "Each misspelled word, bad apostrophe": Ibid.

page 105 "The problem arose when": Rob Irvine, "Trust the Post: Beware of the New New," *Daily Post*, April 14, 2005.

page 105 When Pope John Paul II passed away: Craig Silverman, "The Pope Gets Immorally T'd Off," April 14, 2005, Regret the Error, http://www.regret-theerror.com.

page 117 "There are 175 billion barrels": "The Oil Sands Of Alberta." *60 Minutes*. January 22, 2006.

page 118 "There is something so magical": Tamara Slomka, "Writer's Block," *Ryerson Review of Journalism* (Spring 2003), http://www.rrj.ca/issue/2003/spring/397/.

page 119 "Deploying numbers skillfully": Max Frankel, "Innumeracy 2," *New York Times*, March 5, 1995.

page 119   "It is instructive that many": Scott Maier, "How Sources, Reporters View
           Math Errors in News," *Newspaper Research Journal* (Fall 2003): 49–63,
           http://findarticles.com/p/articles/mi_qa3677/is_200310/ai_n9274650/.

page 119   "Mathematics is not primarily a matter": John Allen Paulos, *A
           Mathematician Reads the Newspaper* (New York: Anchor Books, 1995), 3.

page 120   He conducted a mail survey: Scott Maier, "How Sources, Reporters."

page 120   A 2007 study by Mark Ashcraft: Julie Steenhuysen, "Bad at Math? Worrying
           Makes You Even Worse," Reuters, February 20, 2007.

page 120   "For example, incorrectly reporting": Maier, "How Sources, Reporters."

page 121   "A toll-free number to a non-partisan": Mike Clark, "More on the Election and
           That Really Bad Telephone Number," *Florida Times-Union*, November 7, 2004.

page 121   "Ask accountant Marvin Vissman": Sharon Burnside, "Please Correct Me If
           I'm Wrong," *Toronto Star*, May 7, 2005.

page 122   "I never said a word": "Just Imagine! Paper's Mistake Had Man Believing
           He Won Lotto," August 20, 2006, Canadian Broadcasting Corporation,
           http://www.cbc.ca.

page 122   "We have no reason to doubt": Alan Allnutt, "Note to Readers," *Gazette*
           (Montreal), August 23, 2006.

page 123   "Let's face it, we often": Victor Cohn, "News and Numbers," Foundation for
           American Communications, http://www.facsnet.org/tools/ref_tutor/news
           andnumbers/index.php3.

page 123   "We can be better reporters": Ibid.

page 123   Writing in *Harper's* in 1964: Otto Friedrich, "There Are oo Trees in Russia,"
           Harper's, October 1964, 63.

page 124   "We are in the midst of an epidemic": "Attorney General Alberto R.
           Gonzales Announces Implementation of Project Safe Childhood Initiative,"
           Department of Justice press release, May 17, 2006.

page 124   According to *Legal Times*, he said: Jason McLure, "Numbers Game: Gonzales
           Launches DOJ Project Safe Childhood with Mysterious Figure," *Legal Times*,
           May 22, 2006, http://www.law.com/jsp/dc/PubArticleDC.jsp?id=114777
           0329023.

page 124   It received an answer: Ibid.

page 125   Journalists aren't supposed to pay for stories: Craig Silverman, "Gotcha!
           Dateline's Predator Problem and the Lobotomy That Caused It," *Huffington
           Post*, June 12, 2006.

page 125   After being contacted for comment: McLure, "Numbers Game."
           http://www.law.com/jsp/dc/PubArticleDC.jsp?id=1147770329023.

page 125   "Was it just a WAG: Ibid.

page 125   "For some reason the number 50,000: Ibid.

page 125   In a subsequent interview: "Prime Number," *On the Media*, National Public
           Radio, May 26, 2006.

page 125   "An interesting phenomenon of these numbers": Ibid.

page 126   Maier reported, "Journalistic innumeracy": Maier, "How Sources, Reporters."

page 126   "We were told not to come here without": Richard Wexler, "Understanding
           Child Abuse Numbers," *Nieman Reports* (Spring 1993), 20

page 127   "The panic he had helped start": Ibid.

page 127   Wexler reported that a 1990 study: Ibid.

page 127   But the 50,000 figure remained: Timothy Harper, "Where Are the Missing
           Children?" Associated Press, May 30, 1982.

page 127　Two years later, the AP was still: Bill McCloskey, "Experts Say National Approach Needed to Find Missing Kids," Associated Press, February 7, 1984.

page 127　There's no way there's 50,000": Claire Spiegel, "Missing Children," *Los Angeles Times*, May 28, 1985.

page 127　"The first step towards finding": Wexler, "Understanding Child Abuse Numbers," 21.

CHAPTER 6

page 138　"British commuters take note": "'Toothing' for Hi-Tech Sex with Strangers," Reuters, April 18, 2004.

page 138　It was "where strangers on trains": Ibid.

page 139　Recent years have brought sources: James Savage, "'Naked Skydivers' Article Was Hoax," May 12, 2006, The Local, http://www.thelocal.se.

page 139　a man passing himself off as an executive: Craig Silverman, "BBC hoaxed," December 6, 2004, Regret the Error, http://www.regrettheerror.com.

page 140　Other examples found Slate.com and the BBC: Craig Silverman, "Slate Falls for Cows with Accents Hoax," May 4, 2007, Regret the Error, http://www.regrettheerror.com.

page 140　*Sports Illustrated* reporting that a West Virginia: Craig Silverman, "Sports Illustrated Corrects Dirty Hoax Report," February 5, 2007, Regret the Error, http://www.regrettheerror.com.

page 140　*Toronto Sun* reporting that a fake virgin: Craig Silverman, "Virgin Hoax Fools Media," May 19, 2006, Regret the Error, http://www.regrettheerror.com.

page 140　and a Massachusetts paper saying a student: Craig Silverman, "Student's Hoax Leaves Paper Red," December 28, 2005, Regret the Error, http://www.regrettheerror.com.

page 140　"Bernadette Planting was reunited Tuesday": Will Albritton, "Fat, Blind Fish Reunited with Thankful Owner," *Fresno Bee*, May 9, 2007.

page 140　"Journalists are trained to be skeptical": Cyndee Fontana, "'Reunion' Turns Out to Be Just One Big Fish Tale," *Fresno Bee*, May 10, 2007.

page 142　I bowed to an unreliable source: Craig Silverman, "Pilfered Post-its Don't Compare to Data Theft," *Globe and Mail*, May 7, 2007.

page 142　The *New York Post* quoted "Heywood Jablome": Neil Graves, "Get a Cuppa Joe & Check Your Dough," *New York Post*, May 1 , 2001.

page 142　Two years later, the *Post and Courier*: James Scott, "Protesters Overshadowed by Media, Police," *Post and Courier*, April 13, 2003.

page 143　In 2007, the New York *Daily News*: Michael O'Keeffe and Teri Thompson, "Masters Not Same Without Martha," *Daily News* (New York), April 8, 2007.

page 143　To explain one questionable aspect: Shelley K. Wong, "Paul Vance, Co-writer of 'Itsy Bitsy Teenie Weenie Yellow Polka Dot Bikini,' Dies at 68," Associated Press, September 26, 2006.

page 143　Just a day after the story's: Frank Eltman, "'Itsy Bitsy' Songwriter Complains That an Impostor Stole the Credit for the 1960 Hit," Associated Press, September 27, 2006.

page 143　Van Valkenburgh's widow said: Ibid.

page 144　In a strange twist, however: Byron Calame, "The Wrong Man: Deception, Mistaken Identity and Journalistic Lapses," *New York Times*, March 26, 2006.

page 144 Using the *Times'* archives, Calame: Ibid.

page 144 "The *Times*'s decision to treat": Ibid.

page 145 Leonard Downie, the top editor: Leonard Downie, Jr., "The Guidelines We Use to Report the News," *Washington Post*, March 7, 2004.

page 146 On December 20, 2001, she reported: Judith Miller, "An Iraqi Defector Tells of Work on at Least 20 Hidden Weapons Sites," *New York Times*, December 20, 2001.

page 147 On April 21, 2003, reporting from within: Judith Miller, "Illicit Arms Kept Till Eve of War, an Iraqi Scientist Is Said to Assert," *New York Times*, April 21, 2003.

page 147 "She is possessive of her sources": Franklin Foer, "The Source of the Trouble," *New York*, June 7, 2004.

page 148 Daniel Okrent, the paper's first: Daniel Okrent, "Weapons of Mass Destruction? Or Mass Distraction?" *New York Times*, May 30, 2004.

page 148 The note began by saying that: "The Times and Iraq," *New York Times*, May 26, 2004.

page 148 In summarizing a 1999 conference session: John F. Kelley, "May the Source Be with You" (conference summary, Nieman Foundation for Journalism at Harvard University, 1999 Watchdog Journalism Conference, Cambridge, Mass., May 15, 1999).

page 151 "I started fabricating stories": Kate Jackson, "Confessions of a Teenage Fabulist," *Maisonneuve*, January 10, 2007.

page 151 "In total, I wrote nearly a dozen": Ibid.

page 152 In her essay, "Kate" wrote: Ibid.

page 152 In 2007 she was working in film: Ibid.

page 152 A few paragraphs down comes the inevitable: Janet Cooke, "Jimmy's World," *Washington Post*, September 28, 1980.

page 153 Jack Kelley, a former foreign correspondent: Blake Morrison, "Ex-USA Today reporter Faked Major Stories," *USA Today*, March 19, 2004.

page 153 In November 2005, for example: These and other incidents are compiled in the annual plagiarism round-ups at RegretTheError.com.

page 153 One of the stranger incidents was revealed: Craig Silverman, "Updated: Toronto Star and Two Other Papers Lift Decade-Old Item, Run It as New," Regret the Error, http://www.regrettheerror.com/2006/01/when_we_came_ac.html.

page 155 "It's patently obvious where they got this story": Randy Cassingham, e-mail interview with the author, January 1, 2006.

page 156 "There is no graver breach": "Reuters Drops Beirut Photographer," August 8, 2006, BBC News, http://news.bbc.co.uk.

page 158 That, wrote Parry, "meant I couldn't": Kate Parry, "Can a Writer Unintentionally Plagiarize?" *Star Tribune*, November 19, 2006.

page 159 "Reacting to a right-wing blog, the newspaper": "Star Trib Plagiarism Probe Clears Writer," Associated Press, December 17, 2006.

page 159 Jayson Blair, the disgraced former *New York Times*: Dan Barry, David Barstow, Jonathan D. Glater, Adam Liptak, and Jacques Steinberg. "Correcting the Record; Times Reporter Who Resigned Leaves Long Trail of Deception," *New York Times*, May 11, 2003.

page 161 His editor was not pleased: Seth Mnookin, *Hard News* (New York: Random House, 2004), 117.

page 161 "Anyone who has used a database": Jack Shafer, "Fib Newton," Slate.com, October 29, 2002.

page 162 "AP's spokeswoman Kelly Smith Tunney: Ibid.

page 163 "the very public reprimand of Pulitzer Prize–winning": Judith Sheppard,
          "Playing Defense," *American Journalism Review* (September 1998),
          http://www.ajr.org/Article.asp?id=3440.

page 163 "In the wake of the Blair affair": Richard C. Wald, "How to Worry About
          the Blair Affair," *Columbia Journalism Review* (July–August 2003),
          http://cjrarchives.org/issues/2003/4/times-wald.asp.

page 163 "One way to define the past ASNE year": Peter Bhatia, "2004 ASNE
          President's Speech," April 20, 2004, American Society of Newspaper
          Editors, http://www.ASNE.org, April 20, 2004.

page 164 "Isn't it time to say enough": Ibid.

page 164 "The feedback was very positive": Peter Bhatia, telephone interview with
          the author, March 12, 2007.

CHAPTER 7

page 167 "The most newsworthy event": Mitchell Stephens, *A History of News* (New
          York: Harcourt Brace, 1997), 95.

page 167 "in October 1525 criers in Paris": Stephens, *A History of News*, 77.

page 167 A January 2006 report by *Editor & Publisher*: Joe Strupp, "Obits Find New
          Life," *Editor & Publisher* (January 1, 2006).

page 168 Erik Bergengren wrote in *Alfred Nobel*: Erik Bergengren, *Alfred Nobel: The
          Man and His Work* (London: Thomas Nelson and Sons, 1962), 108.

page 169 Kenne Fant wrote in *Alfred Nobel*: Kenne Fant, *Alfred Nobel: A Biography*
          (New York: Arcade Publishing, 1993), 207.

page 169 "We have found several obituaries": Olov Amelin, e-mail message to the
          author, December 21, 2005.

page 169 Pinter, who was already suffering: Sarah Lyall, "Pinter Awarded Nobel,"
          Associated Press, October 14, 2005.

page 170 "Of the demonstrably wise there are": Ron Powers, *Mark Twain: A Life* (New
          York: Free Press, 2005), 583.

page 170 "If Mark Twain dying in poverty": Ibid., 584

page 170 "The report of my illness": Ibid., 585.

page 171 Baseball great Joe DiMaggio: "Rudyard Kipling," Biblio.com,
          http://www.biblio.com/authors/611/Rudyard_Kipling_Biography.html.

page 171 He had been confused with: L.A. Johnson, "Web Site Keeps Track of a Very
          Vital Statistic of Celebrities—Their Mortality," *Pittsburgh Post-Gazette*,
          August 24, 1998.

page 172 It began, "Alan Abel, a writer": "Alan Abel, Satirist Created Campaign to
          Clothe Animals," *New York Times*, January 2, 1980.

page 172 "An obituary in *The New York Times*": "Obituary Disclosed as Hoax," *New
          York Times*, January 4, 1980.

page 172 "A Los Angeles police spokeswoman": "Britney Death Hoax Fools Fans,"
          June 14, 2001, BBC News, http://news.bbc.co.uk.

page 174 "After the reporter reported": Jeff Jarvis, "People, People Who Need People,"
          April 7, 2004, BuzzMachine, http://www.buzzmachine.com.

page 175 Another Web site, Dead People Server: Abe Vigoda's entry is online at
          http://dpsinfo.com/dps/vnames.html#avigoda.

page 175 "The rule of thumb is the impact": Joe Strupp, "Obits Find New Life," *Editor &
          Publisher* (January 1, 2006), 44–47.

page 176 "Not long after Davis": Ibid.

page 177 Staffers in the office of congressional: "AP Web Site Source of Erroneous Reports of Hope's Death," Associated Press, June 6, 1998.

page 178 CTV political expert: Les Perreaux, "Newsnet Reports Lucien Bouchard Dead, Then Retracts News a Minute Later," *Canadian Press*, September 8, 2005.

page 178 In a press release, Radio-Canada: Radio-Canada/RDI, "Important Clarification—Radio-Canada Asks CTV for a Retraction," press release, September 8, 2005.

page 180 "Wasn't it Mark Twain who wrote": "This Ted Carlson Is Alive and Well," *Corvallis Gazette-Times*, November 2, 2005.

CHAPTER 8

page 187 Adams-Wade referred to Thompson-Frenk: Norma Adams-Wade, "Tolerance to Reign at Spiritual Conference," *Dallas Morning News*, June 15, 2005.

page 187 Her totals for 2004 found: Christine Chinlund, "2004 Was a Better Year for Globe Accuracy," *Boston Globe*, January 10, 2005.

page 188 As Paul Moore, the public editor: Paul Moore, "We Regret the Errors—Some More Than Others," *Baltimore Sun*, December 25, 2005.

page 188 "At first, Frank Calabrese thought Tuesday's": Jon Yates, "No Way, It's Not That Frank Calabrese," *Chicago Tribune*, April 27, 2005.

page 189 "It's just that Frank built": Ibid.

page 189 It carried the playful headline: Ibid.

page 190 The *Tribune* reported the filing and quoted: "Tribune Co. Sued by Man Misidentified as Mobster," *Chicago Tribune*, April 28, 2005.

page 191 Roughly twelve months earlier: John Bebow and Jon Yates, "Front-Page Bike Photo Didn't Show Lombardo," *Chicago Tribune*, April 28, 2005.

page 191 "At first glance, there are certainly": Ibid.

page 192 "I couldn't believe it": Ibid.

page 193 Writer Mark Brown contacted Halprin: Mark Brown, "Someone Should Tell That Other Newspaper This Man Is No Clown," *Chicago Sun-Times*, April 28, 2005.

page 193 "We sincerely regret our mistake": Bebow and Yates, "Front-Page Bike Photo."

page 194 The commentator had read the address: H.G. Reza, "When Blame Knocks on the Wrong Door," *Los Angeles Times*, August 25, 2005.

page 194 The *Los Angeles Times*, which broke: Ibid.

page 196 "I did not realize when I gave his address: The apology is online at: http://www.john-loftus.com/apology.htm.

page 200 She was identified as Ginger: "Why She Left Him," *Us Weekly*, March 21, 2005.

page 201 Nick Paton Walsh, the *Observer*'s: "Apology from Newspapers Sought by Crash Survivor," *Irish Times*, October 26, 2005.

page 202 The *Observer*'s story ran with the headline: The story was later removed from the *Guardian* Web site.

page 202 Denying that the *Sunday Independent*: "Apology from Newspapers Sought."

CHAPTER 9

page 213 "There's only one made it out": "Elation Turned to Tragedy as 12 Miners Discovered Dead, One Survives," CNN transcript of *Anderson Cooper 360*, January 4, 2006.

page 214 "You hear about the fog": "West Virginia Miners Situation; Hatfield Press Conference; Governor Manchin Press Conference," CNN transcript, "Breaking News," January 4, 2006.

page 214 The Associated Press sent a story: Allen G. Breed, "Families Say 12 W.Va. Miners Found Alive," Associated Press, January 3, 2006.

page 215 "Wow," he said, according to: "Trapped Underground: Mine Rescue Mission." CNN transcript of *Anderson Cooper 360*, January 3, 2006.

page 215 "That is incredible news": Ibid.

page 217 "Modern newscraft, addicted to technology": David D. Perlmutter, "Mine Rescue Lesson: Just Say 'Don't Know,'" Editor andPublisher.com, January 5, 2006, http://www.editorandpublisher.com/eandp/columns/shoptalk_display.jsp?vnu_content_id=1001806170.

page 219 In early December 1967: "Hamilton Naki, an Unsung Surgical Pioneer," *Economist*, June 9, 2005.

page 220 In its obituary of Naki, the *Economist*: Ibid.

page 220 As the *New York Times* noted: Michael Wines, "Accounts of South African's Career Now Seen as Overstated," *New York Times*, August 27, 2005.

page 220 On March 29, 1993, the Associated Press: Sahm Venter, "Hamilton Naki: From Gardener to Surgeon," Associated Press, March 29, 1993.

page 220 Barnard said that doctors who work: Ibid.

page 220 More important, he was a symbol: "Injustice Weakens Our Defences," *Sydney Morning Herald*, June 20, 2005.

page 221 In late August, the *Los Angeles Times*: "Obituaries; S. African Hamilton Naki Did Not Assist in 1st Heart Transplant After All, News Reports Say," *Los Angeles Times*, August 31, 2005.

page 221 Professor David Dent, acting dean: David Dent, "Obituary Was Historically Inaccurate," letter to the editor, *British Medial Journal*, September 3, 2005.

CHAPTER 10

page 225 It described how their father: Jayson Blair, "A Nation at War: Military Families; Relatives of Missing Soldiers Dread Hearing Worse News," *New York Times*, March 27, 2003.

page 225 As the paper's exhaustive report: Dan Barry, David Barstow, Jonathan D. Glater, Adam Liptak, and Jacques Steinberg, "Correcting the Record; Times Reporter Who Resigned Leaves Long Trail of Deception," *New York Times*, May 11, 2003.

page 225 Brandi Lynch told the *Times*: Ibid.

page 226 Sources also decline to request: Scott Maier, "Setting the Record Straight: When the Press Errs, Do Corrections Follow?" *Journalism Practice* 1, 1 (2007): 35.

page 226 "Your online archive is the true final": Michael Jesse, "Note from the Chair: The Church of the True Correction," *News Library News* 25, 1 (Fall 2002), http://www.ibiblio.org/slanews/nln/nln02/fall/chair_notes.htm.

page 227 Benjamin Harris who published the first: Walter Lippmann, *Liberty and the News* (Vancouver: University of British Columbia Press, 1995), 8.

page 229 By 1973, roughly one paper: D. Charles Whitney, "Begging Your Pardon: Corrections and Corrections Policies at Twelve U.S. Newspapers" (working paper, Gannett Center for Media Studies, 1986).

page 229 As former *Times* assistant managing editor: Linda Amster and Dylan Loeb

McClain, *Kill Duck Before Serving: Red Faces at The New York Times* (New York: St. Martin's Griffin, 2002), xiv.

page 230 "Early Wednesday morning, the *Voice* learned": "Editor's Note: What Happened to That Cover Story?" *Village Voice*, http://www.villagevoice.com, March 1, 2006.

page 230 The Associated Press said he: Richard Pyle, "Former New York Times Executive Editor A.M. Rosenthal Dies at 84," Associated Press, May 11, 2006.

page 230 The *Los Angeles Times* wrote: Elaine Woo, "A.M. Rosenthal, 84; Venerated Editor Recast the N.Y. Times," *Los Angeles Times*, May 11, 2006.

page 231 "These days, everything we publish": Gail Collins, "A Letter from the Editor: It All Goes on the Permanent Record," *New York Times*, October 2, 2005.

page 232 "In the fall of 2000, Joseph Lelyveld": Dan Barry, David Barstow, Jonathan D. Glater, Adam Liptak, and Jacques Steinberg, "Correcting the Record; Times Reporter Who Resigned Leaves Long Trail of Deception," *New York Times*, May 11, 2003.

page 232 Landman sent staff an e-mail: Ibid.

page 232 After the *Times* introduced a toll-free number: Linda Amster and Dylan Loeb McClain, *Kill Duck Before Serving: Red Faces at The New York Times* (New York: St. Martin's Griffin, 2002), xv.

page 232 In 1982, a study found that: Maier, "Setting the Record Straight."

page 234 In responding to a reader letter: Sally Baker, "Punishing Reporters," *Times* (London), November 12, 2005.

page 235 "McCormick acknowledges that the electronic media": John D. Solomon, "Errors on Air," *American Journalism Review* (August–September 2003), http://www.ajr.org/article.asp?id=3094.

page 236 "any potential error will be looked at": Vaughn Ververs, "E-Mailbag: How Does CBS News Handle Corrections?" March 29, 2006, CBS PublicEye blog, http://www.cbsnews.com/sections/publiceye/main500486.shtml.

page 237 "Last night we brought you the story": "Correction on Picture of Man Accused in Child Pornography Case," September 2, 2006, KSL TV, http://www.ksl.com.

page 237 A 1998 survey by the American Society: "Examining Our Credibility: Perspectives of the Public and the Press," American Society of Newspaper Editors, 1998, http://www.asne.org/index.cfm?id=2632.

page 237 A 2005 survey saw two-thirds: Maier, "Setting the Record Straight."

page 237 A survey released in 2004 found: "Examining Credibility in Canadian Journalism," Canadian Media Research Consortium, 2004, http://www.cmr-cccrm.ca/english/research.html.

page 238 "The news profession apparently sees it": Maier, "Setting the Record Straight, 33."

page 238 Maier wrote that the research results: Ibid., 40.

page 242 Steyn said he "dictated this apology": "Mark Steyn on the Plight of Lileks, the Plight of the Conrad Black Trial, and Whether the Election in France Is Good News or Bad News," transcript of *The Hugh Hewitt Show*, May 11, 2007.

page 243 "The principle is a simple one": Ian Mayes, "Trust Me—I'm an Ombudsman," *British Journalism Review* 15, 2 (2004), http://www.bjr.org.uk/data/2004/-n02_mayes.htm.

page 243 During his tenure, he received: "Writing Wrongs: Guardian Readers' Editor Ian Mayes," *Press Gazette*, January 12, 2007.

page 243 "When I started, the whole": Ibid.

page 244 "People remember that [correction] in a way": Robert Barr, "Pioneering British Correction Column Wins Own Following," Associated Press, December 18, 2000.

page 246 "An Oct. 1 editorial referred to": Patrick McGann, "Attack Ad on a Dead Dad Demeans McMorris," *Lewiston Morning Tribune*, October 7, 2004.

page 247 "In last week's My North West": Craig Silverman, " In the Dirt," November 8, 2006, Regret the Error, http://www.regrettheerror.com.

page 248 Recent articles in this column may have": "Sven: An Apology," *Sun*, October 13, 2006.

page 248 "Sunsport would like to take this": "Owen Hargreaves: An Apology," *Sun*, July 3, 2006.

page 248 "In previous issues of this newspaper": "France—An Apology," *Daily Star*, July 5, 2006.

CHAPTER 11

page 265 Proofreaders were "the best-educated": Linda Amster and Dylan Loeb, *Kill Duck Before Serving*" (New York: St. Martin's Griffin, 2002), xii.

page 266 "You'd turn on 10 Linotype machines": Carl Schlesinger, telephone interview with the author, March 20, 2007.

page 266 "For any statistical table [like stocks]": Ibid.

page 267 "During that period there was a great sense": Ibid.

page 267 "Etaoin shrdlu" are "the 'words' formed": Margalit Fox, "David Weiss, Who Filmed Hot Type's Last Days, Dies," *New York Times*, August 16, 2005.

page 267 "Proofreaders were," in the words: David House, "Earning People's Trust Daily—or Not," *Fort Worth Star-Telegram*, December 17, 2006.

page 268 "Their roles were absorbed by technology": Ibid.

page 268 "Back in the day, newspapers had proofreaders": Wayne Ezell, "Can Grammarians Help Us?" *Florida Times-Union*, November 19, 2006.

page 268 "Now most pages are 'proofed' by an editor": Ibid.

page 269 "I am concerned about what seems": Ian Mayes, "Open Doors: Talking on the Homophone," *Guardian*, December 27, 1997.

page 269 One *Times-Union* reader, a reference librarian: Ezell, "Can Grammarians Help Us?"

page 270 "I have a friend who was": Harold Simon, "The Scourge of Spell-Czech," *Ventura County Star*, September 19, 1997.

page 270 "Our *Star*, and possibly most papers": Ibid.

page 271 "You would have to dig": Schlesinger interview.

page 271 When asked about the secret: "Former Proofreader Audrey Stubbart Dies at 105," Associated Press, November 14, 2000.

page 272 "I love to find mistakes": "At 104, a Computer-Connected Editor Works On," Associated Press, December 29, 1999.

page 272 "She was an inspiration to all of us": "Former Proofreader Audrey Stubbart."

page 272 "When they make consistent mistakes": Ibid.

page 272 "We think that whatever's been hard for us": "At 104, a Computer-Connected Editor."

page 273 "When the original copy was exhumed": Paul Gallico, *Adventures of Hiram Holliday* (New York: Knopf, 1939), 16.

page 274 The *Globe and Mail*, which broke the story: Grant Robertson, "Comma Quirk Irks Rogers," *Globe and Mail*, August 7, 2006.

page 274 The contract stated that the agreement: Ibid.

page 274 "In olden times, lawyers would have": Mark Liberman, "Lawyers in Need of
Linguistic Training," August 7, 2006, Language Log blog,
http://itre.cis.upenn.edu/~myl/languagelog/archives/003425.html.

CHAPTER 12

page 275 "A number of early research departments": Sarah Harrison Smith, *The Fact
Checker's Bible* (New York: Anchor Books, 2004), 9.

page 275 "The checker, or researcher": Otto Friedrich, "There Are oo Trees in
Russia," *Harper's*, October 1964.

page 275 "The theory of fact checkers is that even": Richard Blow and Ari Posner,
"Are You Completely Bald?" *New Republic*, September 26, 1988, 23.

page 276 "Checking is ... sometimes regarded": Harrison Smith, *The Fact Checker's
Bible*, 9.

page 277 "Pound for pound, the most mistake-packed": Ariel Hart, "Delusions of
Accuracy," *Columbia Journalism Review* (July–August, 2003),
http://backissues.cjrarchives.org/year/03/4/hart.asp.

page 277 "the Vatican" of fact checking: Blow and Posner, "Are You Completely Bald?" 23.

page 277 It began, "Edna Millay's father": Griffin Barry, "Vincent," *New Yorker*,
February 12, 1927.

page 278 In fact, the letter was the result: Harrison Smith, *The Fact Checker's Bible*, 10.

page 278 "What with our making fun of other publications": Ibid., 10.

page 278 The ad appeared in the *New York Times*": Linda Amster and Dylan Loeb
McClain, *Kill Duck Before Serving: Red Faces at the New York Times* (New
York: St. Martin's Griffin, 2002), xi.

page 278 Thomas Teal, who worked as checker: Blow and Posner, "Are You Completely
Bald?" 24

page 279 "Every cartoon is fact-checked for accuracy": Emily Gordon, "Ask the
Librarians: The Debut," July 25, 2006, Emdashes blog, http://emdashes.com.

page 279 "OCD is the whole ball game": Anne "Dusty" Mortimer-Maddox, telephone
interview with the author, January 10, 2007.

page 279 "I'm German," he offered with a smile: Robert Scheffler, interview with the
author, *Esquire* offices, New York, November 15, 2006.

page 280 "Fact checkers at *Esquire*": Blow and Posner, "Are You Completely Bald?"

page 280 The *New Yorker's* current head of fact checking: Judith Sheppard, "Playing
Defense: Is Enough Being Done to Prevent Future Journalistic
Embarrassments?" *American Journalism Review* (September 1998),
http://www.ajr.org/Article.asp?id=3440.

page 280 "It's not that we don't make mistakes": Peter Canby, e-mail message to the
author, November 7, 2006.

page 280 "Their prowess for languages may be": Adeel Hassan, "Annals of the Anal:
Fact-checkers at *The New Yorker* and Elsewhere," *New York Review of
Magazines*, Spring 2002, http://www.nyrm.org/2002/.

page 281 "There were five errors in two and a half columns": Antony Shugaar, "Truth
or Consequences," *Columbia Journalism Review* (May–June 1994),
http://backissues.cjrarchives.org/year/94/3/facts.asp.

page 281 When he was editor in chief: Blow and Posner, "Are You Completely Bald?" 25.

page 281 "I knew nobody would notice": Ibid., 24.

page 281 The writer of the piece sought: Friedrich, "There Are oo Trees in Russia," 63.

page 282 "I am in jail and allowed send only one cable": Ibid.

page 282 "I'm hazy on the 17 phone calls": Davin Coburn, telephone interview with the author, January 26, 2007.

page 282 In July 1980, *Esquire* ran an article: Blow and Posner, "Are You Completely Bald?" 23.

page 282 "The baker got very irate and said": Ibid., 23.

page 283 It was a dose of irony, considering: Ibid., 25.

page 284 "I knew how the system worked": "Stephen Glass: I Lied For Esteem," *60 Minutes*, August 17, 2003, http://www.cbsnews.com/stories/2003/05/07/60minutes/main552819.shtml.

page 284 "It's not a secret," he said: David Cohen, interview with the author, *Playboy* offices, New York, November 15, 2007.

page 285 "By the time you are done": Davin Coburn, telephone interview with the author, January 26, 2007.

page 285 "The Internet has revolutionized": Coburn interview.

page 285 "However their accuracy may vary": Harrison Smith, *The Fact Checker's Bible*, 31.

page 286 "Things are a little different": Cohen interview.

page 286 *Time* magazine, as well as *Newsweek*: Liza Featherstone, "Chucking the Checkers," *Columbia Journalism Review* (July–August 1997), http://backissues.cjrarchives.org/year/97/4/checkers.asp.

page 287 "The people who used to be": Ibid.

page 287 According to the magazine's spokesperson: "Recall," *Fort Worth Star-Telegram*, May 12, 1997.

page 287 By the summer of 1997, Marta Dorin: Featherstone, "Chucking the Checkers."

page 288 The Time Inc. layoffs of January 18, 2007: Nat Ives, "289 More Jobs Eliminated at Time Inc.," *MediaWorks*, January 18, 2007.

page 288 "In the past, every piece of copy: Harrison Smith, *The Fact Checker's Bible*, 150.

page 288 Both *Playboy* and *Esquire*, two magazines that still: When I visited these magazines in November 2006, *Playboy* had one fewer full-time person, and *Esquire* had two full-time checkers along with a full-time freelancer, down from a high of "six or seven" years earlier, according to Robert Scheffler (Scheffler interview).

page 289 "It is clear that fact checking": Leslie Lucas, "A Checkered Present," *Ryerson Review of Journalism* (Summer 1999), http://www.rrj.ca/issue/1999/-summer/296/.

page 289 "They had this really stupid idea": Ibid., http://www.rrj.ca/issue/1999/summer/296/.

page 289 "I want to take a moment to acknowledge": Jeromy Lloyd, "Checking Out," *Masthead*, July–August 2006, 11.

page 290 "It has allowed us to be a lot more current": Ibid., 11.

page 290 "Readers have a feeling that magazines": Cynthia Brouse, telephone interview with the author, January 4, 2007.

page 291 "I can't see how you can put out": Lucas, "A Checkered Present," http://www.rrj.ca/issue/1999/summer/296/.

CHAPTER 13

page 295 "We start with the facts instead": Jeremy Miller, telephone interview with the author, March 21, 2007.

page 295 "For a writer, this huge, suddenly vocal": Gary Kamiya, "The Readers Strike Back," Salon.com, January 30, 2007.

page 295 "A writer privileged enough to publish": Ibid.
page 296 "Fortress newsroom was the walled enclave": Steven A. Smith, "Fortress Journalism Failed. The Transparent Newsroom Works," November 23, 2005, PressThink, http://journalism.nyu.edu/pubzone/weblogs/pressthink.
page 297 The report aired just two months": "New Questions on Bush Guard Duty," Transcript, *60 Minutes II*, September 9, 2004, http://www.cbsnews.com/stories/2004/09/08/60II/main641984.shtml.
page 298 One Power Line reader identified himself: "The Sixty-first Minute," September 9, 2004, Power Line, http://www.powerlineblog.com.
page 298 "As is standard practice at CBS News, each of": Mark Halperin et al., "Playing for Harvard: The Second Draft of History Is Usually Better Than the First," September 10, 2004, ABC News, http://abcnews.go.com.
page 298 "As is standard practice at CBS News, the documents": Ibid.
page 299 As journalists worked: "Documents Suggest Special Treatment for Bush in Guard [post 47]," September 8, 2004, Free Republic, http://www.freerepublic.com.
page 299 "I am saying these documents": Jonathan V. Last, "What Blogs Have Wrought," *Weekly Standard*, January 27, 2004, http://www.weeklystandard.com/Content/Public/Articles/000/000/004/640pgolk.asp.
page 299 "'60 Minutes' Documents on Bush Might Be Fake": Ibid.
page 300 "The server hosting Power Line crashed": Ibid., http://www.weeklystandard.com/Content/Public/Articles/000/000/004/640pgolk.asp.
page 300 "My point... was simply to prove": Hunter, "TANG Typewriter Follies: [9/12/04 BREAKING UPDATE]," September 10, 2004, Daily Kos, http://dailykos.com.
page 300 Charles Johnson of Little Green Footballs: Howard Kurtz, "After Blogs Got Hits, CBS Got a Black Eye," *Washington Post*, September 20, 2004.
page 300 He told the *Washington Post*: Ibid.
page 300 Howard Kurtz, the *Post*'s respected: Ibid.
page 301 That day, CBS reported, he admitted: "CBS Statement on Bush Memos," September 20, 2004, CBS News, http://www.cbsnews.com.
page 301 CBS president Andrew Heyward released a statement: "CBS Statement on Bush Memos," September 20, 2004, CBS News, http://www.cbsnews.com.
page 301 That evening, Dan Rather: "Dan Rather Statement on Memos," September 20, 2004, CBS News, http://www.cbsnews.com.
page 302 In 2006, Charles Johnson of Little Green Footballs: Charles Johnson, "Reuters Doctoring Photos from Beirut?" August 5, 2006, Little Green Footballs, http://littlegreenfootballs.com/weblog.
page 302 "I'm just getting familiar": Mark Powell, e-mail message to the author, October 12, 2006.
page 303 "Keep an eye on bloggers": John Leo, "Flogged by Bloggers," *U.S. News & World Report*, July 28, 2002.
page 303 In a post about the *U.S. News*: Nick Denton, "We Can Fact-check Your Ass," July 29, 2002, Nick Denton's personal Web site, nickdenton.org.
page 304 Get something wrong or report something: Layne e-mailed me (June 12, 2007) to confirm his quote. He also added, "I had been working exclusively as an online journalist for several years at that point, so I do admit to encouraging the online journalists (and later, the 'bloggers') to bring Evil Elite Print Media to task for whatever sins. Now that everything is online journalism, the rallying cry is happily forgotten."

page 305   According to a passage from Irvine's book: Michael Massing, "Who's Afraid of Reed Irvine? The Rise and Decline of Accuracy in Media," *Nation*, September 13, 1986.

page 306   "He was always concerned about the media: Cliff Kincaid, telephone interview with the author, May 15, 2007.

page 306   David Brock founded it in 2004: "Who We Are," Media Matters for America, http://mediamatters.org.

page 306   "We don't pretend to read the minds": Eric Boehlert, telephone interview with the author, May 16, 2007.

page 307   Then, a few days after we spoke: Eric Boehlert, e-mail messages to the author, May 18, 2007, and June 6, 2007.

page 307   "want the press to get better and be more responsible": Eric Boehler, telephone interview with the author, June 9, 2007.

page 308   Kincaid said one of the faults of Media Matters: Kincaid interview.

CHAPTER 14

page 312   "The public expects more than just talk": Christine Urban, "What the Follow-up Research Tells Us About the Accuracy Initiatives," *American Society of Newspaper Editors Credibility Handbook*, August 12, 2002, http://www.asne.org/credibilityhandbook/brt/accuracyinitiatives.htm.

page 319   "Earlier versions of this article gave an incorrect": John Holusha, "Huge Profit at Goldman Brings Big Bonuses," *New York Times*, December 12, 2006, http://nytimes.com.

page 321   "It's just a great reassurance of our staff's": David House, telephone interview with the author, May 23, 2007.

page 322   "My great dream is that iThenticate": Ibid.

page 323   "As a geek myself, I searched": Tom Glocer, "Trust in the Age of Citizen Journalism" (speech, Globes Media Conference, Tel Aviv, December 11, 2006), http://tomglocer.com/.

page 323   Glocer emphasized that the search: Ibid.

page 323   "Perhaps this will help rivet attention": Wayne Ezell, "Can Grammarians Help Us?" *Florida Times-Union*, November 19, 2006.

page 323   "heard from roughly 80 readers": Wayne Ezell, telephone interview with the author, June 5, 2007.

page 324   "[The Good, the Bad & the Ugly] openly admits": Bridget Johnson, "An Interview with Reuters' King of Odd News," no date, About.com: Journalism, http://journalism.about.com.

page 325   "Almost every day, *The Chronicle* hears": "Correct Me If I'm Wrong . . .: 'Pilotless Drone,'" SFGate.com, January 29, 2007.

page 325   "This is about listening to your readers": Robert Levine, "Media Talk; Readers Call Newspapers. These Are Their Stories," *New York Times*, January 29, 2007.

page 326   "When I brought Auros' name up": Jack Shafer, "Slate's Fact-Checking Department," *Slate*, March 1, 2007, http://slate.com/.

page 327   "Mr. Howe. I'm looking at the Monday": "Correct Me If I'm Wrong . . .: 'Pilotless Drone.'"

page 329   "I would like to see us say": David Broder, *Behind the Front Page* (New York: Simon and Shuster, 1987), 14-15.

page 329   "We might even find ourselves": Ibid.

Index

About the Author

CRAIG SILVERMAN IS A JOURNALIST and the founder of RegretTheError.com. His writing has appeared in publications including the *New York Times, Editor & Publisher* online, and the *Montreal Gazette,* among others. He is a columnist for the *Globe and Mail,* Canada's largest national newspaper, and *Hour,* a Montreal weekly.

Error Report Form

TO REPORT A MISTAKE IN THIS BOOK, please complete this form and mail it to Regret the Error, 4844 Jeanne Mance, Montreal, Quebec, Canada H2V 4J7. (Those without Internet access can also contact me at this address to submit an error or noteworthy correction from other media.) This form is intended as a means by which those without e-mail access can make a request for correction. If you would also like to receive all corrections to this work via mail, please check the box below and fill in your mailing information. Again, this option is reserved for those who are not able to report and access corrections at RegretTheError.com. Anyone with Internet access should use the Web site rather than this form. It is faster and easier to use.

Name: _____

Address: _____

City/ State or Province: _____

ZIP/Postal Code: _____

Country: _____

❏ Please mail me corrections to this book.
❏ List my full name as the submitter of this correction on your Web site.
❏ List only my first name.
❏ Don't cite me at all.

CORRECTION, PLEASE!

Mistaken sentences/facts: _____
_____
_____
_____
_____

Correct information: _____
_____
_____
_____
_____

Chapter(s): _____

Page(s): _____